I
Romans

1

A History of Denial

Five Snapshots

Before exposing the crooked framework of Roman denialism, I will present five episodes or texts that span the period from the fifth to the thirteenth century and illustrate how Byzantines used the ethnonym Roman, especially in contexts that juxtaposed Romans with others. Who used it? With reference to whom? And what were the criteria that justified its use? What made someone a Roman in Byzantium? In a previous monograph I examined the political dimension of this problem, arguing that the Byzantines were Romans because they were members of a specific polity that derived its origins and distinctive political ideology from ancient Rome.[1] This book will add an ethnic dimension to that definition: the Byzantine Romans were also an ethnic group. This proposal is far removed from the picture presented by many Byzantinists, but it emerges with striking clarity and forcefulness from the sources. The following texts were chosen to highlight the ethnic aspects of Romanness in Byzantium. They are not eccentric, but they do reveal more explicitly what is taken for granted in other sources, and there are more like them that I could have chosen. I present them here, before the exposé of the field's habits of denial, to show what kind of evidence

Byzantinists have to circumvent in order to continue to deny that the Byzantines were Romans.

1. *The election of the emperor Anastasios in 491.* When the emperor Zeno died in 491, the people of Constantinople assembled in the hippodrome along with some military units in order to meet with the empress, patriarch, and magistrates of the court. Among other demands and acclamations, the people called for a new emperor who would be both Orthodox and of the Romans. The empress assured them that she had instructed the magistrates and senate to select a man who was Christian, Roman, and endowed with every virtue. After a brief speech by the empress, "everyone cried out, 'May you be blessed with all good things, Roman woman *(Romaia)*, if no foreign element *(xenon)* is added to the race *(genos)* of the Romans.'"[2]

Why was everyone so concerned to have a proper Roman emperor and prevent foreign elements from occupying the throne? The deceased emperor Zeno (474–491), whose body lay in state in the palace while this exchange was taking place, was an Isaurian from southern Asia Minor. The Isaurians are stereotypically described in Roman sources as mostly uncivilized mountain dwellers. They made good soldiers, but were perceived by many as violent, greedy, and insufficiently Romanized. Even though they were Roman citizens like everyone else in the empire, "Isaurians and Romans" could be juxtaposed as different categories, and the former could be labeled an *ethnos* (people, ethnic group, or nation).[3] In 468, the emperor Leo issued a law against private persons keeping armed slaves, private armies, and their own Isaurians.[4] In 473, there was a massacre of Isaurians in Constantinople when an incident in the hippodrome sparked violence.[5] Zeno's background was a liability. A contemporary Syriac chronicle states bluntly that palace officials hated him "because he was an Isaurian by birth."[6] His native name was Tarasis Kodissa, which he changed to get ahead in imperial politics. The people of Constantinople at first refused to make him a partner in imperial power at the request of the emperor Leo, and he came to power indirectly, as the guardian of his son, Leo's grandson, Leo II, who died prematurely. Within a year of his accession, Zeno was temporarily deposed by rivals while Constantinople erupted in another massacre of Isaurians.[7] These pogroms suggest that people believed that they could tell who was an Isaurian, indicating that they were regarded as a distinct ethnic group.

This background explains the popular concern to appoint a real Roman to the throne in 491. Thus, not all the inhabitants of the empire, or subjects of the emperor, were regarded as Romans, even if they were legal citizens.[8] There were people within the empire, even in the armies, court, and imperial family itself, whose ethnicity made them seem foreign to the majority of Romans. Whether this was how the Isaurians also felt or whether it was only prejudice on the part of the Romans, the Isaurians were seen as *xenoi*, "foreigners." At the same time, as revealed in their exchange with the empress Ariadne, the Romans viewed themselves as a *genos*, a term that can be translated in many ways but whose root is family kinship or belonging to the same species; the modern term *race* might even work in some contexts. We will revisit these terms. In 491, at any rate, the Roman *genos* did not want any "foreigners"—even from within the empire—to take the throne.

The person eventually elected in 491 was Anastasios (491–518), a native of the city of Dyrrachion (classical Epidamnos) on the Adriatic coast. Presumably, nothing about his origins seemed ethnically foreign or posed an obstacle. Still, within a few years of his election, if not immediately, Anastasios put it about that he was a descendant of Pompey the Great, as the name ran in his family.[9] Thus, to prove his Romanness, Anastasios claimed to be biologically descended from a general of the Republic. He also expelled leading Isaurians from Constantinople and launched a full-scale imperial war against their homeland, pacifying it once and for all.

2. *The return of the Roman captives taken by the Avars.* The second collection of the *Miracles of Saint Demetrios of Thessalonike*, written by an anonymous priest in seventh-century Thessalonike, tells the story of some provincial Romans taken captive by the Avars in the Balkans. The Avar khan resettled them in Pannonia, where they intermarried with Bulgars, Avars, and other "ethnic" types (*ethnikoi*) and produced offspring.

But each child received from its father the ancestral traditions of the Romans and the impulse of their *genos*. And just as the *genos* of the Jews grew in size in Egypt under the Pharaoh, so did it happen with them: the tribe *(phylon)* of the Christians increased through the Orthodox faith and holy baptism. Speaking among themselves about their ancestral homeland, they lit in each other's hearts the secret hope that they might escape.

Sixty years after their parents had been captured, the leader of this group, who had been appointed by the khan, "learned that this large people longed to return to its ancestral cities, and he formed plans of his own. He took this Roman people and the ethnic proselytes, as is said in the book of the Jews about the Exodus under Moses, along with their possessions and weapons, and moved against the khan."[10]

It does not matter whether these events occurred as reported, which we have no way of knowing. For our purposes, what matters is the way in which they are reported, and what made sense to the author and his audience to say about these provincial Romans and how they imagined the coordinates of their Romanness. Here too the Romans are a *genos*, marked as separate from the *ethnikoi* by their ethnonym, customs (ἤθη), religion, and strong affective memory of their ancestral homeland, to which they yearned to return. This homeland was not Constantinople, but the Roman Balkan provinces from which they had been removed. This Roman *genos* was animated by its own "impulse" or "drive" (ὁρμή), which is an interesting approximation of what we might today call an "identity." The narrative is also infused with a religious ideology modeled on a scriptural template. The Roman captives are imagined as a new people of Israel in Egyptian exile. This effectively fuses their religious and ethnic distinctiveness, as in the Old Testament. In the Septuagint, *ethne* translates *goyim*, the non-Jewish "nations," or gentiles. Thus the Christian Roman *genos* is juxtaposed to the pagan *ethnikoi*. Under these circumstances, Roman and Christian identity overlapped in terms of the demographic they encompassed, especially when the enemies of Rome were non-Christians, but they were by no means equivalent existentially: they differed precisely in the way that any ethnicity differs from a confessional religion.

The narrative logic of this tale assumes that members of the *genos* did not normally intermarry with ethnic types, which highlights their ethnic exclusivity, but in captivity they might have had to do so. It is significant that the children produced by these mixed marriages came to identify as Romans, as their upbringing was shaped by Christianity, Roman customs, and their parents' narrative of a lost homeland. Thus, belonging to the *genos* was not strictly a matter of descent. Despite one's ancestry, it was possible to be raised as, and thereby become, a Roman. Romanness was ultimately a function of culture (including religion) and a patriotic sense of belonging to the broader Roman community, a sense that was reinforced by a connection to an imagined, distant homeland: it was a group defined more by narrative than by blood. We will later explore how foreigners could be absorbed and assimilated into the Roman ethnic community. Even so, the language of *genos* and of racial exclusivity could still be used regardless of this subtle distinction, as the next snapshot shows.

3. *Konstantinos VII Porphyrogennetos' zoology of nations*. In the mid-tenth century, the emperor Konstantinos VII assembled a text whose purpose was to instruct his son and heir Romanos II how to deal with the foreign nations that surrounded the Romans. Chapter 13 of this text gives advice on how to cleverly and even deceitfully turn away foreign demands for imperial vestments, Greek fire, and royal brides. The basic excuse—a lie—is that an angel of God instructed Constantine the Great to place a curse on the altar of Hagia Sophia against giving any of those things away: "Never shall an emperor of the Romans ally himself in marriage with a nation whose customs differ from and are alien to those of the Roman order, especially with one that is infidel and unbaptized, unless it be with the Franks alone."[11] At this point Konstantinos counters the objection that his predecessor and father-in-law Romanos I Lakapenos had in fact made a marriage alliance with the Bulgarian tsar. His argument is that Romanos I was a man of humble origins who did not properly understand the customs of the Roman court. Konstantinos concedes that Romanos may have countered that the Bulgarians were Orthodox Christians "just like us" (i.e., us Romans), but this response does not

pass muster with Konstantinos, who cannot overlook "this innovation in the polity of the Romans."

> For each nation *(ethnos)* has different customs and divergent laws and institutions, it should consolidate those things that are proper to it, and should form and activate the associations that it needs for the fusion of its life from within its own nation. For just as each animal species mates with its own race *(homogeneis)*, so it is right that each nation also should marry and cohabit not with those of a different tribe *(allophylon)* and tongue *(alloglossoi)* but of the same tribe *(homogeneis)* and speech *(homophonoi)*.[12]

Today this position might be deemed isolationist, xenophobic, and racist, and certainly nationalistic. It goes beyond the idea of the nation as a community of values and postulates biological kinship as its foundation. Konstantinos even compares the nations of the world to different animal species. His logic defines the Romans as one nation *(ethnos)* among others. Konstantinos does not say that they are qualitatively different or better than others, though presumably he did believe it. He defines nations by customs, laws, institutions, language, and intermarriage, which makes each nation also into a "race" or "tribe" *(genos* or *phylon)*. This is a fundamentally secular conception. At the end of the chapter, he offers a taxonomy of the traits that define nations, mentioning "their genealogies, customs, way of life, and the position of the land they inhabit and its climate."[13] This presumably applies to both Romans and others.

Konstantinos' concept is equivalent to standard modern definitions of the nation.[14] Byzantinists are disingenuous when they say that the Byzantines would have been "surprised" to hear themselves described as a Roman nation.[15] As we will see, they consistently claimed to be precisely that. Instead, they would have been surprised by the modern error that "Roman" was somehow a multiethnic category. This modern idea would have sounded to them like a contradiction in terms, as for them Romans and foreign ethnics were separate categories.

Konstantinos also violates the modern expectation that a Byzantine would point to religion as his defining trait. He does not single out Orthodoxy, probably because it would have undermined his separation of Bulgarians and Romans. The Bulgarians, to whom Romanos I Lakapenos gave his granddaughter as a bride, were also Orthodox Christians. Konstantinos thus breaks the link between *genos* and religion that we saw in the *Miracles of Saint Demetrios*. Language is now promoted as a chief distinguishing trait. But the modern ecumenical reading of Byzantine Orthodoxy as somehow transcending ethnicity is misleading too. By the middle period, the Church prohibited marriages between Orthodox and non-Orthodox, on the grounds that "one must not mix things that are discrete."[16] The latter over time came to include many of the empire's neighbors, such as the Armenians and even the Latins. Thus the rules of the Church regarding marriage tended to partially reinforce the kinship basis of the Roman community.

Overall, it appears that the Romans defined themselves as a nation through a constellation of customs, traits, and practices (including religion) and by a shared homeland or geographical location. At each time, they highlighted the elements that worked best to distinguish them from other nations given the circumstances. Sometimes it was their religion, sometimes their language, and sometimes it could even be their hats.[17]

4. *The emperor Andronikos I Komnenos' plan to kill all his enemies.* As Andronikos I (1183–1185) was growing unpopular and the polity was speaking out against him, he convened a council of state where he proposed to execute his political enemies "along with all who are related to them by blood." His son Manuel opposed this, arguing that the decree, if literally enforced, would lead to the death of the entire Roman population—τὸ Πανρώμαιον—and not only of all the Romans but of some foreigners too. Specifically, he argued that the family of each of the accused extended from one relation to the next, through biological relatives and in-laws, in a long chain of affiliation such that eventually all the Romans would have to be killed, and the number of victims would be "infinite" (ἄπειρον). This was hyperbole, but his reasoning reveals that the totality of the Romans (what he calls the *Panromaion*) was for him not a small group but rather a national or ethnic community defined by *genos* and constituted mostly

through kinship. As some Romans were married to "ethnic types" (ἐξ ἔθνους), quite a few of the latter would perish too.[18] Manuel would know this, as he was married to a Georgian princess.[19]

5. *Ethnic enclaves in the thirteenth-century Balkans.* In 1246, the town of Melnik was contested between the emperor of the Romans at Nikaia and the Bulgarian tsar. The majority of the population, however, were ethnic Romans. The historian of the Nikaian empire, Georgios Akropolites, makes their leading citizen deliver a speech to the rest, reminding them that "the emperor of the Romans has rights over us, seeing as our territory belongs to the empire of the Romans ... moreover, we all originate in Philippopolis [they had been resettled in Melnik by a previous tsar] and we are pure Romans when it comes to our *genos* (καθαροὶ τὸ γένος Ῥωμαῖοι)."[20] The concept of a "pure Roman" is striking. Conversely, Akropolites admits that Bulgarians living under the Roman empire of Nikaia naturally "wanted to side with people of the same race as themselves *(homophyloi)* and cast off the yoke of those who spoke a separate language *(alloglossoi)*"—the Romans—"for whom they harbored a deep hatred."[21] Ethnicity in these cases was not decided by imperial affiliation but by cultural traits such as language, historical memory, and perceptions of ethnic kinship. The Nikaian Roman historian did not try to paint every subject of his emperor as a loyal Roman; instead, he revealed that states and ethnicities did not perfectly line up in those chaotic times.

The most straightforward conclusion to draw from these testimonies is that the Romans of Byzantium saw themselves as an ethnic group or nation, defined in the same way that ethnic groups and nations are understood by modern scholars and sociologists: they had their own ethnonym, language, customs, laws and institutions, homeland, and sense (even if imagined) that they were related by kinship and taxonomically different from other ethnic groups. These testimonies come from many centuries that span the long history of the empire's existence; they reflect the voices of provincials and Constantinopolitans alike and are taken from different genres of evidence. Even if we want to hold off momentarily on the specific conclusion that the Romans of Byzantium were an ethnicity or nation, these five moments still give us prima facie reason to believe that they were Romans in some deeper sense than the merely formal one of belonging to an empire that called itself, at the top, "the empire of the Romans." We can certainly say that most Byzantines had something to do with being Roman. It does appear difficult to deny this.

Yet denial is precisely what a dominant strain within Byzantine Studies has long advocated, developing strategies for refusing to accept the obvious. One strategy is suppression, or just looking the other way. The testimonies presented above, along with many others like them, are rarely discussed, mentioned, or even cited in most works of Byzantine scholarship that purport to be studies of identity. The issue of Roman identity is instead often transposed to a religious or even metaphysical level, where we find much talk of God crowning the emperor, something called the *oecumene (ecumene)*, and End-Time fantasy. These denialist acrobatics operate at such a high level of abstraction that the *genos* or *ethnos* of the Romans is obscured from sight. The Byzantines' claim to be Romans has also been branded an act of deception. We now have "critical" studies that argue that all this Roman business was nothing more than a literary game played by a small elite in Constantinople. Such research draws its conclusions without offering close readings of actual discursive claims to Roman identity made in the sources, such as were surveyed above.[22] It does not so much brush them aside as pretend that they do not exist. As it cannot offer any positive evidence in favor of its thesis, it relies instead on the existing predisposition to doubt that the Byzantines were "really" Romans. The sources are full of claims to what can only be called a Roman ethnicity, but modern scholarship on Byzantium suppresses them or denies their significance.

What is going on?

A Thousand Years of Denial

Before the mid-eighth century, the Latin west casually accepted what we call Byzantium as the empire of the Romans, or the *res publica Romana*. There were lingering traces of Latin bias against the eastern "Greeks," but at this time they were marginal.[23] This changed during the second half of the eighth century, when the popes pivoted and sought to replace the patronage of Constantinople with that of the Franks. At this point, the term *Graeci* began to displace *Romani* in western references to the eastern empire.[24] This intensified when some Frankish kings began, if at first only sporadically and uncertainly, to claim for themselves the title of emperor of the Romans. By the ninth century, both popes and western emperors were, in their official correspondence, actively questioning the right of the eastern emperor to call himself emperor of the Romans.[25] As papal and imperial German ambitions began to draw more heavily on Rome's prestige, hegemonic apparatus, and language of power, they saw eastern claims to them as an obstacle. Above and beyond their mutual rivalry, the popes and German emperors had a common interest to exclude Constantinople's claims to the Roman tradition. Thus, the easterners were increasingly reclassified as *Graeci*, a term that in ancient Latin literature conveyed negative connotations that were now reactivated, connotations of treachery, effeminacy, excessive sophistication, love of luxury, verbal trickery, and cowardice.[26] To avoid calling the emperor of the Romans by his true title, western authors invented a number of alternatives, such as *emperor of the Greeks* and *emperor of Constantinople*. Those would remain the dominant terms in the west until the nineteenth century, at which point they were replaced by *Byzantium* (see below). Naturally, the eastern Romans disliked being called Greeks. One emperor even threw papal emissaries into prison for bearing letters that addressed him as such.[27]

The issue was not merely one of east-west rivalry over the titles and the prestige of Rome. Independently of the eastern claim, in the emerging cultural world of Latin-Catholic Europe the memory of Rome had become a paradigm and common reference point by which diverse polities, peoples, languages, and churches were coordinated.[28] Beyond the imperial projects of popes and German kings, the idea of Rome was one of the few things holding the west together, to the degree that it had any common identity. The east, however, was excluded from this club, as its engagement with Rome was configured in vastly different ways than the ideas evolving in the west, so differently that it could not interface with the ongoing western reception of Rome. Eventually, it made no intuitive sense in the west to think of the eastern empire as a shareholder in the Roman tradition, and these intuitive axioms were carried forward and entrenched in scholarship. The process was neither instantaneous nor universal. There were always Latins who recognized the eastern empire as Roman and its people as Romans. But over time their numbers thinned, and the crusades intensified the anti-Greek bias. Cut off by language, the Byzantines were unable to participate or keep up with Latin intellectual developments, including the cultivation of Roman law, while their Church was increasingly perceived as deviating from the standards of the Church of Rome. An element of charged sexual polemic further cast the *Graeci* as unworthy candidates for the legacy of Rome,[29] and the conquest of Constantinople in 1204 and subsequent dismemberment of their empire made the previously rhetorical humiliations real. The sack of Constantinople was regarded by some in the west as payback for the sack of Troy: the Franks, related to the ancient Romans via a Trojan genealogy, were getting back at those perfidious Greeks.[30]

To make a long story short, western medieval observers and polemicists constructed an image of Byzantium that functioned as a discourse of orientalism parallel to that directed against the Muslim east. It was a package of distortions and strategic misunderstandings that stripped Byzantium of its claim to Rome and eventually also justified its conquest, exploitation, and (failed) attempts at conversion by western powers. This image continued without interruption down to the nineteenth century, when the field of Byzantine Studies came into being, even though it had evolved in the meantime. This is not the place to tell that story in detail. Suffice it to say that, to a considerable degree, that field was at first a systematization of preexisting prejudices: biases with references.

The polemic against the medieval "Greeks" had, in the meantime, been intensified by the thinkers of the Enlightenment. Montesquieu and Gibbon cast the "empire of the Greeks" as a steady decline from the peak of ancient Rome. Yet it is fascinating that "on the odd occasion when in his opinion "the Greeks" get something right (such as winning a battle), Gibbon will consider reverting to 'Romans.'"[31] Otherwise, in Enlightenment thought Byzantium became a symbol for all that could potentially still go wrong in Europe's triple inheritance from antiquity: Byzantium was populated by degenerate Greeks, whose language had declined; it was a corrupt New Rome, run by scheming eunuchs and women; and it was retarded by a superstitious form of Christianity that was addicted to icons and hair-splitting theology. Montesquieu, Voltaire, Rousseau, Hegel, and many others indulged in cringeworthy comments about this extinct medieval civilization, which they deployed strategically as an archetypal antithesis of the enlightened state and society that they hoped to see emerge in the west. Perhaps this imaginary Byzantium of the philosophers was not supposed to be historical at all: it functioned as a screen on which they could safely project all that they feared and disliked about their own world and its pitfalls, a dystopian mirror for the early modern nation-state.[32]

Be that as it may, this strategy pushed a historical civilization deeper into the mud of western polemic. The Enlightenment created an even more negative ideological crucible for the study of Byzantium in western scholarship, which effectively perpetuated medieval biases. Byzantium was still intuitively seen in terms of its Greek ethnicity and deviant faith (which we call Orthodoxy), and there was little esteem for either. The idea that the Byzantines might legitimately be Romans, not just in an abstract sense of titular continuity but as an ethnicity, appears preposterous under this light. The Byzantines spoke Greek, did not rule in Rome, and were not Roman Catholics. Thus, they had nothing to do with Rome in terms of language (and so ethnicity), geography, or religion. This view has become for many a form of "mental wallpaper,"[33] the "most hardwired instincts [that] have usually been left out of the spotlight of inquiry."[34] But sometimes the most obvious and natural positions are the most ideological. They require otherwise sensible historians to get into impossible contortions in order to deny the Romanness of the Byzantines, all because they accept "intuitive" premises over the plain evidence of the sources.

This perspective was distinctive to the west but was adopted by many medieval Slavs too, who had closer ties to the medieval west than many scholars realize.[35] The Byzantines themselves, by contrast, consistently claimed that they were Romans. Had their *genos* survived to modern times and developed its own scholarly traditions, there would inevitably have been a reckoning between it and these western ideologies. I suspect that these hypothetical modern *Romaioi* would have gained the upper hand and forced some recognition of their claim. The Arabs, who did not share in Latin biases, also regarded the Byzantines as *Rum* (Romans). In fact, in order to claim the ancient Greek intellectual tradition for themselves and deny it to the Greek-speakers of their own time, some Arab intellectuals were keen to deny precisely that the Byzantines were Greeks, because they were their rivals for the ownership of that tradition.[36] This was a different kind of denialism. Arab histories presented an alternative Byzantium, more accurate in some ways than the Latin version and more distorted in others, but the key point here is that they had no doubts that it was Roman. Yet for better or for worse, Byzantine Studies is a western artifact, not an Arab one, and was designed to buttress and promote western ideological claims.

Until the later nineteenth century, the standard names for Byzantium in western historiography were "empire of Constantinople" and "empire of the Greeks." The term *Byzantium*, while coined in the sixteenth century and put to occasional use after that,[37] displaced the medieval terms only after around 1850 and through a process that is poorly understood; in fact, hardly anyone knows how crucial the nineteenth century was in this story because of the prevailing error that "Byzantium" became dominant in the sixteenth.[38] I suspect that among the reasons for this switch to Byzantium was the creation of a modern Greek state in the 1820s. By midcentury, the Greeks were agitating to reclaim Constantinople and re-create the "Greek empire" that was their birthright. Because such a state would have come at the expense of the Ottoman empire, the weakest link in the fragile post-Napoleonic imperial order, western powers were opposed to this idea, and some even perceived it as a Russian plot. The Crimean War, which was fought against Russia by France and Britain, two states that played a foundational role in the development of western scholarship about Byzantium, led to an intensification of Russophobia in the west and the fear that the tsar was using his Orthodox clients in the Balkans to create a Russian-dominated Greek Orthodox empire centered on Constantinople.[39] The historiographical term *the empire of the Greeks* could be seen as legitimating these aspirations and fueling the Greeks' Grand Vision of imperial instauration. "Byzantium," by contrast, was more neutral and less inflammatory and gradually replaced the ethnic name for the empire after the Crimean War.

Thus, whereas western historiography had, until ca. 1800, accepted the continuity of "Greek" ethnic history from antiquity to the present, including Byzantium within this continuum,[40] when Byzantine Studies developed as a scholarly discipline in the later nineteenth and twentieth centuries this notion was no longer part of its core paradigm. The Greek ethnic element was played down, which is why our histories still refer to ethnically neutral "Byzantines," a fictitious generic category that avoids the complications of both the Roman and the Greek labels. The emphasis was instead placed on imperial ideology and on Orthodoxy. Whereas surveys of Byzantium written in the eighteenth and early nineteenth centuries saw it as the medieval state of the Greeks, in the twentieth century the emphasis shifted to it being an "Orthodox" empire and society. The baton of Hellenic continuity was passed, in the mid- to later nineteenth century, to nationalist historians of the new Greek state. Still, the "Greek" option abides as a fallback position within the western scholarly tradition,[41] though ultimately it can be only a loose way of talking as it is not backed by any theory of ethnicity or proof. "Greeks" can be only a temporary placeholder, *faute de mieux*, for Those Who Must Not Be Named.

In some quarters, the Greekness of Byzantium was not only soft-pedaled or quietly dropped, it was aggressively rejected. A virulent Slavophobic agenda led the German historian Jakob Philipp Fallmerayer (1790–1861) to deny that any racial continuity existed between the ancient and the modern Greeks. In his view, Byzantium had been taken over by Slavs and Albanians who half-learned how to speak Greek and whose descendants were masquerading as modern Hellenes.[42] As is well known, this attack prompted modern Greek historians to rehabilitate and appropriate Byzantium as a medieval Hellenic empire in order to buttress Greek racial continuity. Thus, as the west was moving away from the paradigm of the "Greek empire" and toward the ethnically vague notion of Byzantium, nationalist historiography in Greece ensconced the old ethnic model in its official view of the past. While there is skepticism about this model in Greece today, the empire's official Hellenization in national discourse was possible only because western historiography had already stripped it of its Romanness. Some Greek national historians still go through the same motions of dismissing the testimony of the sources and ridiculing the idea that Greek-speaking Orthodox people can "really" be Romans. By stripping off that false label, they hope to expose the Greek underneath.[43] These moves were pioneered by western medieval writers and are still with us. For different reasons, therefore, both western and national Greek historiography have an interest to engage in denialism.

In sum, the western names for Byzantium during the past thousand years were the products of politics, ideology, and powerful interests, ranging from the papacy and German emperors to the Great Powers of modernity. Their goal was not to promote understanding but to prevent Byzantium from getting in the way of ideological projects. We have still not escaped from this framework.

The Quandaries of Denialism

Two opposing forces tug at us when we consider the Romanness of Byzantium, and a synthesis of the two appears to be logically impossible. Scholars who step between them are inevitably wrenched in contradictory directions and end up in contorted positions. The first and historically dominant of these two forces is the denial of the Byzantines' Romanness. This position finds it absurd—literally and intuitively nonsensical—to believe that Byzantium and the Byzantines were Roman in a meaningful sense. The second position is reflected in the Byzantine sources, according to which not only the empire in general but also the majority of its population were ethnically Romans. In the sources, and for anyone who follows them, this position is uncontroversial and intuitive. The Byzantines *were* Romans. They did not merely "call themselves" by that name in an artificial way or to deceive someone who was looking in.

There is no viable middle ground between these two positions, and efforts to mediate between them produce only weirder variations. That is why the state of the field regarding this question is chaotic and why positions are taken on seemingly arbitrary grounds. I will give one illustration. Before World War II, George Ostrogorsky, a Russian historian active in Serbia, wrote a history of Byzantium in German that became a standard work for decades afterward. In it, he correctly defined the Byzantine way of life as the product of three main elements: Roman, Greek, and Christian, which interacted in different ways and occupied different parts of the culture.[44] This banal definition long formed the basis for college courses and general discussions of Byzantium. It is repeated, for example, by a contributor to a small introductory volume written for nonexperts to celebrate the Dumbarton Oaks Research Center. A second contributor to that same volume, however, who advocates a Greek reading of Byzantium, states that the empire had only "a double nature": Greek and Christian.[45] This demotion to two elements is not exclusive to Greek historians. In a general introduction to the Byzantines, Averil Cameron, a professor of Byzantine history in the United Kingdom, stated that their culture was based on two elements: Greek and Judeo-Christian. Yet later in the book she states that the Byzantines continued to refer to themselves as Romans. The strange implication is that the collective name by which they referred to themselves, along with its historical, political, and possibly ethnic connotations, did not count as one of the constituent elements of their culture.[46]

When Ostrogorsky referred to Byzantium's Roman aspect, he meant "the Roman imperial framework," a more limited conception of its valence than will be advocated in this book. According to his model, the Byzantines, whatever their ethnicity, actively engaged with or passively lived within a formally Roman structure of government. But even this limited notion is subject to apparently random revisions. For example, Cameron, without offering any elaboration, says that "the Byzantine administration was Greek in character."[47] This is perplexing, as there was nothing like the Byzantine administration in previous Greek history and its practices derived entirely from Roman imperial administration. Besides, how is an administration "Greek in character"? This corresponds to no analytical category known to classicists or Hellenists.

The reason behind these variations and seeming arbitrariness is that the field has not yet had a scholarly discussion of the problem of the Romanness of Byzantium, a discussion in which models are based on the primary evidence, terms are defined, evidence is analyzed as to the scope of its relevance, and rival views are juxtaposed and evaluated. There is no body of critical scholarship to act as a center of gravity for a sustained systematic discussion. In its absence, unexamined intuitions fill the gap. This section will offer a critical survey of the denialist trend in Byzantine scholarship, which, for all the havoc it has caused, is not without an amusing side. I will map the terrain of opinion, highlighting its failures and quandaries by using mostly recent publications in English, although comparable moves are made in all relevant languages. I make no bones about belonging to the Romanist camp, which I discuss at the end. Even proponents of an authentically Roman Byzantium have not defined their position precisely or consistently, leaving it too in an inchoate state.

The denialist position is basically only a continuation and rationalization of western medieval views of Byzantium. It is, moreover, utterly unselfconscious and unreflective of this fact. It has never critically examined the origins of its basic assumptions and does not know its own history, of which I offered an extremely condensed summary in the previous section. In treating its biases as natural and intuitive truths, the denialist position is strictly ideological. But these biases are contingent upon specific choices. Had German emperors and medieval popes not developed imperial ideologies of their own that lay exclusive claim to the Roman tradition, setting into motion an avalanche of polemic against the eastern empire, there would be no "Byzantium" in our history books today, no bizarre claims that the Byzantines lied or deluded themselves into thinking that they were Romans. This tradition of denial is unusual in a number of ways, and I will mention one here. A problem in many scholarly fields is that experts identify too closely with their subjects and reproduce their views uncritically, for example when Greek historians highlight the glories of ancient Hellenism or when Roman historians "side" with ancient Roman imperialism. In the case of Byzantine Studies, it is the reverse: through an academic equivalent of Stockholm syndrome, the field has adopted the perspective of those who denied Byzantine claims, derided the empire, destroyed it, and then denigrated it for centuries.

One formulation of medieval denialism, that by the German emperor Louis II in 871, shows both how similar it is to its modern counterparts and how problematic western medieval assumptions could be to begin with. The specific diplomatic context was one of those recurring altercations between the western and eastern emperors (in this case the great-grandson of Charlemagne, Louis II, and Basileios I, the founder of the Macedonian dynasty) over their titles and rights to the Roman mantle. Louis could go only so far as to call Basileios the "emperor of New Rome," while calling himself "emperor of the Romans" (this concession—that Constantinople was also Rome in its own way—would become increasingly hard to sustain in the west in later centuries). In brief, Louis argues that he has the right to be called emperor of the Romans and Basileios does not. Along the way, he makes some arguments that may strike us as modern, by which I mean only that they appear in modern scholarship. Modern scholars do not take them from Louis' letter, which few read, but from a common store of misleading ideas.

Our concern is not with the arguments that Louis advances in support of his own claim to the title of Roman emperor, but with the arguments that he makes toward the middle of his letter against Basileios' claim to it. "The Greeks," he states,

> have ceased to be emperors of the Romans on account of their bad opinions when it comes to religious faith. Also, not only have they abandoned the city and the seat of empire [Rome], they have also abandoned the Roman people [i.e., of Rome] and the language itself [Latin], having migrated in all ways to a different city, seat, people, and language [Greek].[48]

Louis and other western writers offered additional arguments against the Greeks' claim to the imperial Roman title, but these modern scholars would be reluctant to reproduce. For example, Louis maintains that he has a better claim to the title because it was bestowed on him by the pope, whereas in the east the so-called emperors were sometimes acclaimed by the senate, the people, and the armies.[49] In making this argument, Louis displayed how out of touch he was with ancient Roman tradition. In this particular aspect, eastern practice adhered to authentic Roman notions of acclamation,[50] whereas western practice did not; and only a staunch Catholic theorist would support a theory of imperial legitimacy through papal coronation. To give another example, the western *Annals of Lorsch* claimed that the imperial title was available to be assumed by Charlemagne because the eastern ruler at the time was a woman, Eirene, who clearly did not count, making the throne effectively vacant.[51] None of this is relevant anymore, nor is Louis' claim that the "Greeks" had lost the right to the Roman title because of their bad religious opinions.

The part of Louis' letter that codified the bedrock of western denialism for centuries is its claims about ethnicity, speech, and geography. Louis assumes that Basileios' subjects are "Greeks" and calls them that throughout the letter. While he concedes that an emperor of the Romans could be appointed from among the Greeks, Spaniards, or Franks, he promotes the city of Rome as the deciding criterion, in part because it theoretically fell within his realm and also because his letter was possibly ghost-written by Anastasius the Librarian, a native of Rome who had an ax to grind against Byzantium.[52] Basileios could not be emperor of the Romans because his people were not Romans either by ethnicity or language and also because Basileios did not hold the city of Rome.

Similar views were expressed by Liudprand of Cremona, who visited the court of Nikephoros II Phokas as an emissary of the German emperor in 968 and wrote a satirical and hostile account of his experience. When Nikephoros was angry at the pope for addressing him as emperor of the Greeks, Liudprand disingenuously responded that the pope had actually wanted to flatter him: yes, Constantinople had been founded by Romans, but since you have now changed the language, customs, and dress, the pope feared that he might offend by calling you Romans.[53] Liudprand knew perfectly that the Byzantines called themselves Romans, and only pretended that he was surprised to hear it. What is important, however, is that he too frames the issue as one of ethnicity, pointing to language, customs, and dress. In the eyes of a western observer, these indicia proved that the Byzantines were Greeks.

Consider how little had changed by the time of Gibbon, eight hundred years later. For Gibbon, "the Franks and Latins . . . asserted, with some justice, their superior claim to the language and dominion of Rome. They insulted the aliens of the east who had renounced the dress and idiom of Romans; and their reasonable practice will justify the frequent appellation of Greeks" [i.e., by Gibbon himself in his narrative].[54]

One goal of this book will be to argue that these assumptions, especially when converted into quasi-scholarly arguments by modern historians, reflect a mistaken view of Roman identity; are not grounded in the Roman tradition that Byzantium inherited from antiquity; and directly contradict fundamental axioms of modern research in the humanities and social sciences, especially regarding ethnic identities. Before delving into the heart of the case, I want to illustrate the persistence of these views across wide swaths of the field and the invidious ways in which they work. Anyone who has read much Byzantine scholarship will have encountered them many times, but it is still illuminating to see medieval biases echoed by scholars, who profess to be baffled at the Byzantines for continuing to "call themselves Romans" when we supposedly know that they "really" were not. For example, the holder of a named chair in Byzantine Studies wrote that "the inhabitants of the successor empire in Constantinople paradoxically never ceased to refer to themselves as Romans—paradoxically because the language of administration and literature was . . . Greek."[55] Others echo the claim that the empire was cut off from the alleged "source of its ideology," meaning the Roman west, or "cut off from the cradle of its Roman ideology, the city of Rome." Yet even after that its inhabitants still "stubbornly" called themselves Romans.[56]

The criterion of "Italy" is interesting because it exposes both the origins of modern denialism and the hypocrisy at its heart. Rome and Italy had ceased to be the deciding or even a relevant criterion of Romanness already in the second century AD, as Romans at the time had already realized: a Roman general of Antiochene origin even said that "Rome was wherever the emperor was."[57] In the third century, Romans filled the entire empire, emperors stopped living in Rome or even visiting it, and they began to call their provincial capitals "Rome." Rome was now a world, not a city.[58] No contemporary source for the fourth, fifth, sixth, seventh, or eighth century suggests that to be Roman you had to live in Rome, be from Rome, or control Rome, and no modern scholar of those centuries thinks so either. In a period when the emperors came from the provinces and spent their entire reigns there, St. Jerome declared that, when it came to (Roman) authority, "the world outweighs the city."[59] But when popes and German emperors in the ninth century begin to assert the centrality of Rome to Romanness, suddenly and conveniently modern scholars also discover that lost criterion and use it to discredit Byzantine claims to Romanness. Needless to say, the eastern Romans, who were the product of the globalization of Romanness between the second and the fourth centuries, were unaware of this criterion.[60]

In order to deny Byzantine Romanness, some modern historians defend the invented term *Byzantine empire* as appropriate not only for the sake of convention or as only a period of Roman history, but on substantive grounds, because—I have italicized some crucial words—

> it underlines that both empire and people were distinct from their Roman forerunners—*it does not matter that the Byzantines almost always called it the Roman Empire and themselves Romans*. The essence of this distinction between Roman and Byzantine is to be found in the capital city of Byzantium, where a new culture and political system were forged out of old materials. . . . Abandoning Rome and the West to the barbarians meant that *Romanitas*—what it meant to be a Roman—was being drained of meaning.[61]

The resemblance between ancient Rome and Byzantium is described by the same historian as "superficial and schematic," a mere "illusion of the continuing unity of the Roman world around Constantinople."[62] This is then washed down with disparaging comments, another legacy of the Enlightenment: "Byzantium turned out to be the weakest of the medieval civilizations, with the least to offer in terms of originality and development."63 We should turn to Venice if want to find true splendor.64

Denialism has, then, developed its own terms of art, such as "Byzantium," along with specialized methods of evasion. The most common method in introducing the Byzantines is to say that they "called themselves" or "referred to themselves" as Romans, but for the modern historian to not then call them that herself. This is done, for example on the first page of the recent *Oxford Handbook of Byzantine Studies*.65 A corollary of this practice is to put the name "Romans" in quotation marks. This is a truly weird habit, if we think for a moment what it would look like if applied to any other historical people who had a strongly held, widely attested, and quite serviceable name. It is also out of sync with modern efforts to restore indigenous names to groups that have been marginalized in western perceptions of history (e.g., Inuit for Eskimo). In the case of Byzantium, this odd practice of circumlocution and quotation marks plants invidious doubts about whether the Byzantines "really were" who they thought and said they were.

Denialism is often coupled with moral censure. A professor of Byzantine history writes that the Byzantines "pulled off one of the greatest deceptions in history, presenting their society in terms of absolute continuity with the past: to very end they insisted on describing themselves as 'Romans' as if nothing had changed since ancient times."66 For this historian, the fact of "change" makes the Byzantines' claim to be Romans an act of deception. He does not, however, also present us with a methodology by which we can tell how much and what kind of change can support such a conclusion. Rome had "changed" also between Scipio and Cicero, Cicero and Hadrian, and Hadrian and Constantine. Even historians of ancient Rome these days are not sure how much continuity lies beneath the massive changes that the city experienced. As Harriet Flower put it, "How can the archaic community of the Romans be said to be the same republic as the one that conquered Carthage or the one described by Cicero?"67 Either all should count as Roman, or we must reduce history to a series of unconnected microslices defined by ever narrower frames of reference. In coping with this problem, William Harris, a historian of ancient Rome, writes that, "Almost everything changes [in Roman history], not only the sources and the material culture, but the principal language and the dominant religion. But that is a challenge, not an excuse."[68] Byzantium is part of that challenge, as Harris recognizes.

A recent book-length study finds that what it meant to be Roman in antiquity varied by period, region, and context, and calls for the plural study of Roman *identities*. Emma Dench concludes that study with a warning that points directly, in my eyes, to Byzantium:

> Any notion of an "end" to my account of Roman identities is obviously problematic. We have, it is true, hinted at the emergence of strikingly different formulations of identity at the end of the period considered. . . . I would be very weary of positing a decisive break with the past, or a definitive shift towards "global" identities, or anything of the sort.[69]

In other words, modern scholars of ancient Rome—one standard by which we might evaluate the Romanness of Byzantium—are more open to change and variation within Roman tradition than are Byzantinists. The latter should have been leading the charge but, shamefully, have been in steady retreat. They may fear that claiming Byzantium as Roman will elicit resistance from historians of ancient Rome. Based on these recent studies, however, I expect that we will be pushing against an open door.

"Change" is one arbitrary criterion invented ad hoc to justify a preexisting prejudice. There are others. Some affirm that Byzantium was "too small" to be authentically Roman.[70] Again, there appears to be no methodology in the whole of Ancient Roman Studies that justifies this conclusion: How small can Rome get without ceasing to be Rome? No ancient historian has addressed this question. It is only an arbitrary criterion of what it means to be "authentically" Roman that is designed to exclude Byzantium. Here is another, even more bizarre, criterion: "The Greek East, despite its self-identification as 'Roman,' does not appear to have been concerned with oral sex at all."[71] I admit that I cannot reconstruct the logic here. Other scholars have claimed that the sources of Byzantine law had lost the "spirit of Roman law,"[72] while an older study of Greek urbanism asserted that

Constantinople ceased to be a Roman city because of the inherent evil of the Byzantine empire.[73]

A claim such as that, made before World War II, may seem to have no place in our scholarship, and there is growing recognition among historians of the continuity between Rome and New Rome. Yet monographs and textbooks continue to rely on Enlightenment caricatures of Byzantium in order to periodize history in moral-political terms. Byzantium, for example, does not count as a real Rome because it was too despotic and oriental. It reached back to the empires of the ancient Near East in order to find models for its "distant ruler with a heavy hand brandishing a strong religious ideology ... even more so than [it did to] the earlier Roman empire." Another recent study calls Byzantium an autocratic and theocratic state that had moved from orthodoxy to fundamentalism and fused religion with politics in a way that would not be undone until the Enlightenment, whose roots lay in the medieval west. These are not cranky fringe publications but academic monographs published by mainstream presses.[74] Such perceptions are entrenched and widespread. The leading historian of the Hittites could write (in 2002) that the Hittites failed to produce anything like the "paranoid despots of imperial Rome ... to say nothing of the succession of grotesque monsters who occupied the throne of Byzantium."[75] I wrote to him and asked which monsters he had in mind, but I did not receive an answer. Moralizing views of history still inform scholarly periodizations.

The denialists' criteria are so diverse—small, Greek, oriental, evil—that they are patently pretexts for a preexisting position. They are not drawing on some foundational study that rigorously established the case but are instead inventing ad hoc criteria to patrol the borders of a separation that they feel they must enforce. Their individual positions face substantial methodological problems. In no case do they offer supporting reasons why the criterion they choose is relevant or able, even if it were true, to prove that the Byzantines were not Romans. The most disarming evasion that I have come across recently, in a recent book on Byzantine collective identities no less, is that the name "Roman" could not be considered because there are simply too many attestations of it. After all, the author adds, it had to do only with imperial ideology and not identity.[76] This nicely

A HISTORY OF DENIAL

illustrates how the modern view of Byzantine Romanness as an almost metaphysical concept inhibits research into its actual meaning.

Denialism results in baffling expressions, as historians try to occupy the nonexistent space between western prejudices and the unambiguous evidence of the Byzantine sources. We are told, for example, that despite their "shrunken circumstances," the Byzantines "found it difficult to abandon their sense of being *Rhomaioi*, 'Romans.'"[77] What offstage narrative is implied by this odd statement? It is as if some force were pushing them to abandon their sense of who they were, and they were *almost* at the point of doing so, but in the end they could not quite bring themselves to do it. This sounds instead like a displaced metaphor for what is going on in modern scholarship: We would like to abandon the term *Roman* in dealing with the Byzantines, but we cannot quite do so, because it is written all over the sources. Consider also the emperor Herakleios, who, we are told, "did not consider his empire to be a Near Eastern state"—which is correct, because he lacked such a concept (so why is it mentioned?). Instead, "it was a Roman one, however vague that was in his mind."[78] But we are not told why Herakleios would have had a vaguer notion of the Romanness of his empire than any previous emperor. In reality, it is we who have a vague understanding of the matter and project it onto them. Yet we pretend it is the other way around: that we know the real, inner, deeper truth about who the Byzantines really were, whereas they were trapped in outdated labels and self-deception.

As we have seen, denialism works its invidious ways through adverbs such as "stubbornly," "paradoxically," "vaguely," and "technically." "The Byzantines always termed themselves Romans, since their empire was the direct continuation of the ancient Roman empire, technically at least."[79] Here a distinction is implied between who the Byzantines claimed they were, which is only a technicality, and some other putative essence of their identity that we know and they did not. But maybe they *did* know and were only pretending all along. In no less than the Presidential Address delivered at the American Philological Association meeting of 2004, it was asserted that Byzantium was only "outwardly Roman [and was] increasingly incoherent and unable to match its sense of self to its reality because it knew too clearly what it was and what it had been."[80] Here the implication of deception is raised again, as the Byzantines seem to have known that they were no longer "really" Romans and that by 600 AD "all the *romanitas* had gone out of it [their empire]."[81] The footnote to the published version of the address implies that in reality they were Greeks.

One modality of denialism for "containing" the Romanness of Byzantium is to restrict it to the rarefied space of imperial ideology and propaganda, as if it had nothing to do with the majority of the empire's inhabitants. Byzantinists quickly reach for the emperor's titles when they have to explain the appearance in the sources of the ethnonym "Romans." The discussion can then be transposed to a theological level and linked to ecumenical visions, End-Time scenarios, God's plan for the salvation of mankind, and the like.[82] In this way, the Roman name was a purely formal matter that operated "officially" (another one of those tricky adverbs).[83] It was a function of "the consciously antiquated language of the sources."[84] This trope of a formal reality—that is, an unreal reality—is invoked when Byzantium exhibits traits that do not fit the model that scholars have constructed for it (including rationality, classicism, freedom, continuity, and the like). They are exorcised by being labeled as purely nominal, official, antiquarian, or "paradoxical." This is a tool for sweeping away "stubborn" facts that do not fit the model. In our case, that fact is nothing less than who the Byzantines were.

In drawing a distinction between an "official" view of reality promulgated by the "antiquarian" texts of the court (on the one hand) and the identity of the majority of Byzantines (on the other), scholars are again implicitly following the lead of partisan medieval observers such as Louis II. Louis, we recall, intuitively saw the subjects of Basileios as "Greeks." The only thing even *potentially* Roman that he saw in Byzantium were the titles and propaganda of the court, and even those he was concerned to deny. Likewise, a strain of modern scholarship views the Roman identity of Byzantium primarily in terms of "official" imperial theory, court titles, and diplomacy, a sphere that naturally excluded the majority of the population.[85] A variant of this position uses modern "critical theory" to argue that Roman identity in Byzantium was limited to the literary elite in

A HISTORY OF DENIAL

Constantinople.[86] However, such conclusions can be drawn only in analytical frameworks from which most or all of the evidence has been excluded. As we will see, and as the field has always known, claims to Roman identity in Byzantium are abundant, extend in scope well beyond the court and elites, and consistently point in the opposite direction: the ethnicity or nationality of the majority of the population was Roman, as indicated already in the five snapshots presented at the head of this chapter.

Who were the Byzantines, then?

One approach is to see them as a vast enigma. Consider a classic paper by Paul Magdalino, "Hellenism and Nationalism in Byzantium." Magdalino presents a number of texts that strongly suggest that Byzantium was a nation-state and harbored forms of nationalism. He does not deny these impressions or even their reality, but he leaves the matter open when he finds that he cannot answer the question, "What 'nation' did it represent?" He does not consider the possibility that it might be the very nation—the Roman one—that his sources are constantly talking about. That group is simply not on his radar, so he concludes that "the question of ethnicity was left open," which we have already seen was certainly not the case.[87] In this case, denialism has rendered the Romans invisible, as if they never existed.

Another approach, which we have seen already, is to follow the western lead and call the Byzantines Greeks, or rather to characterize them as Greek in some loose way that does not call for a rigorous analysis of their ethnicity. With the exception of a tiny number of intellectuals in the later period, the Byzantines themselves did not think they were Greeks and resented the name, which was imposed on them by the Latins.[88] It is not a coincidence that the name Greeks is used for the Byzantines far more frequently by scholars who work on the later period of the empire. This is not because they follow the lead of those two or three Hellenizing Byzantine thinkers. Rather, the later period was when the Latins colonized the Byzantine world and left more sources about their "Greek" subjects, allies, and enemies, making it easier for historians to simply follow the western lead. Translations of Byzantine texts sometimes even render *Romaios* as "Greek."

Yet commitment to the Greek ethnic identification has been tepid among western historians since the late nineteenth century. They do not intend for it to legitimate arguments of ethnic Greek continuity from antiquity to the present, to buttress diachronic histories of the Greeks, or to "claim" Byzantium for the Greek nation. *Greek* is just a superficially plausible term to use instead of *Roman*, and is legitimated by western medieval sources. A recent book series called "The Edinburgh History of the Greeks" and featuring volumes of outstanding quality almost became an exception to this pattern. The series editor insists that the series will focus "on the history of a people, the Greeks, and not a place, Greece," but the author of the Byzantine volume, Florin Curta, heads this off immediately in his introduction by making clear that his volume on the years 500–1050 AD is a history of *Greece*. He correctly explains that these were Romans, and so "the Greek people" do not appear in the book.[89]

The chief tool that modern Byzantinists have invented in order to remove Romanness from the picture, while still remaining within the Byzantines' conceptual horizons, is to highlight Orthodox Christianity as their chief and, in some cases, their only identity. In relation to their Romanness, this works in one of two (equally arbitrary) ways. Either Romanness is denied, in the usual ways, after which we are told that the Byzantines' "real" identity was Orthodoxy, or else the two are identified: what the Byzantines meant when they said that they were Romans was that they were Christians.

Neither of these interpretations withstands scrutiny. As we will see, the Byzantines perfectly well understood the categorical difference between their ethnicity and their religion. For example, they knew that the Romans had once been pagans and they knew, especially after the conversion of Bulgaria in the ninth century, that there were Orthodox people in the world, even within their empire, who were not Romans. This was not a difficult distinction to make and it caused no confusion. The most that can be said about this interpretation is that these two identities—ethnic and religious—overlapped in Byzantium, so that in many contexts there was no reason to distinguish between them. It was between the seventh and the ninth centuries especially, when Byzantium was surrounded by non-Roman infidels, that these two identities most closely fused. We should expect them to do so. But this is not what the scholarship is getting at. It wants to sweep Romanness under the rug of Orthodoxy in order to hide it from sight.

The distinction between Roman and Orthodox identities will be discussed with reference to the sources in Chapter 2. But it had to be mentioned here, in the survey of denialism, because that is the context in which it functions. As "Roman" was taken off the table in the ninth century, and "Greek" became a problematic national category in the nineteenth, historians of the twentieth were left with nothing besides "Orthodox" to fill the gap when they have to explain to their readers who or what the "Byzantines" were.

By contrast, the Greekness of Byzantium remains a matter of national importance for some modern Greek historians. In addition to adopting the regular tropes of Roman denialism, they like to cite the small number of late Byzantine intellectuals who made gestures in the direction of a Greek identity, and they privilege the role of language in its definition, for what else could Greek-speakers have been if not Greeks?[90] But this isolates one component of a culture (language) in order to support a predetermined position. As this book will argue, however, names used for languages and ethnicity do not always overlap, and the Byzantines increasingly called their language not Greek but *Romeika*, or "the language of the Romans." For us it is "Greek"; for them it was "Roman." In time, therefore, ethnic identity overcame linguistics (the Swiss and Austrians are not Germans; the Indians and Americans are not English; and so on).

In sum, the field of Byzantine Studies suffers from an acute form of what is commonly called cognitive dissonance: while knowing that Byzantium was the Roman empire and that the Byzantines called themselves Romans, it carries on as if neither statement were "really" true. To cope with this unpleasant predicament, it has devised various evasions and terms of art by which it can confuse the issue—enough, at least, to avoid drawing obvious conclusions. These tropes are part of the catechism that Byzantinists are trained to intone in order to prove that they have mastered the subtleties of the field. And it invites the interpretation that the Byzantines were deceiving themselves in the matter of their Romanness, or attempting to deceive others, opinions that have been affirmed by otherwise serious historians. Thus, who the Byzantines were is a question that continues to defeat the field, because many of its practitioners have taken the Byzantines' own answer off the table.

Outside the Echo Chamber

No ideology, however pervasive, can entrap everyone all of the time. Historians of Byzantium have to work with sources that clearly and powerfully refute the fictions of denialism. Inevitably, a steady and distinguished line of Byzantinists have pushed back against its paradigm, or have made statements that do the same effectively, whether intended as a repudiation of it or not. These scholars deserve mention both for recognition and because more work needs to be done beyond what they did toward documenting, clarifying, and theorizing Byzantine Romanness, which these scholars noted and accepted but generally passed by on their way to other scholarly goals.

During the second half of the nineteenth century, historians transitioned from calling the eastern Roman empire "the empire of the Greeks" to calling it "Byzantium." Honorable mention should be made of E. A. Freeman (1823–1892), who advocated the latter term as a way of avoiding the misleading ethnic term "Greek." More than most modern historians, Freeman explained in detail how the empire was Roman, so for him "Byzantine" was just a way of saying "east Roman."[91] But for most other scholars, "Byzantine" was becoming a term that avoided both ethnic Greek entanglements and the empire's Romanness. No sooner had "Byzantium" established itself as the paradigm and name of the new field than John Bagnell Bury (1861–1927) protested against it in the preface to his history (1899) of what he called the Later Roman Empire between 395 and 800 AD, insisting that there was no break that justified a new label. That label, he correctly foresaw, would lead to unwarranted conclusions.[92] Bury was the best "Byzantinist" of his generation and his narrative histories still hold up well.[93] By 1923, when he edited the volumes of the *Cambridge Medieval History* devoted to the "Eastern Roman Empire," he had come around and accepted the new label, but only as a concession to convenience. He was emphatic in the preface that, for all the cultural continuity between ancient Greece and Byzantium, the inhabitants of the "eastern" Roman empire were Romans who spoke a *Romaic* version of Greek, lived in Roumelia (formerly Romanía), and were known to the Arabs as Rum. It was the western empires of Charlemagne and his descendants that had a tenuous claim to the name of Rome.[94] Bury knew exactly the sources of western denialism.

To my knowledge, however, Bury did not explain *how* the Byzantines were constituted as a Roman people (i.e., by what criteria) or what this meant to them beyond pride in the continuity of imperial history. Such an exercise would probably have been beyond the analytical tools available to him at the time, and would have spoiled his excellent prose standards. Steven Runciman (1903–2000) was briefly Bury's student and like him learned Byzantine history primarily from the sources. He was also willing to defend Byzantium against medieval biases, an instinct that would shape his later history of the crusades. In his first book, on Romanos I Lakapenos (1929), Runciman went further than Bury in trying to explain how the Byzantines were Romans. The following passage is worth quoting:

> It may seem paradoxical to urge the nationality of the Empire while insisting on its cosmopolitan nature; certainly, if nationality implies a common ethnological past the Byzantines had none. But such a past is not necessary, as today the United States of America is witness; and in Byzantium the tradition inherited from the world-empire of Rome gave the Byzantines a national unity that overpowered ethnological divergencies—a national unity far more real than any that was to exist in Western Europe till the days of the Reformation. Every Byzantine citizen, were his blood Greek or Armenian or Slav, was proudly and patriotically conscious that he was Ῥωμαῖος. . . . This nationality even tended to mould its people according to one fixed form; and it is as possible to talk of Byzantine characteristics as to talk of Roman and British characteristics.

Writing in 1929, Runciman was not able to frame the question with quite the precision that we would want, but the answer that he proposes makes perfect sense. Specifically, on the previous page he had set out to discuss the "many different races" that lived in the empire, alternating in his discussion among the terms race, nation, tribe, purity of blood, and origin. In his view, Byzantium "mixed" these "ingredients" together and produced from them a single "nation" like that of the United States. It would be a "ruinous misconception," he urged, to deny that Byzantium had a "nationality," which he correctly identified as that of the Romaioi, even though he evidently had trouble in defining the elements that composed it. I would also disagree with him if he meant that *all* inhabitants of the empire were Romaioi in this sense. As we will see, the empire contained ethnic minorities that were regarded as non-Roman by the majority and probably by themselves too. This fact explains the slippage in Runciman's vocabulary, especially between blood and nationality. Postwar historians do not believe in Greek blood or Armenian blood (or at least they say that they do not). But for 1929, when the apparatus of the term "ethnicity" did not yet exist, Runciman's formulation of the distinction between ethnic background and nationality is not bad.

Not even the straitjackets of Balkan nationalism were capable of blocking the truth fully from sight, especially from scholars who spent most of their time reading the primary sources. Consider Ioannes Sykoutris, an exceptional Greek philologist (1901–1937). The formation in which the Greek people lived in the medieval period, he says, was the state of the Romans.

> This [i.e., the label "Roman"] was not merely a conventional [name] or outward form. The Byzantine state was not the creation of the Greek spirit or the Greek nation. It was the continuation of this state [i.e., of the Roman empire] which was founded by the Roman people and subsequently governed by the Caesars. Its organization, army, legislation, its language (at least in the beginning), its traditions, the spiritual principle that infused it, its consciousness (for the most part), its name, its influence on neighboring peoples, etc. etc. were all Roman.[95]

He goes on to say that all Byzantinists should have a thorough grounding in ancient Roman history and the Latin language. That might actually be one way out of this mess.

The German historian Hans-Georg Beck (1910–1999) also devoted a part of his research to rehabilitating Byzantium as a genuinely Roman society, especially in the article *Res Publica Romana* (1970) and in the long book *Das byzantinische Jahrtausend* (1978), which is probably the best book ever written on Byzantium. Beck was not concerned with the Byzantines as a Roman ethnicity or nationality but rather with how their political society was, at core, Roman. I have presented a version of this thesis, albeit significantly modified, in a separate book, and so I will not dwell on it here.[96] Beck deserves mention in an honor roll of Byzantinists who took Byzantine Romanness seriously. His ideas have not had the impact that they deserved.

During the past generation individual voices have also spoken up in support of the Byzantines' Romanness. For example, Evangelos Chrysos told the Nineteenth International Congress of Byzantine Studies (Copenhagen, 1996) that the Roman aspect was not limited to imperial ideology and the court "but had also become the point of reference in the personal field of self-consciousness of the normal citizen." References to the Romans as a *genos* in a great variety and large number of texts "demonstrate a sense of some sort of 'ethnic' identity and solidarity of all the citizens of the entire empire."[97] This is entirely correct, but the problem with these programmatic statements is that they are scattered across the literature and are presented without systematic elaboration or confrontation with the distortions that pervade the field. It is thus easy for them to be lost or missed. Another interesting trend that I have noticed is that they are increasingly made by major scholars but in fields adjacent to Byzantium, for example by historians of Rus' (Simon Franklin),[98] southeastern Europe (Florin Curta, who also definitely counts as a Byzantinist),[99] the Arabs (Hugh Kennedy),[100] and the medieval west (Chris Wickham, whose range is broader).[101] These scholars are seeing something in the sources that appears to be invisible to those trained by graduate programs in Byzantine Studies. Writing about a different set of problems, Noam Chomsky has often commented on the extraordinary expertise and mental discipline that it takes to systematically deny the obvious (e.g., that all U.S. presidents since World War II have been war criminals). We may be in a situation where professional training is providing the blinkers and blind spots that denialism requires, and that it is flourishing especially among the community of Byzantinists even as it is losing ground among outsiders.

Still, there are hopeful signs of change. There is a growing recognition that periodizations that erect a wall between Rome and Byzantium can cause us to miss important links and continuities.[102] I am also increasingly coming across acknowledgments in books from many fields, including popular books, that the Roman empire did not entirely fall in the fifth century but continued on in the east until 1453. This may be banal and trite, but it pushes back against a major pillar of a certain view of history according to which "the" Roman empire fell in the fifth century; that is, the western one, the only one that was presumably "really" Roman. Students who encounter the new paradigm are increasingly beginning to wonder in what sense the eastern empire was "Roman" too, especially when its sources, which they can now increasingly access in good translations, are chock-full of Romans. Unfortunately, Byzantinists are not well positioned to answer this question for them.

There are also signs that nonexperts are beginning to catch on that we have been bullshitting them. U.S. historian Clifton Fox wrote a paper called "What, If Anything, Is a Byzantine?," which recognizes that "the names by which things are called are important in shaping our interpretation of reality. People are often surprised to discover that historical labels which define the past are inventions of later scholarship and ideology.... The people of the 'Byzantine empire' had no idea that they were Byzantine. They regarded themselves as the authentic continuators of the Roman world: the Romans living in Romania."[103] Likewise, philosophy professor Kelley Ross has created a sprawling but lively website dedicated to the many ways in which historians have distorted the Roman nature of Byzantium, where he seeks to uncover what lay behind the smoke screen of modern labels.[104] It is alarming to realize that most professional Byzantinists are unable or refuse to state these basic facts in plain words, far less communicate a sense of intellectual excitement about them. Intelligent nonexperts have had to read against the grain of our scholarship in order to discover the truth.

I close with a scene in Tom Holt's comic historical novel *Meadowland*, told by a Byzantine eunuch escorting two Varangian guardsmen. No Byzantinist has ever put it better:

> Kari shrugged. "It's like I always say," he replied. "You Greeks are bloody clever, but you haven't got a clue."
>
> I was getting just a little tired of these Northerners' attitude towards my people and my City. "For a start," I said, "you can stop calling us Greeks, when we're the great and indivisible Roman Empire, and we've been in business for just on a thousand years—longer, if you don't make a distinction between the Empire and the Republic, which was founded seventeen hundred and eighty years ago—"
>
> "You can't be Romans," Kari interrupted. "Rome's in Italy. And it's hundreds of years since Rome was part of the empire. And you don't talk Latin, you talk Greek, and none of you are Italians. In fact, most of you aren't even Greeks any more, you're bits and pieces of all sorts of things, all bundled up together and cross-bred, foreigners in your own City. Which is silly, if you ask me."
>
> I tried to look all dignified and aloof, but I've never had the knack. "Being Roman is more a state of mind than a simple accident of birth," I said. "It's something you aspire to. We tend to judge a man by where he's arrived at, not where he came from."[105]

2

Roman Ethnicity

*Nam civium Romanorum omnium
sanguis coniunctus existimandus est.*

Three More Snapshots

Three more snapshots bring the contours of Byzantine Romanness into focus and fill in more of the picture outlined by the five snapshots offered at the head of Chapter 1. What personal and social "content" made someone a Roman in Byzantium, beyond the formal labels of state (being a subject of the "emperor of the Romans") and law (being a Roman citizen)?

6. *Juxtaposing Franks and Romans.* The historian Agathias, writing around 580, presented an idealized image of contemporary Frankish society. He did this by, first, postulating that they were in all ways similar to "us" (i.e., "the Romans"), and then noting some of the ways in which they differed. This parity did not, however, remove the Franks from the category of "barbarians" in his eyes, but at least they were not nomads. I quote the passage and then extract its implications for the kind of group that the Romans constituted for Agathias.

> The Franks are not nomads, as some barbarians are, but their polity and laws are modeled on the Roman pattern, apart from

which they uphold similar standards with regard to contracts, marriage, and religious observance. They are in fact all Christians and adhere to the strictest orthodoxy. They also have magistrates in their cities, priests, and celebrate the feasts in the same way as we do; and, for a barbarian people, they strike me as extremely well-bred, civilized, and as practically the same as ourselves except for their uncouth style of dress and peculiar language.[1]

Agathias offers a global, comprehensive definition of who the Franks are as a people by deploying the categories of classical ethnography and applying them to a base-Roman template, which is then adjusted to reflect the distinctive aspects of Frankish culture and society. According to him, a people—today we might say an ethnic group or nation—is defined by its polity, laws, religion, customs, morality, language, and dress. The Franks and Romans are equivalent entities on this level: they fill out all the same questions on the census, but check different boxes under some of them. It is interesting that dress and language, rather than more abstract qualities such as politics and civilization, are singled out as the chief markers of difference between the two. Conversely, while religion is listed among the categories, Christianity is not a quality that can distinguish the Romans here, for the Franks shared that with them; it is instead dress and speech that chiefly mark difference.

Yet kinship was also an issue. In Snapshot 3 of Chapter 1, Konstantinos VII saw the nations of the world as basically separate species of animals that should not intermarry, making one exception for unions between Romans and Franks. Even so, the two people did not have a common ancestry; they were a different *genos*. The twelfth-century historian Ioannes Zonaras says something interesting about this. He quotes the sixth-century historian Prokopios of Kaisareia as saying that the Franks were not part of the Roman *genos* because they belonged to the German *ethnos*. Prokopios had indeed said that the Franks were Germans, but he had not gone out of his way, as Zonaras does, to deny that they were related to the Romans; that would have been too obvious in the sixth century. In other words, Zonaras wanted to make it extra clear that Franks and Romans were not ethnically related, possibly in reaction to affirmations, such as we find in Agathias, of the "cultural kinship" between the two leading powers of the Christian world.[2]

7. A Byzantine colony in ninth-century Italy. An early twelfth-century addition to the history of Ioannes Skylitzes notes that Basileios I (867–886) founded the city of Kallipolis (Gallipoli) on the coast of southern Italy by resettling people there from the city of Herakleia on the Black Sea coast. "This explains why that city still uses Roman customs and dress and a thoroughly Roman social order, down to this day."[3] "Roman" is again defined through the same ethnographic terms: one can tell who is a Roman and who is not by the presence or absence of mundane ethnic traits such as dress. Not everyone in Byzantine southern Italy was a Roman, and these, then, were the criteria by which one could tell the difference. The passage has two additional corollaries. First, it implies that a provincial population from the Black Sea coast, and not only the populace of Constantinople, could serve as a benchmark for Byzantine Romanness, especially when transplanted to Italy, where the population was ethnically diverse. Second, the author expects that, barring major disruption, the town's ethnic profile would abide during the three centuries between its foundation and his own time. In the local Italian context, this implies a continuity in settlement. "The persistence of 'local' or 'indigenous' traits, habits, styles, and so on constitutes a kind of descent,"[4] and therefore a kind of ethnicity. The bishops of Gallipoli remained "Greek" until the later fourteenth century.[5]

8. Saint Neilos is taken for a barbarian. The tenth-century saint Neilos the Younger was from Rossano, Calabria, a predominantly Greek-speaking city in the farthest corner of the empire. One day he found a fox pelt thrown by the side of the road and, for reasons known only to himself, tied it around his head. In this way, he went around the town and no one recognized him. "Some children saw him dressed like that and began to throw stones at him, saying, 'Hey you Bulgarian monk!,' whereas others called him a Frank and some an Armenian."[6] His vita does not explicitly say that he or his compatriots were Romans, but that was the implied standard against which ethnic difference was judged. As Florin Curta has observed about provincial Greek hagiographies, their "audience was 'Roman.' Clearly, there was no reason to stress the obvious."[7] The common ethnonym was so immanent that it could be taken for granted, which must be factored into any analysis of its valence for the Byzantines.

Whether we read an implied default Romanness into this passage or not, what is significant is that provincial populations, including children, were willing to make ethnic assignments based on headgear or other distinguishing peculiarities of appearance. It is a bad sign for the position of ethnic minorities in the empire that their first instinct was to throw stones at foreigners. But the point here concerns ethnic sensitivities and the way that provincials read ethnicity into apparel. Byzantine authors, for example the emperor Konstantinos VII (Snapshot 3), typically refer to the "customs" of the Romans that, among other traits, defined them as a nation. Language was one such trait and dress was another. A son of the Bulgarian tsar Petar, returning from a stay at the Roman court, was killed by a Bulgarian border guard because he was wearing Roman clothing.[8] This may have been a reference to elite court dress. But there are stories that take us down the social ladder. We hear of spies sent out by the Persians and later the Muslims who were "dressed like Romans," could speak the Roman language, and were sent out to mingle among provincials.[9] Approaching a Roman city in foreign clothes could get one arrested and interrogated as a spy.[10] The story of Neilos reminds us not to seek ethnicity exclusively or primarily in textual notions and definitions: for most people it was a function of tangible, audible, or visual attributes, such as headgear. Ethnic distinctions were activated in real time, on the ground, and were not, as they misleadingly appear to us, abstract academic constructs. For people at the time, they verged on being physical.

In the fourteenth century, the historian Nikephoros Gregoras complained in his *Roman History* that during the reign of Andronikos III Palaiologos (1328–1341) everyone, whether they worked in the fields or the palace, wore strange hats: Latin, Serbian, Bulgarian, or Syrian, each according to his taste.[11] Writing about a later reign, he complained that the same confusion extended to all dress worn by the Romans, such that, from his dress alone "one could no longer tell whether a person was a Roman or belonged to some other *genos*."[12] Here too Romans are imagined as one among a crowded field of equivalent, if not equal, ethnic groups or nations, and the borders between the members of the set could be policed by normative concepts regarding what was appropriate for each.

Ethnicity in the Black Hole

The snapshots presented above and in Chapter 1 strongly suggest that the Romans of Byzantium were an ethnic (or national) community. The remainder of this chapter and Chapter 3 will confirm this preliminary conclusion by mapping out, both geographically and socially, whom the Roman sources included and whom they excluded from the Roman community. We will pay attention also to the criteria that justified inclusion and exclusion. The factors that we will find, taken together, suggest that the Romans were an ethnic group that demarcated itself against other ethnic groups by roughly the same criteria that are used by modern scholars to discuss ethnicity.

This approach and the conclusions it produces are far removed from the consensus that prevails in the mainstream of Byzantine Studies. But we are justified in disregarding that consensus for two reasons (there are others, but these will suffice). First, ethnicity has never been a topic of focused, systematic, and theoretically informed research in Byzantine Studies. I know of no study that tries to understand the ethnicities of the Byzantine empire in a way that aligns with fields of research in which the study of ethnicity is more advanced. Indeed, there are almost no studies, whether books or articles, that combine the words "ethnicity" and "Byzantium" in their title. Instead, we have only woolly comments made in passing, usually embedded in general surveys of the culture, and they lack both proof and an explicit theoretical framework. Second, these comments tend to be bipolar: while they deny the existence of the Roman people, when it comes to the empire's ethnic minorities (e.g., Jews, Armenians, Arabs, Turks), they classify them in a naïve, unreconstructed way as "natural" entities. They present us with the implausible picture of a society that had an undefined and nameless majority alongside manifest minorities that can easily be identified and named.

Consider Cyril Mango's popular introduction, *Byzantium: The Empire of New Rome*. Mango refers without difficulty to the Slavs, Armenians, and other minorities of the empire, but when he turns to the bulk of the population, he says that it "had been so thoroughly churned up that it is difficult to tell what ethnic groups were living where."[13] Let us set aside that Romans are invisible to him, which is typical of the field. What is more revealing is that he seems to recognize a fixed set of preexisting ethnicities that may either be living separately (and so can be identified by name) or they are mixed up. This mixture does not for him raise the possibility of a new ethnicity emerging out of the "churning," or of a possible loss of a previous ethnicity compensated by the acquisition of a new one (i.e., Armenians ceasing to regard themselves as Armenians and becoming Romans). Instead, churning creates only an epistemological impasse by making it hard to trace the (ideally) separate history of the preapproved real ethnicities. A mixture cannot, in this model, ever result in an ethnicity of its own. Mango imagines the world's ethnicities as a fixed set that includes Slavs and Armenians (as natural entities that do not need to be problematized) and excludes Romans. No reason is given for this distinction. It has no basis in the primary sources, which treat Armenians and Romans as formally equivalent ethnic categories.

In reality, all ethnic groups, both those that are on Mango's radar (Slavs and Armenians) as well as those that are not (Romans), emerge from churning, because there are no "pure" ethnicities. Granted, in 1980, Mango was not familiar with ethnogenesis, the study of how ethnic groups emerge from a fusion of other groups and elements (though, as we saw at the end of Chapter 1, Steven Runciman had in 1929 identified the United States as a nation that lacked a single "ethnological" background). But consider Averil Cameron's *The Byzantines*, published in 2006. Cameron states explicitly that the Byzantines were not an ethnic group despite the fact that "they called themselves 'Romans.'"[14] Roman ethnicity can be denied without any argumentation,[15] but Cameron does give a reason, namely that "the population had been thoroughly mixed for many centuries."[16] In other words, Cameron does not believe that an ethnic group can have a mixed background, which means that she is unfamiliar with all research about ethnicity since World War II. Like Mango, she intuitively talks about the Slavs, Armenians, and Jews of the empire as ethnic groups, which means she thinks they were unmixed, or pure. It has apparently still not sunk in, by 2006, that every ethnicity is the result of mixture, and that ethnicities are not biological entities but social constructs that emerge, disappear, fuse, and break up. Cameron is likewise operating with a preapproved list of ethnicities, and the Romans are not on it. What the sources treat as the Roman people she sees as an agglomerated jumble of presumably denatured ethnicities. A mess of that kind can have no name, at least not a "real" one.

Denialists can "see" ethnicities that have a modern equivalent, but "Romans" who lack a modern nation to stick up for them must remain nameless. We thus face the problem of an unidentified majority, which appears as a kind of black hole: in scholarship, it gives off no light of its own, but its shape can be traced in negative by what surrounds it, such as foreign barbarians and internal ethnic minorities. Slavs, Armenians, Jews, and Bulgarians can somehow be seen as distinct from it, but it itself remains nameless. The two problems in this picture of ethnicity and empire are Roman denialism on the one hand and a naive and unreconstructed view of other ethnicities on the other. Chapter 5 will show that some in the field still treat ethnicities as fixed races whose essence is transmitted biologically. Yet a big shift has taken place since the early twentieth century in the study of ethnicity to which Byzantine Studies eventually has to adjust. Some background is necessary.

In the aftermath of World War II, the humanities and social sciences rejected the view that race—or biological traits that are passed on genetically—can determine or explain the cultural, moral, or political makeup of groups and individuals, and therefore their histories and identities (who they think they are). This consensus was codified in a series of statements on the "race concept" that were promulgated after 1950 under the aegis of UNESCO and signed by dozens of leading scientists and scholars. To be sure, the race concept is a potent historical force for societies that believe in it, but scholars have largely recognized that it is a fiction. Instead of seeing history as the interaction of fixed races or immutable nations, scholarship in most fields has turned its attention to the ways in which social forces cause certain groups to coalesce and emerge as historical entities and agents. The concepts of "ethnicity" and "identity" were developed in order to provide a flexible framework for the study of groups that are identified (by themselves or by others) as different from their neighbors in terms of culture or descent (or both). These concepts facilitated a shift from objective to subjective factors. Ethnic differences are seen as historically constructed, not hardwired into groups or individuals. No group is "pure," as all emerge and evolve through intermarriage with others, by merging, splitting off, and reassimilating, or change their identities in response to circumstances. Seneca wrote that "every day there are names of new nations, and old ones go extinct or are absorbed into more powerful ones . . . all peoples have become confused and mixed up."[17] He attained this realization in part because many Romans viewed their own nation as a mixture and melting together of prior ethnic groups.[18]

For example, before the Roman conquest, Italy was populated by many ethnic groups such as the Etruscans who had their own ethnonyms, traditions, polities, languages, and a sense of difference from the Romans and each other. Centuries after the Roman conquest, by contrast, their polities and languages were mostly extinct, and they had become Latin-speaking members of a more expansive Roman state, and no less Roman than anyone else. They had not been biologically replaced with Romans; rather, their culture had changed in ways that made them into Romans. Consider also the inhabitants of Asia Minor, for example the Carians in the southwest. Successive cultural changes transformed them first into Greeks, then into Romans, and later into Turks. It is arbitrary to assume that any one of these phases represents their "essence." Those who argue that the Byzantines were "really" Greeks and not Romans forget that the Greeks of Asia Minor had not always been Greek. The geographer Strabo said that the Carians were among the first in that land to "try to live in a Greek way and learn our language."[19]

As ethnic and other identities are social and cultural constructs, a group can change its name and narrative without necessarily receiving an influx of new "blood." Most scholars accept this thesis, and I suppose most Byzantinists do too, at least in theory.[20] In practice, however, many continue to think of ethnicity or identity generally as a function of blood, by which presumably they mean genes (the biology is outdated too here). I take it that the primary audience of this book accepts the postwar paradigm and wants to learn how it plays out in the case of Byzantium.

Yet Byzantine Studies has not fully made the transition to this postwar model. I will mention two reasons for this failure. First, the field rarely engages with scholarship on ethnicity: from the nineteenth century onward, it displays a continuous tradition of identifying the constituent ethnic groups of the empire in fixed racial or national terms. I discern no rupture in this tradition corresponding to the irruption of newer models. Second, much of this scholarship consists of, or relies on, the national historiographies of modern countries that have ideological stakes in identifying members of their nation in the Byzantine "mix." Countries that are geographically situated in territories of the empire still promote official historiographies that rely, whether explicitly or in more coded ways, on racial views of the past and these are injected into the international conversation about Byzantium. The stakes for them range from establishing the continuity or purity of the nation to documenting its claim to specific territories and highlighting the greatness of its past. To be fair, these countries did not participate in the excesses of western "scientific race theory" and were not responsible for World War II; in some cases, they were its victims. It would be hypocritical for the west, given its legacy of racism, genocide, colonialism, and slavery, to police the parochial nationalism of Balkan, Turkish, and Caucasian views of history. Still, those views are backed by national institutions that naturalize the diachronic existence of their ancestral groups. By contrast, the Romans of Byzantium lack that advantage *and* face the sanctions of denialism.

Some basic definitions are necessary at this point to get us up to speed. Ethnic groups are defined by a constellation of factors that converge to produce a unique cultural profile, though groups can always be found that lack one or two of these factors. They include a belief in a shared ancestry and history, a common homeland, language, religion, cultural norms and traditions, and an ethnonym to tie it all together along with a perception of difference from outside groups (who are often viewed negatively or as a threat) and a normative ideal of solidarity in the face of this threat.[21] There must also be evidence that these components, or indicia of collective identity, are understood by the group as the salient criteria of inclusion and exclusion. The ethnonym typically acts as their lynchpin, as in "the homeland of the Romans," "the language of the Romans," and so on for religion, kinship structures, customs, and the like. The argument made in the first part of this book is that the Romans of Byzantium were an ethnic group because they had, and knew that they had, these components of ethnicity. This was not just a matter of passive recognition. There were contexts in which ethnicity spurred a course of action because it situated its bearers within a charged narrative. In the episode from the *Miracles of Saint Demetrios* that we saw in Snapshot 2, this incitement to action is intriguingly called the "impulse of the *genos*." It incited the second generation of captive Romans to return to the homeland.

The factor on which there is most uncertainty among scholars today is the belief in a common ancestry. Some regard it as paramount for an ethnicity, but most now downplay it in favor of some combination of other elements.[22] Either way, shared ancestry is understood to be a group belief, not a fact of biology. A society's myth of descent is malleable and can accommodate the absorption of new groups. For example, people can invent ancestors or choose which aspects of their past to highlight for the purposes of constructing new social identities. As we will see, the Romans of Byzantium referred to their shared ancestry even though they knew that they had absorbed foreigners in large numbers.

There is considerable overlap between this understanding of ethnicity and conventional definitions of nationality, to the point where some scholars believe that in certain contexts they cannot easily be differentiated.[23] I think that Byzantium was one such case. In previous publications, I offered a provisional argument that the Romans of Byzantium constituted—and were aware that they constituted—a nation.[24] This made their state, which they called Romanía, or the state or land of the Romans, into a nation-state. The accumulation of additional evidence and continued study of recent theoretical literature on the existence of premodern nations has convinced me that this model is valid, despite objections that stem from outdated models according to which nations are an exclusively modern phenomenon.[25] Yet my discussion of ethnicity in those earlier studies adhered to theoretical definitions that I no longer believe are helpful. I therefore wish to modify my position regarding the *kind* of nation that these Romans were.

In my previous publications, over ten years ago, I adhered to a model of ethnicity that required a belief in a shared ancestry. Now, the Byzantines, like the ancient Romans, regularly took in foreign groups, gradually absorbed and assimilated them, and were, moreover, aware of the fact that they did so.[26] Many Byzantine Romans did not hide the fact that they had foreign ancestors. I therefore concluded that the Romans of Byzantium must have constituted a civic nation rather than an ethnic nation. In the former, integrative political structures and a shared culture take the place of ancestry in the core definition of the group. In retrospect, I believe now that I drew too sharp a distinction between ethnic and civic nations and underestimated how often and emphatically the sources point to a kinship-based view of Romanness—the *genos* of the Romans. At the time, I thought that this was just a loose quasi-ethnic way of speaking about what was in reality a civic polity, but I now believe that it was a straightforward expression of ethnic Romanness. My error was in not taking the Romans' own rhetoric at face value enough and in expecting strict and rigorous thinking on their part about collective ancestry. Ethnicities are, after all, based on subjective perceptions, which do not always respect the facts of history, in this case the fact of ethnic mixture. These Romans were certainly a nation, but they represented themselves as an *ethnic* nation more than I originally thought.

Civic nations, it turns out, are just as likely to represent themselves as ethnically defined communities even when they "know" that their ancestry is mixed. As Max Weber suggested, "It is primarily the political community, no matter how artificially organized, that inspires the belief in common ethnicity."[27] Such a community can overlook its mixed background in order to represent itself as an ethnicity. In this way, the Romans could represent themselves as a kinship community *and* a nation. The present book will study this representation under the category of ethnicity, leaving aside the more contested category of the nation, to which I will devote a separate monograph in due course. Even though the two categories are functionally equivalent in this case, as stated above, the literature on the nation tends to focus more on its sustaining institutions. That other book will therefore study the eastern Roman nation as a function of governmentality.

My argument for a Roman ethnicity will focus on the middle Byzantine period while occasionally linking up to the early and later periods. It should be noted, however, that the later Byzantine period has had a somewhat different reception in the scholarship, as it is discussed more casually in ethnic terms. The reason for this is that in the later period Byzantium was visited—or inundated—by westerners who may have called the Romans "Greeks" but regarded them unambiguously as an ethnic group. Consider a Latin account of Constantinople, probably from the later eleventh century. It says that the City contained many *gentes*—Greeks, Armenians, Syrians, Lombards, English, Dacians, Amalfitans, and Franks—but the Greeks occupied the largest and best part of the City.[28] The medieval sources viewed these Greeks as having their own customs, language, homeland, ancient ancestors, and faith—the components of an ethnicity. Apart from the label and its derogatory uses in western sources, the Byzantine Romans would have agreed. Thus, as it is easy for western scholars to follow the lead of western sources, discussions of the later period tend to ethnicize the Byzantines more, albeit at the cost of calling them "Greeks." It is hard to decide whether this misreading is better than the field's denialism: it gets the analytical category right, even if it does so for the wrong reason and so mislabels it with the wrong name.

Honorable mention goes here to Gill Page's 2008 book *Being Byzantine*. Based on the unambiguous testimony of the sources, Page saw that ethnicity was a core aspect of Byzantine *Romanness*, though at times she presents it as a phase of being Greek, for example in the subtitle (*Greek Identity before the Ottomans*, earning the book a translation into modern Greek).[29] Setting that glitch aside, she uses a modern understanding of ethnicity to study the evolution of the Roman ethnic group in the chaos of the post-1204 world. And yet, for all that the book is cited often, its core reading of Roman ethnicity has had little impact on the field. For example, no one has set out to ascertain whether the model works for the period before 1204 (it does).[30] In this connection, it is curious that, when they reach the period after about 1200, even staunch denialists admit that "the Byzantines" suddenly acquired an ethnic identity, though even then they do not always tell us its name. Nor do they tell us how this ethnogenesis happened. In the course of a page, we can go from a multiethnic Byzantium with an artificial, purely nominal Roman identity, to a Byzantium with a dominant (but unnamed) ethnic identity, and the prior insistence on multiethnicity vanishes.[31] In reality, no substantive change took place. We need to balance out our views of the culture before and after 1204. The capture of Constantinople by the crusaders intensified preexisting traits in some contexts and weakened them in others, but it did not bring a new people into being.

What, then, is the methodology for establishing the historical existence of a premodern ethnic group? The strongest arguments work through discursive evidence, that is, claims that *this* person or group belonged to this ethnicity because of such and such criterion. It is sometimes argued that the existence of an ethnic group can be established only through such evidence. Ethnicity can be expressed through material culture or physical descriptors, but without the ethnonyms and discursive claims to them it is difficult to know whether an ethnicity existed in the first place to which the material evidence can be attached.[32] In our case, Roman denialism has blocked the archaeological study of *Roman* Byzantium, so we must begin from the written sources and defer the material evidence for now. As it happens, Byzantine sources do occasionally offer approximate definitions of Romanness by listing its main elements, and these suggest strongly that it was an ethnicity (see, e.g., Snapshots 2, 3, 6, and 7). The authors of those texts were able to do this in part because the categories of ancient ethnography were similar to those used by modern scholars, and in part because they could observe firsthand what made Romans distinct.

These are useful texts, but we do not need to rely exclusively on them. Roman claims in Byzantine literature are abundant and come from a wide range of authors, writing in many geographical locations, social contexts, genres, and linguistic registers. They are extraordinarily consistent in the picture that they paint of the Roman community. The criteria for belonging to this community were not being continually reinvented along radically different axes in different periods, nor were they fiercely being contested among different constituencies within Romanía, as has recently been argued, for example, about early Frankish identity.[33] To be sure, Byzantine Romanness had its own history of change and evolution that remains to be told, but it was one of shifting nuance and emphasis; the general framework remained stable.

What we need at first, then, are general "maps" of who was included and who excluded from the Roman community, in order to establish its contours. When we then scrutinize the grounds for such inclusion and exclusion, between the sixth and the thirteenth centuries, we find that they correspond closely to the requirements of an ethnicity, as set by modern theoretical definitions. In this way we will triangulate the coordinates of Byzantine Romanness by using multiple texts and points of view. In the next section we will consider *who* made the relevant claims on which the analysis rests, to ensure that we are not adopting the perspective of a narrow group that may have had an interested reason to project a distorted view. Fortunately, this is not so, and we do not even need to rely exclusively on Byzantine sources to make the case. Arabic sources will be used to reinforce the picture painted by the Byzantines.

A word, finally, on the Greek words *ethnos*, *genos*, and *phylon*. It is correct and expected to say that they do not always correspond to the modern concepts of race, ethnic group, tribe, or nation, even though sometimes they do.[34] These terms are used loosely in texts to refer to different kinds of groups, no matter how they are constituted, so we might read about the *ethnos* of locusts, women, philosophers, or Christians. But in the relevant context and the right kind of text, they often bear senses that approximate to notions of race, ethnicity, nation, or kinship. *Genos* in particular refers literally to a person's birth and can establish an ethnic claim. Therefore, while we should not rely absolutely on these terms to establish a thesis about ethnicity, we should not deny that in the right discursive context they reflect a roughly equivalent concept. Again, we do not have to accept the Byzantines' claim that they, as Romans, were all related to each other. But we have to recognize that their profession of this belief qualifies them to be counted as an ethnic group. The argument will therefore not be philological but based on the presence of the substantive components of ethnicity in Byzantine society and its self-representation.

Who Was Included?

In 212, the *Constitutio Antoniniana* made almost all free people in the empire Roman citizens.[35] The principle was subsequently enshrined in Roman law, for instance in the *Corpus* of Justinian, that "all who are in the Roman world are Roman citizens." This was translated into Greek in the *Basilika*, the Byzantine version of the *Corpus* that was made into law in the late ninth century, to which an interesting scholion was appended that reflected the transition between a world ruled by the Romans and a world in which all were Romans: "Those who live within the circumference of the Roman world, namely those who are under the authority of the Romans, even if they do not live in Rome, are still Roman citizens on the basis of the decree issued by the emperor Antoninus."[36] This legal criterion of Romanness excluded slaves and some barbarian groups who entered imperial territory after the *Constitutio*.[37]

In looking for Romans, citizenship is a place to start, but many scholars of the later empire do not find legal definitions to be, in themselves, compelling. It is conventional to say that Roman citizenship became effectively irrelevant when it was extended to everyone, that it remained in the background where no one really noticed it or cared about it, except for a few jurists. While this issue is not my primary focus here, the assumption is not necessarily correct. For example, the universal grant of citizenship shaped the rulers' perceptions of the empire and its subjects, affecting the very nature of governance. As Caesar in Gaul in the 350s, Julian reminded his cousin, Constantius II, that "no matter where they are born, all [subjects of the empire] partake of Rome's constitution, use the laws and customs that were promulgated from there, and by virtue of these facts are its citizens."[38] As we will discuss in the second half of this book, "empire" and relations of imperial domination represent the rule of one ethnic group, nation, or religious community over a number of other groups who are understood by the ruling group to be different. When all became Romans, even if only legally, Rome ceased to be an empire and became something else, whose precise nature remains to be explored. Studies of late Roman imperial rhetoric and ideology have documented a shift from an empire of conquest, in which non-Romans were the "slaves" of their Roman masters, to a global state beaming universal solicitude to all subjects. Emperors presented themselves "as populist monarchs whose care extended not merely to privileged groups of imperial citizens but to *all* their subjects."[39]

Nor did universal citizenship necessarily remain a legal concept that only certain high-placed functionaries of the state knew or cared about. Discussing St. Paul's claim to Roman citizenship in Acts of the Apostles 22:25, John Chrysostom reminded his congregation that "those who held that honor in that era enjoyed great privileges, and not everyone held it. They say that everyone was made a Roman under Hadrian, but formerly it was not so."[40] We can draw a mixed set of conclusions from this: Chrysostom confirms that Roman citizenship was, indeed, no big deal in his own time since everyone had it, but he also reveals that his audience did in fact know that they were Roman citizens and perhaps imagined that universal citizenship had always been the case in the empire, prompting his historical commentary.

The argument of this book that the Byzantines knew themselves to be Romans will not take its stand on citizenship. Victory in that battle would be swift and decisive, but the spoils would be meager without a deeper analysis of Roman governmentality. I believe that Byzantine society was structured on a fundamental level by Roman legal concepts and their ongoing modulation by the state. But that would take us in a different direction. A legal definition tells us little about ethnicity. For example, we saw in Snapshot 1 how Isaurians in the fifth century were regarded as a separate ethnicity even though they were Roman citizens of the empire. One might theoretically imagine that a multiethnic agglomeration of peoples, marked by diversity of culture, ethnicity, religion, and language, could coexist beneath the formal umbrella of Roman citizenship. This is, in fact, what many scholars of Byzantium believe. Thus, we must demonstrate more than a legal homogeneity for the majority Roman population. Inclusion and exclusion—Roman and non-Roman—were defined and perceived in Byzantium primarily on ethnic grounds, not legal ones. So let us sketch the contours of the Roman community, geographically and socially.

Certainly, the majority of the population of Constantinople were Romans and regarded themselves to be such. One could cite hundreds of passages from texts of all kinds that refer to the Roman "people" (i.e., *populus*) of the capital. We have seen the people's collective demand that the empress Ariadne appoint, in 491, a true Roman to the throne (Snapshot 1). I limit myself to one more such text, which has the advantage of recording, or claiming to record, the people's own collective expression of being Roman. The *Book of Ceremonies*, compiled in the tenth century, records and prescribes the acclamations and antiphonal chants that were to be uttered by the people of Constantinople, the imperial herald, and the representatives of the teams before the races. Among the many things to be said at such occasions, the emperors are called "the beloved of the Romans" and "the joy of the Romans."[41]

The majority of the provincial population are also clearly called Romans in the sources. As many of the sources recount military history, these Romans often appear in accounts of barbarian raids, in which provincials living by the frontier are captured. For example, Prokopios (sixth century) says that "the Gepids held the city of Sirmium and almost all the cities of Dacia . . . and enslaved the Romans of that region."[42] Likewise, when the Slavs raided Thrace, they enslaved many of the Romans there, one of whom, apparently an average person, Prokopios calls "a Roman man" in the singular.[43] He also tries to calculate the total number of the Roman victims of the barbarian raids in the Balkans under Justinian: "More than twenty times ten thousand of the Romans who lived there were either killed or enslaved."[44] This was an exaggeration, but it means that Prokopios and his readers found nothing incongruous in the notion that there were hundreds of thousands of Romans in one set of provinces. As these were only the victims, the total population of provincial

Romans would have been imagined as much bigger. Theophylaktos Simokattes (seventh century) claims that Slavic raiders carried away "a great haul of captive Romans" from provincial towns in the Balkans.[45] The historian and later patriarch Nikephoros (eighth century) notes that provincial "Romans" in Asia Minor were captured by invading Persians.[46] Jumping ahead to a later period, the Bulgarian tsar Kaloyan (d. 1207) styled himself "the Roman-Slayer ('Ρωμαιοκτόνος)" in imitation of the Roman emperor Basileios II, the Bulgar-Slayer. The thirteenth-century historian who tells us this, Georgios Akropolites, says that the tsar took on the name after destroying many cities in Thrace and capturing or killing their Roman inhabitants.[47] In such texts, the provincials are casually assumed to be Romans.

These historians refer to provincial Romans in other contexts too, not just military. In a geographical digression on Lazike (Kolchis), Prokopios reaches the border between that non-Roman land and the empire and says that "Romans live in the adjacent land, whom people also qualify as Pontians."[48] In other words, their Romanness was primary and their provincial identity (as inhabitants of the province of Pontos) was a qualification of it: they were the Romans of Pontos. In the *Secret History*, Prokopios refers often to the Roman victims of Justinian, and calls them a race: "No Roman man" managed to escape from that emperor, whose evil "fell upon the entire race (ὅλῳ τῷ γένει)." Elsewhere Prokopios refers to Romans "who lived in distant lands," including "in the countryside."[49] Prokopios' continuer Agathias refers to the (ancient) Pelasgian ethnic origin of the people of the city of Tralleis in Asia Minor, "yet," he adds, "the townspeople (ἀστοὶ) should not now be called Pelasgians but rather Romans." This was a case of "Romanogenesis": turning Pelasgians into Romans. This claim could be made only if "Roman" was understood as categorically equivalent to the previous ethnic label of the population.[50]

Romans were assumed to live in the provinces during the middle period too. For example, the eleventh-century historian Attaleiates commented that the elephant paraded in the capital by Konstantinos IX Monomachos (1042–1055) delighted "the Byzantioi [i.e., Constantinopolitans] and the other Romans who happened to see it," the latter logically being Romans not from the capital, like Attaleiates himself (who was from Attaleia).[51]

The ethnonym was not limited to provincial *men*, as opposed to women. In the 830s the emperor Theophilos admitted thousands of Khurramite (Iranian) warriors into the empire. In order to integrate them, the emperor enrolled them in the army and "arranged for them to marry Roman women" in the provinces where they were settled. The historians who report this must have assumed that there were thousands of Roman women of marriageable age in the provinces, and we will meet one of them in Chapter 4.[52] Moreover, in Snapshot 4 we examined the reasoning of Manuel Komnenos, who imagined the totality of the Roman population as a network of kinship associations, obviously including the women too.

The ethnonym was not limited to people of a certain class or occupation. An icon-painting monk of the ninth century was called "one of our Romans" and "a Roman by *genos*," when that monk was requested by the Bulgarian king.[53] In the thirteenth century, the emperor Ioannes III Doukas Batatzes wanted to reduce his trade deficit and ordered that his subjects were to buy "clothes produced only from the Roman land and by the hands of Romans"—the latter are here textile workers, likely women.[54] The Romans who appear most frequently in narrative sources, given their emphasis on war, are soldiers. They are called Romans by the historians and addressed as such in direct speech by their officers. These speeches are reported by the historians, who may be suspected of embellishing them with patriotic Roman sentiment. But it is impossible to believe that they simply made up an attribution of Roman pride to the soldiers of the empire and kept this pretense up for a thousand years. The military manuals actually instruct generals to address their soldiers in the following way: "Roman men, let us stand firm and unyielding."[55] Konstantinos VII sent a speech in 958 to be read aloud to the army and it addresses them as Romans too.[56] The soldiers themselves took obvious pride in this name. In some episodes, they are shown begging their commanders to let them fight "so that they could show themselves to be worthy of the name Romans."[57] There is no good reason to suspect literary artifice.

To be sure, soldiers were agents of the Roman state and were extensions of the emperors' will, so the emphasis on their Romanness in this context does have a formal, institutional aspect. But it was not limited to that. In the middle period, most of the soldiers were recruited and stationed in the provinces, and their concerns as soldiers reflected, to a considerable degree, the concerns of their families and local communities.[58] The financing of their service involved many people in their upkeep and support, which later resulted in legal arrangements and land classifications. If the army rosters of the middle period listed between one and two hundred thousand men, and if we assume that each was supported by a farm or family unit of between four and six people (at least), this means that between half a million to a million provincials were tied to the arrangements that the state made for soldiers, whom our sources emphatically and consistently call Romans. They were the protectors of the provincials whom our sources also call Romans, as we saw above.

Economically too Romans could be found at all levels compatible with legal freedom. Consider a decree of Nikephoros III Botaneiates (1078–1081) that is reported by the contemporary historian Attaleiates. That emperor released from certain debts to the imperial fisc "all Romans, wherever on earth they lived, and thereby made them into free Roman citizens."[59] The theory behind the passage is that debt is a form of slavery, but what interests us here is the implication that the Roman community was geographically expansive and also included people who were close to insolvency, or actually in that state: they were on the verge of slavery, but the emperor made them "free Romans" again.[60] This is a case where Romanness is inflected by citizenship in that it concerns a relationship mediated by law, whose purpose is to restore the perks of freedom. The historian Ioannes Kinnamos (twelfth century) likewise recorded how the emperor Manuel I Komnenos (1143–1180) prevented Romans from taking out loans by positing their freedom as collateral, for he "wanted to rule over free Romans, not slaves."[61] Romans could therefore be quite poor, but one step above legal slavery.

In fact, we have some documents of manumission from Byzantium. Two of these from the eleventh century and one from the twelfth state that when the slaves are freed they become "free Roman citizens."[62] These new Romans would occupy the bottom of the social scale, thus the salient distinction between Roman and non-Roman was between free and slave, not elite and nonelite. Moreover, based on these texts we can say that the language of citizenship and freedom was not limited to Constantinople because one of these cases is from southern Italy and the other from the eastern reaches of Asia Minor; the third, from the twelfth century, is from Thessalonike or Constantinople.

We do not, then, find Romans only or even primarily in Constantinople, as is sometimes asserted. There is no evidence that the Romans of the capital were more Roman than those of the provinces.[63] Being Roman had nothing to do with social or economic class, occupation, or gender. There were poor Romans, rich Romans, freedmen Romans, soldier Romans, and icon-painter Romans. The legal aspects of Roman citizenship were not especially prominent in constituting this community, although they did occasionally come into play. In sum, the size and shape of the Roman community was that of an ethnic group or nation.

Who Was Excluded?

Rather than a scarcity of Romans, we may now face the embarrassment of too many Romans. Some historians believe that everyone living within the empire or under the emperor's jurisdiction was automatically a Roman, which turns what appears to be an ethnonym into an abstract formality.[64] One scholar labeled this "a broad, flexible, open-ended concept of 'Romans' (in the statist sense),"[65] in which Roman is defined purely in relation to the state. Stripping Romanness of any specific cultural or ethnic content in this way is another way of denying it. This approach sometimes veers into Orthodox fiction. According to one reading of Byzantine identity, there was no place in Orthodox Byzantium for the distinction between Roman and barbarian.[66] This replaced the ethnic exclusions that are so prominently on display in the Byzantine sources with modern ecumenism.

Yet contrary to these formulas, not everyone living within the empire or serving the emperor was regarded ethnically as a Roman. The Byzantine empire was inhabited by both Romans and non-Romans, and the latter were designated by separate ethnic names and frequently associated with stereotypes. Speros Vryonis has rightly questioned "the often heard generalization that in Byzantium ethnic affiliation was insignificant ... that the inhabitants of the empire felt that in effect they were all Romans and Christians." To the contrary, they "were quite aware of ethnic distinctions among the population."[67] Moreover, recent attempts to cast the early Byzantine empire as "color-blind" when it came to ethnicity have also elicited legitimate pushback: ethnic differences, for example between Goths and Romans, played a significant role in political conflict.[68]

Ethnic others fell into three main groups. First, there were elite men at the court who held offices and commanded armies but who were regarded as ethnic foreigners or had an origin that differentiated them from mainstream Romans, for example the Persarmenian Narses under Justinian; the Armenian Artabasdos under Leon III; the Saracen Samonas under Leon VI; the Norman Rouselios under Michael VII; the Georgian Pakourianos under Alexios I Komnenos; and many more. Mere service was not enough to make one a Roman. However, some officers of foreign origin were more or less Romanized and, if they settled within the empire, their descendants could quickly become indistinguishable from other Romans through processes of assimilation that we will discuss in Chapter 4.

Evidence for foreigners serving at the imperial court even while they were perceived as "ethnics" or "barbarians" is abundant and comes from all periods. In 542, Justinian released "barbarians who are subject to our polity" and who held the rank of *illustris* from the requirement of ratifying their marriages via a contract (i.e., they could use intent alone).[69] Thus holders of the highest imperial rank could still be seen as barbarians and treated separately from a legal point of view. A manual for organizing court receptions from 899 pays separate attention to "all of the *ethnikoi* men who serve the emperor, such as Khazars, Arabs, and Franks ... who are to enter dressed in their proper ethnic garment, which they call *kabbadin*."[70] Dress rules were here enforced to highlight ethnic differences. Interestingly, they were all required to wear a single garment that marked them out as a single class, rather than their respective ethnic apparel. These men may also have occupied an ambiguous legal area. In the collection of legal rulings made by the eleventh-century judge

Eustathios Romaios, we find the case of a Georgian *ethnikos* who, despite having a high title at the court, had not followed "the law of the Romans" in drawing up his will. In addition to whatever customs defined this man's foreignness in Romans eyes, such as his native language, this titular may not even have been operating as a Roman citizen.[71] The *Life of Saint Basileios the Younger*, a fictional tenth-century saint, mentions one Konstantinos, a *primikerios* (a court position usually given to eunuchs), "whom everyone called The Barbarian because he was an *ethnikos*."[72] *Ethnikos* refers to his foreign origin and not his religion, as he was fervently pious. He was called The Barbarian even though he owned a mansion in the City and was important at the court. Dress, law, and names could be used to mark these men out as different.

Emperors could appoint both Romans and foreigners to official positions. If Byzantium was a predominantly Roman-ethnic state, we should expect there to have been a degree of prejudice directed against these foreigners at the court, as their success bred resentment among the "native-born." Indeed, we find such sentiments in the sources.[73] They were all the product of specific circumstances and should not be taken as the Romans' default view of the ethnics among them. Chapters 4 and 5 will show how open Byzantium was to foreign settlement and even to groups of immigrants and refugees who were willing to adapt to Roman norms. But the very possibility that the Romans could express such prejudice on ethnic grounds indicates that this was not, at bottom, a nonethnic society but rather a Roman-ethnic one with minorities. In some cases, emperors made a point of restricting certain positions to Romans.[74]

The second category included ethnic or foreign military units. Roll calls of Byzantine campaign forces in the sources will sometimes list, beside the Romans, various ethnic units such as Huns, Armenians, Pechenegs, Rus', Varangians, or others.[75] For example, in 1088 Alexios I Komnenos exempted a monastery from the billeting of soldiers, "including both Roman and *ethnikoi* allies, such as Rus', Varangians, Koulpingoi, Inglinoi [from England], Franks [Normans], Nemitsoi [Germans], Bulgarians, Saracens, Alans, Abasgians, the Immortals, and, in sum, all other Romans and foreigners."[76] Such lists refute the notion that whoever served the emperor in a formal sense was considered a Roman, regardless of his ethnicity. Some foreign groups served in the imperial army for long periods but still remained ethnically distinct in the eyes of the Romans. Our sources either give their names or simply call them generically the *allophyloi* (people of another race), *ethnikoi* (foreigners), or "barbarians."[77] The army could be described collectively as consisting "of men of the same race *(homophylon)* along with the foreigners *(xenikon),*"[78] or "of Romans and soldiers from the *ethne.*"[79] In his laws, Justinian distinguished between "our officers and soldiers and the others, the ethnic types who are allied to our polity."[80] Arabic sources often make the same distinctions, for example between "Roman and Armenian" soldiers serving under imperial officers, which proves that they were not imaginary or textual artefacts of elite writing but grounded in contemporary perceptions of ethnic difference.[81] On the Roman side, these distinctions were not devoid of moral or patriotic valence. For example, Leon VI advised his generals that, if they should have any *homophyloi* of the enemy in their own army (i.e., men of the same race as the enemy), they were to remove them to a different place before the battle through some plausible pretext.[82] The assumption is that men of the same race might stick together and betray the Romans. On the other hand, Leon admits that foreign spies caught in the Roman camp may be either Romans (suborned) or *allogeneis* (men of foreign birth).[83] He assumed that his men could tell them apart.

These categorical distinctions shaped how the Romans perceived their own armed forces. In his speech addressed to the army in 958—which was probably meant to be read out by criers—Konstantinos VII reminds the soldiers that there are units of barbarians (ἐθνικοί, ἔθνη) fighting alongside them, so the rest should fight bravely to impress the courage of "the Roman *genos*" upon both them and the *homophyloi* (men of the same race, i.e., us Romans).[84]

The third and most populous category of non-Romans were ethnic communities that lived in the empire and were subject to imperial institutions. These more than the others broke the equation between being a subject of the emperor and being a Roman. Indeed, it is only because of them that we can call the empire multiethnic to begin with, to whatever degree that term is justified. For example, we saw in Snapshot 1 how the Isaurians were regarded as a non-Roman ethnic group in the fifth century. Unfortunately, we do not know the Isaurian point of view, which was likely not uniform. In middle Byzantium, the Romans perceived other groups as foreign even when they were part of the empire, including the Slavs, Bulgarians, and Armenians. The question at the heart of the question of "empire" is precisely how the Romans governed these non-Roman groups. But before we can study that relationship, we need to know its parties.

Evidence for the existence of non-Roman ethnic groups within the empire will be presented in Chapters 6 and 7, which will be case studies focusing on the tenth and eleventh centuries. Suffice it to say that the Romans continued to identify these groups by their ethnic names even when they were subjects of the emperor; juxtaposed them to themselves in ways that suggest that they were analogous, nonidentical groups (e.g., Romans and Bulgarians, or Romans and Armenians); identified them as foreign on the basis of birth, culture, language, and religion (where relevant); and spread negative ethnic stereotypes about them.

Here I will note two cases of ethnic prejudice that directly belie the claim that all notional subjects of the emperor were regarded as Romans. In the historian Agathias (sixth century), one of the Roman defendants on trial for the murder of the Laz king Goubazes bursts out with the following inflammatory statement: "Every barbarian race *(phylon), even when it is subject to the Romans*, is totally different from us in mentality as well as in the order of its laws."[85] The speaker was clearly exaggerating for effect. Even other Romans would take this to be an extreme statement coming from a murderer, but it merely sharpens a conventional and widespread perception of difference. In the eleventh century, Eustathios Boïlas wrote in his will that "I became an emigrant from the land which bore me [Cappadocia], and I went a distance of one and one-half weeks from my fatherland. I settled among alien nations with strange religion and tongue."[86] He means the Armenians who lived in the empire's now-expanded eastern provinces.

Conversely, there were circumstances in which assuming an ethnicity might have been advantageous, even if the claim was false, for example in order to register in a military unit for Goths that enjoyed various privileges.[87] Psellos claimed that magicians and charlatans

ROMAN ETHNICITY 63

had no real skill but gave out as credentials their "ethnic origins, the one claiming to be an Illyrian, the other a Persian."[88]

If the formal criterion of being subject to the emperor does not identify anyone as a Roman, we must look for different criteria. Conversely, Romans could retain their ethnicity even outside the empire, when they were in barbarian captivity, at least for a few generations. This reinforces the point that imperial jurisdiction and Romanness did not always overlap. In Snapshot 2, we discussed the story in the *Miracles of Saint Demetrios* of the provincial Romans who were enslaved by Avars yet managed to preserve their identity in foreign captivity and through intermarriage, until their descendants yearned to return home. Consider also a story that is told about Michael I (811–813). That emperor was approached by two groups of refugees who wanted to settle in the empire, one a group of Bulgars "who picked up, departed from their ancestral dwellings, and came to the land of the Romans," while the other were "some of the Romans who had been taken captive [by the Bulgars] in the previous war, had escaped their captivity, and had now come back to their homelands."[89] Their identity was obviously not a function of the title claimed by their ruler at any time. They were Romans who desired to return to the Roman homeland.

A Prima Facie Ethnicity

Let us triangulate our results so far and see what kind of group these Romans formed. The Roman community apparently included most provincials regardless of gender, class, or occupation, except for those who are noted as belonging to specific ethnic groups, such as Slavs, Bulgarians, and Armenians. Language, religion, and other cultural attributes such as dress were occasionally used to mark, justify, and police these differences. The Romans could also be imagined as a community of descent and kinship, though they could at times absorb and assimilate members of other groups. When cut off from their homeland, they could sustain their group identity for at least a few generations.

There is only one type of group that fits this contour: it is an ethnic group (or a nation, depending on the definition). It is important to be explicit about the force and limitations of this conclusion. It is a prima facie model that accounts for the overall shape of the Roman community that is reflected in the sources; for the patterns of inclusion and exclusion that demarcated it from other groups of the same analytical order; and for some of the ways in which its members talked about their in-group. We have also encountered some of the specific criteria of inclusion and exclusion, that is, the contents of the identity in question, and these too strongly suggest that we are dealing with an ethnicity. In much scholarship on ancient and medieval ethnicities, especially the extinct ones, this mere outline is often sufficient to establish the historical existence of such a group, at least on a presumptive basis. In our case, the surviving record is large enough that, in Chapter 3, we can go further and discuss the individual ethnic indicia in more detail.

If the Romans of Byzantium thought of themselves as a group that fits modern definitions of ethnicity—and it seems that they did—that suffices for present purposes. In addition to the evidence for this conclusion, we have the fact that they sometimes called themselves an *ethnos*, or a *genos*, a word that, whether literally or metaphorically, stressed the kinship of their community. However, the way in which they used these two words bears further comment.

The eastern Romans had a dual way of talking about *ethnos* that may cause confusion. In one sense—according to one modality of discourse—they followed the ancient ethnographic tradition in using the term *ethnos* for any group that was constituted by a more or less specific cluster of what we would call ethnic traits, such as a distinctive language, religion, political organization, ethnonym, social mores, possibly shared descent, and the like. In this conception, the Romans of Byzantium were only one such group among many others. But there was a different sense in which the Romans stood on one side of a divide and all the foreign "nations" (*gentes, ethne*) collectively stood on the other. This usage had two roots that came together in Byzantium. The first was the ancient convention of dividing the world between Romans and conquered *gentes*.[90] The second was an Old Testament model that divided the world between the Chosen People and the "gentiles" or "nations," which in Greek was translated as "the *ethne*" or the *ethnikoi* (plural).[91] Here the Byzantines, as

Christian Romans, were a new Chosen People surrounded by hostile *ethne*, who were typically regarded as savage, heathen, and inferior.

For example, in the exchange between Louis II and Basileios I that we discussed in Chapter 1, Basileios seems to have argued in his original (lost) letter that Louis could not be the emperor of the Romans because he came from a *gens*, one of the nations. Apparently, this implied that the Romans were a people who stood apart from the rest. In surviving texts that reflect this division, the Romans call themselves not an *ethnos* but a *genos* or a *laos* (a people).[92] There were weaker and stronger versions of this model. The stronger might imply a full theory of the Byzantines as a new Chosen People on biblical lines, while in the weaker the *ethne* were just barbarians who surrounded the Roman empire and who might even be Christians themselves.[93] Either way, the Romans never ceased to perceive the world as fundamentally divided between "the nations" and "our own people," or "the nations" and "the *genos* of the Romans."[94]

We therefore have two models: according to the first, the world is full of ethnic groups or nations and the Romans are one among them, even if a superior one, while according to the second the incomparable *genos* or *laos* of the Romans (or Christians) is surrounded by a sea of hostile *ethne*. Needless to say, the second view is more amenable to the sacralization of Byzantine identity and its elevation from the mundane world of nations and ethnic groups into a more transcendent realm of theological abstraction, a move that many scholars prefer. Compared to the paratactic equivalence of the old ethnographic model, the ancient imperialist-biblical model took a more exclusive stance, which may have verged on treating the in-group as exceptional: ethnic traits mattered for foreigners only, while the Christian Romans provided the nonethnic norm against which the others were measured.[95] This is like whites today who believe that ethnicity and ethnic studies apply to minorities, to brown or black people, not to what they implicitly take to be the "norm," that is, their own whiteness.[96]

The two models, however, are not incompatible. They were merely two different ways of talking about ethnic difference, the one paratactic and the other hierarchical. Calling the Romans "a people of God" who were distinct from "the nations" is perfectly compatible with the Romans also being an ethnic group. It means only that they viewed themselves as unique and superior to all others. As mentioned above, this model preferred the word *genos* for the superior group. But in ancient and Christian texts, *genos* too could refer to peoples, ethnic groups, and nations.[97] *Genos* even *highlights* ethnicity as its etymology stresses kinship bonds over other aspects of group cohesion, so the national *genos* is effectively an extended family.

Moreover, the argument for a Roman ethnicity is not based primarily on lexicography but on the presence and awareness of ethnic indicia, and the latter could just as well be marshaled under the term *genos* as the term *ethnos*. Besides, the biblical image of the Jewish people surrounded by many hostile "nations" has functioned throughout Christian history as an archetype for the formation of exclusive ethnic or national identities and as a model for medieval and modern nations.[98] In fact, it was possible even within the biblical paradigm to refer to Christian Romans as an *ethnos* so long as one added the adjective "holy," which apparently canceled the negative associations of the biblical word *ethnos*.[99]

Outside this biblical paradigm, *ethnikos* was a banal term in Byzantium, as it just meant a foreigner, a non-Roman; it was not always linked to theological views of history. I will cite two instances. The name of the frontiersman Digenis ("Of Dual Descent") is explained by the poet by the fact that he was an *ethnikos* on his father's side and a Roman on his mother's.[100] This poem is as close to the vernacular and even folk level that we can get for this period (ca. 1100) and it proves beyond a doubt that being a Roman was, at least in part, understood to be a matter of descent. In a normal field of studies, this passage alone would suffice to establish ethnicity as a base sense for how many Byzantines saw themselves to be Romans (even a single specimen of life on Mars suffices for a big conclusion). The second example occurs in a thirteenth-century chronicle, where the author lists all the categories of people an emperor wanted to benefit. Each pair, in its complementarity, is meant to convey the sense of *everyone:* "Urban and rural, slave and free, noble and common, *ethnikos* and Roman, poor and rich, worthy and unworthy, and every person of whatever station in life."[101] The pairing of Roman and *ethnikos* as an exclusive complementary pair means that "Roman" encompassed both rural and urban Romans, rich and poor Romans, and so on.

I have been told by many colleagues that the Byzantine Romans could not have been an ethnic group because they never called themselves an *ethnos*, only a *genos*. I have encountered this claim in print only once in recent reading,[102] but it seems to be widespread, a kind of urban legend that circulates in the field. It is conceptually flawed in two ways: first, because *genos* could also potentially refer to an ethnic group and, second, because the conclusion that the Romans were an ethnic group does not depend on whether they used this word or that, but on whether they distinguished Romans from non-Romans on the basis of what we would identify as ethnic traits. Moreover, the claim is factually wrong, as we have already seen. While *ethnikos* usually referred to foreigners, the Romans are called an *ethnos* and treated as one among many ethnic groups in a wide variety of texts, including histories, horoscopes, religious disputations, and military manuals. We saw the emperor Konstantinos VII call his Romans an *ethnos* on the grounds of language, kinship, and the full taxonomy of ethnographic indicia that he was willing to apply to foreign people too.[103] Both Romans and others, then, were frequently understood to be categories of the same order.

Of interest here are the lists of nations or ethnic groups produced by some authors, in which Romans are listed paratactically among others. Referring to the missions of the Apostles, John Chrysostom listed Scythians, Thracians, Romans, Persians, Moors, Indians, and Egyptians.[104] He may have been thinking here of the Romans of ancient Rome rather than of his own contemporaries, but in the end it makes no difference: what matters is the type of category that the word signified in his usage and that of his contemporaries (and, besides, the relevant Romans in the New Testament were those addressed by Paul in Greek and not in Latin, so they were more like Byzantines). The sixth-century author known as Kosmas Indikopleustes, who championed the divine supremacy of the Roman empire, refers in a similar context to Bactrians, Huns, Persians, Indians, Bulgars, Goths, Romans, Franks, and others.[105] Similar lists, updated for the times, were produced down to the fifteenth century, and the Romans feature in them as one among many Christian *ethne*.[106]

Moreover, the Romans of Byzantium did often imagine themselves as an extended kinship group. This was the basis for Manuel's objection to the proposal made by his father Andronikos I Komnenos to execute all his enemies and their entire families: such a plan would eventually kill "all the Romans" (Snapshot 4). We hear of people who were "Roman by birth." For example, in the lay *Digenis* a girl says that she fell in love with a man of Roman birth, and Digenis is said to be Roman on his mother's side only.[107] We hear of people who were Romans by birth but had been raised among foreigners, where they had become culturally foreign.[108] If being Roman was a function only of cultural profile, then these kinds of statements would not be possible; so too if being Roman meant only that one was a subject of the empire. Birth and descent counted. Conversely, we hear of men who were foreigners by birth (e.g., Italians, Turks, or Tzanoi) but who were raised as Romans and effectively treated as such.[109] Birth *was* a factor, though it could be overcome by acculturation, a dynamic to which the sources were sensitive, as we will see throughout.

It was also possible, in some contexts, to imagine the Romans as a large family. The national Roman collective could rhetorically take the place of one's birth family, a sure sign that we are in the presence of a national ideology. For example, an orator of the late thirteenth century, Maximos Planoudes, decided to talk about the Roman *genos* as a whole when he came to the part in his speech reserved for an emperor's parents and ancestors. The nation appears here as the king's proper family.[110] In 867, the patriarch Photios self-consciously reached back to classical antiquity in order to bestow upon Michael III the title "father of the fatherland" *(pater patriae)*, adding that he surpassed Cyrus and Augustus in that role.[111] In his verse epitaph, Basileios II (976–1025) boasted that throughout his long life he had "guarded the children of New Rome" by marching along the frontiers.[112] These were the paternalistic aspects of a ruling ideology that saw the Roman community as an extended family. The language of kinship could, then, be applied generally to the relationship that bound Romans together, including the relationship between all Romans and their state.

This explains the intuitive logic displayed in texts according to which Romans should side with Romans and not with foreigners, and that preference should be given to people of one's own *genos*, *ethnos*, or *phylon* (add the prefix *homo-*) and not to those who were "other" (add the prefix *allo-*). More texts than can be surveyed here urge such an ethic of national solidarity, a reminder that the Romans needed given their propensity for civil war.[113] I highlight two military manuals to show how state policy and hortatory rhetoric built on and tried to evoke Roman ethnic solidarity. The military author Syrianos (ninth century) says that defensive war brings salvation to "the people of our own race" *(homophyloi)*. We must fight back, he says, for our enemies attack our religious faith and fatherland *(patris)*, and we have to fight "on account of the love that we have for each other. . . . We have to do what is just, for we are Romans and we should imitate the virtue of our ancestors [the ancient Romans]."[114] Syrianos sometimes addresses his audience directly as "Roman men."[115] Defensive war by the state was therefore not only justified but required in order to protect people of the same race, an extended family. This effectively cast the empire as a large "fatherland" *(patris)*, or homeland of the Roman people.

These were not expressions of an exclusive military fraternity. The imagined "family" here was the Roman nation as a whole, not just the army corps. In his military manual (ca. 900), Leon VI echoed the sentiments of Syrianos and wrote to his generals that when the enemy ravages "our land . . . it is right to take up war on behalf of our subjects . . . your brothers."[116] As the empire was surrounded by non-Christian enemies between the sixth and the ninth centuries, appeals to Roman patriotism and Christian solidarity effectively overlapped. For Leon, devotion to Rome and to Christ went hand in hand (he had not yet fully processed the conversion of Bulgaria, which threw a wrench into this equation for him). He too uses kinship language in talking about fighting on behalf of the homeland and the faith. For example, heralds should instruct the army that "the war is on behalf of God, and the love that we have for him, and for the entire *ethnos*. It is, moreover, on behalf of our brothers in the faith and, if this applies, for our women, children, and fatherland. They should say that the memory of those who excel in war on behalf of our brothers' freedom will be eternal."[117]

How much weight should we give to these expressions of Roman kinship and how did they operate? There are two ways in which a nation of this size may imagine itself as a kinship group. The one is horizontal, in real time: Romans today are born from other Romans. As we saw, the Byzantines certainly had the notion that one could be born a Roman, Ῥωμαῖος τὸ γένος, as opposed to, say, a Turk, Τοῦρκος τὸ γένος. The other way is vertical, reaching back to the distant past: according to this schema, Romans are collectively descended from the ancient Romans. Did the Byzantine Romans believe that they were collectively descended from the ancient Romans too?

This is harder to document. It probably formed only a vague aspect of Romanness in Byzantium; I doubt many people thought about it in explicit terms. But it was presupposed in many discursive practices. Merely by calling themselves Romans they asserted a continuity between themselves and the ancient Romans, whose default, unreflexive mode in traditional societies was genetic. In many contexts, the Byzantines called these putative ancestors "the ancient (πάλαι) Romans," to distinguish them from the Romans of their day, that is, themselves, but also to underscore their continuity. The historian Attaleiates, for example, wrote a long comparison between ancient and modern Romans to prove that the latter, his own people, failed to live up to the standards of glory set by their ancestors.[118] Such comparisons were not limited to the authors of classicizing histories. The ninth-century monk Euodios wrote the martyrdom of the forty-two military martyrs of Amorion, who were killed after the Muslims took that city in 838. He saw his world as divided between the Romans and the Ishmaelites, and he has the saints at one point speak and refer "to the Romans of old, who conquered the entire world."[119] They were making the point to their Muslim captors that one did not need to have the one true faith in order to win a war. Likewise, the provincial author, a monk, of the life of the southern Italian saint Elias the Younger (tenth century) has his hero admonish an imperial general to restrain his men, and in order to persuade him he cites the example of virtuous ancient generals, including Scipio, "who was also a Roman general,"[120] that is, *like you*.

Political continuity could also be taken to imply biological continuity. Consider Justinian's comment on the title "satrap" used in one of his four Armenian provinces: this, he says, "was not a Roman name, and was unknown to our ancestors, but was introduced from some foreign polity."[121] Moreover, Byzantine chronicles trace the history of the Roman polity from antiquity to the Byzantine present without break or ethnic rupture. The symbolic "bridge" between the two was the career of Constantine the Great, who built New Rome and, according to the Byzantine imagination, populated it with nobles whom he brought from Elder Rome.[122] This may have been enough to establish a sufficient or symbolic link of biological continuity between the two Romes. Also, as we will see in Chapter 3, Byzantine writers called Latin their "ancestral language," which implies that they viewed the ancient Romans as their own ancestors. By contrast, when they talked about the ancient Greeks, whether in works of elite literature or just in church, they referred to them in a distant way, as a people of the ancient world who were no longer around in the present, the way we might talk about ancient Egyptians or Phrygians.

In some contexts, biological continuity from ancient Rome was asserted more explicitly, for example in the army. In a speech to his army, the emperor Julian in 363 referred to the conquerors of Carthage and Spain—over five hundred years before—as "our forefathers."[123] In 589, the bishop of Antioch, Gregorios, restored order to an army that had mutinied by addressing the soldiers as "Roman men" and challenging them to prove that they were true Romans and not the "illegitimate children" of their ancestors, who included Romans of the Republic such as Manlius Torquatus.[124] A church liturgy for fallen soldiers, dating probably from the tenth century and produced in the provinces, refers to the sanctified heroes as the "offspring of Rome," calling them also the foundation of the *patris* and the entire *genos*.[125] During the passage of the Second Crusade in 1147, the emperor Manuel I Komnenos warned the German king Conrad not to pick a fight with the Romans, that is, his own people, whose ancient "ancestors" had conquered a large part of the globe, including the Germans of that time.[126] In military contexts, therefore, when the Byzantine sources mention "ancestors" they often mean the glorious Romans of old.

This link functioned rhetorically, but we should not dismiss it for that reason. Rhetorical appeals are emotive and must correspond to something. And ancient Roman ancestry was invoked in other contexts as well. When emperors and elite Byzantines concocted fake genealogies, they tended to claim ancient Roman ancestry, though by no means exclusively. We saw in Snapshot 1 how Anastasios I claimed descent from Pompey the Great, and similar claims can be traced down to the Palaiologan period.[127] This was part of Byzantium's "Roman impulse," and it could justify actions in nonmilitary spheres too. For example, a hostile source reports that the emperor Theophilos (829–842) was going bald and therefore decreed that "no Roman" should wear hair longer than below the neck; for this, he invoked the practice of "the Roman ancestors, who wore their hair in this way."[128] This was rather antiquarian, but the story—or the emperor's policy, if we accept it as historical, or the author's joke, if that's all it was—presupposes an ethnic notion of what it meant to be Roman and a normative standard derived from ancient Rome. None of it would make sense if the Byzantine Romans did not believe that they were in some way descended from the ancient Romans.

The fiction of kinship and descent from the ancient Romans was only one side of the picture, however. As we will see when we turn to assimilation in the second part of this book, Byzantium was also capable of absorbing groups and individuals whose ancestry was partly or even wholly foreign and treating them as fully Roman, so long as they adopted and exhibited the requisite cultural traits; that is, so long as they *became* Roman through acculturation. Such people might appear in the sources as "a Turk by *genos*, but raised as a Roman."[129] We have seen that the captive Romans in the *Miracles of Saint Demetrios*, who longed to return to their Roman homeland, were the offspring of mixed marriages, and so too was Digenis Akritis, the borderland hero. Acculturation, therefore, could override ancestry, leading to assimilation.

This had a long history in Roman tradition. More than any other ancient polity, Rome incorporated foreign peoples and admitted them to its citizenship and name, even though some Romans did talk about blood purity. That claim is not extensively documented, but it was made.[130] The dominant logic, however, was of assimilation. A community formed through social consensus, and that moreover knew itself to be so formed, could nevertheless still cast itself as a community of descent. As has been written about ancient Rome:

> All Romans, no matter their origins, were in a sense descended from Romulus.... Commitment to the community allowed one to become part of that community.... Loyalty to the group was more important than biological ties in the construction of Roman society.... The myth of shared descent was by nature permeable.[131]

It remained permeable in Byzantium too, for the myth of shared descent and the assimilation of foreigners could coexist. It was common for premodern groups that formed through political integration to insist that they had a common origin, even in the face of the known facts: "Genealogical appeals are important for ethnic reasoning not because kinship and descent are ubiquitous or necessary aspects of how ethnicity or race were conceptualized in antiquity, but because they offer a central way of communicating a sense of ethnic/racial 'fixity,' essence, and continuity."[132]

A Fiction of the Sources?

The discussion has so far used explicit textual claims to outline the contours of the Roman community. People were included in it or excluded from it based on what are unambiguous ethnic criteria, as opposed to (say) criteria of occupation, gender, location, or socioeconomic status. We will flesh those ethnic criteria out in Chapter 3. One question remains to be asked here: Who made those "explicit textual claims"? We must ask this because it is theoretically possible, however unlikely, that this ethnic Roman community is a fiction of the source material. Historians should be suspicious of sources. In

1975, Cyril Mango referred to Byzantine literature as a "distorting mirror," because its conventions of literary artifice distorted the historical reality that it ostensibly presented.[133] For example, many authors who wrote in a high register of Greek used concepts and even just a vocabulary that made their world appear more like classical antiquity than it really was. This insight was effectively a precursor to the Linguistic Turn, an understanding that dawned on many scholars in the 1980s and 1990s that our sources are literary artifacts that represent reality in ways that are conditioned by genre, various linguistic and cultural conventions, and political agendas. We do not have immaculate windows to Byzantine reality, but highly structured (and thereby "distorted") images of it. Was Roman ethnicity one of its fictions?

In a recent iteration of the denialist thesis, Ioannis Stouraitis has asserted that it was. According to him, a tiny number of elite authors in Constantinople somehow conspired to manufacture a false picture, a rhetorical fiction, that the population of the empire constituted a homogenous Roman nation. However, he presents no actual evidence in support of his thesis, only assertions drawn from modern "critical theory." He does not define this elite, which is a real problem for his thesis because the elite of the capital was drawn from the provinces. Nor does he explain why they would engage in such a distortion, or the mechanisms by which they perpetuated the fraud. Also, he couples this thesis with another one that directly contradicts it, namely that Romanness was claimed exclusively by the (tiny) ruling class in Constantinople, in contrast to the majority of the population, who were "ethno-culturally diverse." He ignores the fact that the sources distinguish between Romans and ethnic minorities inside the empire, and even at the court. Moreover, the sources clearly do not limit Romanness to an elite, referring, for example, to "the leading men in the City [or state] and all who were of the Roman race." In the end, the elite theory fails because it is not based on the sources and because it proposes a complex and incoherent solution to a nonexistent problem.[134]

But the methodological question remains: Who produced the sources that tell us about Roman ethnicity? And did their representation distort it in ways for which we can perhaps correct? The answers to these questions are that, first, our sources were produced by such a wide variety of people across time, space, class, and language that no conspiracy to produce a "homogenizing discourse" can be suspected. We have evidence from outside Byzantium too, specifically from the Arab and even Latin worlds, that most Byzantines were ethnically Roman. And, second, there is reason to believe that the discursive practices of the Byzantine elite *downplayed* the Romanness of the majority. They did not exaggerate it, far less invented it. Ethnic Romanness ran even *deeper* than our sources suggest. This discussion, then, is a good opportunity to expand the circle of the evidence and go closer to the ground.

The usage patterns of the ethnonym *Romaios* that we surveyed above are not found exclusively in elite authors writing in Constantinople, and many of these had provincial origins anyway. The same patterns are found also in texts that possibly originated in the provinces, including in the poem *Digenis*, whose instinctive and patriotic commitment to Romanía we will examine in Chapter 3; and texts that certainly originated in the provinces, such as a liturgy for fallen soldiers and much hagiography. For example, in his *Life of Saint Ioannes the Hesychast*, Kyrillos of Skythopolis (sixth century), a monk at St. Saba near Jerusalem, says that a Saracen raid against the provinces of Arabia and Palestine seized "as captives many tens of thousands of Romans."[135] Kyrillos had no investment in the discourses of Roman power propagated by the court. In the fantastical fifth- or sixth-century *Life of Saint Epiphanios of Salamis*, the saint comes from a poor family of peasants in the province of Phoenicia who did not have enough to eat. Yet when he comes to the court of the Persian king, he warns the king not to fight against the Romans, "for if you move against the Romans you will be moving against the Crucified one." When he departs, the king tells him to "go in health, Epiphanios, Glory of the Romans! (ἡ δόξα τῶν Ῥωμαίων)."[136] This provincial text is not written in a high style, but clearly made the point—to us as well as to later Byzantines—that a poor provincial was a Roman, and a patriotic one at that. In the ninth-century *Life of Saint Nikolaos the Younger*, a provincial work, the first-person plural pronoun "we" is used in reference to "the Romans" when barbarians invade the empire; the same happens in the ninth-century *Life of Saint Petros of Atroa*.[137]

Provincial Syriac texts from the sixth century tell the same story. The Church of Zeugma, in Mesopotamia, wrote a letter to the Church of Edessa about an omen that concerned "you, us, and all Romans" (a goose had laid an egg with the inscription "the Romans will conquer"). This letter was then copied into the so-called chronicle of Pseudo-Joshua the Stylite, a Syriac text written by an official in Edessa that is as straightforwardly pro-Roman as any Greek or Latin history written in Constantinople.[138] It proves that members of a local church on the fringes of empire saw their fates as entwined with the victories of the Roman armies and considered themselves and their fellow provincials to be Romans.

Examples can be multiplied, and more evidence pours in if we tap the riches of Arabic literature, which consistently called the Byzantines Romans *(Rum)*, distinguishing them from other ethnic groups who lived near or among them, such as Slavs, Armenians, or Bulgarians.[139] Already in the eighth century, Arab writers listed the Romans among the "ethnic categories," so alongside the Persians and Copts.[140] In their detailed testimony about Byzantium, Arab ethnographers and other writers treat the inhabitants of the empire, whether high or low, Constantinopolitan or provincial, as *al-Rum*, unless they belonged to one of the aforementioned ethnic groups. The ninth-century Arab essayist al-Jahiz quotes a Turkish general who made the point that Rum and Slav differ in the same way that Arab and non-Arab differ, not in the way that different kinds of Arabs differ.[141] Byzantine slave women in the Arab world were called "Rum women" and juxtaposed to other ethnicities, such as Slavs and Franks.[142] Texts mention slaves of Rum ethnic origin who had previously not been nobles but had practiced lowly professions, such as blacksmiths.[143] Al-Jahiz also claimed that the Rum of his time were good not at science but at the humble "handicrafts of turnery, carpentry, painting, and silk-weaving."[144] He was not writing about an elite here—of generals, statesmen, and orators—but the general Rum population. Arab writers knew that there were civilian Rum in the towns and countryside of the empire as well as soldier Rum and elite

Rum.[145] Arab ethnographers often relied on the testimony of visitors to the empire, none of whom reported that the Rum were limited to a small elite in the capital. They also traded with, captured, and interrogated the Rum, but if they found non-Roman ethnic identities among them that fell beneath the notice of our allegedly elite Byzantine sources, they failed to report it.

Moreover, Arab writers saw the Romans as a kinship group. The ninth-century Baghdadi poet Ibn al-Rumi claimed that he had Roman ancestors, and that his maternal uncles were Persian, but his paternal uncles were Romans.[146] A similar case is provided by the poet Abu Firas, a cousin of the Hamdanid prince of Aleppo Sayf al-Dawla. In the 960s, Abu Firas spent time as a captive in Constantinople. As it happens, his mother was Roman, a slave woman of his father, though Abu Firas defensively claimed she was a free woman. At any rate, he refers to her as Rum, which again proves that this was, in Arab eyes, an ethnic category, not one of class.[147] In this respect, therefore, the Arab and the Roman sources agree. However, the Arab writers cannot have been collaborating with the Byzantine elite to perpetuate a fiction of Roman ethnicity. They called them Romans because that was their self-professed ethnicity, whether in the army, the court, or the countryside.

The same conclusion emerges even from some Frankish or Latin sources. Despite their general tendency to call the Byzantines "Greeks," sometimes the real name sneaks through. This happened, for instance, when a western power wanted to keep the Byzantines loyal to an alliance and so softened the exclusion of the name Roman. In his diplomatic letters, the German emperor Friedrich II usually called his Byzantine counterpart Ioannes III Batatzes, his ally against the pope, "the emperor of the Greeks." But in one letter of 1250 he indignantly recounts how the pope had excommunicated Batatzes and all his subjects—"all the Romans subject to you, shamelessly labelling as heretics the most orthodox Romans, from whom the Christian faith had spread originally to the four corners of the earth!" It was an occasional piece of flattery, to call his correspondent by his own ethnic name.[148]

This slip occurred in contexts that had nothing to do with Constantinople or the court. The *Chronicle of the Morea* is an early fourteenth-century poem that recounts the conquest of the Peloponnese in the aftermath of the Fourth Crusade and the history of the Frankish principality of Achaea during the thirteenth century. In the Greek version of the poem, the Byzantines are called Romans throughout, including both the current subjects of the emperor and his former subjects now ruled by the French in the principality. These Romans are called a *genos* throughout the poem and are defined by traits that were shared by all Byzantines, for example religion (e.g., v. 470: "to make all Romans obey the pope," i.e., because they were Orthodox); ethnic stereotypes (e.g., vv. 593–594: the *genos* of the Romans is crafty and faithless); and speech ("the language of the Romans"—what we call Greek—is here called ῥωμαίικα: v. 4130, i.e., "Roman-talk"; cf. v. 5207). Romans and Franks are juxtaposed as different but comparable types, and references are made to the "local Romans" of the Morea (e.g., v. 1424).

Why does this poem deviate from the standard western practice of calling the Byzantines Greeks? The French version of the *Chronicle*, for example, calls them *grecs*. This question has not been fully investigated, but the most recent study supports the priority of the Greek version of the poem over the French (the latter was likely a translation and adaptation of the Greek).[149] This was, then, a Frankish text, reflecting the typical prejudice against the Romans (Byzantines), but it was composed in vernacular Greek by a Moreot Frank, who was possibly bilingual. In his poem he reflected local usage, including the fact that the Greek-speaking Orthodox population of the empire and its former provinces (such as the Peloponnese) called itself Roman and spoke *romaïika*.

Additional proof is provided by the poem *Dittamondo* written by the fourteenth-century Florentine poet Fazio degli Uberti. This didactic poem takes the form of an exploration of the known world. When the narrator reaches Macedonia he meets a local with whom he speaks in a demotic form of Greek, transcribed directly into the poem. "Do you speak Frangika?" (i.e., any Romance language), he asks the local. The latter answers "*Ime roméos* (εἶμαι Ῥωμαῖος, i.e., I am a Roman)."[150] What he says immediately after that is harder to make out, but this testimony should lay to rest any doubt that the Byzantines called themselves Romans. Their enduring Roman ethnicity peaks through the cracks of western labels straight through to the Ottoman period. For example, the traveler Richard Chandler admitted in the eighteenth century that the Greeks of Athens called themselves and their language "Roman."[151] French writers, such as Voltaire and Raffenel, made the same admission.[152]

In sum, we are not dealing with a "distorting mirror" here or some elite "discourse" twisting reality for obscure reasons. There is no conceivable reason or mechanism that would enable Byzantine writers from the provinces and in many genres to conspire for over a thousand years to misinform their readers (and posterity) about the ethnicity of the majority population of their own society. This mechanism would, moreover, also have to explain how and why foreigners who were often the enemies of Romanía, such as the Arabs and occasionally the Franks too, supported this national discourse of homogenizing Romanness, if it corresponded to no existing Romans. And the testimony of other foreign observers can be added to theirs.[153] In addition, the conspiracy theory would have to explain why local "Greeks" in the Ottoman empire still referred to themselves and their language as "Roman," as reported by western observers whose instinct and bias was to call them Greeks.

Insofar as ethnicity is established primarily through discursive claims, which must be written in texts or inscriptions in order to reach us, we cannot hear the voice of the majority of the population. But Roman claims are made in all types of surviving sources, even those that bring us closest to the provincial ground level. They occur as far down the social scale as the sociology of Byzantine writing allows us to see, and there is no reason to believe that those claims then disappeared below the threshold of literacy. We have found no connection between being Roman and being able to read and write. Provincial saints' lives, for example, assumed that the majority of the population (barring ethnic minorities) was Roman and that "we" were the targets of barbarian raids against "the Romans." They sometimes expressed patriotic sentiments of loyalty and prayer for the emperor of the Romans.[154]

In other words, these texts testify not only to Roman ethnicity but also to Roman patriotism. This was deeply embedded in provincial society. Beyond the hundreds of thousands of people who were sustained by and identified with the imperial state's military infrastructure, religious services across the empire also typically ended in prayers on behalf of the emperor and for victory in war over the barbarians; the Church was a willing participant and supporter of imperial ideology.[155] Derek Krueger's words of caution about religious differentiation in Byzantium are also relevant to the question of possible ethnic differentiation: "The religious lives of the elites and of the masses were not truly distinct. Rather, all Byzantines participated in a shared system of religious practice.... The religious lives and outlooks of the lower ranks of the clergy, in particular, may not have differed so greatly from those of their lay parishioners."[156]

Besides, there was not a single elite in Byzantium. Generals, statesmen, and courtiers were invested in the Roman ideology of the imperial state because it underpinned their social status and power. But the literary elite based its status on the ability to write formal, purist Greek. It was this Hellenism that constituted their elite status, not their Romanness, which was "common" by comparison, in both senses. As Chapter 3 will show, in two crucial respects the literary elite's stylistic preoccupations led it to *underplay* the Romanness of their world. Compelled to avoid vernacular terms and write as if they lived in ancient times, they had to pretend not to know what common people were calling the state in which they all lived and the language that they all spoke at home: *Romanía* and *romaíika*.

3

Romanland

Neque apud civis solum Romanos, qui et sermonis et iuris et multarum rerum societate iuncti sunt.

What traits were used to distinguish Romans from others in Byzantium? Here, in chronological order, is a list of the indicia that we have seen already, to which I add some additional sources:

Agathias (sixth century): polity, laws, religion, customs, morality, language, and dress (Snapshot 6).
The Miracles of Saint Demetrios (late seventh century): descent (partial), upbringing, narratives of group history, the homeland, Orthodoxy, and customs (Snapshot 2).
The western emperor Louis II (871): "the Greeks" differ in religion, geographical location, language, and peoplehood.[1]
Leon VI (d. 912): Slavs and Romans differ in customs, language, religion, and modes of rule.[2]
The patriarch Nikolaos Mystikos (d. 925): Romans and Saracens differ in their way of life, habits, and religion.[3]
Konstantinos VII (d. 959): customs, laws, religion (specifically baptism), language, birth, a native territory, and biological descent (Snapshot 3).
The Lombard bishop Liudprand of Cremona (tenth century): the "Greeks" were distinct by language, customs, and dress.[4]

Eustathios Boïlas (eleventh century): Romans and Armenians differ in homeland, religion, and language.[5]

Digenis Akritis (ca. 1100): Romans differ from Saracens by birth, language, religion, temperament, and fatherland.[6]

Addendum to the chronicle of Skylitzes (twelfth century): customs, dress, and social order (Snapshot 7).

The Frankish *Chronicle of the Morea* (thirteenth century): "Latin and Greek [actually "Roman" in the text] ethnicities are defined . . . in terms of contrasts in physical appearance, character, religion, language, and culture."[7]

Konstantinos Akropolites (fourteenth century): the hypothetical St. Barbaros, when he was still a Muslim, was "diametrically opposite [to us] in terms of language, race, laws, and customs . . . a barbarian in his race, his manners, his roughness."[8]

Nikephoros Gregoras (fourteenth century): Barlaam the Calabrian had to grow a beard and change his language, dress, manners *(ethos)*—in a word, "everything"—when he decided to move to Byzantium and fit in.[9]

The list remains fairly consistent from late antiquity to late Byzantium, and many more statements to the same effect could be cited. Although each of these writers adduced a different combination of traits, they would presumably agree on a compound definition that included all these elements. This means that it was possible in Byzantium to refer individually or in combination to Roman ancestry, Roman customs, the Roman laws, the Roman way of life, Roman dress, the Roman political order, the Roman religion, the Roman language, the Roman homeland, and so on. Indeed, each such element is attested individually and frequently in the sources. These are the indicia of Roman ethnicity, the things that one would point to if asked, "What makes you (or anyone) a Roman?" They were what separated Romans from others. (Interestingly, they do not include "being subject to the emperor," the bloodless formal definition preferred by many modern scholars.) Individuals could always be found who exhibited only some of these attributes, and they might make for interesting case studies in "hybridity" or what not. As we will see in Chapter 4, there were always in Byzantium populations that were crossing those multiple boundaries on their way to becoming Roman, and so were often in a state of in-betweenness. But this was not the case for the majority of the Romans. For them it was not any one of these qualities that was decisive, but their combination as a distinctive cultural profile and, in addition, the recognition by both insiders and outsiders that this combination underpinned their ethnicity.[10]

Foreigners who came to Byzantium, as well as its own native minorities, encountered a dominant culture that understood itself to be Roman in these very ways, which are both general and specific. The present chapter will discuss some of the key indicia of Roman ethnicity, specifically homeland (or one aspect of it), language, and religion. It will then conclude with a brief look at antiquity and the process that had originally created all these Greek-speaking Romans in the east, which we can label a "Romanogenesis." This will set the stage for the discussion in Chapter 4 of the ongoing assimilation of foreigners and minorities to the dominant Roman ethnicity.

The Vernacular Ontology of Romanía

A national homeland can be discussed under many different aspects, as no nation imagines and valorizes its own homeland in quite the same way as its neighbors, given the uniqueness of its history and landscape of memory. For example, there might be that one place of special importance, often sacralized, which generally stands in symbolically for the nation as a whole. Constantinople may have played this role for Byzantium, in addition to being its imperial capital. There was in addition an infrastructural territory, demarcated by borders and treaties and defended by armies. This was the territory controlled by the state, within which operated its fiscal and judicial systems of governance. More than in any other medieval state, Roman writers evince a strong and clear understanding of this concept.[11] The institutional homeland largely overlapped with a looser sense of the homeland that the sources label simply "the land of the Romans" or "the territory of the Romans," for example when it was invaded by barbarians. This expressed the ethnic distinction between "us" and "them" in terms of territory. References of this kind are so abundant in the sources that we can safely conclude that these

Romans thought of land or territory as an integral component of their collective existence.

Here we will focus on a specific and striking terminological development, namely the emergence of the name *Romanía* ('Ρωμανία), which may be translated as "Romeland" or, better, "Romanland." This name first appears a century after Caracalla's grant of universal citizenship, so precisely when the inhabitants of the eastern empire—and especially the inhabitants of the regions that would form the core of the future Byzantine empire (i.e., the Balkans and Asia Minor)—were adjusting to their new identity as Romans and coming to terms with the global Roman community. Ontologically, this new name ("Land of the Romans") recognized that the world was now full of Romans and extended their collective name to their territory as a whole, and not just to the inert territory but also to the state and society that they collectively formed. It is a striking instance of a national territory being conceived and defined into existence in lands where the name had never before existed or applied. This development was based on the (new) civic identity and, ultimately, the new ethnicity of its majority population. Moreover, the name originated from below, from the habits of vernacular speech, and not among the late Roman literary elite. This is what average Romans called their homeland, territory, and polity, in which they were shareholders. What we call Byzantium, the Byzantines called Romanland.

Byzantinists have excluded this name from their technical vocabulary, to say nothing of using it in the titles of their books. It remains the elephant in the room, known to many nonexperts but apparently not to specialists in the field. The Byzantines offer it to us as a perfectly viable and widely attested name for their state, political society, and national territory, a name, moreover, that stems from and points directly to their Romanness. Yet we prefer other terms that are both invented and misleading ("Byzantium," "medieval Hellenism," etc.). There is not a single article in print on the meaning that "Romanía" has in the Byzantine sources or on its scope and variants. The name does not appear in Warren Treadgold's *A History of the Byzantine State and Society* (1997) or in the collective *Oxford Handbook of Byzantine Studies* (2008), for all that each has over 1,000 pages.[12] This reveals a bad conscience, for the name cannot be missed in the sources. It appears in hundreds of them written in all genres of literature as well as in the documentary evidence. As the name highlights the Romanness of the Byzantines and the Roman origin and nature of their polity, scholarship has banished it with a silence that is both embarrassing and culpable.

By contrast, there *are* a few studies of Romanía as it appears in the *Latin* sources of the age of the crusades, when Byzantine territories came under western rule.[13] This imbalance in coverage reveals the underlying ideological bias. The Byzantines apparently have no right to a Romanía of their own, but western rule in their lands legitimates the use of the term by scholars. Studies of the Latin empire of Constantinople and its Italian residents use the name Romanía freely and without explanation.[14]

Byzantine Romanía was, as we will see, a name of *popular* origin and part of the mental landscape of the average Roman. Only later did it enter the vocabulary of more elite sources, which shied away from vernacular terms until they could no longer avoid them. Or else they artificially classicized it into the pseudo-archaic adjectival substantive *Romaïs*.[15] Thus, because of its stylistic conventions, which aimed to reproduce a pure form of Greek by imitating Attic grammar and carefully avoiding vernacular terms and neologisms, the Byzantine elite actually downplays the vernacular Romanness of the general population.

The name first appears in the fourth century and was likely in circulation even before that. It is important to stress this, because frequently cited and even standard studies assert that it first appears in the sixth or seventh century.[16] Yet in our earliest sources, the name Romanía does not burst on the scene. It is used casually, almost quietly, by mid-fourth-century authors who assumed that it did not require explanation for their readers, which means that it must have been in circulation for some time before its first appearances. Moreover, the texts in which it first appears are not highbrow. Classicizing texts would avoid the name for some time still, suggesting that it was first used widely on the street and not in fancy declamations.

The first texts are Athanasios of Alexandria's *History of the Arians*; the *Passion* of the Gothic saint Saba; and Epiphanios of Salamis' *Panarion*. Let us see how they introduce and use the name. Athanasios is, as always, railing against the Arian heretics of his time, and in this passage he accuses them of spreading their "madness" as far as Rome itself, "without any reverence for the fact that Rome is the metropolis of Romanía."[17] Romanía here can mean only the empire as a whole. This is imagined as an extended colony of Rome the "mother city," which is technically correct, as metropolitan citizenship had been extended to every free citizen in the empire in 212 AD. The jurist Modestinus had opined, in the aftermath of that seismic shift, that "Rome is our common *patria*," a view enshrined in Justinian's *Digest* and later again in its official Greek translation, the *Basilika* (ca. 900).[18] This meant that a Roman was to feel at home everywhere in the empire, in Romanía. It is fascinating that, two centuries before Justinian, the view that the empire was basically an extension of the city of Rome had already been naturalized within Christian Egyptian priests' view of the Roman world. Athanasios addressed his work primarily to monks and clerics and expected them to understand the concept of Rome being the metropolis of something called "Romanía," which was where they lived. The name could therefore be used in a purely internal frame of reference, not as a perception of the Roman world from the outside. Egyptian Christians, who were now Roman citizens whose religion was favored by the imperial court, knew that they lived in and were part of "Romanland."

Athanasios' contemporary, the pagan philosopher and orator Themistios also said, in 366, that "the empire of the Romans should be imagined as a single, unified city."[19] A late third-century orator had expressed this in striking language, while pointing to a map of the world: "We see nothing foreign in it."[20]

This shift had marked the end of Rome as an empire—understood as the domination by Romans of non-Romans[21]—and its transformation into something that called for new terms. Romanía was among them. Cliff Ando has produced precise definitions of the nature of this transformation, and we need only plug the new name into them to understand Byzantium. "What sort of state," he asks, "was the empire, when Rome ceased to rule over anyone?"[22] "One might even say that it ceased in any meaningful way to be an empire. It became, rather, something like a state . . . with a uniform law of persons and legal culture, both penetrating universally throughout its territory."[23] He notes that "the empire was late to develop a conceptual and linguistic apparatus with which to describe itself as a unified political space or articulate claims to sovereignty over a unified territory and unitary population."[24] The people who developed that apparatus were the provincials themselves, and, for their state, they settled on the proper (ethnic) name of Romanía.

Our second text is the *Passion* of the Gothic saint Saba, which was written before 379 in the land of the Goths, north of the Danube, by an author who knew ecclesiastical Greek and the conventions of hagiography. The text takes the form of a letter addressed to the Church of Cappadocia. At one point, it refers casually to a Gothic Christian who was avoiding the persecution by spending time in Romanía; also, at the end of the narrative, a Roman official transports the saint's remains from the *barbarikon* to Romanía.[25] This text reveals more aspects of the name's ontology. Socially, we observe that it was familiar to provincial Romans writing in a low-level register of Greek, even to those who were active among the Goths outside the empire itself. Geographically, it could refer to the Roman provinces in the Balkans and Asia Minor, and stood in contradistinction to the lands inhabited by barbarians, here Goths, who dwelled in the *barbarikon*.

Goths had "Gothia" and Romans now had "Romanía." Although Romans generally regarded themselves as superior to barbarians, these pairs—ethnonym plus eponymous homeland—were strictly homologous: "the Romans" were an ethnicity in their own right with their own homeland and territory, and they lived next to the homelands of other groups. The Roman homeland, however, had at least one feature that set it aside from the others and made it superior to them in the eyes of the Romans themselves: it was fundamentally a community of law. In fact, in a decisive way, it had been brought into being through a law of universal enfranchisement. The fifth-century historian Orosius (writing in Latin) tells a story about the Gothic king Athaulf's idea to abolish Romanía and replace it with Gothia. But he realized that, in order to do that, he would have to abolish Roman law, which would make his new state not a state at all.[26] When he tells this story about Gothia and Romania, Orosius stops to apologize for the "vernacular" terms that he will stoop to using *(ut vulgariter loquar)*. This is more confirmation that these terms rose up from below; they did not trickle down from elite levels. It was perhaps not the only term to which this happened. It has been argued that the use of *dominus* for the emperor began in the second and third centuries "in texts commissioned by middling social strata, such as military officers, freed slaves, and mid-ranking civilian officials, then percolated upward to the higher echelons of the imperial aristocracy."[27] Something similar happened in the case of *Romanía*.

Epiphanios, bishop of Salamis (on Cyprus), wrote the *Panarion*, a massive catalogue and refutation of all heresies, in 374–377; it too is not a work written in high-register Greek. He mentions Romanía in two complementary ways. The first is geographic: Romanía encompasses the seas and lands of the empire and it is mentioned when people, ideas, or goods come into it from outside.[28] We should generally be prepared to see Romanía named largely in contexts that juxtaposed it to something else. There was less reason for authors to mention it when they were writing about events occurring wholly within it. Even so, they did, as we saw with Athanasios. Romanía also defined the territorial scope of the Roman state. For example, Epiphanios says that an emperor would send a letter out "to the whole of Romanía."[29]

The *Panarion* is also not written in a highbrow register, which supports the idea that Romanía was a name that these ecclesiastical authors picked up from the vernacular of their time. It was already in wide circulation by the mid-fourth century, from Egypt to Cyprus and the Danube frontier. It is likely, therefore, that it originated in the third century AD, in both Greek and Latin, and its rise was connected to the universal extension of Roman citizenship and the creation of a global Roman community. In the second century, the orator Ailios Aristeides had already foreseen that "you [the leaders of Rome] have made 'Roman' mean not the citizen of one city but the common name of an entire *genos*."[30] This foreshadowed a Roman ethnogenesis as well as the proliferation of "duplicate Romes" in the provinces, culminating in the making of a New Rome in 330 AD, Constantinople, a branch office of Old Rome in the east. The eastern empire was not called Roman after its new capital,[31] but rather the reverse: it was the globalization of Rome in the third century that enabled the empire to replicate its capital city in a provincial environment that had already become Roman. The basis for this leap of the imagination had been laid in the east before Constantine broke ground on his new capital. The roots of Romanía had been put down before they sprouted a New Rome.[32]

One of the mechanisms that made Romanía possible was the transfer, or rather the extension, of local civic affiliations to a global scale. In the classical Roman empire, cities were the primary foci of political identity. In the Byzantine Roman empire, Romanía took their place by casting itself as a vast city. Already in the second century, Aristeides had praised the Romans for turning the entire world, the *oikoumene*, into a single unified city.[33] Athanasios in the fourth century imagined Romanía as the vast hinterland of a single Roman metropolis. And in the early fifth century, the pagan Latin poet Rutilius Namatianus again praised Rome for "creating a single fatherland out of many diverse nations: what was once a world, you have made into a city."[34] In the past, Rome had been praised for gathering into itself all good things from across the entire world that it had conquered, and thereby becoming a "cosmopolitan" city.[35] In a reversal of that trope, the world itself had now become like a city. This world has been unified politically to such a degree that it becomes equivalent to a common "fatherland," a *patris (patria)*, and would therefore receive patriotic devotion.

The next section of this chapter will discuss expressions of patriotism in Byzantium that were directed at Romanía as a whole. Here I wish to explore further the concept of Romanía. We have seen that, while the name designated a geographical entity, that entity was understood quasi-legally as a "colony" of its "metropolis," and administratively as representing the scope of the emperor's jurisdiction. By 500, if not earlier, Romanía was also the name given by the people in the streets of Constantinople to the polity to which they belonged, in which they were shareholders and in which they believed that they had a right to intervene. In 512, part of the population of Constantinople rose up against the emperor Anastasios and began to chant, "A different emperor for Romanía!" Then, after they found their man, they chanted, "Areobindos as emperor for Romanía!" In the

Nika Riots of 532, the people, rising up against Justinian are recorded as chanting "Probos as emperor for Romanía!"[36]

These fascinating episodes reflect crucial developments. First, we note again the popular use of the name Romanía. Here we see it literally spoken by the people in the streets, recorded in two chronicles (Malalas, the *Paschal Chronicle*) that, although not written in vernacular Greek, are not highbrow either. We can be fairly confident that they are recording the very words that were spoken. Classical authors in the same period such as Prokopios were still avoiding these popular neologisms. Prokopios' successor Theophylaktos, for example, uses the term only once, in a letter of the Persian shah Khusrow that he quotes.[37] This linguistic profile reinforces our initial assessment that "Romanía," as an ideological construct, originated among and rose up from nonelite social strata. This is not to say that Prokopios and his kind did not participate in the ideology of Romanía; they merely expressed it in different ways in their high-register idiom. Second, there is the "constitutional" angle: the people believed that they had a legitimate say in the political fortunes of the state at the highest level, where emperors were deposed and appointed.[38] Calling the state Romanía linked their own ethnic-political identity to its very name and reinforced their legitimate claim to intervene in its fortunes.

Third, the grammar of Romanía also compels attention. In antiquity, the normal way to name a collective political entity or state was through the (plural) ethnonym of the people who constituted it: the *demos* of the Athenians, the *populus Romanus*, or simply the Lacedaemonians, the Macedonians, and so on. Where modern historians tend to say Athens and Sparta, thinking along the lines of France and Germany, ancient authors referred instead to the Athenians and the Lacedaemonians. But the early Byzantines had made a curious conceptual leap in this regard: they had imagined an abstract noun-entity named after themselves and made it the focus of political activity and contestation. I will argue in a separate study that the Byzantine abstraction and personification of Romanía was categorically equivalent to modern practices of imagining and naming the nation-state.

Here let us stick with the grammar. It is also curious that the people invoked Romanía in the dative and not the genitive. They wanted a different emperor *for* Romanía, not an emperor *of* Romanía. The distinction is important. "The dative proper is largely personal and denotes the person who is interested in or affected by the action . . . [it] is not often used with things; when so used there is usually a personification or semi-personification."[39] In other words, Romanía was not imagined as an inert thing subject to the power of the emperor, something that belonged to him, but rather as a quasi-personalized entity with a stake in the selection of the emperor. In 512 and 532, new emperors were being proposed for the benefit of Romanía. The normal way of referring to the emperor was as "the emperor of the Romans," which revealed that he was defined by and beholden to a specific ethnopolitical community. The dative use of Romanía preserved that personalized delimitation. Territory, state, and people were coextensive. As a comparative study of empires put it recently, after the universal grant of citizenship in 212, "imperial citizenship had multiple meanings—a legal status with obligations and protections, a source of pride and honor, a sense of cultural superiority, a personal bond with state power and with other citizens even over a huge space. The polity could exist in the persons of its members, not just in the group of servitors around the emperor or his rivals for power."[40]

That "personal bond . . . over a huge space" is revealed by an inscription from Sirmium, carved in about 600 in horribly misspelled Greek: "Christ, Lord, help the city and stop the Avars, and protect Romanía along with the person writing these words, Amen."[41] It was not just the people of Constantinople who had a personal stake in the fortunes of Romanía. That identification extended across the national territory, including both center and periphery. There is no reason to equate Romanía with Constantinople. Referring to the uprisings of 512, Malalas says that they took place "in Constantinople and in every city of Romanía."[42] These were parallel events occurring simultaneously across the national territory. Likewise, at banquets in the palace to celebrate the emperor's anniversary the people chanted that "the City and the whole of Romanía is delighted."[43] In the eleventh century, the patriarch Keroularios accused a personal enemy of fighting against both the imperial City *(basilís)* and Romanía.[44] The City was understood as the capital of a national territory named after its dominant ethnic group.

The name Romanía continued to be used in a banal geographical sense, referring to the territories belonging to the Roman state, but also to that state itself. In this sense, Romanía was always entered through the borders of the empire, not at the gates of Constantinople.[45] It had "edges" that lay along its frontiers (e.g., the Black Sea).[46] It was juxtaposed to foreign lands, such as "the Armenias"[47] or, as we saw, "Gothia." In times of war, Romanía was identified as "our lands": it was a target of attack by enemies and the object of defense by the Roman armies.[48] Land conquered by Roman generals could be described as a "gift and dowry brought to Romanía," as if the general were a suitor seeking its favor.[49]

The foreign evidence again confirms the picture presented by Roman texts. The Arab geographer al-Masʿudi (tenth century) wrote that the *Rum* called their country *Armania* (Romanía).[50] Arabic-speakers did not typically use that term, which is why he reports it. Usually they called it *bilād al-Rūm*, which means the "lands (or towns) of the Romans" or, basically, "Romanland." Thus, they too, like the Romans, took the people to be primary and named the land after the people, as did the Persians *(diyār-i Rūm)*.[51] In Hebrew texts it is likewise called *Romaniyah*, which is just a direct transcription of what Jews heard it called in common parlance.[52] And the French version of the *Chronicle of the Morea* begins by declaring its theme as "la conquest de Costantinople et de l'empire de Romanie" (the Greek version of the chronicle uses the term *Romanía* over a hundred times, exactly as we would expect in a vernacular Greek text).

In sum, the name functioned in many ways like that of a modern nation-state. This hypothesis is confirmed by the various ways in which individual Romans could be said to interact with it. An emperor might be "zealous on behalf of Romanía" in both foreign relations (e.g., war) but also domestically, to reform "Roman affairs."[53] A donation may be made to a monastery by a widow to commemorate her husband's "exertions on behalf of Romanía."[54] Romanía was, then, by no means an inert territory or land. It was a quasi-personified entity that could compel devotion and personal toil. Like any nation-state, it was conceived as an abstract "person" with interest and claims. In a chrysobull to a monastery on Mt. Athos (ca. 1102), Alexios I Komnenos justified the operation of state officials by citing "the most pressing needs of Romanía."[55] His grandson Manuel I Komnenos (1143–1180) late in his reign required his high officials to swear an oath regarding the succession that included this clause: "I will make every effort in all contexts and in all ways to promote the honor of your beloved son and of Romanía."[56] This dual conjunction again emphasizes that the Roman empire was not a mere expression of the court, a set of personal relations existing between the emperor and his men, but a broader abstract entity representing the collectivity of the Romans. When Isaakios II Angelos (1185–1195) made an agreement with the Genoese, the text of the chrysobull that he issued contained dozens of references to Romanía as the entity with which—or with *whom*—the Genoese were negotiating: his Romanía has territories, interests, fleets, and is the sort of thing to which one can be friendly or hostile.[57]

Romanía was, then, a territory, a jurisdiction, a state named after a people, and an abstract national entity that had needs and honor; it was something to be defended and on whose behalf one might toil and labor. If it existed in modern times, we would have no difficulty in identifying it as a nation-state. Its name emerged at popular levels of speech and was only later adopted by the official language of the state. This is the exact opposite development from what so much denialist scholarship assumes, namely that Romanness was held only by court elites, and was projected downward by them.

Just as some historians erroneously postdate the first appearance of the name Romanía to the sixth or seventh centuries, others mistakenly date its adoption as the "official" name of the empire to 1102, specifically to the chrysobull by Alexios I cited above.[58] Yet a chrysobull of 1074, containing the draft of an agreement between Michael VII Doukas and the Norman terrorist Robert Guiscard, also stipulates (twice) that Robert and his heirs must remain dutiful "both toward my kingship and Romanía" (emperor and state, we must remember, were not the same).[59] This chrysobull was no place for terminological innovations, which means that use of the term was older still. But it is also not clear by what standards we can distinguish between official and unofficial uses. Do the people of Constantinople, acting in their collective capacity as the *populus Romanus*, count as official? Must "official use" be linked to chrysobulls or to texts written in purist Greek? The military manual of Nikephoros II Phokas (963–969) also uses the name,[60] as does Konstantinos VII Porphyrogennetos in a dossier of notes for his son and heir Romanos II that goes by the modern title *De administrando imperio*. It is significant in this connection that Konstantinos draws attention to the fact that he wrote these notes in a "plain" style, not "Atticizing for display, but rather in a common and vernacular way of speaking."[61] Was it this choice that enabled him to use the vernacular name Romanía?

In other words, the term *Romanía* remained in vernacular use *for over six hundred years* before it was "officially" adopted by emperors in their own texts and pronouncements. To be sure, the Roman chancery and formal prose were conservative. But this delay in adoption strengthens the argument made above that the term *Romanía* was of popular origin and that it reflected the average Roman's perception of his or her polity, and the word's grammar reflected the ways in which those average Romans interacted with their state. *Romanía* was long established in everyday speech as the key term that mediated interactions between the state and its subjects.

Patriots for Romanía

If Romanía was the recipient of national loyalty, we would expect to find expressions of patriotism directed toward it. Indeed, many survive, and we saw earlier how Roman-Christian patriotism was assumed by the authors of military manuals.[62] I will present three more texts here that reflect the variety of genres, authors, and contexts in which such sentiments are found. This variety indicates that Roman patriotism was not limited to one period, social context, or discursive mode. These texts also refute the notion that Byzantines had only a local sense of patriotism and were united solely by the coercive force of a distant imperial state, with which they did not identify. To be sure, patriotism is a tricky concept to use in a premodern context, being entangled with questions regarding the state's penetration of society and its ability to marshal sentiment on a popular level. Still, theoretical squeamishness and an excess of defensive hedging should not lead us to deny the obvious. I have therefore chosen three provincial, non-Atticizing texts.

The first is from the sixth century by a Christian geographer and scriptural exegete from Alexandria conventionally known as Kosmas Indikopleustes, whose theology deviated from that promulgated by Constantinople (he has been called a Nestorian). He takes a theological view of the "kingdom of the Romans," based on biblical prophecy. According to Kosmas, who expresses great pride here, the kingdom of the Romans will never fall because it was born at the same time as Christ precisely in order to promote God's designs for the salvation of mankind. The idea was old among Christian writers, but its chief prior exponent, Eusebios of Kaisareia, had not been led by it to express a great enthusiasm for the empire itself.[63] Kosmas, by contrast, is effusive, and identifies with Romanía personally. Because Augustus and Christ coincided, he says,

> the kingship of the Romans partakes in the honors of the kingdom of our Lord Christ, and surpasses all other kingships of this world, to the degree, of course, that that is possible for this world. It will remain undefeated until the consummation of the world.... To be sure, barbarian enemies will, at times, attack Romanía, on account of our sins and in order to correct our ways, but its kingship will remain undefeated through the strength of the Almighty.[64]

This was an explicitly theological Roman patriotism.

Kekaumenos, by contrast, was a retired imperial official of the eleventh century who, in the 1070s, wrote a book with advice for other officials and the emperor. He deliberately eschewed high-register prose, denied possessing an elite Hellenic education (*paideia*), and viewed imperial affairs from a provincial Balkan standpoint. He comes across as a staunch Roman patriot. Do not fear death, he says, if it is on behalf of the fatherland (*patris*) and the emperor, a statement that would be taken as the very measure of a nationalist mentality if it occurred in a modern author.[65] The Roman formation in battle, he avers, is the best and safest of all, while the navy is "the glory of Romanía."[66] Kekaumenos had a complicated family history, including ancestors who were, as he says, "enemies of Romanía," but this did not shake his own loyalty.[67] Kekaumenos had a strong sense of the national Roman interest. For example, he did not believe it was "in the interests of Romanía" for the emperor to award high titles and offices to foreigners; from that policy, "Romanía has suffered much harm." The highest titles and offices should go to Romans, and when that happens "Romanía flourishes." Another one of his ancestors, he adds, "toiled mightily on behalf of Romanía and was honored" with high office by the emperors.[68]

This language is consistent with how the Romans generally thought of Romanía: it was an entity with its own interests, it could be benefited and harmed, and it was the object of supreme devotion on the part of individuals, even to the point of self-sacrifice. None of this would strike us as noteworthy if we had not interposed two errors between us and them, namely that Byzantium was not Roman and that nations are exclusively modern phenomena. Otherwise, Kekaumenos' outlook was probably banal.

The name Romanía appears frequently in the quasi-vernacular heroic poem *Digenis Akritis*, which celebrates the exploits of the brawny frontiersman Digenis. This frequency is not surprising, given that the action takes place in the borderlands between the empire and the Arab lands, with much movement back and forth. We are again at the "edges" of Romanía, not the center.[69] Digenis' father was a Muslim emir who abandoned his family, faith, and country for the love of a Roman girl who stole his heart, and for her sake he moved to Romanía. In the poem, the name Romanía encapsulates all aspects of the emir's conversion and move. Whereas at first he was "full of wrath against Romanía," he later admits to the girl that "for love of you I came to Romanía."[70] Here is how the poet captures the transition.

> In this state, that marvelous emir looked with contempt on fame and the highest commands, forgot his kinsmen, his parents, and his fatherland *(patris)*, and renounced his faith for the love of a

girl. . . . He who was once an enemy was now revealed as a slave of love. He moved to Romanía on account of his beloved.[71]

The emir now expresses a strong affective identification with Romanía, calling it "beautiful" and linking it to his love for his wife, son, and new religion.[72] This is, after all, what a *patris* is. When the former emir is about to leave his mother, she tearfully asks him whether miracles happen in Romanía that are comparable to those that are performed at the Prophet's tomb. The emir answers her heatedly with a Christian sermon, and then sharply declares, "Mother, I'm now returning to Romanía."[73] Romanía provided him with a global frame of reference for his new life.

Some historians who realize that the nation is not an exclusively modern phenomenon have to make an effort to prove that the premodern states with the potential to be considered national entities had corresponding national names.[74] In the case of Byzantium—that is, Romanía—the name has been there all along, well attested, and its national import is obvious on the face of the evidence. Not only that, the national name's philology reveals it unquestionably to have originated and been used primarily at nonelite levels, affording us a rare glimpse into the lexical and grammatical structures of the average Byzantine's Romanness. All we have to do in order to see it is overcome the ideological filters and barriers created by centuries of denial and obfuscation.

Latin and Romaic: Two Roman Languages

In ancient ethnography, language was sometimes regarded as a more important component of ethnicity than homeland. For example, it is included in the famous list given by the Athenians in Herodotos of what all the Greeks have in common, along with blood, religion, and customs, whereas homeland is not.[75] In Roman texts, "language" (*glossa*) is sometimes used as a synonym for "ethnic group" (*ethnos*).[76] The ethnic communities living on Mt. Athos could be called languages instead of nations.[77] The *Life of Saint Neilos of Rossano* (tenth century) divides Christian believers into "those of the same race" as the saint (*homophyloi*) on the one hand and "those who speak a different language" *(alloglossoi)* on the other.[78] Writing to a friend who had left the capital, Psellos asked, "If I were an Italian or a Briton living among many foreign people speaking many different languages, would I not exchange them all for a single person of the same *genos?*"[79] On the other hand, language was not the sole criterion for ethnicity. A Roman could speak a foreign language and even be bilingual without ceasing to be Roman,[80] while, conversely, foreigners could speak Greek without thereby being regarded as Romans. For example, the tsar of Bulgaria Simeon (d. 927) could speak Greek because he had spent part of his childhood at the imperial court, and perhaps he thought that this entitled him to make a bid for the Roman imperial throne. The Romans tried to strip him of all his credentials, including that of language. A Roman orator specified that "Symeon spoke in a way that was for the most part barbaric, and he committed many solecisms."[81]

Two incidents from military history show how language could be used to literally patrol the boundaries between ethnic groups. In a war with Persia in the late sixth century, the Romans gave their barbarian allies a password, the name of the Mother of God *(Theometor Parthenos)*, so that they might know each other in battle and not "mistake their allies as enemies and kill them because of their difference in *genos*."[82] In the twelfth century, when some Roman commanders attacked the Turks at night, they issued the password *sideron* (iron), which only the Romans could pronounce. The historian remarked that this allowed them to recognize the *homophylon* (people of the same race) based on their *homophonon* (speaking the same language), because the inability to say the word proved who was *alloglotton* (a foreign-speaker).[83] This was the Roman equivalent of the shibboleth story in the Old Testament: even minor differences in speech patterns could lead to the execution of an out-group member.[84]

But in the case of the Byzantine Romans there was a twist in the otherwise straightforward equation of language and nation. In antiquity, the main language of the Romans, the Roman language, or "Roman," was Latin. Latin could also be called the language of the Latins, or some variation thereof. Even though many ancient Romans, especially elites, also spoke Greek, so much so that they referred to "our two languages," Latin was regarded as "the language of the

Romans," an idea that continued into Byzantine times.[85] This meant that Byzantine authors, who wrote in Greek, referred to what had effectively become a foreign language to them, Latin, as the language of the Romans, even though they were now the Romans, in fact the only Romans in the world, except for those of Rome in Italy. They referred to "the language of the Romans" whenever someone in a narrative spoke Latin (which included both conversation and formulaic acclamations by the army or imperial subjects), as well as when the author had to use a technical term or the name of an office that was derived from Latin. These foreign terms jarred with the purist Hellenic diction to which many elite Byzantine authors aspired. All this has been laid out in a persuasive study by Carolina Cupane.[86]

Two areas of Byzantine life were seen as especially "Roman" from a linguistic point of view because they contained a greater density of Latin terms: these were law and the army. Law was sometimes even called the study of the Roman matters or the Italian science. Byzantine legal dictionaries could be called "collections of Roman words."[87] By contrast, the Byzantines called the language in which they spoke and wrote "Hellenic" or "Greek." Some of them knew that it was the *koine* dialect.[88] In its spoken forms, however, it was a heavily Latinized version of Greek. Thousands of Latin terms for everyday objects and activities had entered the Greek language between the second and the sixth centuries, and many of them survive still in spoken Greek.[89] To write formal Greek, Byzantine authors had to learn to filter those terms out so as not to sound too vernacular—or too Latin—just as they avoided the term *Romanía*.

While this usage was conventional, it sometimes put the Byzantines in an awkward situation. Why would "the language of the Romans" be different from the language currently spoken by the Romans? This was, after all, what western critics (such as popes and German emperors) brought forward in order to deny that the Byzantines were really Romans. In a famous letter of 865, Pope Nicolaus I scolded the emperor Michael III for calling himself the emperor of the Romans when he did not speak the language of the Romans (i.e., Latin); it seems that Michael had even denigrated the Latin language in his now lost letter.[90] Some modern Greek scholars make the same error: the Byzantines were really Greeks, they assert, because they spoke Greek.

The Byzantines had ways of addressing this mismatch of language and ethnicity, but it should be noted that at no point did this discrepancy cause them to doubt whether they were Romans. Until the end of the empire and beyond, they were unpersuaded by western polemics on this point. Moreover, our understanding of ethnicity should give to the Byzantines themselves the right to decide which of their cultural attributes constituted their ethnicity and how. Here the evidence is clear: they did not see their ethnicity as defined by their language, but the reverse.

One device was to qualify Latin as "the *ancestral (patrios)* language" of the Romans, implying that it was no longer the language that they used, but was the language of their ancestors. This reinforced the ethnic connection between the Byzantines and the ancient Romans. We can even observe the invention of this linguistic ancestry, which occurred at the same time as the rise and establishment of the notion of Romanía. Consider, for example, Themistios, who was a leading member of the Senate of Constantinople and a Hellenist (pagan) philosopher in the fourth century. For all that he was deeply embroiled in Roman things, he had not yet "converted" to a Roman ethnicity, just as he had not converted to Christianity. He begins one of his speeches addressed to the emperors with a declaration that he has not found it necessary to master the "ruling language" because his "ancestral Greek language was sufficient."[91] But two centuries later, the referent of linguistic ancestry had changed from Greek to Latin, even among intellectuals from the Greek east whose native language was Greek. The scholar Ioannes Lydos was from western Asia Minor and was awarded a chair of Latin in Constantinople under Justinian. Even though he wrote in Greek, he lamented that the administration of the empire was being conducted increasingly in Greek and not in "the ancestral language of the Romans," Latin.[92] The seventh-century historian Theophylaktos, a native of Egypt writing in Constantinople, frequently refers to Latin as the ancestral language.[93]

This usage implied that at some point the Romans had stopped using their ancestral language and began to use Greek instead. We can observe that switch in real time in some of the laws of the emperor Justinian, who contributed to that switch. Justinian commented on the reasons behind his decision to stop issuing his *Novels* in the "ancestral language" of the Romans and to use Greek instead: it was now the language of the majority of subjects.[94] Looking back at this switch four centuries later, Konstantinos VII wrote that emperors after Herakleios (610–641) "Hellenized [i.e., used Greek] to an even greater degree and cast off their ancestral Roman language."[95]

It is impossible to know how many average Romans in Byzantium knew that the language of their ancestors had been Latin. But the mentality of those who did is interesting. To maintain the fiction of their Roman ethnic origin, and to reinforce the obvious truth of imperial continuity, they were willing to posit a rupture in the linguistic continuity of their own ethnic history. This proves how deeply they identified as Romans: no self-identifying ethnic "Greek" would ever refer to Latin as his ancestral language. This is not without parallel in other times or parts of the world, mutatis mutandis. The ancestral language of Greek-speaking Jews in antiquity was Hebrew. The ancestral language of Ireland is Gaelic. Latin in Byzantium can be seen as such a "talismanic" ancestral language, analogous to Hebrew among postbiblical Jews: "a national language that is not spoken by most of the nation."[96] This talisman was invoked when authors had to explain the name of a Latin office, a vernacular Latin term that linked Romanía to its ancient roots, or the ritualized acclamations that preserved many Latinate fossils within spoken Greek.

However, the fine distinction between the ancestral and current language of the Romans likely preoccupied few Byzantines. The majority of the population was, in the middle Byzantine period, coming to a more straightforward view of the relationship between their Romanness and their language. Not caring for the historical claims of Latin or the niceties of linguistic accuracy, they began on a popular level to call their (Greek) language "Roman," because they were Romans and that was their language. It is likely that they were doing so for a long time before our sources catch up to the fact. This corresponds to how popular speech pioneered the name Romanía for the national state of the Romans, before more official types of discourse caught up.

In spoken Greek, the change to naming the language "Romaic" was complete and comprehensive by 1250. We have two foreign sources for this development, which come from different parts of the former empire and are independent of each other. The *Chronicle of the Morea*, composed by Greek-speaking Franks in the Peloponnese, calls the (Greek) speech of the locals Romaic (ῥωμαίικα).[97] On the other side of the Aegean, in Muslim-ruled Asia Minor, Sultan Veled (Walad, late thirteenth century), the son of the great Persian poet Jalal al-Din Rumi, wrote a poem in which he addresses a beautiful woman in Greek, so she can understand him; he precisely transcribes his words of seduction in which he calls the language Romaic (ῥωμαϊκά).[98] Thus, independent Frankish and Persian witnesses, living at opposite ends of the former empire, attest that the language of the Byzantines was being called *romaika* or *romaïika* among provincials who had nothing to do with the literary conventions of the imperial court. The attestation of this term in non-Roman sources signals that it may have been *too vernacular* to appear in texts written in high-register Greek, even if it had been in use for many centuries. Here again our elite sources downplay the extent of popular Romanness. In this case they may have done so not only to avoid the newfangled term *Romaic*, which came from vulgar Greek, but also because they positively wanted to retain the talismanic valence of claiming a connection to Latin as the language of the Roman ancestors.

There is no reason to think that the *Chronicle of the Morea* or Sultan Veled were reflecting a new convention in calling Greek "Romaic." This is what they heard and learned from provincial Greek-speakers in the post-Byzantine Peloponnese and Asia Minor. Now, those two regions had parted ways in 1204, so the name used for their language by provincial Romans was probably already in place before then, and possibly before the 1070s, when the Seljuks first overran central Asia Minor.

This development was bound to happen. A Roman ethnic group was eventually going to start calling its language "the language of the Romans." Even court sources sometimes did this. For example, when the biography of the emperor Basileios I (written in the tenth century) says that barbarian spies were sent out using Roman dress and language, the latter was obviously Greek.⁹⁹ And while it was common for Byzantine authors to describe terms of Latin origin that were used in contemporary spoken Greek as "Roman" words, they could also explain Greek technical terms as being words in the language of the "Romans," that is, the (Byzantine) Romans of their own day.¹⁰⁰ On a vernacular level, the poem *Digenis* says that the hero's father, a Saracen by origin, knew "the language of the Romans," also meaning Greek.¹⁰¹ And when the Georgian general Gregorios Pakourianos endowed a monastery in Bulgaria in 1083 after years of imperial service, he used *romaikos* for the Greek language and script of the charter.¹⁰² This was a usage that he likely picked up during his years of service, not from an education in formal Greek. This reinforces the conclusion that "Roman" was the name given to their language by average Romans in the mid-eleventh century, and possibly earlier too. This evidence refutes the notion that spoken Greek came to be called Romaic only in the Ottoman period.¹⁰³

Romaic as "Greek" appears more frequently in the later Byzantine period. For example, the translation of the romance *Apollonius, King of Tyre* is (strangely to our ears) called a "translation from Latin into Roman" (μεταγλώττισμα ἀπὸ λατινικὸν εἰς Ῥωμαϊκόν).¹⁰⁴ Roman was here juxtaposed to Latin. In addition to being a vernacular term for Greek, Romaic may also have been a term for vernacular Greek as opposed to Attic or elite Greek. Elizabeth Fisher has brought attention to a translation of an *Apocalypse of Daniel* made from Arabic into Greek by a certain Alexios around 1245. A second Greek translator of the text commented that Alexios had transposed the text into "Hellenic, which is to say into Romaic." The second translator accordingly tried to elevate the style into a higher register of Greek.¹⁰⁵ Romaic may here stand for a less elevated form of Greek, closer to what was being spoken. This distinction persisted, on and off in various contexts, until recently. A priest in Serres in the seventeenth century drew a firm contrast between Romaic and Hellenic writing, the latter accessible only to teachers and scholars. In the early years of the nineteenth century, it was still seen as bizarre to call the spoken language "modern Greek" rather than "Romaic, which is how the entire nation calls it." And a Russian newspaper in 1821 distinguished between ancient Greek and modern Greek, calling the latter "Romaic."[106] Philologists were already comparing Romaic Greek to classical Greek on the one hand and to Latin on the other.

This Roman "nation" continued to exist during the centuries of Ottoman domination and, contrary to widespread belief, was never fully subsumed within a pan-Orthodox community (the *millet* of Rum). The Romans continued to be set off by roughly the same ethnic markers as they had in the past, if no longer by a separate state of their own. Consider, for example, how one hostile text describes the patriarch of Constantinople, Raphael I (1475–1476), who was of Serbian origin: "The people hated him, because of his habitual drunkenness and also because of his speech, as he did not speak *Romaíika*, only Serbian; as we said, he was from Serbia and spoke Serbian, whereas he spoke *Romaíika* only imperfectly."[107] These distinctions were observed by non-Romans too. The seventeenth-century Ottoman travel writer Evliya Çelebi also classified as an ethnic Roman (*Rum* or *Urum*) whoever spoke what to his ears sounded like the *Rumca* language.[108] The eighteenth-century travel writer Richard Chandler admits in one place that the nation he has been calling Greek really calls itself, and its language, "Roman."[109]

According to the evidence presented above, the Greek language began to be popularly called Romaic no later than the eleventh century, and possibly earlier. We may be able to confirm this development and move it earlier in time with the help of Hebrew and Arabic evidence, though this will require further research by specialists. Byzantine Hebrew texts of the middle and later periods typically call Greek "the Roman tongue *(lšwn rwmi)*," as the Jews of the empire are also conventionally called "the communities of Romanía."[110] It is likely that the Jews were using the same name to refer to the language as was being used by their Christian neighbors, so it would be useful to date the earliest emergence of this usage among them. Arab authors too, writing outside of Romanía, often refer to the language spoken by the Rum as *bi-lisāni l-rūm* ("in the tongue of the Romans"), in some cases distinguishing it from the Greek used by the ancient authors, which for them was *al-yūnāniyya*. Intellectuals in the Arab Muslim world debated what the relationship was between the two languages, and al-Ya'qubi (d. 897) even claimed that the

"Roman language" had replaced Greek after the Roman conquest.[111] It would be interesting to know if *bi-lisāni l-rūm* was merely an Arabic rendition of what Romans whom they met—including soldiers, merchants, and captives—were calling their own speech ("the language of the Romans").

Be that as it may, the evidence presented above shows that the Romans' ethnic self-understanding eventually overcame the terminological distinctions between Greek and Roman that they had inherited from antiquity, and created instead a separate, and quite fascinating, distinction between Roman and Latin. Their ethnicity and ethnonym overcame the conventional linguistic classification of their language. One of the main arguments used by western medieval writers and their modern followers to prove that the Byzantines were "really" Greeks is the fact that after about 600 they spoke Greek. This argument is also welcome to the modern Greek national interpretation of history, because more than anything it seems to authorize the rebaptism of the Romaioi as Greeks. As Greg Fisher has written, "the legacy of modern nationalism and modern ideas about linguistic identity can colour our understanding of how other, older, or different, cultures perceived themselves."[112] Yet for most of their history the Byzantines did not think that their language made them Greek; to the contrary, their ethnicity as Romans made their language "Roman," or Romaic.

The Byzantines' self-understanding in this matter did not deviate from ancient Roman precedents. In ancient Rome, Latin was at times invested with the aura of traditionalism but—and the following point cannot be repeated too much—there was never any requirement that one know Latin to be a Roman. Greek had always been a part of Roman culture and the Romans often referred to their "two languages," Greek and Latin.[113] Interestingly, even Byzantines of the middle period could refer to their "two languages, Greek and Roman," in some contexts, for example law.[114] The terms Roman and Latin were thus asymmetrical, and they remain so today. A study of ancient Roman literature might include Greek texts. A recent survey of Roman historiography, for example, begins with a senator writing in Greek (Fabius Pictor) and ends with both Greek and Latin historians of the later empire.[115] What was new about the Byzantines was not that they were Romans who spoke Greek but that they were Romans who had lost touch with the Latin tradition. That was an interesting development, though it emerged over the course of centuries.[116]

Instead of arguing that the Byzantines were not really Romans because they did not speak Latin, we should be saying instead that the Byzantines had *two* Roman languages, one the language of their ancestors (Latin) and another their language in the present (Romaic).

Religion and Ethnicity

It was well understood in Byzantium—I believe by the entirety of the population—that the two labels Roman and (Orthodox) Christian did not signify the same thing, even though they overlapped when one was looking only at the Romans. Considerable efforts were made to fuse them together, for example in the title of the emperor, which became "faithful-in-Christ emperor of the Romans." So too, provincial hagiographic texts could refer to the golden age before Islam "when the empire of the Romans was governed well by both orthodox doctrines and an excellent political system."[117] Between the sixth and the ninth centuries, when the empire was surrounded mostly by barbarians who were also infidels, emperors could address their subjects as Christians rather than Romans in some contexts, because the two names pointed to the same population.[118]

Yet it was known that those two names were not equivalent and did not always overlap. For example, the Romans had formerly been quite hostile to the Christians. The average Byzantine would have been regularly reminded of this by the stories of the martyrs that were told in church, as they heard about cruel Roman officials gruesomely torturing Christian saints. Indeed, some early Christian literature is hostile to Rome, and in it "the name Roman and the name Christian are completely opposed."[119] Conversely, there were many Christians in the present who were not Romans: the Franks were at first regarded as fellow Catholics (though not Romans) and then, when their Church began to deviate from received tradition, there were also the Bulgarians, Serbs, Georgians, and others. These were

Orthodox but not Roman. Byzantine writers were quite capable of expressing the difference between their ethnic and religious identities. This did not require complicated theoretical distinctions on their part but was a matter of course. Already from the reign of Constantine, Christians were being divided into "Romans and *allophyloi*" (those of another race, e.g., Persians).[120]

Over time, Byzantine Romanness and Orthodoxy were closely intertwined and mutually encompassed each other: being Orthodox was part of the "customs and laws" that defined a Roman, while at the same time the Romans regarded themselves as the most important Christians in the world. Moreover, between the later sixth and mid-ninth centuries, the empire was surrounded on almost all sides by non-Christian peoples, so that "Roman" and "Christian" temporarily had the same boundaries. Roman patriotism could take the form of Christian zeal and vice versa. At such times, there was no compelling reason to distinguish the two conceptually. Roman and Christian could be used interchangeably not because they meant the same thing but because they referred to complementary identities of the same group of people.[121] That changed after the ninth century, especially with the conversion of Bulgaria.

All this is fairly straightforward and would not require much comment or excite any controversy were it not for the difficult circumstances in which the denialist tradition found itself when it morphed into a scholarly discipline of study in the late nineteenth and especially the twentieth century. Until the early nineteenth century, the west had been happy to relabel ethnic Romans as ethnic Greeks and leave the matter there, viewing them as Orthodox Christians as well. As we saw, the developments of that century made those labels problematic. The "Byzantines" were then uncoupled from any strong sense of Greek ethnicity and historians began to assert that they had no ethnicity. This left unresolved the problem of the pervasive ethnonym "Roman." Some scholars decided to sweep this under the Christian rug, a move that is made in one of two contradictory ways, both false and arbitrary, that nevertheless have the same result. According to one fiction, "the Byzantines" *were not* Romans anymore *but rather* Christians, whereas according to the other when the Byzantines said they were Romans they *meant* only that they were Christians.[122] I hope it is clear by now that these unnecessary acrobatics obfuscate what is in fact an unproblematic situation: the Byzantines were Romans who were also Christians. This picture emerges clearly from the evidence and no reason has been offered why we should not take it at face value. Instead, there is only an entrenched and ideological obsession to deny that the Byzantines were Romans, by any pretext necessary. This impression has been given prima facie plausibility by the massive attention that was paid during the twentieth century to the Orthodox aspects of Byzantine civilization compared to the minimal attention (or negative attention) paid to its Roman aspects.

That the terms are not strictly interchangeable emerges when we try to replace one with the other in all contexts: saying that someone was a Christian by birth might make some amount of sense, but saying that he spoke the language of the Christians or dressed like a Christian does not. Let us look at some texts that reveal that Roman and Christian were not interchangeable. In the ninth century, Petros of Sicily wrote a treatise on the beliefs of a heretical group, the Paulicians, who had established a military stronghold at Tephrike in eastern Asia Minor, which he seems to have visited. He reports that they called themselves Christians and called "us" Romans in a religious sense. The Paulicians, in other words, were trying to depict Byzantine Orthodoxy as the "Roman religion," not the true Christian faith; they had repurposed an ethnic label as a religious one. Petros, a priest, was baffled and outraged at this switch. He said that they were misusing "our ethnic name" in a religious sense in place of the main one that we use for our faith ("Christians").[123] This encounter forced a Byzantine to confront his ethnic name being used as a religious label, and he thought it was completely wrongheaded.

The Bulgarians, Serbs, and Rus' also converted to Byzantine Orthodoxy, but the Byzantines never regarded them as Romans. There is abundant evidence for this, and it is consistent.[124] I will give an example from the most remote province of the empire and another example from Constantinople. First, the *Life of Saint Neilos of Rossano* (tenth century) reports that when this southern Italian saint traveled to Rome he found a monastery twelve miles from the city "where a few brothers who were of the same race as he lived" *(homo-*

phyloi), that is, fellow Greek-speakers. And the local clergy in Latin-occupied Constantinople told a Catholic cardinal in 1206 that they could, if they wanted, leave the City for one of the Byzantine successor states in exile or for "the lands of the barbarians who share our faith," such as the Bulgarians or the Rus'.[125] A clear explanation was offered in the fifteenth century by Ioannes Kanaboutzes, who explained that

> one is not a barbarian on account of religion, but because of *genos*, language, the ordering of one's politics, and education. For we are Christians and share the same faith and confession with many other nations, but we call them barbarians, I mean the Bulgarians, Vlachs, Albanians, Russians, and many others.[126]

There were always foreign Christians inside the empire to remind the Romans of the distinction. For example, in his monastic foundation Typikon (1083 AD), the Georgian general Gregorios Pakourianos boasted that he had fought against the Pechenegs, who attacked "not just Romanía but every *genos* of the Christians."[127]

The distinction between Roman and Christian did not require a contrast with foreigners, as it could be made on grounds that were purely internal to Byzantine culture. For example, *heretical* emperors were sometimes praised as good rulers when it came to "the affairs of the Romans" while being condemned for oppressing Christians through their bad religious policies.[128] In condemning the rebel general Leon Sgouros, the historian Niketas Choniates puts into the mouth of his brother Michael a speech that distinguishes between the man's Christian and Roman identities: "It was not fitting for one who was called a Christian and who was reckoned among the Romans to wage war against the Romans, unless he were paying mere lip service to Christ's name and was, in his heart, far removed from those who are named after Him, while, as for being Roman, he was like them only with respect to his dress and speech."[129] A true Roman would not only wear Roman dress and speak the Roman language (Greek), he would also be loyal and patriotic toward his fellow Romans. As a Christian, on the other side of the equation, he would exhibit appropriate moral qualities. In the early fifteenth century, the emperor Manuel II Palaiologos likewise noted that "we are Romans and Christians by *genos* and baptism"—that is, respectively.[130]

There is, therefore, no reason to postulate an either/or between Roman and Christian or a false equivalence of the two. For the Byzantines, it was instead a both/and situation. For example, it was sometimes underscored that Byzantine civil wars were fought between people who were "*both* of the same race *and* the same faith."[131] Leon VI advised his generals not to break agreements with the enemy because it would be a shameful thing for Romans to do when "the other *ethne*" are upholding their end of the bargain—"for Romans, moreover, who are also Christians."[132]

A monastic founder of the later eleventh century, Nikon of the Black Mountain (near Antioch), cites his Roman ethnicity as proof that he is Orthodox (i.e., Chalcedonian), in what had by then become a confusing ethnic and denominational situation in the east. He states that he himself was never curious about the fine points of doctrine but had received the faith "entire from the start and from his ancestors: these were not people who had been raised and lived in any of the places and lands where the heresies are all mixed up together, but were a Roman root (ῥίζα 'Ρωμαίων), via the grace of Christ."[133] Nikon, who was probably from Constantinople, configures his Romanness as a function of ancestry (i.e., ethnically) and uses this in turn to establish his Orthodoxy. Here we can see how ethnicity and religion, while not being the same thing, are mutually reinforcing. They are also mutually exclusive of both ethnic and doctrinal others, a dynamic that we will observe when we turn, in the second part of this book, to examine the imperial rule by Orthodox Romans over their non-Roman subjects.

When twentieth-century historians of Byzantium played up Orthodoxy and occluded the Byzantines' ethnic Romanness, they made it impossible to explain both foreign and domestic relations between Romans and non-Romans. Ethnic Romanness was swapped out for "universal" Christian ideals that created an alleged "ecumenical" state. These terms were never defined, but the general sense was that the "Romans" (i.e., Orthodox) could not have formed an ethnic group because they were committed to ecumenical ideals.[134] However, this model could not explain any of the policies of the state or the ethnic exclusivity and cultural chauvinism of its majority population. It also naively overestimated the degree to which Christianity is capable of creating universal communities of faith that transcend ethnic differences. Historically, it has tended to underwrite exclusivist national ideas and movements just as often as it has created bridges between peoples and cultures.[135] There is no reason to assume that it would have weakened, replaced, or subsumed Roman ethnicity. If anything, it reinforced the Romans' sense of superiority, even toward other non-Roman Christians.

There is an "ecumenical" bias in modern scholarship about Byzantium, by which I mean an assumption that Byzantine Orthodoxy was premised on those passages of the New Testament that gesture toward ethnic inclusiveness rather than the books of the Old Testament that present the Chosen People as superior to all the rest. Many studies of Byzantine identity begin with quotations from the New Testament and use the alleged "universal" or "ecumenical" spirit of the Christian message to define the realities of the Byzantine state and society. From this, the conclusion is drawn that the Byzantines did not see the world in ethnic terms and so ethnicity played no role in Byzantine social history, which flies in the face of all our evidence.[136] Because of these misconceptions, historians have not investigated the degree to which even Byzantine Orthodoxy complied with state projects that targeted other Christians or cultivated an ethnic Romanness that was premised on a categorical distinction between the Romans and "the nations," especially when the latter were also Christians.[137] The Byzantine Church has sometimes rightly been seen as a "national Church," as it was a pillar holding up the Roman imperial establishment, but its history and practices have not yet been studied from that standpoint.[138]

These are big issues that will likely be explored more when scholarship opens the question, as inevitably it will, of Romanía as a national state. I here consider a few ways in which the Roman context shaped the habits, thoughts, and practices of Orthodoxy in the empire. One area that has been studied, for example, is how religion was used to boost morale in the army, fusing patriotism with religious faith even when the war was against other Christians.[139] It is often difficult to distinguish between "sacred war" and Roman nationalism, as the soldiers are addressed emotionally as both Romans and Christians. Moreover, the militarization of religion was not limited to army camps. Prayers on behalf of the Roman emperor, expressing the hope that he will defeat the barbarians, are expressed in many saints' lives.[140] During ordinary religious services, Romans throughout the empire made similar prayers. "The church and its public worship came to provide an enduring and frequent forum in which the average Roman subject voiced his loyalty to the emperor . . . a common experience in the daily life of the provinces and capitals."[141] This was certainly expected in sermons preached before the emperor or in the capital. The patriarch Photios explicitly states at the end of his Holy Friday homily that God brought forth the emperor specifically for the well-being of the *genos* of the Romans.[142] The emperors asked their subjects to pray for them generally but also during specific crises. Special prayers, for example, were ordered or offered in Egypt in support of the war, probably during the Arab invasion, as we know from a papyrus fragment, and Byzantine prayer books contained specialized prayers to be recited in times of "barbarian invasion."[143] Ethnic distinctions were strengthened by religion.

The celebration of the liturgy throughout the empire was also framed in imperial terms. The so-called Liturgy of St. Basil, the one used primarily by the Byzantine Church between the sixth and the eleventh centuries, contains a section of prayers (the Anaphora) with the following words: "Remember, Lord, our most religious and faithful emperor . . . strengthen his arm, exalt his right hand; make his empire mighty; and subject to him all the barbarous people that delight in war. . . . Remember, Lord, all rule and authority, our brothers at court and all the army."[144] A military service of the tenth century prays to the Lord: "Save your people . . . grant victories to the emperors against the barbarians, and guard your polity through the cross."[145] Recited regularly by imperial subjects, such prayers bound their religious devotion to Roman projects of empire that rested on the cardinal distinction between "us" and the barbarians. This is an ethnic-imperial aspect of the "formation of the self" in Romanía that has not yet been explored.[146] In this respect, what took place and was intoned in churches throughout the empire was the same as what happened in the hippodrome in Constantinople, when the people came face to face with the emperors and acclaimed them in the same religio-national terms. Heralds, the representatives of the teams, and the Roman people would there engage in a long set of acclamations that called down God's assistance for the emperors of the Romans, who are also called "the beloved of the Romans" and "the joy of the Romans." It included the following: "We thank you, Christ our God, for breaking up the plots of the foreign *ethne* and crushing our enemies at war."[147]

Whatever "ecumenism" may have been embedded in key Christian texts was likely a dormant option for most Byzantines. Their liturgy, institutions of governance, and entertainments in the capital expressed a strong awareness of a hostile world of *ethne* "out there" from whom they, the Roman people, were protected by their emperor, army, and God. Christianity was the religion of the Romans, a component of Romanness in many contexts. "Religion is not, and cannot be, a person's all-encompassing identity."[148]

Romanogenesis in Retrospect

The contours of Roman ethnicity should by now be reasonably clear. We need much more research on its cultural content, "the cultural stuff" that makes up an ethnicity,[149] namely the institutions, social conventions, and practices that most Romans regarded as distinctive to their *genos* at any given moment in their history. The second part of this book will turn to the non-Roman ethnic groups living in the empire and explore how some of them could become Romans by acquiring this "stuff." This kind of assimilation implied that ethnic differences could be overcome, that non-Romans could, in time and by accepting a new cultural profile, become Roman. Before we look at how the state enabled this process and how it was viewed by the Byzantines, a reminder is in order that *all* the Romans of Byzantium, or their ancestors, were the products of precisely such a process. There was a time, after all, when the core regions of Romanía had no Romans. How had it come to be filled up with Romans?

This section will eschew an objective analysis of that transformation and focus instead on what the Byzantines themselves had to say about it. Still, it is worth keeping in mind that this is a major question in ancient history that has not yet been answered satisfactorily. Plausible terms for it include *Romanization, Roman ethnogenesis*,[150] or *Romanogenesis*, namely the process by which people who formerly had other ethnic, national, legal, political, and cultural identities became Roman in those categories and let their previous identifications lapse. That this did happen during the Roman empire is understood, although it has not yet been fully theorized or explored, especially for the Greek East.[151] Here is an example of how modern historians acknowledge this process:

> When peoples were conquered, incorporated into provinces and, in due course of time, became part of an integrated empire, this entailed a process of ethnic disintegration or decomposition. This is the essence of "Romanization." The Nabataeans, the Idumaeans, and the Commageneans in the east, the Allabroges in the west, all disappeared as ethnic entities.[152]

To theorize the final outcome of this Romanogenesis, historians are even beginning to experiment with the concept of "nation," previously a dreaded word.[153] A separate book can (and should) be written on how the Roman nation that we call Byzantium came into being in the Greek east. Here I would like to focus on what later Byzantine sources said about it. Having access to abundant narratives from antiquity, Byzantine authors knew that Asia Minor, for example, was once not Roman, and then was full of Romans, such as themselves. How had that happened?

We discussed the legal aspect of this transformation in Chapter 2. But beyond acquiring a Roman legal status, how had the subjects of the empire acquired a Roman ethnicity too? Sources available to the Byzantines touched on aspects of this process. In his commentary on the book of Daniel, for example, Hippolytos (third century) tried to explain why the prophet did not offer a species-image for the nation, the Romans, that would terminate the sequence of world empires. The Babylonians, he explains, were a single nation *(ethnos)* and so were the Persians, which is why the prophet figured them as individual animals. "But the beast that rules now is not a single *ethnos*; rather, it is drawn from all tongues and from every *genos* of people, all of whom are called Romans." Therefore, the prophet offered a composite image of them.¹⁵⁴ In this text, written probably soon after the *Constitutio Antoniniana*, the Romans are understood as a single entity consisting of many ethnic groups; they are a plural *ethnos*. But this later shifted toward greater ethnic unity.

In time, the mere name "Roman" was accompanied by a more "thorough" Roman profile, as the fourth-century philosopher and court orator Themistios put it. He astutely outlined this transformation in a speech arguing that the Goths who were then being settled in the empire, admittedly not under the best circumstances, could, in time, become regular Romans, just as had happened to the Galatians of Asia Minor. The Galatians had once been ferocious Gallic barbarians, but were now ordinary Romans, no different from any others. Here is how he put it:

> Look at these Galatians, the ones in the Pontos. These men crossed over into Asia under the law of war and, having depopulated the entire region on this side of the Halys, settled in this territory which they now inhabit. And neither Pompey nor Lucullus destroyed them, although this was perfectly possible, nor Augustus nor the emperors after him; rather, they remitted their sins and assimilated them into the empire. And now no one would ever refer to the Galatians as barbarian but as thoroughly Roman. For while their ancestral name has endured, their way of life is now akin to our own. They pay the same taxes as we do, they enlist in the same ranks as we do, they accept governors on the same terms as the rest, and abide by the same laws.¹⁵⁵

Let us focus on the factors highlighted here as facilitating Romanization. First, the Roman leadership did not try to destroy the Galatians but sought to integrate them into the Roman order (ἐν μέρει τῆς ἀρχῆς ἐποιήσαντο). Second, their way of life had adjusted to a Roman norm. Third, they lived under the same laws, taxes, and administrative arrangements as other Romans, and as a result the Galatians were eventually regarded as fellow Romans and no longer as barbarians. In sum, becoming Romans was a process of integration by which one acquired the name, customs (including language), laws, and political order as other Romans, all of which went far beyond mere citizenship. By the end of the process, the only thing that differentiated the Galatians from other provincial Romans was their "ancestral name," which was normalized within the Roman order as the name of a province. They were just Romans from the province of Galatia. This is what an early Byzantine model of ancient Romanization might look like.[156]

By the early fifth century, if not before, this had resulted in the extinction of many local ethnicities and their replacement with a Roman one. Discussing the issue of ethnic diversity in his own time, Augustine (d. 430) asked rhetorically in a homily: "Who now knows which nations in the Roman empire were which, when all have become Romans and all are called Romans?"[157] Unlike Hippolytos, there was no longer any reason to insist on the composite nature of the beast. Provincials were not only *called* Romans, they *were* Romans. To be sure, Augustine was not an author who was available to later Byzantines, and he was saying this to highlight the relatively greater importance of the difference between Christian and non-Christian.[158] But it is nevertheless fascinating that he could say this. It matches what we find in eastern sources, for example the historian Agathias' explanation of how the inhabitants of the city of Tralleis should now be regarded as mainstream ethnic Romans, regardless of who their ancestors were.[159]

Before looking at later Byzantine views of this process, it is, as always, worth considering Arabic perceptions, in this case that of Mas'udi (d. 956), which is substantially correct. He is talking about the Greeks:

> [We rehearsed] how they [the Greeks] were defeated by the Romans *(al-rūm)* and were absorbed into their society *(jumlatihim)*, such that [the Greeks'] name vanished and there ceased all mention of them, and all of them were renamed Romans *(nusiba l-jamī'u 'ilā lrūm)* after their defeat by the emperor Augustus.[160]

The Greeks were absorbed by the Romans in antiquity, just as we will see in Chapter 4 that other ethnic groups were absorbed by the Byzantine Romans.

Turning now to later Roman views, in his treatise *On the Themes*, the emperor Konstantinos VII provided an antiquarian gazetteer of the empire's provinces, drawing on classical texts and ancient ethnography and mixing with them a few recent developments. The first theme he discusses is the Anatolikon, which encompassed most of north-central Asia Minor. It is inhabited, he says, by five nations (*ethne*), the Phrygians, Lykaonians, Isaurians, Pamphylians, and Pisidians. Of course, these were not true ethnic groups in middle Byzantium, only the antiquarian names of Roman provinces. But Konstantinos makes an important qualification: "When the Roman yoke fell upon them, they were all subjugated and became compact [or mixed together: συμμιγεῖς] under one authority," namely the Roman one.[161] The many had been mixed together into one. Konstantinos does not specify whether the five prior nations had ceased to exist and had become some other new thing, or whether the result was simply a composite of the five. It is, nevertheless, fascinating to see him take note of this issue, even if only in a passing remark.

The most interesting account of ancient Romanization is contained in a set of letters by the patriarch Photios (ninth century). In two letters (nos. 246–247), Photios explained to his correspondent Euschemon, the bishop of Kaisareia, how St. Paul could have been a Roman, which Euschemon was inclined to doubt on the grounds that Paul was a Jew from Tarsos in Cilicia. He later wrote a longer and more elaborate version of the argument (*Letter* 103), which is addressed more generally: "To anyone who asks how is it that we can't convict the divine Apostle of falsehood when he says that he is both a Jew and Roman, having Tarsos as his native country at one point but being born at Rome in another."[162] It is in fact quite possible to doubt the claim of Acts—not made in the epistles, not even in Romans—that Paul was a Roman citizen.[163] But Photios maintains that Paul did not lie when he called himself either a Jew or a Roman. Let us look at his argument.

Photios begins *Letter* 103 with arguments from plausibility that we can pass by (namely that Paul would not have risked lying about this because he was being attacked by the Jews as a liar, and also that the Jews did not deny that he was a Roman citizen, thereby tacitly conceding his claim: ll. 5–40). The main question is conceptual rather than factual: How could Paul simultaneously be a Jew, a citizen of Tarsos, and a Roman? (ll. 41–44). Photios maintains that there is no problem here. Paul was a Jew by *genos* (family or race) and by being raised in the Mosaic Law; his fatherland *(patris)* was Tarsos, because he was born there; and, finally, he both was and was called a Roman because his father had obtained citizenship formally either through a Roman grant or by paying money (ll. 45–49). Thus Paul was not born "at" Rome but was born into the Roman name (i.e., citizenship) and the Roman polity (ll. 51–54).[164] Photios is explicit that "in those days, the dignity [of Roman citizenship] was enjoyed not only by those who were born at Rome but also by those to whom its name was formally granted by law or payment" (ll. 60–62). Moreover, it was not only individual men but entire cities and even cities of a foreign *genos (allogeneis)* that could acquire the Roman name. Photios cites the example of the city of Philippi, whose citizens called themselves Romans (ll. 63–75). Although he does not say so, we know that the city was made a Roman colony in the aftermath of the famous battle there in 42 BC. Photios does, however, make excellent use of the narrative in Acts 16:16–24 in order to show the adoption by the Philippians of a Roman identity. Paul had driven a spirit out from a local slave girl, which had enabled her to predict the future. Her owners took him to court, accusing him, a Jew, of trying to spread practices that were unlawful for "us Romans." The text clearly shows that the locals had embraced a kind of Romanness, expressing it in the first person.

After more arguments from narrative plausibility (ll. 76–111), Photios asks a side question: "Was he not then a Christian too? But of course he was." This, however, was a name that he bore on behalf of his religion *(threskeia)*, a different kind of identity (ll. 112–117). So Paul's profile is, in Photios' account, shaping up to be compound: a Jew by race or ancestry, a Tarsian by place of birth, a Roman by citizenship, and a Christian by religion. This is interesting because it resonates with the multiple identities born by many Romans in Photios' own time. Some Romans, for example, had a foreign ethnic ancestry (e.g., Armenian or Slavic), were Christian Orthodox in their religion, Hellenic by language (especially if they were educated), and their national, political, and legal identity was Roman.

Photios concludes the letter by trying to make Paul an ethnic Roman too, though he does this in a half-hearted way. He offers a tale according to which Paul's Hebrew tribe of Benjamin had sent colonists to Italy in prehistoric times, including one Ros, the ancestor of the Romans (ll. 118–134).[165] Photios himself is skeptical of this tale, but it is interesting that he, an ethnic Roman, imagined that Paul's legal Romanness needed an ethnic aspect. His letter is also interesting in that it lays out a conceptual foundation for having two, three, or more *patridai*, or fatherlands, albeit configured along different existential aspects (ancestry, place of birth, religion, civic-ethnic). It is unlikely that Photios knew Cicero's theory of the two *patriae*, or two fatherlands, of each Roman, namely his place of origin and the Roman *res publica* as a whole.[166] Photios' analysis replicates that distinction, which is due to the fact that both authors were thinking within the common paradigm provided by the Roman polity to which they belonged. That paradigm tended to produce similar effects, even if separated by a millennium. Both Cicero and Photios lay down a path by which both individuals and whole cities could become Roman.

The letters to Euschemon provide more historical and conceptual support for this mode of analysis. In the brief *Letter 246*, Photios distinguishes among the Apostle's various fatherlands. First, he was a citizen of heavenly Jerusalem through his love of Christ. Second, his distant ancestors were from the Judaean village of Gischala, which made this his *patris* through the link provided by birth. Third, Tarsos was also his *patris* as he was born there. Finally, the Romans were so magnanimous that they bestowed their name and citizenship even on people who were not of the same *phylon*, or race, as themselves. In this way, Paul's parents acquired Rome as their *patris* and polity through "human laws," as opposed to the bonds of ethnicity. This is what Paul meant when he told the centurion that he was "born a Roman." Thus, Paul had not only two *patridai*, but three (or four, if we add heavenly Jerusalem).

In *Letter* 247, Photios mentions the Apostles Barnabas and Apollos in order to draw a distinction among the affiliations that one has by ancestry (e.g., a Jew), by place of birth (e.g., a Cypriot), and through residence in a city (e.g., an Alexandrian). After applying this distinction to Paul, he makes the point about the city of Philippi: it managed to glorify itself with the name of Rome even though, as a Macedonian city, it had no kinship relation with Rome. In this letter, Photios also raises the example of the historian Josephos. He too was a Jew whose *patris* was Jerusalem, but he acquired Roman citizenship, which he signaled through the name Flavius (after Vespasian, his patron). In fact, when Jerusalem itself was renamed Aelia Capitolina by Hadrian and made a part of the Roman polity, it too "put on a Roman *genos*, so that all of them, even though their *ethnos* and their *patris* were of a different race, were registered in the Roman polity."[167] Jerusalem had thereby acquired a Roman identity. We can detect in Photios' language his pride in being a Roman in the same tradition, as he claims that all these people and places were "honored and dignified" at receiving the Roman name (ἐπισεμνύνουσι).

Among all Romans, Photios thought the hardest about the conceptual issues posed by Romanization in antiquity. He did so because he had to defend the Apostle against the accusation of lying about being Roman. In order to do so he had to draw analytical distinctions among different types of affiliation (such as ancestry, city of origin, religion, and citizenship) that ancient and medieval thought tended, by default, to lump together under the rubric of a single unified identity. In the process, Photios also provides a flexible analytical framework by which we can understand the articulated complexity of Romanía itself, which was absolutely a Roman civilization, albeit one that was not located physically in Italy, did not speak Latin, nor practiced ancient Roman religion. Photios tried to understand how one could acquire a Roman *genos* and *politeia* even if one's *phylon* was originally foreign. He correctly distinguishes between being Roman and being Christian, and provides a model by which one can acquire Roman ethnicity without a Roman ancestry. If ancestry was necessary, it could always be invented. Jews had, after all, colonized ancient Italy.

II
Others

4

Ethnic Assimilation

Roma est,
civitas ex nationum conventu constituta.

The Roman polity in all of its phases—Republic, early empire, Byzantium—was capable of absorbing foreigners, including the inhabitants of conquered lands, barbarian armies defeated on the frontier, and refugees, settling them according to its own modes, and, over time, making them into mainstream Romans. It was a literary cliché that Rome was formed from a mixture of nations.[1] Absorption and assimilation were among the driving mechanisms by which Rome expanded from a town on the Tiber to the world of Romanía. At the end of Chapter 3, we saw how Romans looked back to antiquity and tried to describe aspects of this process of Romanization which had led, ultimately, to themselves. The corollary of that process was the extinction of most ancient ethnicities, which now existed only as antiquarian trivia or geographical-administrative labels. Yet the process of absorption and assimilation did not stop in antiquity. It continued apace in Romanía, in real time, and was not just a distant memory. Foreign groups were admitted or imported into the empire by the emperors, whereas others, who had invaded and settled on Roman territory between the sixth and the eighth centuries, primarily in Greece, were also absorbed back into the Roman state. This chapter will trace and analyze the twin processes of ethnic extinction and Romanization in Byzantium, the necessary corollaries of ethnic assimilation, which have been little studied.[2]

The previous chapters, on Roman ethnicity, were necessary to set the stage for a study of assimilation. That is because Byzantium, if stripped of its Romanness, presents no majority identity *to which* refugees, resettled groups, immigrants, or absorbed populations could adapt and assimilate. Unless we can follow the sources and talk about them as becoming Roman, the process remains hazy and unmoored from any specific commitments. People did not cease being Khurramites, Pechenegs, or Armenians in order to become generic "subjects of the emperor" or "Byzantines," an invented and bloodless label. Other groups, by contrast, refused or avoided assimilating to the dominant ethnicity of Romanía, creating the conditions for Roman imperial rule over ethnic minority subjects.

I will here anticipate the major conclusions of this chapter and set the stage for Chapters 6 and 7, which will look at groups that did not assimilate. Some empires, for example the Achaemenid Persian and the Ottoman, were premised on the management and enforcement of difference among conquered populations: different groups were expected to abide, and be defined, by their own religious, local, or national traditions, as permitted by the ruling class of the empire. They lived according to a differentiated legal system, and the culture and identity of the conquering ethnic group was never extended to a large portion of the population. The same groups that went into the empire at its creation by and large came out of it upon its dissolution. Romanía was not such an empire. Compared to other premodern states, the Roman state had the most success at extending the culture and identity of its metropolis to its provincial populations, and not only to their elites. As we will see, through a combination of policy on the one hand and the largely passive but pervasive and enduring operation of institutions on the other, it turned "barbarians," who had initially entered the empire as members of different ethnicities, into Romans.

To a degree, this was brought about through imposition. The Roman state was keen to convert its domestic population to Orthodoxy (even though it was usually indifferent toward converting those outside). Orthodoxy, moreover, embedded these people within ecclesiastical, imperial, and other structures of governance and also promoted the spread of the Greek language. Romanía, moreover, had a single and uniform legal system that did not allocate rights and opportunities to its Orthodox citizens based on ethnicity. The newly assimilated could rise to high places within the empire's ecclesiastical, administrative, and military ranks. As a matter of policy, the empire actively incorporated the leadership of previously foreign groups into its own high commands. Although the court was willing to tolerate a degree of cultural difference among the first generation of ethnic elites that it brought onside, those leaders were invariably Romanized quickly, establishing new priorities, precedents, and incentives for the rest of their people.

The methods and outcome of barbarian settlements remained strikingly constant throughout a millennium of Roman history. In the fourth century, the authorities "demanded hostages, directly recruited able-bodied men into military service, separated leaders from their peoples or killed them, transported the peoples a safe distance from their homelands, and split them into smaller groups to effect the disintegration of tribal structures."[3] Not all Romans were happy that foreigners were being settled among them by the emperors, and so these policies receive special attention in imperial propaganda of that period. Emperors were praised for "taming" the barbarians, settling them as agricultural labor, and "admitting them to our laws," and even for "bidding them to become Romans."[4] The exact same policies and politics are described and justified by Eustathios of Thessalonike eight hundred years later, in his long funeral oration for Manuel I Komnenos (d. 1180). These men eventually made this foreign land their home, became inhabitants of our cities, soldiers in our armies, and grafted their offspring onto the vine of the Romans. They became patriots who risked their lives on behalf of the Roman homeland.[5]

Logically, for new Romans there must have been interstitial moments in the transition between their previous ethnicities and full absorption. We should be able to glimpse such moments in the sources. What did they look like? Let us consider some examples. In the sixth century, the historian Agathias refers to Aligernos, the brother of the last king of the Goths in Italy, who decided to defect to the empire. Specifically, he decided to "join the Roman *res publica* (πολιτεία) and to discard his present state of danger along with his barbarian customs."[6] Aligernos may stand for the moment of decision, as represented here in his mind by a Roman author. For someone further along that process, Agathias offers the example of one Theodoros: "by ethnic origin he was from among the Tzanoi, but he had been raised among Romans and had already lost his barbarian manners; even though they were his ancestral ways, he had now changed his way of life to a more civilized manner."[7] In the late eleventh century, Argyros Karatzas held the highest offices in the army and provincial administration: he was a "Scythian [steppe nomad] by birth, but otherwise a man of wisdom, virtue, and truth"—that is, despite his birth he was civilized, "one of us."[8] In the twelfth century, one Prosouchos is described by the historian Kinnamos as a "Persian by *genos* [i.e., a Seljuk], but having a Roman upbringing and *paideia*." Ioannes Ises, another "Persian by *genos*, had a Roman upbringing and way of life (δίαιτα)."[9] These men, who probably came from ethnic elites, could set an example for the rest of their people. Agathias is explicit about this in the case of Aligernos: "He set an example of good judgment for the rest of his people."[10]

Entire foreign groups, and not just individuals of elite ethnic background, were also embedded within Roman institutional matrices of governance that favored the adoption of Roman cultural norms, such as Orthodoxy, the Greek language, and identification with the Roman polity. The prestige, wealth, and opportunities for advancement offered by the Roman armies, Church, court, and other instruments of the state provided strong incentives to ethnic conversion. The processes of assimilation that we will discuss below took effect over the course of generations, usually two or three, though sometimes over the course of centuries. They regularly produced the same outcome: the extinction of previous ethnicities and their replacement with a Roman one. Only a few groups managed to survive this process, whether through tenacity (Jews) or size (Bulgarians). After all, Romanía never fully recognized, far less "celebrated," cultural diversity within its territory, maintaining instead the fiction that it was the polity of the Roman people (i.e., Romanía) and never in theory or title the empire of the Romans, Bulgarians, Slavs, Armenians, and so on. This chapter will investigate how that fiction of ethnic homogeneity tried to reproduce itself in reality.

The Khurramites: A Textbook Case

In the 830s, a large force of Khurramite warriors sought refuge in the Roman empire. The event and its aftermath are well documented in both Roman and Arab sources. The Khurramites were mostly Iranians from Azerbaijan whose religious beliefs mixed deviant Islam and Mazdakian Zoroastrianism.[11] They had waged war against the Abbasid caliphate for years but had been defeated and were on the verge of annihilation. Their best option was to move to Romanía. The Khurramites thus were a combination of refugees and warriors. The initial group is said to have been 14,000 strong, and more of their compatriots joined them subsequently, soon bringing the total up to 30,000. Even if these numbers are inflated, which is always possible in medieval sources, we are certainly dealing with thousands of men, including many hardened warriors. No women are mentioned, though it is possible that they brought some with them. The emperor Theophilos (829–842) enrolled the Khurramites in the Roman army and used them in military operations against the empire's eastern enemies. They served him reasonably well for a number of years but, toward the end of his reign, Theophilos became suspicious of them: he arrested their leader, who had taken the Greek name Theophobos, and decided to break them up into smaller units of 2,000 men and disperse them among the themes (the militarized provinces of the empire), where they would be commanded by Roman officers. In the words of a tenth-century history, "He caused them to be scattered and divided up."[12] It is also possible that they had suffered great losses in battle, so there were fewer of them to absorb.[13]

Another Roman historian, Genesios, writing about a century after the Khurramites entered the empire, used interesting language to describe their fate: "They were dispersed and almost entirely vanished."[14] The word ἀφανισμός also means "extinction." But Genesios was not imagining their physical destruction or failure to reproduce. Instead, he had in mind the extinction of the Khurramites as a distinct group within the empire. They were not killed, but absorbed.

They ceased to exist as Khurramites, or "Persians," which is what the Romans (accurately) called them. Moreover, Genesios was right: the Persians are no longer attested as a group in Romanía after the ninth century. The only memory that remained of them were the names of their units, scattered among the themes. And a later chronicler reworking the same sources at the end of the tenth century omitted the references to the unit names, as they had ceased to exist by then too.[15] If the Persians' descendants retained any affective memory of their ancestors, they did not express it in ways that reached our sources. This is significant, because ethnic ancestry of this sort was sometimes remembered generations later by assimilated Romans in other cases that we will consider. But in this case, a group of many thousands was assimilated and lost their identity within a century or less.

It is impressive that Romanía could absorb thousands of men from a group that was initially so different from the mainstream of its own culture, who initially shared no common traits, whether in ethnicity, language, or religion. How, then, was this accomplished? And how did imperial policy facilitate their absorption?

The sources say that the emperor Theophilos registered the Persians in the Roman army rolls, giving regular military commissions to the soldiery and court dignities to their leaders. Even though initially they formed a single "Persian" unit, they were "enlisted among the Romans who went out to fight the Agarenes [Arabs]." The emperor decreed that each of the Persians was to "adjust himself so as to fit in with the Romans" (συναρμόζεσθαι . . . τοῖς Ῥωμαίοις), in part by making it legal for all the Persians to marry Roman women.[16] We would like to know more about this last provision than we do. Were they required to convert to Christianity in order to marry Roman women? This would almost certainly have been expected by the women themselves, by society at large, and especially by the Church, if the latter were to accept such marriages as lawful. A later source, Michael the Syrian, does say that the Khurramites converted en masse to Christianity when they went over to the empire.[17] By that point, their physical survival may have mattered more to them than their religion, as the Abbasids were slaughtering them to the point of real extinction in the east.[18] A similar episode from the tenth century suggests that conversion to Christianity was probably required. Between 10,000 and 12,000 horsemen of the Banu Habib, an Arab "tribe," defected to the empire in the years after 941 with their families, slaves, and livestock, and were followed by more kinsmen in subsequent years. They accepted Christianity, were given lands, and also joined the Roman army in raiding Muslim lands.[19]

I find it harder to believe that the purpose of Theophilos' decree was to permit an extraordinary set of unions between Orthodox women and non-Orthodox men.[20] It is more likely that the decree facilitated, or even coerced, marriages with newly converted but essentially still foreign men, who did not yet speak Greek or understand Roman customs, and whose Christianity would have been skin-deep. It is probable that this decree is mentioned in the *Life of Saint Athanasia of Aigina*, who lived in the first half of the ninth century. After the death of her first husband, "an imperial edict was issued that unmarried women and widows should be given in marriage to foreign men."[21] Athanasia herself had to marry one such foreign man, whom she eventually persuaded to join a monastery. By that point, at least, he was certainly Christian and spoke (some) Greek. An account of the same decree in a different hagiographical text is overtly hostile to Theophilos (who, we must remember, aroused considerable opposition in Orthodox circles also because he was an Iconoclast). It says that he ordered his foreign soldiers to marry the daughters of citizens, even under compulsion, "and this ruined the good fortune of the Romans and put Christians in a hard spot."[22] Theophilos was accordingly called *philoethnes* and *ethnophilos*, "foreigner-lover," by his critics.[23] In other words, there was a nativist reaction, which is what we expect in a polity premised on a strong ethnicity.

Theophilos had two good, pragmatic reasons to order these unions. First, a large force of armed men without access to women would have been extremely dangerous to have in imperial territory. Second, "the purpose of the edict may have been to encourage the assimilation of foreigners."[24] Their children would have been raised Christian by their Roman mothers and would have primarily spoken Greek. Especially after the Persian army was broken up into small units and scattered among the themes, it is likely that these children, and their children in turn, would have been fully acculturated to Roman norms. There would have been no institutions to preserve and perpetuate Khurramite religion and identity.

As John Haldon has written, the Khurramites "were settled and subjected to the same conditions of fiscal and civil administration as native Byzantine populations" (i.e., Romans).[25] Those institutions had particular and specific ways of categorizing people and structuring their relations to each other and to the state, all of which were expressed in the technical vocabulary of the Roman administration. At first, this language, like their new religion, would have been a superficial imposition under which their previous cultural life carried on, as best it could under the circumstances. Eventually, both the new religion and the new language, with all their ideological implications for interpersonal and subject-state relations, would have been internalized. We should not underestimate the degree to which "registered" subjects are shaped by the language of public institutions, with far-reaching personal and political implications. We may like to think of the categories of officialdom as external to the self and that private or cultural identities can resist them. But "registration in the military rolls" meant taking on an institutional affiliation that made these newcomers recognizable to the Roman state and to the rest of Roman society. It would have granted them access to opportunities that were previously closed. The pull of that affiliation, however formal it was at first, would have been hard to resist in the long term in a society as interconnected as Romanía.

The locals' expectations also pushed in the same direction. Consider an episode from 380 AD, told by the historian Zosimos. A unit of recently hired foreign Gothic soldiers stationed in Lydia, in Asia Minor, was mistreating local merchants, whereupon they were scolded by Roman soldiers from Egypt, who told them that "such actions did not befit men who wanted to live according to the laws of the Romans." The two units came to blows, and the Egyptians killed many of the Goths.[26]

To assimilate foreign groups, it was especially important to co-opt their leadership. Just as Theophilos gave wives and commissions to the rank and file, he did the same, but on a princely scale, to their commander Theophobos. This man was made a *patrikios* and married to the emperor's own sister (who cannot be securely identified). This not only gave the leadership a stake in the imperial regime but signaled to the entire group that status in the Roman empire was not determined or limited by ethnic origin. Previous scholars identified Theophobos with the Khurramite general Nasr, but Juan Signes Codoñer has offered a decisive argument that Theophobos was in fact Nasr's son, a conclusion that finally resolves the otherwise odd tales told about him in the Roman sources. According to the sources, Theophobos was raised in Constantinople, probably at the court. Signes Codoñer proposes that he was deposited there by Nasr during an embassy to seal a prior alliance between Rome and the Khurramites. This explains why the Roman sources say that Theophobos was properly educated, indeed that he was especially eloquent (i.e., in Byzantine Greek), and also why he would have been a suitable match for an imperial marriage. Theophobos was "more Roman than barbarian," indeed more cultivated by Roman norms than some of the uncouth emperors of that period.[27] Signes Codoñer proposes that he had been raised as a Roman in order, one day, to act as a pro-Roman leader of the Khurramites in Azerbaijan, but we cannot exclude the possibility that some Khurramites were cultivating the option of imperial service and wanted to place one of their own within the Roman hierarchy. Either way, the leader of the Roman Khurramites had been Romanized before they crossed the border, and his prominence at the court would have pointed the rest toward the path of success and assimilation in Romanía.

The Khurramites did not remain a distinct group thereafter in Romanía. But three individual "Persians" are attested in Constantinople in the year 867, when Basileios I murdered his patron Michael III, Theophilos' son, and took the throne. The first, with the Iranian name Artabasdos, was the commander of the palace guard, the *hetaireia*. He is not called a Persian, but it is said that he could speak Persian, which suffices. The avenues of promotion in imperial service had, therefore, remained open to Persian-speakers. The second was Eulogios the Persian, who had a manor in Constantinople, indicating a level of economic prosperity. The third was Iakobitzes the Persian, who helped Basileios murder Michael III. After the murder, the assassins went to the house of Eulogios, who, in turn, took them to the palace and "spoke in his language to Artabasdos the *hetaireiarches*" to get him to open the gates.[28] These three men, then, represent an intermediate stage of assimilation: they were well integrated in Roman society and had diversified their presence beyond the army, but they continued to cultivate ethnic links to each other, expressed through language, from which other Romans were excluded. We do not know whether these three men were descended from the Khurramites who entered the empire in the 830s, but it is plausible. Only one generation after their dispersal by Theophilos, these men may have even been from among the original group, or at least their immediate offspring. Significantly, such Persian networks are not attested in subsequent generations.

Considering the experience of the Khurramites, we can identify these factors as promoting and facilitating ethnic assimilation—or Romanization—in Byzantium: conversion to Orthodoxy; legal equality; the right to marry Roman women; equal integration into the institutions of the state, especially the army; and the right to claim high positions at the court, especially for the leadership. The process was accelerated by their dispersal in smaller groups throughout the themes.

Muslims to Romans

Theophilos was not a genius at absorbing foreign people into the Roman polity; he was only following the traditional Roman playbook. Byzantium was always in need of manpower for both the army and agriculture, and its leadership made concerted efforts to convert and assimilate people who, at first sight, might have appeared as hopelessly foreign. Consider Muslim captives of war, for example. Some were regularly exchanged for Roman captives taken by Arab raiders, but others were pressured or incentivized to convert and resettle on Roman lands. We possess a set of imperial instructions from the tenth century defining the "start-up packages" given to Muslim captives who converted. The magistrates of the themes in which they lived were to give them three gold coins in cash, twelve more for a pair of oxen, and a measure of grain for seed. They were also given land and made exempt from taxes for three years. To promote assimilation, Roman families into which these former Muslims married were also exempted from taxes for three years.[29] In other words, the emperors financially incentivized not only Muslims to convert but Romans to accept them in the most intimate ways. A historian of the Islamic-Roman frontier has seen in this "a Byzantine version of tribal incorporation (in the unit of the family) and an attempt by the central state to encourage sedentarization and agrarian productivity."[30]

Ibn Hawqal's report on the 10,000 Banu Habib who entered the empire and converted in the 940s notes that they too were given good lands, garments, and precious objects by the emperor, presumably as incentives to settle and serve in the Roman army.[31] Moreover, the Roman conquests in the east during the tenth century resulted in the capture of many thousands of Muslims who were resettled in Romanía. It is likely that they either agreed or were forced to convert, and so were treated in the same generous way, or dispersed as slaves if they rejected the offer. But Roman expansion in the east, and the decline of the Arab states, induced a number of Arabs to take up service with the empire and eventually become assimilated (though some may have been of Arabic Christian origin rather than Muslim).[32] Either way, cut off from any Arabic-speaking environment, their descendants would have become indistinguishable from other Romans. In the eleventh century, Psellos corresponded (in Attic Greek, naturally) with a provincial governor named Chasanes (i.e., Hasan), lacing his letters with classical allusions and making no mention of his correspondent's ethnic or linguistic ancestry. Quite the contrary, Psellos contrasts Chasanes' own mild and philosophical manner to the "barbaric habits" of his own lower-class (Roman) subjects in the province.[33]

For the Romans, conversion was supposed to change one's nature. In the striking manuscript illuminations of the Menologion of Basileios II (ca. 1000), Arab persecutors are depicted as foreign and alien, whereas Christian Arabs are depicted in the same way and the same (lighter) colors as Roman saints.[34] This suggests that Romanía was open to ethnic foreigners so long as they shed the most important identifying traits of their ethnicity. Their cultural profile had to become Roman just as their religious one became Christian. The most famous case of such an Arab convert and defector was the father of the frontier hero Digenis Akritis.[35] A great deal of the poem named after that frontiersman focuses on the conversion of his unnamed father, an emir, to Christianity and, beyond his religious conversion, on his assimilation to Roman cultural norms. The latter are emphasized throughout the process of his assimilation, which we should not reduce solely to its religious aspects.

The emir is described as fair and handsome, not black like an Ethiopian, which means that the poem is predisposed to see him as a Roman, just as Christian Arabs are painted in lighter colors than the heathen Arabs in Basileios II's Menologion. The emir already spoke "the language of the Romans," but had, up to this moment in his career, been an enemy of the Romans, leading raids into their territory. For love of a Roman maiden, however, he proclaims his intention to "defect to Romanía and become a Christian," which her brothers accept as "a miracle" demonstrating "the power of the Romans!" But her mother still has concerns: "Will he share the values of high-born Romans . . . or be a wrathful man, like the heathen?" The emir turned out to be handsome and civil enough for his Roman in-laws and started wearing "Roman dress." His mother in Syria reproached him for "renouncing his relatives, faith, and country."[36]

The story of the conversion of Digenis' father reveals that the Romans had cultural expectations too of anyone who wanted to join their society and become a Roman, not just religious expectations. Foreignness in their eyes was not shed by simply reciting a new creed and renouncing Islam. There were, in addition, specific cultural-ethnic indicia (language and dress) as well as norms of behavior, basically being "civilized"—and handsome (Romans were just better-looking). This tale is a romantic fiction and so does not reveal anything about the state regulations and administrative procedures that would have been involved in this defection; also, for narrative simplicity, the story overlooks the emir's men. His case had real-world counterparts, though they appear rather more prosaic. The descendants of the last Arab emir of Crete, for example, became a prominent Roman family after the island was conquered in 961, and they were still active in imperial service a century after the conquest of Crete.[37]

A later fictional tale about a converted Arab Muslim reveals the same assumptions and refutes the belief that the Romans were content with "mere" religious conversion that did not reshape the convert's cultural profile as well. This is the story of one Saint Barbaros (literally, "Saint Barbarian"), who was left behind in western Greece (Aitolia) when his army of fellow Muslim raiders was defeated and repulsed by local defense forces during the reign of Michael II (820–829). His story was written in the fourteenth century as a model for religious *and* cultural conversion. In his initial state, Barbaros represents the exact opposite of the norm, as the text calls him "diametrically opposite in terms of language, race, laws, and customs . . . a barbarian in his race, his manners, his roughness."[38] After his unit was defeated, he wandered the mountains of Aitolia like a wild man, murdering the local farmers. But eventually he was converted by a local priest. Barbaros was so bestial that he could not make proper sounds with his mouth, so the priest taught him Greek. He eventually changed his violent ways. The text says that he "not only" partook of baptism but went even further, cutting his wild hair and taking off his barbarian clothes.[39] At the end of the text, the author beseeches the saint to help "us" (Romans) against the godless Muslims, and to "fight on behalf of our realm, strike down those who are hostile to us, and champion the scepters of our empire."[40]

It says something interesting about Roman society that it was prepared, in both life and fiction, to embrace former Muslims who had so recently been murdering its own people. It accepted them into its territory, its families, and even its worship. Modern Christian states are struggling to do much less even with quite harmless Muslim refugees. On the other hand, Romanía required religious conversion and expected (and usually received) a sincere transfer of allegiance to Romanía, to the point of fighting against one's former Muslim coreligionists. It also encouraged and praised cultural change that made absorbed Muslims seem more like Romans. Modern western states cannot and should not require, expect, or encourage such efforts, as they are committed to the priorities of multiculturalism (at least ostensibly).

However, even after Romanization an ethnic background could be used to tarnish one's reputation. Roman politics could devolve into vicious rhetoric, in which ethnicity was fair game. Consider Konstantinos VII's slurs against some of the officials of his (detested) uncle, the emperor Alexandros (912–913). Hasé and Niketas were brothers who served as provincial governors, in Athens and the Kibyrraiotai theme, respectively (Hasé was murdered inside the Parthenon by the disaffected townspeople). Konstantinos VII, who probably wanted to blacken his uncle's memory, insinuates that Hasé, "who was a Saracen by ethnic origin, was in reality also a Saracen when it came to his attitude, manners, and form of worship." Those two words, "in reality," imply that Hasé presented himself as a Christian, which Konstantinos VII is exposing as a façade.[41] In other words, there were political contexts in which ethnic origins could be used against Romans who otherwise appeared to have assimilated (compare the rhetoric regarding Barack Obama's Muslim background). We cannot settle the issue of whether Hasé "really" was or was not a Muslim, but we can extract from Konstantinos' polemic the notion, seen consistently in our discussion so far, that for the Romans it was not just one's faith that mattered but "attitude and manners" too, that is, social values and one's cultural profile.

Slavs to Romans

Many foreign groups entered Romanía and, like the Khurramites, eventually went "extinct"—to use Genesios' powerful term—including Goths, Vandals, Huns, Slavs, Arabs (e.g., the Banu Habib mentioned above), Armenians, Bulgarians, Turks, Pechenegs, Cumans, Franks, and others. An interesting case is a unit of Goths stationed in Bithynia that is not attested after the ninth century. They are described as Greek-speaking *(Gotthograikoi)* and must presumably have melted away into the general Roman population.[42] In fact, we cannot be certain that this unit retained a sense of ethnic distinction toward the end of its existence in the eighth–ninth century; by that point, it possibly contained Roman recruits in a unit that retained its old ethnic name.

Our discussion of assimilation has focused on individuals and groups that were either hired, transplanted, or admitted by the imperial authorities, and who entered the empire without much disruption, especially in the east. An entirely different history unfolded in Greece, Macedonia, and Thrace, which were settled by Slavic-speakers between the late sixth and the eighth centuries. The extent of their demographic impact on Greece has occasioned exactly the kind of heated debate that one would expect between nineteenth-century German racists and Greek nationalist historians. That Slavs settled in the empire's western provinces is certain, and they possibly did so in large numbers. Some of their tribal names are attested in the Roman sources, especially the *Miracles of Saint Demetrios*, though we do not know if they called themselves "Slavs" (*Sklabenoi*, in Greek). I will henceforth follow the Roman sources and use "Slavs" for non-Roman Slavic-speakers.[43] The Romans perceived these Slavs to be a different ethnicity: they were non-Christian (until converted), barbaric and foreign, spoke a different language, and at least initially were hostile to the Roman state and its subjects.

The sources are so bad that it is hard to visualize the Slavic settlement and how it affected what were core Roman territories. Looking back at that process, some tenth-century Roman texts present it in hyperbolic terms, as if the Slavs displaced the local population entirely.[44] But given the speed of their subsequent conversion, Hellenization, and absorption by the empire, Slavs could not have entirely displaced or destroyed the local Roman population of Greece (including the Peloponnese), Macedonia, and Thrace, but probably settled among it in ways that temporarily disrupted the functioning of the imperial administration. Their demographic impact as such was likely smaller than their impact on the ability of the empire to control and govern those territories, especially in the hinterland. For example, an area that became 50 percent Slavic and was dominated by that group may have lost *all* imperial presence for a while. Thus, parts of these territories fell out of imperial control and had to be regained over time through war and co-optation. The empire did retain uninterrupted control over important cities on the eastern coast, such as Athens, Corinth, and Thessalonike.[45] (A recent genetic study of the Peloponnese finds little evidence of "Slavic DNA," for what that is worth, probably not much.)[46]

Starting in the late seventh century, progressing in the eighth, and then accelerating during the ninth, the empire reestablished direct control over almost the entire Peloponnese, most of southern and central Greece, coastal Macedonia (the hinterland of Thessalonike), and Thrace. As the zone of imperial control and influence expanded, thousands of Slavs became imperial subjects. This entailed violence, to be sure, including military expeditions against the Slavs and the relocation of groups to other parts of the empire, where they could be more easily absorbed. But progress toward their incorporation must also have been accomplished through negotiations, incentives, and peaceful exchange, whether with the imperial authorities or local Romans. Many of these Slavs ultimately became Romans themselves: they learned to speak Greek, accepted Christianity and Roman cultural norms, and were integrated politically and administratively into the Roman polity and imperial institutions of governance. There is no doubt among modern historians that this process did take place, even if many share the usual horror of the terms *Roman* and *Romanization*. But once we overcome that squeamish reluctance, we can say that by the end of this process large numbers of people whose ancestors were regarded by the Romans as barbarian Slavs had become Romans themselves. Ihor Ševčenko summarized it as follows: the Slavs "were made to disappear as Slavs not by the sword alone and certainly not by the encouragement of Slavic letters, but—so we surmise more than we know—by the reimposition of the Greek [i.e., Roman] administration, the introduction of the Greek Church hierarchy, and by the celebration of the liturgy in Greek."[47] We cannot give exact figures for the Slavs who were thus assimilated, but it was a significant portion, especially in the Peloponnese and southern Greece but also around Thessalonike.

It is the process of assimilation that concerns us here, or at least the way in which the Romans viewed it. Unfortunately, this happened during the period in Roman history that produced the fewest surviving sources, so we have only hints, clues, and traces. It is impossible to give a full and detailed account of how the Slavs were "Hellenized" and converted, that is, made into Romans.[48] But that is exactly what the imperial authorities believed that they were doing. Looking back on the whole process around 900, the emperor Leon VI said that his father, Basileios I (867–886), persuaded the Slavic nations "to change their ancient customs: he made them into Greek-

ETHNIC ASSIMILATION

speakers, subjected them to rulers according to the Roman way, honored them with baptism, freed them from slavery to their own rulers *(archons)*, and trained them to take the field against the nations that make war on the Romans."[49]

Such a transformation could not, of course, have been carried out by one man but was the result of a long process; nor was it as complete as Leon implies. His account does not reveal the pushback that conversion and assimilation to Roman norms would have elicited from recalcitrant Slavic pagans, such as were encountered by the emperors of the Franks in the ninth and tenth centuries.[50] Still, Leon's account, even if compressed and driven by a Great Man view of history, expresses a concept of national assimilation. Despite its flaws as history, it reveals the mentality guiding imperial planners, or at least Roman leaders who looked back on the process and interpreted it. We do not see here an empire content to subject and incorporate a foreign people in ways that allowed their foreignness to persist. The result of such a process would more accurately be called a multiethnic empire. Instead, the empire sought to remake the Slavs in its own image. The transformation that Leon imagines extended to many aspects of cultural practice, language, religion, modes of rule, and politics and war. This is national assimilation, not imperial agglomeration.

As it happens, we can glimpse some steps in this process. They are more like tantalizing hints than solid pieces of evidence, but interestingly they all point in the same direction. Moreover, they correspond to the strategies of assimilation that we saw the empire apply to groups that it took in in the east, which reveals a unity of purpose, outlook, and approach despite the different challenges posed by invasive Slavic settlers on the one hand and Zoroastrian refugee armies on the other.

The stages can be seen in the history of one group of Slavs who settled in southern Thessaly, known as the Belegezites (spelled variously). In the early seventh century, when they invaded and settled in the empire, they were hostile barbarians bent on plunder and violence, and they joined an attack by other Slavic groups on Thessalonike in the 610s. By the 670s, however, when the Slavs of the north (the Drogoubites and others) attacked Thessalonike, the Belegezites "seemed"—in the words of the *Miracles of Saint Demetrios*—"to have peaceful relations with the city" and were engaged in trade with it so that the townspeople could be supplied with food.[51] Our next data point comes over a century later, in 799, when we hear of one Akameros (or Akamir), *archon* of the Slavs of Belzitia, who plotted against the empress Eirene in league with the Roman army of the Helladikoi and the exiled sons of Konstantinos V who were at Athens. Scholars have plausibly linked Belzitia to the Belegezites and placed Akamir in Thessaly.[52] Florin Curta has concluded that "the Belegezites had already been drawn into the political developments of the theme of Hellas. Akamiros was no barbarian chieftain, but a client ruler with knowledge of, and influence in, local Byzantine politics."[53]

In literary texts, the title *archon* may have been a way of referring to an independent or quasi-independent barbarian chieftain, but the evidence of seals suggests that this was a title granted by the Roman court to the leader of a group of Slavs who were being brought onside. A number of seals belonging to "*archons* of Greece" have been found, one (from the eighth century) with the definitely Slavic name "Dragoslav." He used the cross and Virgin on his seal, but we cannot be sure that he was a Christian. Another seal of a different *archon* of Greece (from the end of the seventh or early eighth century) belonged to one Petros, who was more likely a Christian and additionally bore the title "consul." Moreover, as southern Greece formed the official theme of Hellas, the Greece in question on these seals was likely Thessaly, a localization attested in Byzantine literary usage. What we are seeing here are the lords of the Slavs of Thessaly being drawn into the imperial system, converted, and given titles. Seals have also been found naming *archons* of the Belegezites, Evidites, and Drogoubites. Nikos Oikonomides explicitly frames these seals within a story of progressive assimilation of the Slavs of Greece. Although we may not know what was happening on the ground among nonelite Slavs, the scarcity of references in the sources after 800 to Belegezites, Sklabenoi, and ethnic *archons* argues in favor of their assimilation; and after 900 there are almost no such references. Around 900, the *archon* of the Bichetai of Greece was Ioannes, an "imperial *koubikoularios*," that is, a eunuch. The Bichetai had by this point been thoroughly integrated into the court system and soon disappear altogether as a distinct group. "The process of their Byzantinization [i.e., Romanization] was practically accomplished, which perhaps explains why they disappear from the sources." To be sure, "the process is badly known: one must infer its existence from the results."[54]

A similar, albeit inevitably more partial process can be observed in the hinterland of Thessalonike. Again we lack details, but the data point in the same direction. The *Miracles of Saint Demetrios* names many Slavic tribes that settled around the city after invading the empire in the later sixth and early seventh centuries. Under Konstantinos IV (668–685), the *rex* ("king") of the Rynchinoi, a man named Perboundos, was living in Thessalonike when he was arrested by the imperial authorities and sent to Constantinople. "The nation of the Sklabinoi, which consisted of two parts, the Rynchinoi and the people of the Strymon [a major river]," joined with the people of Thessalonike in sending an embassy to the emperor to request his release. Whatever their identity at that time, this kind of behavior was characteristic of imperial subjects. Perboundos, moreover, managed to escape from Constantinople because "he was dressed in the Roman way, spoke our language, and could pass as one of our citizens."[55] His ability to pass as Roman is noted in the text because it was probably not typical of the majority of Slavs—yet. We have seen that Romanizing the ethnic leadership was the first step in a more thorough process of assimilation.

In the 670s, the Rynchinoi, Drogoubites, Sagoudates, and other Slavs were attacking Thessalonike (even while, as we saw, the city was buying supplies from the Belegezites). But in around 680 the Drogoubites were sufficiently subject to imperial authority for the emperor to order them to provide supplies to a mixed Romanobarbarian group of refugees who escaped from the Avar khanate.[56] By 904, the Drogoubites and Sagoudates, "living in villages of mixed population," were paying taxes to the city of Thessalonike and were subject to a bishopric. A new theme was named after them before 1000: "Although the ethnic name was eventually transferred to that of an administrative unit, no indication exists that by the time the theme of Drougoubiteia came into being its inhabitants felt, or were regarded by others as, in any way different from those of the neighbouring themes of Veroia and Thessalonike. Did they speak Slavic?"[57] We do not know. As for the Slavs of the Strymon valley, in 688/689 Justinian II settled a number of "Scythians" (Slavs or Bulgars) there to guard the passes.[58]

A brief notice in the tenth-century *Book of Ceremonies* describes how an emperor Michael (I, II, or III; in any case, in the first half or middle of the ninth century) received some Slavs who had rebelled in the otherwise unknown region of "Soubdelitia" and then regretted their actions and sought an imperial pardon. The description of this event makes sense only if they were integrated into the imperial system but still regarded as ethnically distinct and perhaps living under a special administrative arrangement. The reception also featured "other Slavs from the district of Thessalonike," to function perhaps as exemplars of obedience to the emperor.[59] By 904, there were Slavs who were subject to the governor of Thessalonike and other Slavs under the overall authority of the general of the Strymon theme, though the latter seem still to have had their own separate *archons*. Our source for the siege of Thessalonike by the Arabs in 904 accuses the Strymon Slavs of being cowardly, selfish, and corrupt, but it does not ethnicize their flaws: the same accusations could be made against Romans.[60] In the early eleventh century, hostile barbarians are attested near the coast between Mt. Athos and the Strymon (river or theme), but this was during the long war between Basileios II and Bulgaria and their identity is not specified; they may not have been affiliated with the empire at all, not even nominally.[61]

Just as in Thessaly and the Peloponnese (which we will consider next), the dominant trend in the Slavic hinterland of Thessalonike was toward increasing integration into the imperial administration, which enhanced the desirability and promoted the expansion of Roman and Christian cultural traits. The Roman sources, as we have seen, do not shy away from mentioning ethnic *archons* along the imperial fringe or foreign groups such as Slavs or their tribal subdivisions that were settled near areas of imperial control. That is why the silence regarding both *archons* and such tribes in sources after 900 is significant, especially as those sources generally become fuller as the Roman centuries advance. Leon VI's explicit statement that the Slavs were acculturated to Roman norms points to the most plausible explanation for that silence. A strategy, or at least the concept, of acculturation is reflected in the thinking of imperial planners and observers of the time.

However, the evidence does not support the complete assimilation of the Slavs in the north. Alongside the Romans, or mixed among them, there would have been a significant bilingual population as well as exclusive Slavic-speakers, even if by now they were Christian. Western envoys were attacked by Slavs who, in 927, had risen in rebellion against the emperor Romanos I near Thessalonike,[62] while "Slav Bulgarians" are attested at Hierissos (Chalkidike) in the tenth and eleventh centuries.[63] In this connection, we must factor in the gravitational pull of the emerging and nearby Bulgarian empire, with its own Slavic populations. The north remained ethnically diverse, but that odd composite designation—"Slav Bulgarians"—suggests that the Roman state distinguished between its own Slavs and Slav settlers from the Bulgarian empire. In the ninth century, the empire and Bulgaria had drawn up specific treaty arrangements over the control of the borderland Slavs.[64]

By contrast, in southern Greece and specifically in the Peloponnese the newcomers were more fully absorbed into Romanía. The reassertion of imperial control in the Peloponnese definitely involved violence. Our sources document unrest on the part of the "Slavs" or "the nation of the *Sklabenoi*" against the imposition of imperial order in the early ninth century and again in the early tenth century, which prompted repressive interventions by the imperial armies. These were generally successful, resulting in the extension of Roman authority and administration to almost the entire population. Only one ethnic enclave seems to have survived, the Ezerites and the Milengoi around Mt. Taygetos in the south. Konstantinos VII, writing in the mid-tenth century, acknowledges that they were allowed to form a quasi-autonomous region that paid tribute to the empire.[65] The Milengoi are reliably attested thereafter. The *Life of Saint Nikon "Metanoeite!"* reveals that in around 1000 the Milengoi had a *doux*, Antiochos, whose function was probably analogous to that of the Slavic *archons* of central Greece in past centuries. The *Life* labels the Milengoi *ethnikoi*, which probably refers to their ethnic difference in the author's eyes and not to paganism. It is likely that they were

Christian by this point. Still, according to a clever interpretation of the passage describing the death of Antiochos, they may have retained the pagan custom of cremation. Be that as it may, the *Life* definitely presents the Milengoi as ethnically different from the rest of the population of the province, as it stresses their "barbarous nature," not religious differences.[66] Nikon, a firebrand preacher, would likely have agitated against their paganism had they remained outright heathens.

The Milengoi are mentioned again at the time of the Frankish conquest of the Peloponnese in the thirteenth century when they fought on the side of the Romans against the Franks; it seems that the author of the *Chronicle of the Morea*, the Frankish source for the conquest, considered them to be Slavs.[67] Inscriptions from the region dating to the fourteenth century reveal that the Milengoi still retained their ethnonym and leaders (*tsaousios* or *tzasis*) as well as some Slavic personal names (Slabouris, Kopogis); but they were Orthodox Christians, bore Byzantine names, and recognized the emperor in their local inscriptions.[68] A text of the fifteenth century implies that they still spoke a language related to that of the Slavs living by the Baltic Sea.[69]

The Milengoi provide a useful control case for assessing the extent of assimilation and Romanization among other groups, and also for assessing the value of our sources. Had *no* ethnically distinct groups been mentioned in the sources we could legitimately wonder whether the latter were covering up or ignoring a seething mass of ethnic variety. But the ethnic enclave of the Milengoi is mentioned by an emperor, a saint's life, and a later Frankish chronicle (whose coverage, incidentally, roams over the entire Peloponnese). The Milengoi did survive and are mentioned by a variety of sources. This makes it unlikely that other foreign groups survived without being mentioned, at least groups of a size sufficient to retain their ethnic distinctiveness. This is especially so as the sources become fuller in later centuries. To be sure, there are some places, especially the remote mountains of Arcadia, that may well have harbored culturally and even ethnically different groups that passed without notice in our sources. But these would have been small compared to the overall population. When Saint Nikon traveled in Greece and the Peloponnese in the later tenth century, visiting Epidauros, Athens, Euboia, Thebes, Corinth, Argos, and Nauplion, he came across no other ethnic enclaves apart from the Jews at Sparta and remnants of the Arabs on Crete, both groups that we would expect him to find. We cannot, then, accuse the sources of hiding ethnic diversity from us. Our presumption must be that by the tenth century Greece was a mostly "normal" Roman province with a familiar, mainstream culture.

This was a remarkable achievement of Roman policy, and it was in part deliberate, even if we do not know all of its mechanisms. Leon's statement about his father's policy of assimilation reveals that the emperors had a concept of what they were doing, and we must not underestimate the ample timescale on which they did it. The *Miracles of Saint Demetrios* tells a story set exactly two hundred years before Basileios I in which it is assumed that groups of mixed Romano-Slavic ethnicity entering the empire from the Balkans would be "dispersed" by the emperors and resettled in various locations, separated from their previous leadership.[70] This is exactly what happened to the Khurramites in Asia Minor too.

Between the seventh-century world of the *Miracles* and the assimilative policies of Basileios I, the emperor Nikephoros (802–811) had ordered Christians from every province of the empire to sell their lands and relocate to the Balkan Sklabinias, a measure that many resented and took almost a year to implement.[71] This was demographic restructuring on a vast empire-wide scale. We are not told that he ordered mixed marriages too, but that was only a step away from forced relocations to mix the Slavs up with Romans. Premodern empires were perfectly capable of conceiving such strategies and pulling them off. The Assyrian empire, for example, used them to assimilate conquered populations: the administration "settled deportees from the conquered countries [in Dur-Sharrukin], made them speak one language, and commissioned natives of Assyria, experts in all craft, as overseers and commanders over them to teach them correct behavior and the right reverence towards god and king."[72]

The Politics of Slavic Ethnicity

Under the right circumstances, complete assimilation could occur quickly, and the offspring of a mixed marriage could "pass" as a Roman from the start or even just be that. Individual foreigners "often seem to have become Romanised quite quickly, a process undoubtedly assisted by the need to assimilate in respect of belief."[73] But the complex politics of ethnicity could be warped by other concerns. Consider the patriarch of Constantinople Niketas (776–780), who is said to have been a eunuch of Slavic origin: not "a Slav" as such but "from among the Slavs" (ὁ ἀπὸ Σκλάβων). Unfortunately, we do not have more information about this. Niketas' ecclesiastical career before 776 had been distinguished, which means that a Roman of Slavic ancestry could attain high positions by the mid-eighth century. The sources present him negatively, but that was because he was an Iconoclast. If his Slavic origins and inability to pronounce Greek diphthongs were real, they were mentioned only to blacken his reputation further for reasons of religious politics. Had he been an Iconophile, these traits would either have been passed by in silence or presented innocuously. As with Konstantinos VII and the "Saracen" Hasé, we are again in the realm of ethnicity-as-politics.[74]

A figure whom our sources consistently brand as "a Slav" is Thomas the Slav, a general who rebelled against Michael II in 820–823. This was a bitterly fought war, which Thomas lost, and so the press about him afterward was negative. His alleged "Slavic" ethnicity was part of a broader defamation that sought to depict him as leading an army of foreign ethnicities against the empire, that is, as a traitor and outsider in all ways. It is possible that he did receive military support from the Abbasids, but his pitch to become emperor of the Romans depended on domestic support and on himself, as a Roman, being qualified for the throne. He certainly was raised (and probably born) in the empire, but the imperial historical tradition stresses his foreign ethnic roots, a mélange of Slavic, Armenian, and even generic "barbarian" elements. This was ethnicity as polemic.[75] In reality, Thomas may likely have had a thoroughly Roman cultural profile.

On the other hand, there were circumstances in which an ethnic inflection could be advantageous. In the mid-ninth century, Dami-

ETHNIC ASSIMILATION

anos, a "eunuch of Slavic origin," served as the *parakoimomenos* (chamberlain) of Michael III (842–867) and held the high court dignity of *patrikios*.[76] Now, eunuch chamberlains at the court were often *meant* to have a foreign profile—many of them were imported from outside the empire for this reason—so he might have actually been foreign to begin with. Otherwise, Damianos may have cultivated an aura of "otherness" in order to serve more effectively as a buffer between the emperor and his Roman subjects. Ethnicity would here be an asset. We have no proof for this, but it is a possibility.

It was especially in the Peloponnese that the politics of Slavic-inflected ethnicity played out in subtle ways. Now, the Peloponnese, as we have seen, was a great success story of imperial Romanization. Around 900 AD, some of the leading writers, bishops, politicians, and diplomats of Romanía came from the Peloponnese, including Arethas, bishop of Kaisareia, Leon Choirosphaktes, and Niketas *magistros*, all of whom engaged in elite literary activities. This was no remote outpost of imperial culture. Yet the careers of all three were embroiled in nasty controversies at the court. Here I will focus on Niketas *magistros*, a leading representative of the elite Roman culture of his time, because the rivalries that brought about his downfall generated ethnic imputations and insinuations. His alleged Slavic ethnicity occupies that middle ground between history—the settlement of the Slavs in the Peloponnese—and polemical rhetoric, such as we saw directed against Hasé by Konstantinos VII. That emperor was again at the heart of the matter.[77]

Niketas was born around 870 and claimed to be "a Spartan on my father's side and Athenian on my mother's side," though he regarded himself primarily as a Spartan.[78] His letters are full of classical references, more so than in any other collection from this period, and he speaks of classical matters as if they are his own ancestral patrimony, calling himself a Spartan and a Lakonian.[79] His diction, he says, is appropriately "laconic."[80] In one letter he rejects the Bithynian Mt. Olympos (a center of Christian monasticism) as an unpleasant location compared to the more celebrated Olympus in Thessaly, home of the gods.[81] Toward the beginning of his career, Niketas had also written the *Life of Saint Theoktiste*, the first hagiographic fiction of the middle Byzantine period that imitated the ancient romance.[82]

In the frame narrative of the *Life*, Niketas has been sent on a mission to Crete in 910 by Leon VI, whom he calls "the emperor who took with him to his grave the good fortune of the Romans."[83] Niketas had a large stake in Roman affairs, and this statement could have been written only during the turbulent period between Leon's death in 912 and the rise of Romanos I Lakapenos (920–944), whom Niketas personally helped to place on the throne and whose son and later coemperor Christophoros married Niketas' daughter Sophia. Niketas was as Roman as Roman got in the tenth century. He was invested in the view that barbarians and barbarism were the opposite of civilization;[84] he was classically educated, corresponded in Atticizing Greek, and wrote belles lettres; hailed from one of the empire's most ancient and famous cities; and he also served a number of emperors personally on missions, held high court titles, and married into the imperial family.[85]

This eminent profile, however, was dismissed at the court of Konstantinos VII as arrogance and pretension. Niketas is one of the few contemporaries mentioned by name in that emperor's short treatise surveying the antiquarian history of the empire's provinces, the *On the Themes*, where he is attacked in the section on the Peloponnese. Konstantinos says that the grammarian Euphemios smacked down a man from the Peloponnese who thought too highly of his own nobility (εὐγένεια), which was in truth only ignobility (δυσγένεια), through the following verse: "*garazdo*-face, a Slavicized visage." Konstantinos then specifies that the target of this attack was Niketas, who married his daughter Sophia to Christophoros, the son of Romanos I.[86] This section on the Peloponnese is a crucial passage of the work *On the Themes*. A statement occurs here that has resonated in modern debates on Greek ethnic continuity: it is precisely before this passage on Niketas that Konstantinos VII says that "the entire land [of Hellas and the Peloponnese] was Slavicized and became barbarian." We justly wonder, then, is the attack against Niketas merely an illustration of the general thesis of Slavicization (that Slavs settled in Greece), or is the Slavicization thesis actually meant to reinforce the ad hominem attack that follows? But what was the political background of that attack? We know that classical postures and ethnic attacks were politics by other means at the Roman court.[87] That is why we have to consider the political function of these opposing tropes.

Konstantinos VII had good reason to dislike Niketas, for the latter was linked to the house of Lakapenos and had taken part in the coup that brought Romanos Lakapenos to power in 919–920.[88] Romanos then sidelined the heir to the throne, Konstantinos VII himself, for twenty-four years. The scholar-emperor was quite bitter about that when he later assumed sole power in 945. In the *De administrando imperio*, he advises his son not to give brides to foreign nations. But what if someone asks, "Why then did Romanos I give his granddaughter in marriage to Petar, the Bulgarian tsar (in 927)?" Konstantinos answers with a tirade against Romanos I, whom he calls an illiterate low-born fellow, unqualified for office.[89] In his polemics against both Niketas and Romanos, Konstantinos comes across as a royal snob: he labels the former "arrogant" and the latter "impudent," likely because they aspired to positions—*his* position—beyond their "proper" station.

As it happens, the two men were linked by more than Konstantinos' polemical rhetoric. The bride in question, Maria, the one given in marriage to the Bulgarian tsar, was the daughter of Romanos' son Christophoros, and therefore the granddaughter of Niketas himself. These upstarts not only usurped power from Konstantinos, they managed to join their bloodlines to the Bulgarian royal house. Niketas was even dispatched to personally escort the Bulgarian king to Constantinople.[90] The point of such an alliance might have been to solidify the Lakapenos hold on power by projecting it onto the stage of international relations and thus to further sideline Konstantinos himself.[91] (The latter inclined toward a Frankish alliance, which is why he made an exception for Franks in his bridal policy.[92]) It is no wonder that Konstantinos vented against the Bulgarians too, in the *Life* of his grandfather Basileios I (867–886) as "vain boasters" and in *On the Themes* as "God-hated."[93] One suspects that all these accusations of "arrogance" are linked: Slav-faced social upstarts from Greece and Bulgarian pretenders to the throne were all threats to Konstantinos' position, and so he linked them together in his ethnic polemic.

The Slavicization of the Peloponnese served in the works of Konstantinos VII as a way to discredit *domestic* rivals. Conversely,

Niketas' Hellenic rhetoric might well have been one way for social upstarts from the "untamed" lands of the south to legitimate their position. He may have been a Roman of Slavic origin, like the patriarch Niketas, the chamberlain Damianos, and the rebel Thomas. Perhaps that is why he reached back to classical antiquity when he described his own origins in his letters: it was to bypass the settlement of the Slavs while advertising his embrace of upper-class Roman culture, precisely the sort of "civilization" that helped to distinguish Romans from barbarians. And perhaps that was why Konstantinos VII placed his hyperbolic statement about the Slavicization of Greece in the section of the *On the Themes* that is devoted to the Peloponnese, in order to set the stage for the defamation and delegitimization of his political enemy Niketas. As a Slav, Niketas would by definition have been a barbarian, "the opposite of 'civilization' or cultural sophistication."[94] We must remember that the *On the Themes* is devoted to the classical and antiquarian history of the empire's provinces. There was much that Konstantinos could have said about the Peloponnese to make it seem like a bastion of classical culture and thereby reinforce Niketas' classical persona. Instead, we get poems about the upstart "*garazdo*-face" and the Slavicization of the land.

As it happens, we can possibly dig deeper into Niketas' background. A contemporary chronicle tells the story, set around 921, of an "uneducated" Rentakios Helladikos who, under Romanos I, was a relative of Niketas *patrikios* (i.e., our *magistros*). This man is said to have attacked his father and plundered his possessions, before seeking asylum in Hagia Sophia. The emperor Romanos wanted to remove him from the church and punish him, but Rentakios sent forged letters to the Bulgarians promising to defect. We must remember in this connection that the Bulgarians under Tsar Simeon (d. 927) had recently been raiding as far south as the Gulf of Corinth. Rentakios was arrested and blinded.[95]

The Rentakioi were a Peloponnesian family.[96] Helladikos was, then, a relation on Niketas' father's side, the "Spartan" side. The name Rentakios was of Slavic origin, though there is no proof that any people who bore it by this point spoke Slavic.[97] In Rentakios Helladikos' appeal to the tsar, we note again a "sinister" connection

ETHNIC ASSIMILATION   151

to the Bulgarians, which his relative Niketas would solidify through an actual marriage alliance. Note also the seemingly Hellenic name *Helladikos*. It appears, however, that its original form was *Eladikos*, referring to the olive-oil business (these were "oily" men, not *Hellenes* . . .).[98] "Helladikos" was an attempt to classicize the name, which appeared to Konstantinos VII as just more impudence. One Ioannes Eladas had been a member of the regency that had ruled in Konstantinos' place during his minority, possibly another reason for the later emperor to dislike the family as a whole.[99]

It is therefore likely that our Niketas was the same as the Niketas Eladikos *protospatharios* (a court title) who was sent by Zoe in 914 to negotiate with the Bulgarians over Adrianople.[100] This family was all too close to the Bulgarians, to say nothing of their Slavic faces and oily business. It is no wonder that Niketas sought to play up his Athenian and Spartan credentials. In one of his letters from exile, he asked the metropolitan of Kyzikos to send him some olive oil, "which this miserable place lacks."[101]

Niketas *magistros* exemplifies how Slavic ethnicity could be attributed, covered up, or ameliorated in Romanía. It was part of a long Roman tradition of ethnicity-as-politics that stretched back to the days of the Republic.

Conclusions

It was generally bad for a Roman to be branded as an ethnic type. The retention of a foreign language was not something to boast about.[102] In politics, old ethnic affiliations could be dredged up and used against otherwise mainstream Roman rivals. In this chapter we have seen it done with Slavic and Arab ethnic origins, and we will examine the advantages and disadvantages of an Armenian ancestry in Chapter 5. But any association was fair game. The emperor Michael III insulted the patriarch Photios as a "Khazar-face."[103] The empress Theophano called the chamberlain Basileios Lakapenos a Scythian and a barbarian (because of his mother).[104] The poet Ioannes Geometres used Slavic words to insult his enemy Psenas, imputing ethnicity to him, just as Niketas *magistros* was mocked at the court of Konstantinos VII.[105] A candidate for the patriarchal throne in the fourteenth century was insulted as a *Boulgaralbanitoblachos*, a Bulgarian-Albanian-Vlach.[106] A textbook case would be Anna Komnene's attack on the ethnicity of the eleventh-century philosopher Ioannes Italos.[107] This may have played out on the local level too, as when children threw stones at Saint Neilos for wearing what appeared to them to be a Bulgarian hat (Snapshot 8).

In many of these and other cases, it is hard to know whether there was any truth to the ethnic imputation or whether it was invented or exaggerated for polemical purposes. I suspect that in most cases this colorful language was used against men whose cultural profile was mainstream Roman, whatever their ancestry. If this was the case, many Romans would have been vulnerable when the stakes were high and the knives came out. Romanogenesis continued apace in Romanía as refugees, captives, foreign armies, and even invaders who had settled on imperial territory were taken in, absorbed, and admitted into the majority Roman group. The whole process could sometimes be accomplished during the course of a few generations, two or three if mixed marriages were involved, or longer if the foreign population was larger.[108] Assimilation was often messy around the edges, or incomplete, or it left visible traces. All the evidence suggests that the Romans of Byzantium disliked ethnic foreigners, but they were simultaneously willing to admit them into their polity and even their ethnicity. No groups who wished to join were excluded or turned away, even Muslim warriors who had been fighting against the empire.

Becoming Roman entailed far more than just converting to Christianity. It required learning Greek, meeting the demands of the Roman state, and adopting a new cultural and ethnic profile. The Romans expected a complete makeover of potential members of their polity. In modern terms, we would say that Romanía practiced an expansive model of assimilationist membership, trusting in its way of life and institutions such as the Church, army, legal system, and imperial court to gradually make Romans out of foreigners; it did not restrict membership to those who already belonged to the *genos*.[109] But Romanía was not for all that a multicultural state: the Romans had zero respect for foreign cultures as such and recognized no imperative to preserve them. In some sectors of opinion today their policies might be condemned as cultural genocide, even if their openness to refugees might be praised.[110]

One court author described "the polity of the Romans" as "an altar of safety for refugees fleeing savagery to our civility and mildness."[111] He was referring to a group of Bulgar refugees whom the court refused to return to their khan when he angrily demanded it. Many Byzantine texts claim that foreign groups who adopted Roman norms would become civilized in time. This was a proud and uninterrupted Roman conceit, dating to antiquity.[112] It suggests that, even if they were ethnically prejudiced, the Romans were not racists, if we define a racist as someone who believes that traits are ingrained and cannot ever change.[113] To be sure, some policies sparked controversy and pushback, such as Theophilos' order that Roman women should marry Khurramite men. There must have been internal debates about the specific measures. And, as Angeliki Laiou observed, the first generation of such new Romans "remain[ed] under scrutiny, almost on probation . . . rarely assimilated fully. By the second generation, assimilation was far advanced, although some people might remember and mention the non-Roman antecedents of a family."[114]

Laiou was referring to resettlements that involved intermarriage and a new Roman environment for the newcomers. But some cases did not take place under optimal conditions and did not work out, for example the Pechenegs who turned against their Roman hosts in the mid-eleventh century. The frustrated underlying expectations were then revealed: a Pecheneg leader had changed only his clothes, not his soul, complained a court orator.[115] And it could get racist: you can't paint the Ethiopian white after all, said a historian at the time, noting that the Pechenegs continued their old habits of raiding the empire.[116]

Integration was not always successful. Consider the divergent lives of two Turkish children. Both were taken captive in the later eleventh century and sent to the imperial court as presents. The first had been a child soldier fighting against the empire around 1080; the second was captured when Nikaia fell in 1097. They were adopted, given titles, and associated with the imperial family. But the first, Tzachas, was cut off from access to the court when Alexios I seized power, so he reverted to raiding and became the empire's foe, temporarily conquering much of western Asia Minor.[117] The second, Axouch, was given by Alexios I as a playmate to his son and heir Ioannes II. He grew up to become one of the most powerful court officials and the founder of a prestigious and thoroughly Roman family.[118]

The expectation of complete Romanization harbored yet another source of potential conflict: the Romans talked about themselves as a *genos*, a kinship community, yet knew perfectly well that many among themselves had a foreign ancestry. In some cases, this did not matter and was soon forgotten or ignored, but in others it created a potential for ethnic politics and prejudice.

A fascinating case study of this "melting pot" reality is provided by the advice writer of the eleventh century, Kekaumenos. He had served as a high imperial official, mostly in the Balkans, and takes considerable pride in being Roman and serving the interests of Romanía.[119] At one point he advises the emperors not to promote foreigners to high positions because that demeans the Romans who could have been promoted instead. He formulates this as a matter of national interest and pride: "it is not in the interests of Romanía to do this," and "Romanía prospered when the high commands were held by Romans." Yet elsewhere in his book of maxims he casually reveals that among his ancestors were a local lord of Dvin in Armenia (a man of unspecified ethnic background), who captured a fort in Armenia from the Roman general in command there; the latter is said to have called Kekaumenos' ancestor "an enemy of Romanía." He also reveals that another of his ancestors fought for the Bulgarian tsar Samuil against Basileios II during the great wars, before he switched sides. Yet another ancestor, also named Kekaumenos, had fought for Basileios against Samuil.[120] His mixed ancestry in no way diminished Kekaumenos' proud Roman patriotism as expressed in his career and opinions.

5

The Armenian Fallacy

Ita ex variis quasi elementis congregavit
corpus unum populumque Romanum ipse fecit.

In the sixth century, the Roman empire began to pay an increasing amount of attention to Armenia. As part of his ambitious project to make Rome great again, the emperor Justinian created a new field army for Armenia, recruited soldiers there for the wars that he was waging on so many other fronts, and sought to co-opt segments of the Armenian aristocracy by bringing them to Constantinople and giving them offices. Initially, this produced oddities such as an Armenian officer, Gilakios, who led a unit of his countrymen in Italy but could not speak Greek or Latin, so when he was captured by the Goths he could state only his rank, which he had learned by heart after hearing it said many times. Also, the nobleman Artabanes, who had formerly waged war against the empire but had been brought onside, conceived the desire to marry Justinian's niece, which, he thought, would give him a shot at the throne. Disappointed in this hope, he was approached by a relative, Arsakes, a scion of an Armenian princely house also resident in Constantinople, who was planning to assassinate Justinian.[1]

These stories were the preludes of a closer rapprochement between the empire and "Armenia," which was a patchwork of states, provinces, and lordships. This relationship accelerated dramatically in the seventh century, when the empire was threatened by the caliphate and its access to old recruiting grounds in the central and western Balkans were cut off by the Slavs and Avars. The emperors turned increasingly to Armenia to recruit soldiers and officers for their armies and manpower for settlements and agriculture. This led to an influx of Armenians into the empire, including military units (sometimes stationed far from Armenia, for example in southern Italy);[2] fugitives from the wars with the Arabs who fled to Romanía;[3] captives brought back by the Roman armies; colonists who were resettled by the emperors in recaptured lands, such as the Peloponnese, Crete, Cilicia, and the small "Armenian themes" that began to proliferate along the frontier during the tenth century;[4] population drift, during the later tenth and eleventh centuries, from Armenia into the reconquered lands in Asia Minor; and the co-optation of aristocrats, their families, and retinues into the court hierarchy and imperial high command. Finally, in the late tenth and eleventh centuries, in a qualitative leap in expansion, the empire annexed Armenian realms, including Taron, Vaspurakan, and Ani (this will be discussed in detail in Chapter 7).

These events have been studied in many books and articles. In one crucial respect, however, our understanding of the presence of Armenians in the empire has been skewed by the logic of racial nationalism. I define the "Armenian fallacy" in Byzantine Studies as the assumption (which is rarely explicitly acknowledged) that Armenian identity was propagated genetically and could not be lost through cultural adaptation and assimilation. Put in the form of a syllogism: if x is an Armenian and y is descended from x, no matter how many generations have passed between them and no matter the admixture of any amount of what is called "non-Armenian blood," then y is also "an Armenian." This fallacy results in distortions, errors, and oversights. Specifically, it refuses to recognize the Roman cultural profile and ethnicity that many families and individuals acquired after living for a few generations in Romanía. It is thus predisposed to attribute an essentialized Armenian identity to individuals and families based on putative (and sometimes fictitious) "bloodlines." It is unable to recognize that they had in the meantime become Roman, an identity that lacks the same existential weight in its eyes because it sees only blood. "Nationality" is here taken to be immutable, and linked to "stock," that is, race.[5] Second, it assumes that Armenian blood prevails over the blood of non-Armenians, so the offspring of mixed marriages always "are" Armenians. At most, such people are called "of Armenian or partially Armenian origin,"[6] but the other "part" that makes up the whole is never named or researched; it does not reach the same level when it is conjoined with any "part" of Armenian "blood."

The hunt for Armenian bloodlines is a full-fledged modality of research in the field of Byzantine Studies. In 1905 and 1909, scholars such as G. Ter Sahakean and Z. N. Perperean published books on the "Armenian Byzantine Emperors," extending western European modes of racial and nationalist historiography to the history of medieval Armenia. But their books were written in Armenian and so remained inaccessible. It was Nicholas Adontz, writing in French as well as in Armenian a few decades later, who made the search for Armenians in Byzantium into a more scholarly and less romantic nationalist process, though he too was often uncritical when it came to later medieval legends. Just like some of his sources, especially the eleventh-century historian Step'anos of Taron (also known as Asołik), Adontz saw Armenians everywhere and injected them into as many important events as he could. This might have remained a local national project had it not been endorsed a few decades later by Peter Charanis and Alexander Kazhdan.[7] The hunt for Byzantines who were "really" Armenians has been ongoing ever since, though in a number of individual cases there has been pushback against initially uncritical or unfounded claims. Nevertheless, among many scholars, making that connection has now become a knee-jerk reaction: the mere mention of certain names sparks an automatic qualification or subordinate clause labeling them as "Armenians" or as being "of Armenian descent," even when that label or factoid is irrelevant to the discussion at hand or has no foundation in the sources.

This nervous tic is not today confined to nationalist Armenian historians; if it were, it might simply have been ignored along with the fantasies of other nationalist schools of historiography. The habit has spread widely in the field of Byzantine Studies. It has become the sort of thing that one *has* to say, for some reason, and sheer repetition has legitimized it over time. Seeing it done so commonly, one assumes that it must be a meaningful kind of thing to say, even though we are rarely told exactly what it means to say that a particular individual had Armenian "blood." In one sense, this is a product of Roman denialism. Ethnic identities, especially if they bear the name of a modern nation, naturally seem more real and weighty than an insubstantial "Byzantine" identity that has been stripped of its Roman core. This cedes the field to modern nationalist ideologies, which step in to fill the vacuum. It is no wonder, then, that so many Byzantines have the label "Armenian" foisted upon them as their fixed ethnicity, when in fact they were just Romans, some of whose ancestors may have come from Armenia—or not, as we will see in many cases. As most scholars do not recognize the Romans of Byzantium as "real," the drive to Armenianize Byzantium has expanded, seeking ever more frivolous, fictitious, flimsy, or far-fetched connections by which to label as "Armenians" a whole host of Romans, including many about whom no such claim is made in the sources.

It is time for this nonsense to end. It has become a reflex that in most cases is meaningless or false. The present argument aims to bring balance between the Roman and Armenian sides of a centuries-long relationship, and specifically to restore integrity and historical weight to the Roman side of it. It leaves intact the integrity and continuity of the long history of the Armenian nation. To be clear: there absolutely were Armenians inside Romanía, by which I mean people who belonged to the wider Armenian people as that was defined by language, its own Church, principalities, local communities, aristocracy, cultural practices, collective memory, and ethnonyms, whatever variable forms those took—or by a partial combination of those factors. Conceivably, Armenian identity could survive the loss of one or two of these elements. For example, some Armenians belonged to Chalcedonian churches. There is no question that there were many Armenians of this kind throughout the empire, settled in minority communities or serving in the army. As we will see throughout this chapter, and especially at the end, the Romans definitely perceived them as a distinct people, and did not view them favorably overall (though there were exceptions).

THE ARMENIAN FALLACY

But if Armenians stayed long enough in Romanía, especially if they lived and operated in small family groups, they could be assimilated just like everyone else. Over the course of a few generations and through intermarriage, Armenians could become mainstream Romans, whether or not they retained a memory of this one (Armenian) strand in their mixed ancestry. Instead of postulating fixed races, we should rather be thinking along the lines of a spectrum of assimilation, ranging from Armenians in Armenia or elsewhere who were not regarded as Romans; first-generation Armenian immigrants who had settled in Romanía or taken up imperial service; Armenians settled in the empire who were in the process of Romanization; Romans who remembered their Armenian ancestors; and Romans who had Armenian ancestors but did not know or care about that fact. To be sure, in most cases we lack sufficient information to make a precise classification, but a spectrum captures reality better than modern fictions about "blood." We should add two more categories to it: Romans who had no Armenian ancestry but found it advantageous to claim that they did; and Romans who had no Armenian connection but have had it attributed to them by others, either by medieval historians or modern scholars. That last group is far larger than most historians realize.

The fact of assimilation (i.e., Romanization) has often been recognized. It is, however, hard for the field to say exactly what it was that these Armenians were assimilating *to*. We have to grasp for words and typically use the wrong ones because Byzantine Studies has never recognized Romanness as real. "Greek" is the usual stand-in for That Which Must Not Be Named, though it points weakly to language and not to nationality or ethnicity. For example, Armen Ayvazyan correctly pushed back against Romilly Jenkins' racial view of the Byzantine aristocracy:

> Much of [the] ethnically Armenian elite in the Byzantine Empire, in religious and cultural terms, was almost entirely Hellenized [i.e., Romanized] and certainly put imperial interests above the interests of Armenia, while retaining its connection with the Armenian nation only nominally, by and large for

receiving a career support from their rich and powerful compatriots as well as getting authorization of their real or alleged noble origins from Armenian princely or even royal (Arsacid) blood.[8]

Nina Garsoïan likewise cautions that "the degree to which they were still to be considered 'Armenian' is open to question," precisely because of assimilation, for which, when she is not typically calling it "Greek," she once uses the unique word "Constantinopolization."[9] She knows that within two or three generations they had the same profile as the rest of the aristocracy.[10] Some historians have used the correct term for this process: Werner Seibt has not only asked when is an "Armenian" just a normal Byzantine and when does he remain Armenian, he has coupled this question with an explicit acknowledgment of the integrative pull exerted by "the Romano-Greek national self-awareness" of Byzantium.[11] This explicit affirmation of a Roman *national* identity is language that Byzantinists lapse into when they just state what emerges clearly from the sources. The most recent statement on the issue, by Johannes Preiser-Kapeller, correctly denies that there is any point to labeling these people Armenians when their families had been in the empire for generations and had adopted an entirely "Roman" profile, but he still uses the typical scare quotes around the dreaded word.[12]

Despite such concessions, the Armenian fallacy remains strong in the field because its modalities and false premises have never been exposed. Even those who disagree with its general thrust (mentioned above) do not explicitly tackle its fundamental assumptions and preconceptions. The present chapter will continue the discussion initiated in Chapter 4, developing further the notion of Roman assimilation by focusing on the period between the seventh and the early tenth centuries (the imperial expansion of the tenth and eleventh centuries will be discussed separately under the rubric of "empire" in Chapter 7). I will argue that the scholarly trope according to which some Romans "were really" Armenians is a meaningless thing to say in most contexts, unless one holds a racial view of identity. It effaces Roman ethnicity for the benefit of a different, neighboring ethnicity that is construed along racial lines. Finally, going beyond

THE ARMENIAN FALLACY 161

the "melting pot" approach, I will consider how and why otherwise assimilated Romans may have maintained affective or symbolic memories of their Armenian ancestors. What were ethnic ancestors good for in Romanía?

Some Family Chronicles

The evidence allows us to track the assimilation of specific Armenian families only in the case of elites, whose members were visible at the highest levels of power in Romanía. Conversion to Byzantine Orthodoxy, intermarriage, dispersal, and assimilation would have affected nonelites as well, though it is likely that elites were assimilated faster and easier because they came in smaller groups (a family plus retinue), were not settled in compact communities, and intermarried more quickly with Romans. We are fortunate in this connection to possess the *Life of Saint Maria the Younger*, a saint whose family occupied the middle rungs of Roman provincial administration. The *Life* is a family chronicle of sorts and offers a model of assimilation over the generations that we can use as a basic template. The author of the text was not trying to make a point about this process, but was instead concerned about a different set of (saintly) issues. Its basic narrative is therefore unlikely to be the product of politicized distortion.

According to the *Life*, some powerful men of Greater Armenia emigrated to Constantinople during the reign of Basileios I (867–886), where they received honors and offices from the emperor. Among them was Maria's father, who had two sons and two additional daughters. He managed to marry off the other two daughters before he died, but not Maria, who was raised by her mother (2). We do not know whether Maria was born in Armenia, but she was raised in Constantinople. We also do not know the ethnicity of her mother. If Basileios gave wives to these Armenian nobles (as Theophilos had to the Khurramites), then her mother might well have been Roman. In this case, Maria might not have learned to speak Armenian at all. She is never called "an Armenian" in the text: that fact about her ancestry is never mentioned again after the section about her father. Maria's sister married a man named Bardas Bratzes, whose surname is the

Armenian word for Georgian (i.e., Kartvelian, Greek "Iberian"). We do not know this man's identity—he may have been a long-assimilated Roman—but his two names point to a mixed Caucasian background. The sister's marriage was arranged by her father, the Armenian nobleman, so it seems that ethnicity may have played a role in the arrangement. But this was not to be in the case of Maria. Bardas Bratzes introduced her to a friend of his, Nikephoros, a *droungarios* (mid-level officer) in the army, who went to Constantinople to ask her mother for Maria's hand in marriage (2).

There was nothing Armenian or ethnic about Nikephoros. His siblings were named Alexios and Helene, and Helene's daughter was named Sophia (7, 21). Everyone in this story, moreover, is Byzantine Orthodox and speaks Greek. Maria and her husband Nikephoros lived in the Thracian town of Vizye, among other Romans (until he caused her death). That is where the couple made their life together. When Maria identifies herself to a painter in a posthumous vision, she calls herself "Maria from Vizye," not Maria the Armenian (18). When a priest later tells her story to the Bulgarians, he says that "she was from Constantinople, the daughter of noble parents" (24). The Bulgarian later calls her Maria of Vizye (25). Maria and Nikephoros had four children, whose names alternated between Greek and Armenian, which indicated an affective memory of Maria's Armenian past (Orestes and Bardanes, who both died young, and the twins Stephanos and Baanes: 4–6). Stephanos eventually became a monk with the name Symeon, while Baanes, like his father, had a military career. He rose to become "the commander of the army of the Romans" at Selymbria (24–25). When finally there was peace between the Romans and Bulgarians, "everyone rushed to his own fatherland *(patris),*" so Baanes returned to Vizye (27). This man was just a Roman: a Greek-speaking, Orthodox captain in the Roman army whose home was a Roman town in Thrace. He married a woman from a distinguished family (30). It makes no sense to call any of the people in this story Armenians, except for the immigrants under Basileios I. This is "melting pot" assimilation, with some tinges of affective ethnicity (to be discussed below).

The Armenian fallacy would have us believe that Baanes' (hypothetical) grandchildren "were" Armenians. We will scrutinize the operations of this racial logic in a later section. Let us first consider some additional genealogies.

Ioseph Genesios was a historian of the mid-tenth century who wrote an account, *On the Reigns of the Emperors*, covering most of the ninth century in what he believed was high-style Greek, and he dedicated it to Konstantinos VII. Genesios was an Orthodox Roman: he speaks of Romans in the first-person plural and identifies with the Roman order.[13] It is almost certain, moreover, that Genesios' grandfather was the ninth-century high official Konstantinos, who appears many times in the work.[14] Genesios goes out of his way to praise this man and highlights his deeds more than do other sources. He also knows more about his family background than do the others:

> Konstantinos was said to be of Armenian descent (ἐξ Ἀρμενίων ... ἀπόγονον Ἀρμενίων) and was sent to Theophilos [829–842] by his relatives and the rulers of his native land as a hostage and ambassador. Shortly afterwards, on account of the beauty of his soul and body and his noble disposition in all great affairs, he was appointed *droungarios* of the *arithmos*, i.e., of the imperial *vigla*; later he was made a *patrikios*, and finally *logothetes* of the *dromos*.[15]

Konstantinos thus appears to be the exact Armenian analogue to Theophobos, the son of the leader of the Khurramites who was sent to the Roman court to be raised there, learn Roman ways, and serve as a diplomatic bridge. In both cases, these "hostages" stayed in Romanía and had distinguished careers there.[16] We note again the use of moralizing language—"the beauty of his soul and body and his noble disposition"—to counter any foreignness that might be imputed to this man. Moreover, Genesios does in one place call him "the Armenian," but he and his parallel source, the *Life of Basileios I*, sometimes phrase this more carefully: he was "from the Armenians," "was descended from Armenians," or "his *genos* was derived from the Armenians."[17] These were roundabout expressions to designate his *background*, but not who he was in the present.

Konstantinos' two sons were Genesios (not the historian, but his uncle) and Thomas, a high official at the court in the early tenth century, described by the *Life of Basileios I* as "philosophical and incorruptible."[18] It is probable that our historian Genesios was Thomas' son. Genesios is labeled by a later historian as a "Byzantine," that is, a Constantinopolitan.[19] He exhibits in his own work no special attachment to Armenians, whom he mentions as neutrally as any other foreign people. One passage, however, is interesting. When he refers to the Armenian origins of the emperor Leon V (813–820), Genesios digresses to divulge an antiquarian (and fictional) etiology according to which "the Armenians took their name from Armenos, who was from the Thessalian city of Armenion, and had campaigned with Jason."[20] This is not much to go on, but it may reflect a desire on the part of a man who had a bit of Armenian ancestry to ameliorate its potential foreignness by linking Armenians to an ancient Greek hero who served on the *Argo*. It is as much affective-ethnic attachment as we would expect from a third-generation Roman. Other Genesioi are attested in the later tenth and early eleventh centuries—a branch of them were prominent citizens of the city of Trebizond—but they are never called Armenians, and it is not certain anyway that they were descended from Konstantinos.[21] At any rate, Armenian origins are mentioned only for Konstantinos, the first to arrive, and even in his case they are oblique, for it is possible that he was raised in Constantinople. Unfortunately, we know nothing about the women of this family, who would have played a key role in changing its ethnic profile over the generations.

A snapshot of the same progression—from ancestor of qualified Armenian origin to just plain Roman descendant—can be observed in the case of the Mosele family (Μωσηλέ or Μουσελέ, spelled variously, derived from Armenian Mušel). The first known to us is Alexios, who held court titles and military commands and was involved in imperial politics at the highest level in 790. The chronicles, sparse for this period, do not call him an Armenian; for all we know, his family may have moved to Romanía many generations previously. Alexios appears to be a fully integrated member of the Roman high command.[22] The same is true of the next one known to us, also named Alexios, who was active at the court of Theophilos (829–842), married the emperor's daughter, and was appointed *kaisar*, a rank held only by those who were close to the imperial family. This

Alexios is called "an Armenian" in one source, while another gives a detailed background: "He was descended from the race of the Krenitai, a place in the land of the Armenians. . . . He lived on the acropolis [of Constantinople] in the so-called manor house of the Krenitissa woman."[23] Juan Signes Codoñer has plausibly linked the Krenitai to the Armenian city of Karin (Roman Theodosioupolis), which was captured by Konstantinos V in 754; an Armenian source relates that Konstantinos V took a large part of the local population back to the empire and resettled them there. Interestingly, the emperor Theophilos, Alexios' father-in-law, also attacked Karin in the 830s, forcing the city to pay tribute. A local link would have been an asset in this expansion.[24]

The particulars need not detain us here, and other scholars may interpret the place-name Krenitai differently. What we seem to have here is a man active at the highest level of imperial service, who was perfectly assimilated (certainly by language, religion, marriage, and residence) but found it advantageous, in the early ninth century, to remind people of his (ostensible) Armenian ancestry and to live in a manor named after his native land, a form of affective attachment. None of this made Alexios "an Armenian." Rather, he was a Roman who wanted to be seen as ethnically inflected, probably for political reasons. He was possibly two or three generations out from his Armenian ancestors. Later members of the family, prominent in the tenth century, were even further removed from this ethnic origin. An Alexios Mosele was an admiral in 922 and his (likely) son was the *magistros* Romanos Mosele (mid-tenth century). None of the many sources that mention them call them Armenians in any way or hint at their foreign origin or distinctive cultural profile.[25]

Another surname that indicated an Armenian ancestry was Taronites, referring to the mostly Armenian realm of Taron that was ceded to the empire around 968 by the sons of its last native ruler, Ašot III. They took the name Taronites and were appointed to high military posts. To be sure, not all men with the surname Taronites were necessarily descended from its former ruling family, as anyone who moved from Taron to Romanía could call himself Taronites, but whether there were one or more lines does not concern us here. The

Taronites rose to the highest levels of the Roman aristocracy in the eleventh and twelfth centuries. They certainly became Byzantine Orthodox and dropped their native names (whose Greek versions were Pankratios, Asotios, and Krikorikios) in favor of standard Roman names: Romanos, Theophylaktos, Michael, Gregorios, Eirene, and others.[26] They also intermarried with prominent members of the Roman and former Bulgarian aristocracies. The literary record about their later activities contains no references to their foreign origin, other than that encoded in their surname, and it also leaves no doubt that they became normal (if elite) Romans. A Taronites is listed among the "Roman" casualties of a battle with the Turks in 1070.[27] At the end of the eleventh century, Theophylaktos of Ohrid wrote letters to Gregorios Taronites, praising his accomplishments as an administrator and governor who defeated the Franks and the Turks: now, he says with a flourish, it will be seen that those celebrated trophies of the ancient Romans were no myth, as we have among us precisely such a most noble Roman; that ancient Roman spirit is not dead but lives on in you.[28]

Alexios I Komnenos appointed one Ioannes Taronites to a provincial post in 1107, and the description of this man by Anna Komnene reveals a perfectly Romanized gentleman:

> From his early childhood [Ioannes] had been under the emperor's protection and for a long time served him as a secretary. He was a man of active mind, with a sound knowledge of Roman law. . . . If he spoke freely, his censures were not devoid of tact: he was [Aristotle's] ideal of what a dialectician should be.[29]

It is absurd to refer to such people as "Greek-speaking Armenians."[30] We have a nuptial poem from the mid-twelfth century celebrating the marriage of a Taronitissa bride to a scion of the ruling Komnenos dynasty, who is hailed as the pinnacle of Roman manliness. The girl apparently also had some Komnenian ancestry, so the poet, addressing the groom, says that "the maiden is not from a foreign race (φυλὴ ἀλλοδαπή) but from a *genos* related to your father's and a kin-clan," while simultaneously being "the glory of the Taronites" and "from a noble family."[31] It did not get more Roman than this. The

Taronites were a benchmark of Romanness, and no mention is made anywhere in the poem of a foreign origin.

The families of Maria the Younger, Konstantinos "the Armenian," Mosele, and Taronites demonstrate the pace, modes, and extent of Armenian integration into Roman society. Ethnic affiliations attach to the first generation of new arrivals, then give way to only symbolic-affective gestures (the names of children or manor houses), and finally disappear entirely. To be sure, these were all elites (or subelites, in the case of Maria) who sought advancement in Roman imperial service through offices, marriages, and the politics of patronage. Matters would have been different among groups of Armenians resettled in provincial villages. It is possible that such small communities retained their Armenian identity for centuries, though they too could be assimilated if they were dispersed among the Roman population and given strong incentives. Kazhdan opined that Armenian communities in the empire were close-knit, allowing them to retain a sense of ethnic distinctiveness.[32] But the proof for this is weak.[33] Usually, it is negative: a group is mentioned as being settled in a particular location, but is never heard from again. Moreover, Armenian authors evince almost no interest in their compatriots who moved to the empire, whether in groups or as individuals. In part, this may be because Armenian historiography placed a premium on confessional affiliation and increasingly refused to recognize as true Armenians those who joined Chalcedonian churches, which many of them did, especially if they "went Roman."[34] Thus, it is difficult to reconstruct networks linking Roman elites of Armenian descent to their counterparts in Armenia.[35]

The Armenian fallacy, however, primarily mischaracterizes not so much groups (which are virtually invisible) as it does individuals, and their decisions. As these individuals are mostly elites, it is on them that we must focus.

The Fallacy in Action

The Armenian fallacy consists of interconnected and expanding errors. It began by imputing racial-ethnic labels to various Romans on the basis of an alleged ancestry. No number of intervening generations or mixed marriages sufficed to stop the transmission of a fixed Armenian identity through a single bloodline. This approach gained a foothold in part because no scholars were willing to push back on behalf of Byzantine Romanness, which the field has never recognized as such, whereas Armenians were and still are a real nation. Once this axiom was accepted, it began to chew almost methodically through Roman history to find "Armenians" everywhere, expanding like an economic bubble into increasingly riskier and attenuated claims. Armenian identity is now postulated not only on the basis of actual textual claims about a person's ancestry—whatever value we may place on those—but also on the basis of a name, place of origin (anywhere in the eastern provinces of the empire would do), collateral relations, in-laws, friendships, and alliances. Any link, no matter how tenuous, now serves to make one into "an Armenian." Finally, once networks of these alleged "Armenians" were established, historians then began to attribute specific acts and behaviors to the underlying ethnic bond among them, racializing their politics.

This is a house of cards. We have seen that even explicit attributions of Armenian ethnicity in the primary sources may not mean much when it comes to the identity of individuals. Clearly, they meant something or else they would not have been remembered, recorded, or invented, but their existential valence may have been quite different from how they are used in scholarship. Consider the significance of personal names. Prominent men in Byzantine history are often—and in some cases always—labeled as Armenians if they bear a name that was common in Armenia, or which can be etymologized as a calque, translation, or even a distortion of an Armenian name, resulting in some remarkably far-fetched connections that are proffered with a straight face only because the underlying illogic of the fallacy has taken such a strong hold in the field. This methodology of "ethnicity by name" persists even though it has correctly been recognized as problematic.[36] Armenian names such as Bardas and Bardanes were popular and fashionable within Roman society, just as Germanic names had been fashionable between the fourth and sixth centuries and for largely the same reasons: with Armenian noblemen taking positions of military and political leadership, their names became prestigious for Romans. This had happened in previous Roman tradition too, with Etruscan, Oscan, Greek, and other names. The consul of 56 BC, Lucius Marcius Philippus, was not a "Greek." Emperors named Michael and John were not Jews. The states of Massachusetts and Ohio are not more "Indian" than New York and Pennsylvania, and John F. Kennedy was not an Irishman.

Mixed marriages, such as that of Maria the Younger, disseminated common Armenian names further, regardless of the culture or ethnicity of their bearers. Besides, there is a curious double standard at work, in that those specific names were actually of Iranian origin, but no one proposes that their Byzantine bearers were "really" Persians.[37] By contrast, rarer names such as Mosele and Artabasdos may be more reliable indicators of an Armenian ancestry, though not of an Armenian identity in the present.[38] The basic problem with this entire approach is that the presumed etymology of one's name has little or no bearing on one's ethnicity. Consider the tenth-century Roman legal historian Symbatios. It is convention in the field for this name to mark one as an Armenian (Smbat), but Symbatios, who takes obvious pride in the Roman ethnonym and stresses the lines of continuity between his culture and ancient Rome, "would have thought of himself as no less Roman—despite the Hellenized form of his Armenian name—than Cicero or Julius Caesar."[39]

In practice, the Armenian fallacy is more tenuous than this onomastic error. It would be one thing if we had a network of allied individuals at the court *all* of whom had "Armenian" names. That might even be interesting. What we actually find is different. I will expose these problems by scrutinizing Signes Codoñer's recent book on the emperor Theophilos. It is an excellent book that clears up many problems concerning the reign, and I have relied on it and cited it frequently in the present study. One part of it, however, is unpersuasive, namely the proposal that Theophilos' court was dominated by an Armenian faction that acted in explicit awareness of its ethnicity.[40] This is a fiction, and typical of much of the scholarship. Let us see how it is constructed.

The leader of the Iconoclasts at the court of Theophilos was the patriarch Ioannes the Grammarian, a man vilified and cast as a wizard in Iconophile texts, though he is also presented as a formidable figure. Theophanes Continuatus says this explicitly about him: "He was not a foreigner or a recent arrival, but a true native offspring of this Queen of Cities . . . nor did he come from a humble family, but from one that was quite noble, called Morocharzanioi."[41] The name of this family provides no clues as to ethnicity. Based on the rest of this testimony (in a hostile source, no less) it would seem a hopeless task to try and make Ioannes into "an Armenian," far less into "the leader of the 'Armenian' party." But this is exactly what Signes Codoñer does, by pointing to the alleged names of his father and brother (Pankratios and Arsaber respectively): "This links the family with the Armenian Bagratids."[42] No, it doesn't. Even if the name of his father is accurately reported, Pankratioi are attested in Roman service already in the sixth century,[43] and the source that reports his father's name is clearly trying to link the warlock-patriarch to a famous astrologer of the eighth century with the same name; in fact, the name "Pankrates" was a professional name taken by a number of magicians in antiquity.[44] No source calls Ioannes an Armenian, gives him an Armenian ancestry, or claims that he consorted with Armenians, even though that would have been a convenient way to portray him as a sinister outsider in the polemic that was later directed against him by Iconophiles, as was done with Leon V. This is almost proof that the patriarch was not regarded in Byzantine society as an Armenian. Incidentally, his cousin was Leon the Philosopher, a major thinker of the ninth century. Signes Codoñer is reluctant to Armenianize him too but another scholar confidently makes that connection, on the premise that the cousin of anyone whose father had an Armenian-sounding name must also have been "an Armenian."[45]

Signes Codoñer also postulates that "it was important for [Theophilos] to give some satisfaction to the Armenian supporters of his inner group . . . with an 'Armenian' wedding."[46] The marriage to his "Armenian" empress Theodora was arranged either by Theophilos' (probable) mother Thekla or by his father Michael II's second wife Euphrosyne, both of whom Signes Codoñer labels as Armenians. However, no source calls any of these women Armenians or sees them as agents of an Armenian faction, so we must scrutinize the basis for these claims. Signes Codoñer identifies Thekla as an Armenian because she was *possibly* the daughter of Bardanes the Turk, a leading general of the time and, apparently, also one of the "leading Armenians" of the time.[47] However, there is no evidence at all that he was an Armenian. All the sources consistently report that Bardanes was called "the Turk," whatever that meant. Yet because of his personal name, his ethnic moniker is disregarded and he is reclassified as an Armenian, and his alleged daughter along with him (because—remember—if any of your ancestors is an Armenian, you too are "an Armenian"). All this is fiction.

What about Euphrosyne, the daughter of Konstantinos VI and second wife of Michael II? She, Signes Codoñer claims, "was also of Armenian blood, for her mother Maria of Amnia came from a Paphlagonian family of Armenian descent."[48] Note, however, that Maria of Amnia had married Leon IV (775–780), who was not an Armenian, and that Euphrosyne herself had been raised at the court as a princess of the Romans; therefore, she can have been an Armenian only through a distant relation of "blood," but this is sufficient for the fallacy to kick in. Yet what proof is there that Maria of Amnia's Paphlagonian family was "of Armenian descent?" The chronicler Theophanes reports that Maria was brought to the court from the Armeniakoi region, but this refers to the Roman theme of that name, not to her ethnicity.[49] Maria's family is known to us through the *Life of Saint Philaretos the Merciful*, a saintly romance about her father, which does not, however, claim that the family was Armenian; it says only that they lived in the territory throughout which the court sent its men to find a royal bride, namely "the land of the Romans."[50] However, Maria had a cousin named Bardas, which is apparently enough to label her entire extended family as Armenian, including her daughter Euphrosyne, even though she was raised at court. As it happens, the *Life* itemizes the names of everyone in Maria's family, and they are: Philaretos, Ioannes, Hypatia, Euanthia, Myranthia, Petronas, Anthis, Niketas, Petros, Kosmou, Michael, Eirene, Bardas, Eustathios, Helene, and Euphemia. This is a veritable garden of classical Greek and Christian names, but a single Bardas, who is not even here called an Armenian, apparently trumps all the rest in the logic of the fallacy.[51] And that is the entire basis for the claim that Euphrosyne was "of Armenian blood."

What, then, about Theodora, whose marriage to Theophilos was supposed to appease the (alleged) Armenian faction? As the restorer of icons in 843, many texts discuss her, yet none refers to her Armenian ethnicity. As we have seen, for example regarding Maria of Vizye, Konstantinos (the ancestor of Genesios), and Alexios Mosele, an Armenian ancestry was the sort of thing that Byzantine sources could mention without harming the reputations of their subjects; it was not something that had to be hidden. But they say nothing of the sort regarding Theodora. So what is the claim based on? She was from the province of Paphlagonia and her parents were named Marinos and Theoktiste Florina. Signes Codoñer lamely suggests that the name Marinos may have been popular among Armenians, but the key pieces of evidence are, first, that her brother was named Bardas—a name treated like a DNA marker of Armenian ethnicity. Yet her other siblings were named Petronas, Sophia, Maria, and Eirene. This gets us nowhere. The second piece of evidence is that her uncle Manuel—apparently paternal—is in fact said in the sources to have been an Armenian or, rather, "descended from the Armenians."[52] Signes Codoñer concludes that this "confirmed the Armenian descent of her family."[53] But why? Surely we can imagine a number of scenarios that could have included an uncle "descended from the Armenians" (which, as we have seen, still does not mean that he "was" an Armenian). It is significant that the sources make this claim about him only and not about any other member of this well-documented family; they especially do not make this claim about his niece, the empress Theodora. This is true not only in the Roman sources. The thirteenth-century Armenian historical compiler Vardan explicitly calls Manuel a Mamikonian (a leading Armenian clan), but not Theodora or any other member of her family.[54]

The preceding discussion of Theophilos' wider family has exposed the strained logic and fictions that the Armenian fallacy requires, and it undermines the theory that his court was "controlled by Armenians."[55] Two of its prominent members, Alexios Mosele and Manuel, are said to have had Armenian ancestry, but even this does not necessarily mean that they were less Roman than the rest of the court. There is also no proof that they based their actions on their ethnicity (when Manuel had to flee the court at one point he went

THE ARMENIAN FALLACY

not to Armenia but to the caliphate). Interestingly, Signes Codoñer often places the words "Roman" and "Romanized" in scare quotes while treating "Armenian" straightforwardly, as if it did not require similar skepticism.[56] It would be more accurate to do the exact opposite. It is the Armenian claims that are made on behalf of Roman generals in the sources that must be treated as deliberate strategies of distinction among the Roman military elite. At one point, Signes Codoñer correctly warns that "we must be very careful with these genealogies, used by individuals for particular purposes but not necessarily reflecting any real ancestry."[57] Unfortunately, his own methodology ignores this warning.

The Armenian fallacy is pervasive, and I have focused on this one book because it is recent (2014), offers an otherwise excellent reconstruction of a reign, exhibits many of the far-fetched connections and associations that are often used to convert Romans into Armenians, and uses them to build up to a big thesis about the power of "Armenians" at the court. The next step is to postulate that these Armenians behaved in ethnic solidarity: if two men "were of Armenian origin, some kind of special relationship between them is to be presupposed," and "Armenian elites favored marriage among [their] countrymen."[58] But there is no proof for either notion that does not rest on the fallacy. Moreover, it is risky (or worse) to believe that people will "band together" and form a faction based on common ancestry. Armenians were just as divided among themselves.[59]

It has become customary for scholars of Byzantium to attach Armenian ethnic labels to Roman families whose history unfolded entirely within the empire and never in Armenia. This type of racialized thinking is widespread and mainstream. A vigorous debate has taken place on whether such and such a family did or did not have an Armenian ancestry, but rarely is it asked why that one strand of ancestry is treated with such exceptional attention, especially when the families in question and the sources about them made no such claims to an Armenian ancestry. If they did make such a claim, we should ask what it meant in its Roman context. If they did not, and the sources did not either, we should wonder why we deem it so important to make them ourselves. The grounds on which these ethnic origins are alleged are often extremely tenuous, and this whole way of thinking rests on the assumption that "families" have aboriginal ethnicities that in some unexplained way define them forever after.

In the absence of firm historical evidence for ethnic claims, aboriginal ethnicities are modern fictions and so debates over them have an unreal quality. Moreover, recent scholarship has "appreciably reduced [the] more enthusiastic earlier estimates" by Adontz and Charanis regarding the number of Roman families of Armenian descent.[60] The families of Phokas, Dalassenos, Bourtzes, and Doukas have been removed from that list, on which they had been placed originally for the same flimsy (i.e., nonexistent) reasons.[61] Yet we may be skeptical of many who have survived this winnowing process too, for example the Lakapenos, Kourkouas, and Skleros families, whom Byzantinists routinely call "Armenians." Let us look at them.

Romanos I Lakapenos (920–944) is discussed in many Roman sources, but none of them calls him an Armenian. His father was Theophylaktos Abastaktos, who is also not called an Armenian in the single report that we have about him (but because Romanos was of humble origin and is assumed to have been "of Armenian descent," his father has retroactively been reclassified as "an Armenian peasant").[62] However, Liudprand, the bishop of Cremona in Italy who visited Constantinople after Romanos' reign, does report that Romanos was "of humble origin and of the Armenian people."[63] This is odd. Why would no Byzantine source mention this, but we find it instead in a Latin text written by a foreigner? Fortunately, this is easy to explain. Romanos came from the village of Lakapa, which the Romans situated in the theme of Armeniakon (broadly defined). For example, Romanos found a wife for the brother of the Bulgarian tsar, and she was a woman from Romanos' "own homeland in the Armeniakon (Ἀρμενιακῶν) theme."[64] It would be easy for a Latin writer such as Liudprand to muddle the distinction between an Armenios (an Armenian) and an Armeniakos (a resident of the Roman theme of the Armeniakoi), especially as the Byzantines, following ancient conventions, could refer to people from a specific province of the empire as having their *genos* or *patris* there. One could be "an Armeniakos by *genos*" or "from a *genos* of the Armeniakon."[65] These labels were not ethnicities, but designations of a specific provincial origin. It could be said of a woman that she "drew her *genos* from the Opsikion," that is, the theme of that name. No modern scholar has postulated an Opsikian ethnicity on that basis.[66] Likewise, one's *genos* could be from the province Boukellarioi,[67] or, as here, from the Armeniakoi.

If Lakapa has been correctly identified—of which I am not certain—it lay between Kaisareia and Melitene in eastern Cappadocia.[68] In 908, this region was incorporated into the theme of Lykandos founded by Melias (Mleh), an (actual and so-called) Armenian in Roman service. The theme was subsequently settled by Armenians, but this happened long after Romanos I's association with the place, whatever exactly it was (he was born around 870). We are explicitly told that when Melias was authorized to create this frontier theme, "he found the land empty and uninhabited."[69] So we should not project its later (mostly Armenian) demography onto the ninth century, when the territory belonged to the wider orbit of the Armeniakon theme. In fact, there is a good reason to doubt that Romanos' origins in Lakapa (assuming he was from there) had anything to do with his ethnicity. The one thing that we know about his father Abastaktos is that he saved the life of the emperor Basileios I in battle, in 871. Offered a reward, Abastaktos refused offices and titles and asked instead for a *topos basilikos*, which in context probably means imperial land on which to settle.[70] Basileios I was just then creating new themes in the east, specifically the theme Charsianon, which was founded between 863 and 872 in territory detached from Armeniakon that included the future Lykandos.[71] It is therefore likely that Romanos was from Lakapa because his father settled there in an earlier phase of Roman expansion in the region.

Romanos was not "an Armenian." But his alleged ethnicity has been repeated so often in the literature that it has acquired the status of a known fact, even though it is based on the most tenuous of indirect connections. It is therefore all the more important that we not use his alleged origins to explain his policies, as has also been done,[72] especially when we can explain those policies just as well without it. Even if he had (some) Armenian ancestry, we still should not use it to explain his actions. Ancestry is not destiny. That belief is what today we call "racism." It is also a mistaken way of explaining people's actions.

A word of clarification must be said here about the Armeniakon theme and its population. Historians often conclude from its name that its population must have been predominantly Armenian, but this inference can be conclusively refuted. The name of this middle Byzantine theme derives from the name of the field army established much farther to the east in 528 by Justinian to operate in Armenia. The general in command of this army held the title *magister militum per Armeniam et Pontum Polemoniacum et gentes*. When that army was pulled back to Asia Minor during the defeats of the seventh century, it gave its name to the huge new province of Armeniakon (the same happened with other provinces in Asia Minor into which the other field armies were withdrawn).[73]

Neither the original field army created by Justinian nor its descendant thematic army in Asia Minor was named after the ethnic origin of their soldiers, though this error is sometimes asserted.[74] Justinian's edict instituting the army *per Armeniam* survives along with narrative sources about the event, and they all say that the new army was made up of Roman soldiers who were transferred there from Roman armies elsewhere. They were *specifically* meant to replace the inadequate units of local Armenians used by the governors of Roman Armenia down to that point, in order to "make the Roman army less dependent militarily on local levies and the armed retinues of members of the indigenous Armenian aristocracy."[75] It is possible that over time that army did recruit soldiers locally, but that is not where its name came from. The name came from its being stationed *in* Armenia.

When the army retreated from Armenia proper into Asia Minor, it kept its name even though it was now stationed in Roman territories whose population contained a smaller Armenian element (as we will see in Chapter 6). The names of Roman provinces are no sure indication of their ethnic makeup. This is certainly the case with Armeniakon, whose name stems from a Roman army that was created to operate in Armenia but was then pulled back into Asia Minor. But the names of other provinces along the frontier sometimes gestured to what lay beyond them, for example the late Roman Balkan province of Scythia (which was not inhabited by Scythians), the theme of Longobardia (in Apulia), the command of Iberia (which contained only a small part of Georgia, Kartli), and the theme of Mesopotamia. We can perhaps think of the relationship between Armeniakon and Armenia as that between the U.S. state of New Mexico and the adjacent country of Mexico. Many Mexicans live in New Mexico along with American citizens of Mexican origin, but most of the population is neither.

Our imperial geographer Konstantinos VII says that Armeniakon took its name from the Armenian people who lived "adjacent to its border" and that the theme was located "in proximity to them," which is true because Justinian's field army was stationed in Armenia, to the east of the later Armeniakon theme. Konstantinos adds that parts of the theme by Koloneia, that is, the easternmost parts, were inhabited by Armenians.[76] This is significant: Konstantinos VII could distinguish between Armenians and Romans living in the theme of Armeniakon, and the former were in his view a majority in only one small region. Therefore, we should not automatically assume that a person from Armeniakon was also an Armenian. Charanis claimed that the thematic army of Armeniakon "consisted primarily of Armenians," but the passage of Theophanes that he cites as proof demonstrates instead that the "Armenians" were a separate unit from the regular army of the Armeniakon theme, thus directly undercutting his argument.[77] (This sort of confusion could be avoided if scholars were willing to place Byzantium in its larger Roman context. No historian of the later Republic would argue that the *Legio I Germanica* was composed of Germans.)

Roman writers were usually consistent in distinguishing between ethnic Armenians and the inhabitants and soldiers of the Armeniakon theme, even when the two overlapped.[78] Consider the case of "Artabasdos, an Armenian and the general of the Armeniakoi."[79] Sometimes there was slippage between the two concepts, or scribal errors in copying these two words that looked similar, but this does not affect the case of Romanos I Lakapenos. There are also modern scholars, proponents of the Armenian fallacy, who carelessly write Ἀρμενίων ("of the Armenians") when the text actually says Ἀρμενιακῶν ("of the Armeniakoi theme"), and thereby produce more fictitious "Armenians."[80] At any rate, we can now understand the origin of the misleading report in Liudprand.

If we scrutinize the evidence that is cited to prove that other Roman families were "of Armenian descent," we obtain the same negative results, even if we focus on those cases that have been "chosen very conservatively from families still considered of clear Armenian origin, such as the Skleroi (despite the reservations of Kazhdan), Lakapenoi, Kourkouas-Tzimiskai," and others.[81] These are supposed to be the safest examples, but upon inspection they turn out to be flimsy. The Skleros family is often touted as "Armenian," but the evidence for this claim is just as tenuous as for the Lakapenoi, in fact more so. It consists of one early ninth-century Skleros said by a highly unreliable text (the *Chronicle of Monembasia*) to have come from the Roman province of Armenia Minor (not that he was "an Armenian"), and this figure may or may not have been related to the later family with the same surname.[82] No source claims that any later Skleros—say, in the later tenth century—was "an Armenian," though many scholars make that claim.

Beyond their alleged ancestry, however, what exactly are we saying about otherwise fully Roman figures such as Bardas Skleros and Ioannes Tzimiskes when we call them "Armenians" or "of Armenian descent"? Even if one believes in blood—whatever that means— "after very few generations of intermarriages, such as those between the 'Iberian' Phokades and the 'Armenian' Skleroi or Kourkouas Tzimiskai . . . the question of *limpieza de sangre* could hardly be raised."[83] We must, moreover, remember that this entire discussion is conducted in a realm of modern fantasy, since the original sources, which were capable of mentioning someone's ethnicity when it was relevant (and even when it was not), say nothing whatever about "Iberian" Phokades or "Armenian" Skleroi. In fact, in the sources "Byzantines of Armenian origin are ethnically identified as to origin more frequently than are Byzantines of any other origin."[84] This gives us a presumptive basis to treat silence as absence.

Jean-Claude Cheynet correctly observes that "after a few generations nostalgic feelings toward a family's place of origin could gradually vanish. Nothing indicates that the Skleroi of the eleventh century felt the importance of their Armenian roots, or that the

Branades of the twelfth–thirteenth centuries remembered their Slavic origins." Yet in a footnote he adds: "By contrast, during the tenth century, Bardas Skleros' revolt was largely supported by Armenians," the implication being that he was drawn to them (or they to him) on the basis of ethnic affinity.[85] It is common for historians to postulate ethnic affinities in the case of this war.[86] Some versions of the Armenian fallacy here outdo themselves, such as the proposal that Armenians may have supported Skleros because they remembered the Armenian blood of the emperor Ioannes Tzimiskes (969–976), Skleros' former son-in-law.[87] Moreover, the fallacy always has to be selective as, according to some of its other incarnations, Skleros' enemies (the Phokades and the Macedonian dynasty) were also of Armenian descent or Armenians.[88] Did all this Armenian blood cancel itself out at some point, like Buridan's ass? If all Byzantines were Armenian, there could not then have been an Armenian faction among them.

Skleros did in fact receive support from ethnic Armenian units when he rebelled against Basileios II in 976–979 and again later in 989. But his rebel army was predominantly Roman, and he also sought support from Arabs, Kurds, and others, eventually also the Persian Buyids.[89] The prominence of Armenians in his army was due to the fact that he raised his rebellion in the southeast, in regions that the empire had militarized in the tenth century through the settlement of Armenian colonists. There is no reason to think that Skleros' choice of allies had anything to do with ethnic affinity, nor do our sources suggest anything like that. What we have is a rebel general mustering all the support that he could find. Let us keep in mind that Skleros' "Armenian roots" have not been proven, anyway; that the family has a documented history of imperial service since the early ninth century, almost two hundred years before the rebellion, which is more than just a few generations; and that much of that service took place in the empire's Balkan provinces. There is no reason to ethnicize Bardas Skleros' wartime politics.

Many more individuals and families have been ethnicized on the basis of such flimsy or inconclusive evidence, their behaviors then explained on the basis of "race" or "blood." The eleventh-century general Katakalon Kekaumenos—a thoroughly Roman figure—is said in one article to have "still had affinities with his old race," which of course is Armenian.[90] It would be otiose to interrogate all such claims. If the reader has not already been convinced that this methodology is flawed, more examples will not make a difference. The preceding analysis will have served its purpose if the reader, forewarned, approaches this racial fallacy in Byzantine Studies with due skepticism.

"Armenian" Emperors

The consensual mass hallucination that is the Armenian fallacy has populated Byzantine history with a series of alleged "Armenian" emperors. A longer list of them (proposed by Adontz) has been winnowed down by later scholars to a few cases that are "self-evident," including Philippikos Bardanes (711–713), Leon V (813–820), Basileios I (867–886), Romanos I Lakapenos (920–944), and Ioannes I Tzimiskes (969–976).[91] As we saw, however, the case of Romanos I Lakapenos is hardly self-evident, and, when we follow the trail of footnotes for *most* of the rest too, to say nothing of Maurikios (582–602), Herakleios (610–641), or Nikephoros I (802–811), it becomes apparent that these confident assertions are built on sand and have become established only through uncritical repetition. But before we delve into the dubious methodologies by which Armenian emperors have been manufactured, we have again to question what exactly is being asserted. What does it mean to call an emperor an "Armenian" when neither he, his subjects, or any actual Armenians recognized him as such? When no such claim is made about him in the sources? When his language, religion, political affiliation, and cultural profile were all Roman?

The answer to these questions is that we are saying nothing that has any literal content, but it only seems meaningful because it draws its substance from the vigorous claims of Armenian national historiography. This, like modern Greek national historiography, has benefited from the dismissive way in which scholarship treats Roman ethnicity. To clarify, we are not interested here in *past* ancestry but in *present* ethnicity. It was in fact possible, albeit rare, for Roman emperors to have "ethnic" profiles. But these are noted in the sources, as contemporaries were quite capable of making observations about ethnicity. Septimius Severus had Punic North African traits.[92] Zeno was an Isaurian, which was explicitly held against him as making him less than fully Roman.[93] Michael II was said to be affiliated in some way with the heretical sect of the Athinganoi in central Asia Minor and to have followed some of their odd ways; he also seems to have had a speech impediment.[94] Alexios I Komnenos had a lisp.[95] Emperors are the most documented individuals, yet about none is it said that he spoke Greek with an Armenian accent, spoke Armenian at all, or followed Armenian customs in his private life.

The present section will first discuss some emperors to whom I believe Armenian ancestry has erroneously been attributed by modern scholarship. It will then discuss some emperors to whom an Armenian ancestry is attributed in some primary sources and assess the ways in which that factoid is relevant in our understanding of their reigns.

The alleged Armenian ancestry of the emperor Maurikios (582–602) is largely unknown to historians who study his reign, even though it was "proven" by Adontz in 1934 and confirmed by Charanis in 1965.[96] No contemporary source—and there are many—mentions it. They all say that he came from Arabissos in Cappadocia, in the province of Armenia II. A historian writing during his reign, Euagrios, says that his family and name came from Old Rome, which may just be flattery, whereas an eighth-century western historian, Paul the Deacon, says that he was "a Cappadocian by race ... the first emperor from the race of the Greeks," whatever that means.[97] None of the names in his extended family are Armenian. It is only a later list of emperors, possibly from the eleventh century, which says that Maurikios was "by *genos* an Armenian," but this chronicle regularly converts provincial origins into *genos*, according to the ancient convention in the Roman empire that turned provincial origins into artificial ethnicities. Thus the emperor Markianos was "by *genos* an Illyrian," Leo I was "by *genos* a Thracian," Zeno was "by *genos* an Isaurian," Justin I was "a Thracian," Tiberios II was "by *genos* a Cappadocian," and so on.[98] Maurikios was, as we said, from the province of Armenia II, a fact that would have been known to many Romans not only from geography but also because the bishopric of

Arabissos belonged to the ecclesiastical province of Armenia, even in later times.

The "proof" of Maurikios' Armenian origins is provided by a much later set of Armenian folktales told about the emperor. Adontz himself admitted that these tales were unhistorical in almost every way, but he selectively defended the nugget of the emperor's origins in Armenia. Again, every punch is pulled for the purpose of making a Roman into an Armenian. Charanis conceded that the historical emperor Maurikios distrusted the Armenians, and seventh-century sources claim that he formulated aggressive policies against them.[99] Yet he tried to argue around these reports by reasoning that Maurikios' intimate knowledge of the Armenians' bad qualities—the grounds of his hostility—meant that he was one of them. (The same argument has been used by another historian, again with a straight face, for the emperor Nikephoros II Phokas: he was so hostile to the Armenians in his legal and military works that he must have been one himself.)[100] Charanis also has to argue around the fact that Maurikios' Armenian ethnicity is not mentioned by a much earlier, and more sober, Armenian historian, pseudo-Sebeos (of the seventh century). Charanis responds by saying that this does not count because pseudo-Sebeos also does not mention the Armenian ancestry of the emperor Herakleios, which is a sacred cow of the Armenian fallacy. So let us take a closer look at Herakleios.

The Armenian ethnic origin of the emperor Herakleios (610–641) takes the prize for fiction masquerading as history. Even the *Prosopography of the Later Roman Empire*, the standard reference work of the field, asserts that "the family was Armenian," a conclusion that is more tentatively endorsed in the most recent biography of the emperor.[101] The scholarly imagination has here run riot: not only was he Armenian, Herakleios was "related to the Arsacids of Armenia and came from the Arsacid princedom of Carenitis" (i.e., Karin). His Greek name was a translation of Vahagn, an Armenian pagan god sometimes equated with Herakles.[102] He may have been the great-great-grandson of Hovanes Arshakuni.[103] "Presumably he was bilingual"—though it is immediately conceded that there is no proof for that.[104] His politics and military strategy are examined in light of his Armenian ethnicity and his relationship to "his Armenian compatriots."[105]

Just so that we are clear, *there is not a single primary source* that says that Herakleios was an Armenian. The statements in the paragraph above have been woven out of thin air. The biographer I mentioned, Walter Kaegi, admits that "we have no evidence on what Armenian consciousness, if any, Heraclius possessed."[106] But identity without awareness is just racial thinking. The later Byzantine sources call Herakleios a Libyan, because that was where he was based when he rebelled against Phokas in 602, and a Cappadocian.[107] Moreover, none of the names in his extended family are Armenian, and this in an age when Armenian generals in Roman service kept their native names and did not always switch to Graeco-Roman ones. So where does the error come from?

The fiction of Herakleios' Armenian ancestry is based on a single sentence in the historian Theophylaktos Simokattes that refers to the military career of the emperor's father, also named Herakleios. In late 587, Herakleios the Elder was a general serving under Philippikos, the *magister militum per Orientem*. The latter had just found out (in Constantinople) that he had been replaced by Priskos. He wrote to Herakleios the Elder in the east ordering him "to leave the army and return to his own city in Armenia," transferring the army over to Narses, the commander at Konstantine (a city in the province of Osrhoene).[108]

This passage cannot bear the weight that has been placed on it. First, it does not call Herakleios the Elder an Armenian. It says only that "his own city" was in Armenia, which certainly means Roman Armenia, the four (militarized) provinces of that name that were populated by both Romans and Armenians. Second, "his own city" in Armenia certainly refers to Herakleios' command headquarters, not his home town. It would make no sense in the context of the narrative for Philippikos to send Herakleios "home." Herakleios was not being decommissioned but being given orders for moving the army within his command territory. This was exactly how the translators of Theophylaktos understood the passage, one of whom, Michael Whitby, is the leading historian of the wars in question:

Herakleios was being sent back to his headquarters at Theodosioupolis (Erzurum).[109] He was still active in the same military post for the next couple of years: he had not been sent "home."[110] There is no ethnicity here, no proof that "he was born in the region of Karin."[111] The passage says and implies nothing about where Herakleios the Elder was "from." Even if he was "from" a Roman city in Armenia, such as Theodosioupolis, that would not mean he was "an Armenian." Those places had been crawling with Roman soldiers, officers, and their families ever since Justinian established the massive field army *per Armeniam* manned largely (and deliberately) with non-Armenians. Justinian had also established a civilian, legal, and bureaucratic apparatus tasked with imposing Roman law on the four Armenian provinces.[112] As with the theme of Armeniakon, we should not mistake administrative labels with demography and ethnicity. The four Armenian themes had been formed in part by imperial expansion into Armenian lands but also through the subdivision of the former Roman province of Cappadocia. Even if Herakleios' "home" or residence was in one of them—which the passage in Theophylaktos does not suggest—that would say nothing about his ethnicity, and even less about the ethnicity of his son.

Another house of cards collapses here: there is no proof that Herakleios was an Armenian. The seventh-century Armenian historian pseudo-Sebeos, who wrote but a generation later, mentions Herakleios the Elder and his son many times but never says that they were Armenians.[113] As far as I know, no Armenian historian calls Herakleios an Armenian. Never has the Armenian fallacy built up so much on the basis of so little, as it has here.

Ioannes I Tzimiskes (969–976) is also widely considered to have been "an Armenian," but the grounds for this are extremely weak. First, he came from the Armeniakon theme, but the name of this theme, as we saw above, did not reflect its demography. The second reason is his nickname—Tzimiskes is not a family name—which is said in a history written by a Roman contemporary to be an Armenian word referring to the emperor's short stature, in which case he must have earned it as an adult.[114] For all we know, it was given to him by Armenian soldiers serving under him. A much later and far less reliable historian, Matthew of Edessa, claimed that the nickname came from the similar-sounding name of the village in which Tzimiskes was allegedly born, near Hozat in modern Turkey (also in the Armeniakon theme, broadly defined). However, this claim occurs in the midst of a purely fictional romance that requires Tzimiskes to have been born in that area for dramatic narrative purposes. It may simply be an invention based on the similarity of the names and, besides, it does not make Tzimiskes into an Armenian to begin with, and neither does Matthew nor any other source claim that he was one.[115] Nor, as far as we know, was Tzimiskes related to any Armenians. No ethnicity or even distant ancestry can be proposed based on such evidence.

Unlike Maurikios, Herakleios, and Tzimiskes, there are other emperors who are said by roughly contemporary sources to have had Armenian ancestry. Still, in not one case can we say that these were "Armenian emperors" in any meaningful sense. As far as we know, they were all Romans of (possible) Armenian ancestry. None of them exhibits any cultural or biographical traits that would associate him with Armenia. Moreover, individually they present certain idiosyncrasies in their alleged Armenianness that are worth examining.

Philippikos Bardanes (711–713) is said to have been "an Armenian by *genos*" or "a Persarmenian by *genos*." For all we know, he was of Persian rather than Armenian ancestry, but we lack an Iranian lobby to push for its own "ethnic rights" in Byzantine Studies. Our sources for his origin also condemn him for his evil ecclesiastical policies and erroneous theology (Monothelitism).[116] They may be highlighting his ethnicity to make him look more foreign, though there is no reason to think that they were simply inventing it. The move to link his ethnicity and doctrinal views has been made even more explicitly by modern historians.[117] But how far back did Bardanes' ethnic background lie? His father Nikephoros was active at the Roman court in the 660s, under Konstas II, which means that Bardanes was probably born and raised in Romanía; possibly, his father was too.[118] The suggestion that they were descended from the fifth-century Armenian hero Vardan II Mamikonian is a modern fiction.[119] A number of sources testify to Bardanes' tutoring, scholarly interests, learning, and eloquence, which were all in Greek.[120] It is likely, in that age of iron, that he highlighted these attributes of elite culture in order to compensate for his ethnic past, which is why many sources comment on them. We have seen how provincials with possible ethnic origins (e.g., Niketas *magistros*) used classical learning to showcase their Roman credentials.

Philippikos Bardanes is especially interesting in this connection because of his decision to expel all Armenians from the empire, forcing them to seek refuge among the Arabs, though the extent to which this was enforced is unknown. This measure followed upon a decree ordering all Armenians to accept the authority of the patriarch of Constantinople, though it is unclear whether this decree was issued by Philippikos or Justinian II, his predecessor.[121] The perverse illogic of the Armenian fallacy would link this anti-Armenian policy to Philippikos' Armenian ethnicity. In reality, it shows that despite his ancestry he was not, and did not consider himself to be, "an Armenian," as some modern historians call him.[122] Interestingly, a later (tenth-century?) Armenian history does call him "an Armenian noble." Was its author engaging in an early version of the Armenian fallacy, making guesses based on the emperor's name alone? This would explain why the attribution is so vague, lacking the details of family affiliation that Armenian memory so cherished.[123]

Three more emperors are said in the earliest sources about them to have had an Armenian ancestry: Artabasdos (a rebel general who briefly took power in Constantinople in the early 740s), Leon V (813–820), and Basileios I (867–886). We do not know enough about the first to have an interesting discussion of his ethnicity.[124] Leon V's ancestry is said to have been Armenian, Assyrian, and Amalekite (a biblical ethnonym), whatever exactly those terms may have meant in a late eighth-century context.[125] Like Philippikos Bardanes, he was raised in the empire; his father Bardas was a *patrikios* at the court.[126] The tales of his ethnic ancestries are told by later Iconophile texts in order to blacken him further as an Iconoclast heretic, though this does not mean that we can write them off as mere polemic. However, we have no evidence for how Leon V acknowledged, tried to hide or counter, or ameliorated his "ethnic" background as emperor. Matters are different when we turn to Basileios I, however. His dynasty, the Macedonians, produced a phantasmagoric account of Basileios' descent from a royal house of Armenia as well as from

Alexander the Great and Constantine the Great. We are here squarely in the realm of the rhetoric of ethnicity, which means that we must approach the subject from a different angle.

The Politics of Armenian Ethnicity

In Romanía, calling someone an Armenian or claiming an Armenian origin for oneself could be a banal piece of information, but sometimes such claims played into a contested field of ethnic stereotypes, religious animosities, genealogical pretensions, and the politics of belonging and exclusion. To make sense of this chaotic scene, we may start by drawing a general distinction between Roman views of Armenians, including ethnic Armenians who were imperial subjects, and Roman views of Romans who had Armenian ancestry but were in all relevant ways assimilated to Roman norms. The latter category includes almost all the "Armenians" discussed in this chapter. Looking at their careers and diversity, from emperors to saints, it appears that Roman society did not treat them any differently than other Romans. Assimilation was possible and did not carry an ethnic stigma. The Armenian ancestry of these individuals may have been something that they wished to have remembered and associated with their names, though we cannot know. There are a few cases, however, where it was invoked polemically to tarnish their reputations, for example against Philippikos Bardanes and Leon V who were (in retrospect) regarded as heretical and therefore alien to the Christian Roman order.

This stigma was effective because unassimilated ethnic Armenians were generally associated with negative stereotypes. Of course, any people regarded by the Romans as foreign in terms of ethnicity and culture were bound to be viewed negatively. This was certainly the case with the Armenians, starting already in late antiquity. "We live here among Armenian barbarians," wrote the Roman bishops of Armenia II in 458, "who are of the faith, to be sure, but they lack Roman eloquence."[127] But when the Armenian Church refused to accept the Council of Chalcedon, its followers in later centuries were deemed heretical as well as barbarous in Roman eyes, resulting in theological polemics against "the Armenians." These prejudices could combine into vicious images, as we find in a poem attributed to the famous female hymnographer of the ninth century, Kasia (or Kasiane):

> The terrible race of the Armenians
> is deceitful and extremely vile,
> fanatical, deranged, and malignant,
> puffed up with hot air and full of slyness.
> A wise man said correctly about them that
> Armenians are vile when they live in obscurity,
> even more vile when they become famous,
> and most vile in all ways when they become rich.
> When they become filthy rich and honored,
> then to all they seem as vileness heaped upon vileness.[128]

The *Life of Saint Euthymios the Younger* (ca. 900) refers to a monk Ioseph on Mt. Athos as being a simple and good man at heart, "despite his Armenian origin."[129] We see that ethnocultural identifications were present even in this far-off uninhabited corner of the monastic world, in a text written by and for Romans. Armenians were regarded as outsiders even when they were inside the empire. When the empire expanded dramatically in the tenth and eleventh centuries, these slurs could be directed against many of the inhabitants of the new eastern provinces. We have the will of one Eustathios Boïlas who, under adverse circumstances that he does not elucidate, found himself living there in the mid-eleventh century: "I became an emigrant from the land which bore me . . . and I settled among alien nations with strange religion and tongue." He later explains that these were Armenians, whom he mentions right after "snakes, scorpions, and wild beasts."[130]

It is often asserted that the Byzantines respected the fighting prowess of the Armenians, who were allegedly sturdy and valiant soldiers. This probably was the case, given the Armenians' prominent role in the Roman army for so many centuries, but it finds scant expression in Byzantine literature, including in the military manuals and histories. Instead, they are often depicted as unreliable, undisciplined, shifty, and prone to banditry: "The Armenians carry out sentry duty poorly and carelessly ... after all, they are only Armenians."[131] (Conversely, Armenian literature contained plenty of recriminations and stereotypes against Romans.)[132]

These negative images were not limited to elite literature or classicizing tropes that recycled stale ancient polemics. To the contrary, they were produced and most intensely disseminated in the middle Byzantine period, when so many Armenians had entered the empire. We can even speak of popular prejudice in this connection. In the twelfth century, we hear of mimes who performed comic sketches about Arabs and Armenians.[133] With such prejudice at hand, it is not surprising that attacks against emperors and other individuals could also target their (real or only alleged) Armenian origins as aggravating factors. When the patriarch Theodosios Boradiotes made a seemingly underhanded comment to the emperor Andronikos I Komnenos (1183–1185), the latter said, "'Behold our profound Armenian,' because it was said that his family had Armenian roots."[134] Romans of Armenian descent might have faced this commonly, even though they were accepted at all levels of Roman life. This was likely possible because they were not Armenians in any meaningful way.

Still, it is possible that the "melting pot" model does not fully account for the Armenian experience in Romanía. Was it possible for assimilated Armenian-Romans to be proud of their Armenian ancestry? Could it be used to advantage, or even invented for that purpose when it did not exist? This is more difficult to document, but the possibility is enticing. To turn to the field of U.S. sociology, the familiar melting pot model may work as a kind of baseline, but it has been found to be deficient. In particular, it has failed to explain the fact that some groups do not assimilate as quickly or as well as others, or are blocked from assimilating because of racial traits that they cannot leave behind. Some groups may react to persecution or discrimination by withdrawing from the mainstream and forming a separate community (we will see in Chapter 6 that the Paulicians may count as such a group). But other groups, especially from economically better-off immigrant communities, for whom assimilation and "whiteness" is possible, may nevertheless choose to selectively cultivate ethnic networks and affiliations and activate them in advantageous contexts. Moreover, others have failed or refused to entirely forget about their Old World past and continue to cultivate links to it through narratives, ethnic food, dress, and religious customs. This is sometimes called "symbolic ethnicity" and seen as sociologically trivial, for its scope is limited to practices that do not offend the dominant culture.[135] Yet these "white ethnics" (especially Greek, Italian, and Irish Americans) create community organizations and maintain affective ties and networks, for all that they are assimilated to the mainstream.[136]

At present, a sociology of the Byzantine "ethnics" lies beyond our reach, especially when the basic parameters of Roman ethnicity in Romanía are misunderstood by the field on a fundamental level. In addition, we are not in a position to reconstruct the thick context and social valence of ethnic claims, or, in many cases, the biography of those who make them. All I can offer here are some preliminary remarks.

We have seen that gestures of affective ethnicity were made by the first generation of Armenian Romans. Maria the Younger gave half of her children Armenian names. Alexios Mosele lived in a manor house in Constantinople that was presumably named after his city or land of origin in Armenia (whether or not he had ever been there, and more likely not). The language would certainly have been spoken among some assimilated Armenians, just as we saw a network of successfully integrated Persian-speakers in Constantinople in 867. Sometimes origins were remembered, rather than forgotten or actively suppressed. The *Life of Saint Maria the Younger* openly discloses that her father was Armenian but makes sure to reveal that he was powerful and honored by the emperor. The historian Genesios took pride in his grandfather Konstantinos "the Armenian" and sought to praise him at every turn in his narrative. It is also likely that historical sources label individuals as having a (proximate or distant) Armenian origin not only because that was a known fact about them but because they chose to broadcast it and link their name to it. In other words, being of Armenian origin may have had a positive value that pushed against the negative stereotypes that we saw above.

It is not difficult to see what that value was for social elites. Their ethnicity may have been a liability in some contexts in Roman society, but being perceived as nobility or as a member of a royal family (even if only a foreign one) conferred prestige in contexts that may have mattered more to them for political and social purposes. Already in the early seventh century, a governor of Ravenna, Isaakios, took pride in his ethnicity in the epitaph carved on his sarcophagus: "He was the great jewel of the whole of Armenia, an Armenian from a glorious family," but it also says that "he kept Rome safe as a general."[137] This was a Roman general who expressed himself publicly in Greek, even when in Italy, and was certainly Byzantine Orthodox too (he was buried in San Vitale).

The threads of this discussion come together in the emperor Basileios I (867–886). I close this chapter with a closer look at how the politics of ethnicity played out in his case. Basileios was of humble, possibly peasant origin, from Macedonia, which is why he and the dynasty that he founded were called "the Macedonians." He migrated to Constantinople to seek a better life and skillfully maneuvered and murdered his way to the throne. To the extent that the sources allow us to see it, his cultural profile is entirely Roman with no trace of foreign culture, and panegyrical texts written about him during his reign highlight his humble origins to cast him as a new David.[138] But an effort to mythologize this emperor was already under way. When Basileios I died, his son and heir Leon VI composed a funeral oration for him that claimed that he was descended from the royal line of the Arsacids, who were in turn descended from the Persian king Artaxerxes I (465–424 BC), who ruled over a large empire.[139] The Arsacids were, in fact, of Iranian origin, and it was only a later branch of them that ruled Armenia. But Leon's boast lies under the shadow of an infamous scandal. The patriarch Photios is alleged by his enemies of having forged, during the period of his ten-year deposition (867–877), a genealogy for Basileios, trying to flatter his way back into the emperor's favor by tracing his ancestry to the Arsacid Armenian king Tiridates the Great (d. 330), who converted to Christianity.[140] If the story is true, then Leon's funeral oration was based on a forgery.

In the mid-tenth century, when scholars at the court of Basileios' grandson Konstantinos VII produced the *Life of Basileios I*, they fleshed this genealogy out with a full backstory, all of it definitely fictional. To make a long story short, his ancestors were ancient

Armenian Arsacids who moved to the empire at the time of Leo I (457–474) and were resettled in Macedonia-Thrace. Moreover, "they preserved their ancestral nobility and prevented their *genos* from being mixed with others" for centuries thereafter, though they occasionally intermarried with locals. Basileios was also descended from Alexander the Great and Constantine the Great—if you're making it all up anyway, why not add them too?[141]

This incredible story is the main basis for believing that Basileios was of Armenian descent. The claim was recycled in a number of later Roman and Armenian texts, but repetition does not make the original any more true. The Romans generally called Basileios a Macedonian, from his provincial origin, rather than an Armenian, and some Arabic texts call him a Slav. A fierce debate has, predictably, raged among scholars over the issue, as if there could be a single "truth" about his ancestry (the entire debate is premised on the idea of racial purity). Needless to say, the more skeptical one is of court propaganda, and the more one accepts the scandal of Photios' forgery, the less Armenian Basileios ends up looking.[142] Here too the Armenian fallacy has produced its inevitable absurdities: for example, one study proposed that the eastern policies of the empress Theodora (1055–1056), Basileios' great-great-great-granddaughter, were possibly shaped by her Armenian ancestry.[143]

In reality, Basileios' actual ancestry is irrelevant: what matters, as always, is the politics of claims to ancestry. Basileios' son and grandson both advertised his Armenian ancestry, without denying that he was born and raised in Macedonia, and it is likely that Basileios did so himself while he was emperor; otherwise it would be hard to explain why this odd fact was invented about him by his heirs after his death. But why might Basileios have wanted to project an Armenian royal ancestry?

Unfortunately, here we are in the realm of conjecture. First, we must not interpret the Armenian link apart from the others. In the fully developed version of the *Life*, Basileios is descended also from Alexander (which ennobles his Macedonian origins) and Constantine (which burnishes his Roman and imperial credentials). The legends that are told in the *Life* about the young Basileios link him to those figures as well as to Cyrus the Great, David and Solomon, as

THE ARMENIAN FALLACY

well as to prophets of the Old Testament. We know that during his reign Basileios was eager to associate himself with those biblical figures.[144] The Arsacid connection was thus part of a "full-spectrum" propaganda that aimed to confer legitimacy upon this upstart in a wide variety of contexts. As it happens, the *Life of Basileios I* tells of a prophecy pronounced 350 years earlier by one Isaak, another Arsacid, to the effect that an Arsacid would ascend the Roman throne. This prophesy is recorded also in (later) Armenian historiography.[145]

An Arsacid claim may have also given Basileios diplomatic leverage in his dealings with the empire's Armenian neighbors, which might have worked in two ways. First, Basileios was engaged in active warfare near the borders of Armenia against the renegade Paulician sect at Tephrike, which actually had its origins in Armenia.[146] Second, it was during Basileios' reign that Ašot I Bagratuni managed, through skillful diplomacy, to restore the Armenian kingship after a lapse of many centuries and have himself proclaimed king in 884. According to an almost certainly unhistorical later Armenian tradition, Basileios asked Ašot for a crown, the idea being that an Arsacid would want to be crowned by a Bagratid.[147] In reality, it seems instead that Basileios recognized Ašot as *archon* of *archons* and as his spiritual "son," that is, as a subordinate.[148] An Arsacid descent would be useful in this diplomatic context. It is no coincidence that a Roman emperor claimed descent from the ancient Arsacid kings of Armenia just when the status quo in Armenia changed so dramatically.[149] Moreover, at this time we know that Armenian writers were also forging prestigious genealogies for their rulers, which linked them to the Assyrian and Old Testament kings.[150] Basileios' genealogical fictions were perhaps meant to give him leverage.

Looking at the domestic scene, Basileios' Armenian origins were distant enough to not threaten his Roman ethnicity (and, thereby, his ability to claim the throne) but prestigious and hoary enough to rise above the prejudice typically directed at "Armenians." More than most people, an emperor was in a position to choose his ethnicity according to context and deploy it to his advantage both practically and symbolically. We mentioned above the *patrikios* Konstantinos, the Armenian grandfather of the historian Genesios. In a rare episode of reported ethnic solidarity, Konstantinos helped Basileios at an early moment in the latter's career, "being disposed toward him in a friendly way, as his *genos* too was from among the Armenians."[151] Interestingly, when Genesios told the same story he strengthened the connection between the two men, claiming that they were actually related.[152] Genesios was in effect claiming that his grandfather was related to the grandfather of the emperor to whom he was dedicating his history, Konstantinos VII. In this way, "aboriginal" claims of Armenian ethnicity could forge political links that were useful in the present, in the same way that ancient cities used Greek mythology to establish (fictional) ancestral connections when they wanted to establish closer diplomatic relations.[153]

The same kind of insider ethnic connection could, however, just as easily be viewed negatively, if a polemical context activated anti-Armenian prejudices. The *Life of the Patriarch Euthymios* is extremely hostile to Stylianos Zaoutzes, the prime minister appointed by Basileios I to advise his son and heir Leon VI. The text is therefore biased when it reports that Zaoutzes' surname was Armenian and that he was, like Basileios, a Macedonian and Armenian by *genos*, and that was why the emperor appointed him to advise his son.[154] Scholars are right to see this observation as a case of Roman "polemic by ethnicity."[155]

In conclusion, it cannot be doubted that thousands of Armenians lived in the empire, especially between the sixth and the eleventh centuries, served in its armies, and filled its highest offices. "The general consensus continues to be that they were the largest non-Greek unit of that society"[156]—so long as by "Greek" we mean "Roman." However, the field of Byzantine Studies harbors a cottage industry that manufactures "Armenians" left and right. First, specific families and individuals are habitually given Armenian ancestry on flimsy or nonexistent grounds. Second, the field had failed to cope with the reality of assimilation: even "real" Armenians could be Romanized, just like everyone else, and we are fortunate to be able to track this process in the case of specific families over the course of a few generations. By overlooking and even sometimes rejecting the valence of Roman ethnicity in Byzantium, the field fails to distinguish between Armenians proper and Romans who had a (usually distant) Armenian ancestry—among other ancestries that the field does not privilege with the same amount of attention. This habit effaces the role of culture in shaping ethnicity and upholds an outdated racial model. Ethnic claims in Romanía, both real and invented, were political and utilitarian, not biological. It is time for us to retire biological notions of identity.

Personal postscript. Writing this chapter came at the cost of inner conflict. I am fascinated by medieval Armenian history and believe that the Armenians are among the few actual nations of antiquity to make it through all those millennia with a more or less coherent and continuous idea about who they are, a sense that is reflected in their remarkable tradition of historiography.[157] Also, accounts of what Armenians suffered at the start of the twentieth century are enough to make anyone cry. Yet having been raised in a country with a strong national ideology, I can foresee exactly how this chapter will be received by some: as anti-Armenian.[158] This was of course not my intent. I have written this postscript in order to state my purpose directly and emphatically. This chapter calls into question an interpretation of Byzantine history propagated by Byzantinists of all nationalities. When modern Armenian historians first made these claims, they were writing at the birth of their field as a modern discipline, a hundred years ago. It was common at that time to make maximalist claims on behalf of one's nation and claim for it the "great men" of a famous empire. But Byzantinists today should know better than to treat "race" uncritically. If my chapter speaks to current Armenian concerns, it is to debates over diaspora, the loss of identity through intermarriage and assimilation, and the degree to which the future generations of the diaspora in foreign lands still "belong" to the homeland.[159]

6

Was Byzantium an Empire in the Tenth Century?

*Nunc demum iuvat orbem spectare depictum,
cum in illo nihil videmus alienum.*

What Is an Empire?

Byzantium is conventionally called an empire, but it is not at first sight evident that this term withstands critical scrutiny. Beyond mere convention and inertia, there is no systematic investigation of whether or to what degree Romanía fits definitions of empire that are used by scholars who specialize in the history of empires. This field has surged in the past two decades or so, especially after the belated admission that the United States is also an empire of sorts, which has prompted a great deal of comparative work. How "imperial" might Romanía appear if it is brought out of the insular shell of Byzantine Studies and required to play by the rules that have evolved for the comparative study of empires? This will be the first attempt of its kind. I must therefore quote John Haldon, who, in a similar context, wrote that "it is only with some difficulty that I can present a critique of the preexisting literature on the comparative situation and evolution of the Byzantine state, since there is so little to discuss."[1] There is a total lack of theoretical reflection and empirical inquiry on the issue of whether Romanía was an empire.

There are three reasons we might call Romanía an empire, only one of which is a good one. The other two reasons are that it was a direct continuation of the ancient *imperium Romanum* and that its monarch may in some fashion have called himself an emperor (regardless of whether what he ruled was an empire). Let us set these reasons aside for a moment and stick with the more general and cross-disciplinary definition. After all, if we want Romanía to participate in broader discussions about empire, it needs to follow common rules. Limiting the discussion to heirs of the old *imperium* would leave a set of exactly one (or two, if we allow the Germans to crash the party), which is a recipe for isolation.

What is an empire? I distil here from recent bibliography what seems to be a conventional current understanding.[2] An empire is a state that results from the conquest or subjugation by one state or ethnic group of a number of other states or peoples. The conquering state does not have to be a monarchy that is ruled by an "emperor": for instance, democratic Athens and Republican Rome have been studied as empires. Empires do not emerge from the mere titles of monarchs or the political arrangements internal to the conquerors. They are instead defined by an awareness, maintenance, and enforcement of ethnic, cultural, political, or religious differences between the conquerors and conquered. Empire places the two in a hierarchical relationship defined by legal distinctions and differential rights and responsibilities that often entail exploitation based on precisely those differences. The contrast is typically accentuated by the geographical separation of the metropolis or core territory, where the majority of the ruling group or nation lives, from the subjugated peoples who populate the provinces. Therefore, empires are almost by definition multiethnic. "The key marker of an 'imperial' state was thus the degree of 'foreign-ness' perceived to exist between rulers and ruled, conquerors and conquered."[3] And, "empire is differentiated: religiously, nationally, occupationally, and territorially. . . . [It] usually subordinates diverse ethnolinguistic groups or would-be nations."[4] Empires are often large, but it is neither necessary nor possible to specify an absolute requirement of size. The perception that empires are big stems from the fact that they subsume several states or peoples and thus expand the scale of the conquering polity.

Empires are enormously varied within the broad parameters set by this definition, for example in the ways that they exercise control over their provinces (direct vs. indirect, or formal vs. informal). Empires are typically segmented: the various conquered regions are usually not in contact with each other but only with the imperial center, resulting in a hub-and-spoke structure.[5] In the Roman and Byzantine cases, the rim holding the spokes together was the armies along the frontier periphery. A popular recent distinction is that between states that *are* empires and states that *have* empires.[6] For our purposes, I would define this as a distinction between a preexisting state that comes to acquire an empire, which it can lose, whereupon it reverts to being a more circumscribed, possibly ethnic or national polity (ancient Athens, modern Britain, and Napoleonic France are examples of states that acquired empires); and a state that comes into being during the process of acquiring an empire. In the latter case, the loss of empire cannot easily be imagined without a fundamental reconceptualization of the "core" polity, assuming that it can easily be identified (the Sasanian Persian, Arab, and Ottoman empires come to mind here). So *was* Romanía an empire or did it *have* an empire? Or neither of the two?

Imperium and *Imperator*

If we apply the above definitions to earlier phases of Roman history, we obtain some counterintuitive results. Specifically, what we call "the Republic" was far more imperialistic than "the empire." The latter in fact gradually wound down the history of Roman conquests. Also, Rome had an empire long before it had an emperor.[7] But we begin to call it an empire only when it acquires an emperor. The modern taxonomy of ancient Roman history tracks changes in the domestic politics of the *res publica* that are extraneous to the definition of empire that is used by comparative historians today. This is because domestic politics were (and still are) more important in the tradition of western political thought than international relations. Whereas the rest of this chapter will examine Romanía in light of the general definition of empire presented above, we must consider the two other reasons for calling it an empire that I mentioned above, namely that it was the continuation of the ancient *imperium* and that its ruler may have claimed to be an "emperor." These are not good reasons for calling Romanía an empire in a theoretical or comparative context, but they explain why it has conventionally been called that.

The Latin term *imperium*, from which we get the word "empire," did not originally mean that; in fact, it is likely that it never meant that in antiquity. Its original meaning was the power or authority vested in a Roman magistrate. In the late Republic, it could refer to the power of the Roman people as a whole. It was only later, and by extension from this original sense, that it came to acquire a territorial sense, as referring to the lands and people subject to Rome. But even in this sense it did not primarily point to the relation of domination that obtained between Romans and non-Romans. "Subjugation" was not its original meaning and even the emperors used the term *imperium* to refer primarily to the power of their position within the "domestic" Roman political system, not to the rule of Romans over non-Romans. On the other hand, generals who were victorious in battle were acclaimed as *imperatores*, as having conquered their enemy, who was usually a foreign foe. Some received triumphs for this but these were "granted for military success, not for empire-building."[8] So *imperium* could point to what we have defined as empire, but it was not a technical word for it. Moreover, the main "titles" of the Roman emperors were Caesar and Augustus, which did not point to any kind of "imperial" position at all.

Imperium was not among the hundreds of Latin terms relating to politics and public power that entered the Greek language during the early Byzantine period. Thus, after about 600 AD the Romans did not call their territorial state an *imperium*. To be sure, the term had previously been *translated* in various ways into Greek for official use, but those translations referred to the monarchy (*basileia, monarchia*), or to the concentration of power into the hands of the monarch (*autokrator*), or generally to the power or the sphere of command of the Romans (their *ischys* or *arche*).[9] If Romanía was an empire in the sense defined above (a relation of domination among peoples and over territories), then none of these terms *meant* that. They could just as well be applied to nonimperial types of monarchy or just to states in general.

These terms, or a nominalist approach in general, are not going to make Romanía into an empire for us. Moreover, the fact that Romanía was a direct continuation of the ancient Roman *imperium* also does not prove that it was an empire proper, because the ancient *imperium* underwent fundamental changes that call its continued status as an empire into doubt. In 212, all free people of the *imperium* were made into Roman citizens; provincials from formerly conquered peoples increasingly began to fill the highest offices in the state, including the imperial office; there was considerable assimilation of the provincials to the evolving consensus Roman norms; and the emperors and their courts left Rome to reside primarily in the provinces. In these ways, the empire transformed itself from a state in which Romans ruled over non-Romans into a large, unified, and increasingly homogeneous state in which the same rights were distributed across the territory, fractally reproducing Roman social structures regardless of prior ethnicity. Power was no longer exercised by Romans upon non-Romans, whom they had previously called their "slaves." The ruling class, armies, and the emperors themselves were provincialized, while the provinces were Romanized.[10] Exploitation and inequality were no longer a function of territory, the history of subject peoples, or ethnicity.

In many publications, Cliff Ando has argued that, if "empires function through the cultivation of difference" such that "those belonging to the center are equal among themselves in contradistinction to those over whom they [exercise] a collective rule," then Rome after the third century "constitutes a special case."[11] The universal grant of citizenship was "no less than an unprecedented act of imperial self-abrogation," which turned Rome into a different kind of polity.[12] "One might even say that it ceased in any meaningful way to be an empire. It became, rather, something like a state . . . a state that *was*, rather than a state that *had*, an empire—with a uniform law of persons and legal culture, both penetrating universally throughout its territory."[13] Linking Romanía to the tail end of this development will not, therefore, establish it as an empire; quite the contrary.

The official and nonofficial titles of the rulers of Romanía do not signal that they ruled over an empire, that is, over Romans *and* non-Romans. Compare the Achaemenid Persian title "king of kings"; the Sasanian Persian title "king of kings of the Aryans and non-Aryans" (though it is not clear who these subordinate kings were supposed to be); the full titles of the Ottoman sultans that listed all the provinces of their empire;[14] and the long list of territorial and other dependencies still appended to the British and Spanish Crowns. As a Roman equivalent of such lists of conquered peoples or territories we might take the triumphal *cognomina* appended to the imperial title, which named the nations that each emperor had conquered—Alamannicus, Germanicus, and so on. But these indicated only that a people had been defeated in a battle, not necessarily that they had been annexed by the empire and ruled as ethnically different subjects. Moreover, that tradition seems to have lapsed after the seventh century, though it was once revived after a long hiatus, by Manuel I Komnenos, for one occasion in 1166.[15]

Formal titles will not get us to empire, nor are they necessary. After all, not all empires have monarchs with suitably "imperial" titles, nor are they all even monarchies.[16] Byzantinists are wedded to the idea that the Byzantine ruler called himself an emperor and his realm an empire. We take this for granted so much that we use those terms even for its final days when it included only the capital, a few islands, and the Peloponnese. This prompts many historians to comment on the gap between names and reality: "It was an 'empire' in name only."[17] But perhaps it was not an empire even in name.

The core title of the Byzantine ruler was *basileus* of the Romans ("faithful in Christ"), which in plain Greek means "king of the Romans" and was probably taken by his subjects to mean just that: they were the Romans and he was their monarch. Having said that, the *basileus* of the Romans was not any king. Both he and his subjects believed that he was superior to other kings. But this does not mean that he was an "emperor" in the sense that he was an über-monarch who ruled over non-Roman realms. If that idea forms part of our intuition regarding medieval rulers, it comes from the German tradition, not the Roman one. It was the Germans who began the practice of formally promoting the *"rex* of the Germans" to the notional status of *"imperator* of the Romans," but this did not correspond to anything in Roman titulature or practice. The idea that an emperor is a monarch who rules over a number of subordinate kings, barons, dukes, cities, archbishops, and peoples, thus making him the lord of a loosely federated and multiethnic empire, is also a medieval German convention.[18] In Romanía, the *basileus* was primarily the monarch of the Roman people. If at a given time he did not rule over non-Romans, that did not make him any less a *basileus* of the Romans or any less superior in status to foreign kings. Moreover, although his position was understood to be superior to that of barbarian kings, their realms did not have to be parts of his own for that to be the case.

Consider for example the sixth-century political theorist Ioannes Lydos. He claims that the position of Caesar is superior to that of king *(basileus)* because the (Roman) Caesars used to appoint kings to rule the various foreign nations. He is referring here to the tradition of Rome's client kings, whose realms were not governed directly by imperial administrators but which were dependent in various ways. Yet this relationship is not how he *defines* a Caesar. Two chapters earlier he had defined the Caesars in terms of their relationship to the rest of the Roman polity—τὰ κοινά, "the commons." He slots the term *imperator* in here, as the function of commanding the Roman army.[19] None of this requires empire as such, an ongoing relationship of domination of non-Romans by Romans.

In his discussion of whether the Athenian empire was really an empire, Ian Morris correctly warns against approaching the question as "a philological exercise," with the central question being how we translate terms that appear in the sources. This way "we are ducking the analytical challenge." Fundamentally, we should "think of empires as a type of state, characterized by a strong sense of foreignness between rulers and ruled."[20] So was Romanía an empire? Or did it instead only have an empire? In which case, how much of it was empire and how much not?

Empire and Difference in Romanía

To ascertain whether Romanía was an empire we must weigh the balance of difference and domination within it, and we mean a particular kind of difference. The difference between rich and poor is not an imperial relationship, but one of socioeconomic inequality that can exist between Romans. That type of rule may have been exploitative, but it does not make a state into an empire. (Also, we have no reason to think Romanía was more exploitative of its "own" people than other developed states.) "Two different logics of exclusion operated within imperial cores and peripheries—in the former those tended to be exclusions of social status, wealth, gender and citizenship, while in the peripheries exclusions operated along lines of race, ethnicity, and civilization."[21]

The Romans of Byzantium encompassed its Greek-speaking Orthodox population, which was the majority at all times. No cultural, religious, or ethnic differences existed between the Romans of the court, capital, and army and those of the provinces, save for what we would expect: some were wealthier, some more snobbish, some had weapons, and some were farmers. But otherwise there was no ethnic or legal barrier that provincial Romans had to overcome in order to join the army of the Romans, hold office in the state or Church, or rise to the throne. They were not marked as "other" by the ruling elite. They did not, then, constitute a community governed by imperial articulations of difference. Empire must be sought in Roman rule over the non-Romans. Were there enough non-Romans in Romanía such that we can classify it as an empire? Who were they?

There is no shortage of statements in the scholarship that Byzantium was a multiethnic empire marked by extraordinary diversity in both language and ethnicity. These general statements are made by Byzantinists,[22] comparative scholars of empire who rely on them,[23] and authors of historical fiction.[24] The metaphor of an ethnic "mosaic" is thrown about a lot, and I suspect that some historians infer circularly that Byzantium was multiethnic simply from the fact that we call it an empire, because that is what empires are. Some versions of this view project onto Byzantium the image of a Central Asian empire, with tribes, loosely allied to the emperor, wandering its provinces; whereas others project onto it the image of Ottoman Constantinople, a cosmopolitan city of many faiths where Jews, Armenians, and Latins rubbed shoulders with Greeks and Turks, all devoted to commerce. These images are anachronistic and inaccurate, but the very premise of the multiethnic empire on which they rest is also problematic. Consider that no historian of Byzantium has done the actual work to document this alleged ethnic diversity, namely the existence, nature, and size of the "ethnic minorities" whose "very existence challenged the concept of Byzantine uniformity."[25] The present chapter will be the first to do so, and it will argue that these minorities do not greatly compromise Byzantine uniformity.

Before we proceed to an ethnic inventory of the empire, some points of methodology are in order. Claims that Byzantium was multiethnic and multilingual can be made casually because they can be proven true with no effort whatsoever, albeit in a trivial sense. Every society of that size harbors some degree of ethnolinguistic diversity. What matters, however, is its demographic impact. It is routinely asserted, for example, that Byzantine Constantinople was a "cosmopolitan" city in which all manner of ethnicities rubbed shoulders and dozens of languages were spoken. But the proof for this assertion for the period before the influx of Latins in the twelfth century turns out to consist of prisoners of war, foreign mercenaries employed by the emperors, ambassadors, merchants passing through, and a small Muslim community, possibly also of merchants.[26] It is misleading to call this a "cosmopolitan" city, given that its population was in the hundreds of thousands and such groups could not have accounted for much of it. If a capital city claimed to be cosmopolitan, but its diversity consisted only of prisoners, hired guards, foreign ambassadors, and the residents of its hotels, we would not be impressed.

The Ohio State University (OSU), where I teach, has students from over a hundred countries representing dozens of ethnic groups. Yet the university is fundamentally white and Ohioan, which is how most of us here perceive it. In 2016, two-thirds of the student body were from Ohio and fewer than 20 percent were nonwhites.[27] It would be misleading to call this a "diverse" campus. At Rutgers University, the most diverse in the United States, only 40 percent of the student body are white, though the students are from sixty countries, fewer than at OSU.[28] It matters which numbers we choose to shape our impressions. OSU's "diversity" is "truthy": it is not actually true, but a passable impression of plausibility can be made for it.[29] When it appears in brochures, it is a Potemkin diversity. Something similar has been done with middle Byzantium and its capital in our scholarship.

In most truly multiethnic empires, the dominant group is usually a small minority compared to the conquered population, which consists of many groups. Where is the balance point between a multiethnic empire on the one hand and a nation-state-with-minorities on the other? The distinction between the two is not only a matter of relative population (e.g., Roman vs. non-Roman) but also of the institutional maintenance of difference between the two in an imperial context. It would be an odd empire whose population was (say) 80 percent conquerors and 20 percent conquered, and it would also be an odd empire that extended the same rights to many of its conquered subjects as it gave to its own people.

A second point concerns the ethnic nature of Byzantine Romanness. Evidence has already been presented in this book, and will continue to pile up, which proves that "Roman" was not a label held by or projected upon all subjects of the state collectively and indiscriminately. It was not an abstract, "umbrella identity" that could encompass Greek-speakers, Armenians, Slavs, Jews, and whoever else happened to live in territories governed by the state. Rather, it entailed specific exclusions based on language, religion, upbringing, and custom; in sum, it was an ethnicity. It is important to raise this matter again because this error is made on a regular basis by proponents of the idea that Byzantium was a multiethnic empire. For example, one scholar notes that "the empire retained its multiethnic and polyglot character—Greek-, Slav- and Armenian-speakers dominated, but other ethnic/linguistic groups counted themselves as 'Romans' too."[30] But the sources strongly refute this formulation. If an imperial subject was sufficiently foreign as to speak primarily Slavic or Armenian, he would likely have been called a Slav or Armenian in imperial service, not a Roman. Speros Vryonis has correctly pushed back against "the often heard generalization that in Byzantium ethnic affiliation was insignificant . . . that the inhabitants of the empire felt that in effect they were all Romans and Christians." After reviewing the evidence for the Armenians specifically, he concludes to the contrary that the Byzantines "were quite aware of ethnic distinctions among the population."[31] The key difference we are looking for will not be found *among* the Romans but *between* Romans and non-Romans.

It is those non-Romans whom we must find in order to decide whether or not, or to what degree, Romanía was an empire. Moreover, it is not only their existence that counts but the modes in which they were governed differently by the state *because* they were non-Romans. Despite the occasional note of despair at ever cataloguing the empire's ethnic groups,[32] this is not impossible to do. To be sure, precise figures for any part of the population lie beyond our reach, but as we have often seen, Roman sources are sensitive to ethnic difference, whether they were recording it neutrally, engaging in ethnic polemic, or elaborating literary ethnographies. It is possible to compile a kind of ethnic inventory of the Roman empire that tells us generally who lived where. It is extremely unlikely that large non-Roman groups lived in the empire without leaving any trace in the written record. We have to try, within the limitations of the available evidence, to be explicit about the empire's alleged ethnolinguistic diversity. It can no longer be sufficient to state vaguely that it was diverse and, on that premise, classify it as a multiethnic empire without providing any documentation.[33] Some will no doubt insist that there was more diversity on the ground than is revealed in our sources, but this puts them in the awkward position—indeed, an untenable one—of maintaining a general and significant thesis that is unsupported by evidence. Again, the question is not whether Romanía was marked by regional diversity, as clearly it was. The question is how much of that diversity operated *on the relevant analytical level*, that is by creating distinctions between Romans and non-Romans. It is insufficient to find that some Romans lived in the mountains whereas others lived on the plains; we must instead find non-Romans who were ruled differently from Romans.

In fact, the problem all along has not been in finding non-Roman "ethnic" types in Romanía but in finding *the Romans themselves*. There are many studies of Jews, Armenians, Slavs, and others in Romanía, but the problem has been in identifying the "core group" against which they can be seen as minorities or as separate ethnic groups.[34]

Committed to Roman denialism, historians have been unable to "see" the majority of the empire's population, which went by the name "Roman" in the sources. Assuming wrongly that this population could not have been ethnically Roman, it has remained for us a nebulous, undefined mass of "imperial subjects" who are called "ethnolinguistically diverse." But once we recognize them as "real" Romans, then suddenly the contours between them (the core group) and the ethnic others emerge more clearly into focus, just as they do in the sources. Thus, the question of Romanía as a multiethnic empire is but an aspect of the question of its Romanness.

Our search for non-Romans must be guided by the sources. After all, discursive claims in textual sources remain the best way to establish ethnic groups and explore their history under empires. Most non-Roman groups in the empire are attested in multiple sources written in different genres, from different perspectives, and (if we are lucky) in different languages. We do not want to be at the mercy of one type of source. We must also correct for the ancient Roman convention of using pseudo-ethnic language to refer to the Roman inhabitants of a province, as well as be sensitive to changes over time. Methodologically, we are now better positioned to study ethnicity than previous scholarship ever was, especially in Byzantine Studies, which assumed that ethnic groups were fixed or inalienable. We now know that over a few generations, small and large groups could be assimilated to the dominant culture, and some of them were incentivized by the state to do so. Thus, the empire's ethnic profile was not the same from century to century, even if there had been no intervening expansion, contraction, or influx of new settlers. We need to track not only the existence of ethnic groups but their survival or assimilation within the empire.

If we place empires along a spectrum from assimilation to exclusion, all phases of Romanía would be closer to the former end of it. A recent volume on the dynamics of ancient empires links its relative homogeneity to Romanía's extraordinary longevity as a state, correctly in my view.

> The issue of [empires'] success and longevity will revolve around the same key questions: to what extent are empires of conquest

able to impose upon the conquered lands and cultures their own ideological and cultural values and patterns of administration and elite formation and thereby create out of a range of different sociocultural formations a more or less homogeneous set of political values and ideological identities? Of all the "empires" discussed in this volume, the Roman—and its successor in the east Mediterranean basin, the Byzantine—states were perhaps the most successful in this respect.[35]

The authors, Jack Goldstone (a modern political historian) and John Haldon (a Byzantinist), even wonder whether Byzantium was an empire after all, and put the word and its cognates consistently in quotation marks:

The Byzantine "empire" was, in many respects just a small, territorially unified state; its "imperial" aspect was both short lived and occasional, yet it retains the image of an empire because of its "imperial" origins, as part of the Roman imperial system.[36]

This suggests that we should not be satisfied with a classification that stems from a vague "image of empire," especially if that image (whatever its source) is not grounded in Roman realities. The sources, as we have seen, mix imperial with national Roman images of their state. The latter may have a greater claim to its enduring reality. This is what Goldstone and Haldon call "a small, territorially unified state," not far from what I call the national state of the Romans. In fact, there is no Byzantine terminology that straightforwardly translates as "empire," whereas the vocabulary of the Byzantine sources was full of expressions for the nation, polity, state, and monarchy "of the Romans."

Byzantine authors sometimes reveal that their state was more expansive than just the polity of the Romans, that it had what we might call an imperial aspect. In other words, there were two ways of talking about the territory that was under Roman control: one referred to *all* the territory subject to the emperor, whereas the other distinguished within that territory between lands inhabited mostly by

Romans (what we might call a Roman homeland) and lands inhabited mostly by foreigners (but still under imperial governance). These expressions reveal and reinforce the bounded ethnic nature of Byzantine Romanness, and would have been impossible if the latter were of "universal," supra-ethnic scope. For example, Kekaumenos, an eleventh-century author of maxims addressing the emperor, intuitively draws a distinction between "the *themata* of the Romans and the lands of the foreign nations *(ethne)* under your authority."[37] He intends for these two, taken together, to refer to the entirety of what we might call the empire. In other words, not everyone under the authority of the emperor was a Roman. Previous sources can be cited to the same effect.[38]

A similar distinction is drawn in some passages written by Konstantinos VII in his survey of foreign nations around Romanía, *De administrando imperio*. In one place, he refers to three forts in Armenia and says, speaking hypothetically, that "if the emperor were to hold them, a Persian army could not come against Romanía, because these forts happen to lie between Romanía and Armenia and serve as a barrier against armies."[39] Therefore, what we call the empire is for him Romanía plus the foreign buffer territories. In a later passage, he distinguishes between "Romanía itself" or "Romanía proper" and some foreign forts held by the emperor.[40] Sources of the eleventh century also distinguish between the old Roman themes or the "Roman land" and the new "territories" that had been acquired in the recent burst of expansion. The "Roman land" strictly so called included the interior of Asia Minor but not the new territories.[41] This points to the recently developed theoretical concept of "the nation within the empire." Rather than see the two concepts as polar opposites, some historians are finding that historically they often coexist, for example when one creates the other or is nestled within it.[42]

It is not clear whether this "gap" between the Roman homeland and the foreign territories was expressed through technical terminology. In two passages of the same work, Konstantinos seems to draw a distinction between "our polity *(politeia)*" on the one hand (i.e., that of the Romans) and "the entirety of the *arche* (area of command or authority) of the Romans" on the other.[43] Perhaps this hints at a distinction between a more political mode of life for Romans domestically and a more authoritative relationship between them and their subjects. Perhaps *arche* can be translated here as "empire," though more research on this would be required.[44] Other terms could express the same idea, for example, "hegemony": Konstantinos IX Monomachos expanded the boundaries of his *hegemonia* when he annexed parts of Armenia.[45]

In this and the following chapter, I have decided to sketch the ethnic profile of Romanía at two different moments that should provide a striking contrast: the first is 930 AD, when the empire had made significant progress at absorbing some of the populations that had invaded its Balkan territories in the seventh century but before it had made any extensive conquests of its own. The second is 1064, which was the high point of imperial expansion in the whole of the empire's history since late antiquity, not to be matched at any time afterward. Yet by 1064 Romanía had not had enough time to absorb the recently conquered populations. I will look for ethnic difference first in the provinces and then in the capital and the armies. I focus on territories of the empire administered directly by its institutions and not on various outposts and client states that recognized its authority only nominally while remaining self-governed in most ways; the empire might have been present there only by way of a court title bestowed on a local ruler. To be sure, some emperors liked to pretend that these titles literally gave them sovereignty over those client states, and sometimes even spun them into theories of world rule.[46] But this takes us to ideologies of symbolic empire, and not to its historical practice, which is what we are primarily interested in here. Nor do most scholars believe that such claims made specific territories part of the empire. For example, histories of Byzantium do not include histories of, say, Capua, Croatia, and Armenia. Moreover, as client states were not governed by imperial agents, the question of whether they enforced a politics of difference is moot.

We do not, of course, have census information and must rely on literary sources and a tiny number of documentary texts. But we are interested in groups large enough to be statistically significant, not a few clans that may have sought refuge in the mountains near the frontier. If groups had so few dealings with the Roman state or

Roman society at large that they evaded attention in the sources altogether, they probably should not be included in a study of the subjects of the empire anyway. It is unlikely that larger groups altogether escaped the attention of our sources, which were quite attuned to ethnic difference. The documented survival of small minority groups in the provinces is a reassuring indicator that our source basis is not inadequate for this undertaking.

The Ethnic Profile of the Provinces, ca. 930 AD

Jews were a distinct ethnoreligious minority marked by a separate religious organization, different customs, a different national history, and the use of a different language (Hebrew) alongside the Greek vernacular. Byzantine law *both* proclaimed their legal equality as Roman citizens *and* discriminated against them as non-Christians, resulting in an incoherent legal regime that was subject to erratic ecclesiastical or imperial pressure.[47] The core principle was that Jews were subject to the same laws and courts as all Romans, though they were barred from high political positions and the army. But when it came to matters that pertained to their "superstition," they were subject to the jurisdiction of their own religious leaders. Matters of purely internal concern included various contracts, marriage, and inheritance, in addition to strictly religious observances. But the Roman law of Byzantium gave Jewish women two advantages that they enjoyed nowhere else in the Jewish world: they could initiate divorce by appealing to the secular courts, and they could retain control over their own financial assets. The rabbis did not like this—and foreign rabbis were shocked that this was going on among the Roman Jews—but they were powerless to change it.[48] After all, "the rabbis had a vested interest... in viewing their version of the law of the Torah as the only legal system under which the Jews could legitimately live. This meant they regarded Roman law as basically invalid, at least for Jews."[49] But individual Jews and, it seems, their women, did not agree with them all the time. So overall Jews constituted a separate nation, but they could easily integrate through conversion and even pass as Romans in some contexts without it. It is indicative that Jews from Romanía came to be known as Romaniote Jews.

Roman attitudes toward Jews were mixed. Because churchmen wrote a disproportionate number of our sources and religious texts tended to survive better than secular ones, our evidence is slanted toward theological polemic and religious hatred against the Jews. But more tolerant attitudes are attested as well. When the saint Nikon (later tenth century) wanted to expel the Jews from Sparta, a local notable, Ioannes Aratos, opposed this move. Aratos was unsuccessful, but is on record as saying that the expulsion was unjust and unreasonable.[50]

Jews lived in many cities of the empire, and we hear of various attempts by the emperors to forcibly convert them, attempts that are reported in vague terms and never managed to eradicate Judaism from the empire. These attempts may have resulted in emigration or conversion, reducing the number of Jews in Roman society. But the community survived and grew in the phase of Roman expansion in the later tenth and eleventh centuries. This happened both through annexation and Jewish immigration from abroad.[51] While we cannot estimate the size of the Jewish population around 930, a Jewish traveler from Spain, Benjamin of Tudela, gives population figures for the empire's communities around 1170 that add up to about 10,000. Inevitably, there is disagreement about how to interpret this figure (was he counting families or individuals?) and whether to accept it. Some scholars reduce the total to less than 9,000, whereas others would raise it to 75,000.[52] Estimates in terms of the overall size of the population of the empire range from 0.1 percent (a tenth of 1 percent) to 0.5 percent (one half of 1 percent), but such estimates are highly subjective.[53] At any rate, "Jews represented only a marginal element within the Byzantine population."[54] They loomed larger in theological imagination than in real life.

Joshua Holo has masterfully drawn the complex position of the Jews in Byzantine society: "The distinct and corporate nature of the Jews readily comes through in the primary sources.... The minority Jews, in all their complexity, are easily identified in distinction from the majority Byzantines [as] a distinct people with its own religion, calendar and institutions.... To be a Jew was to belong to an ethnic group in every possible sense."[55] "Byzantine Jews defined themselves in relation to their coreligionists in other countries, more than they did as subjects of the imperial state."[56] Therefore, on the one hand "the Jews were not, in any modern sense, integrated; in Constantinople they lived in a separate quarter, they suffered legal limitations, and they underwent episodes of physical violence and forced baptism." But, on the other, "the Jews defied easy dismissal as aliens or foreigners, insofar as they met a very high standard of cultural integration in signal matters of language and autochthony."[57]

Jewish literature of the middle Byzantine period was written in Hebrew, though it survives mostly from southern Italy. Unfortunately, these texts have been more rigorously excluded from modern Byzantine scholarship than their authors were from contemporary Christian society. Some of these authors were clearly in dialogue with the contemporary Greek intellectual scene, though their literary productions followed separate traditions and genres and tended to assert (or presuppose) the distinctiveness of the Jewish community. This is evident, for example, in the works of Shabbatai Donnolo (tenth century) and the long family *Chronicle of Ahimaaz* (Ahima'as), whose partly historical and partly legendary tales cover the ninth to eleventh centuries. It is also likely that the *Sefer Yosippon*, a Hebrew adaptation of Josephos that recounts the history of the Jewish people and was popular with medieval Jews thereafter, was also a product of Byzantine Italy.[58] These texts present a narrative view of Jewish national distinctiveness and would find parallels in the eleventh century in similar texts by Bulgarians and Armenians under Roman rule.

Armenians were among the largest minorities of non-Romans within the empire (along with Slavs, to be discussed below). As we saw in the Chapters 4 and 5, they were subject to the pull of Romanization. Some Romans had Armenian or Slavic ancestry but were not aware of the fact or not interested in it; others were (or were made) aware of this ancestry in ways that inflected their Roman ethnicity (we might call them "hyphenated Romans"); and finally there were nonassimilated Armenians or Slavs who lived in the empire or who had taken up imperial service but retained foreign cultural traits that marked them off from the mainstream of Roman society. They were perceived as foreign, though it is not entirely clear how or whether they were treated differently by the imperial state. We are here interested primarily in this last category, though it is unlikely that we will ever be able to assess its demographic impact.

In a study of the Byzantine aristocracy, Alexander Kazhdan concluded, based on nomenclature and biographical information, that some 10–15 percent of these families were of Armenian origin, or, in absolute terms, 30–45 out of 300.[59] He realized that many of them were assimilated into Byzantine society, but did not fully make the distinction between (past) ancestral origins and (present) identity. In reality, there were few officeholders who personally had foreign origin; most were two or more generations removed. There were a few Armenians from the "homeland" who rose to high positions in the Roman system, but they are found mostly in the seventh and early eighth centuries,[60] not the ninth and early tenth. Indeed, in the Armenian history of Ghewond, covering the seventh and eighth centuries, "fleeing to Byzantium" is presented as a regular option for the Armenian nobility. But we generally do not find ethnic Armenians in the Roman aristocracy of the tenth century.

Moreover, we should no longer postulate ethnic origins on the basis of Armenian-sounding names, as Kazhdan did, and much of the other biographical information on which such origins are postulated is, as we saw in Chapter 5, often twisted out of recognition to yield the desired result. Charanis estimated that Armenians made up about a quarter of the Roman army in the middle period, but he did so by mistaking the (huge) Armeniakon army as an ethnic Armenian army, even though the main source that he cites, Theophanes the Confessor, distinguishes between the two.[61]

There is also no reason to believe that the statistical presence of men of Armenian origin in the aristocracy—even if that could be reliably estimated—reflected the number of Armenians living in the empire. By such Armenians I mean here not Romans of Armenian ancestry but people who could be identified as ethnically Armenian, for example those who were targeted by the stereotypes and prejudices surveyed in Chapter 5. The majority of them lived in the eastern themes, though of course we have no population figures. Modern historians sometimes give the impression that the empire's eastern provinces throughout the middle Byzantine period were predominantly Armenian in this sense, but this is likely quite wrong and it does not correspond to the geography of Armenian history to begin with. Before the Roman conquests—so between the mid-seventh and the mid-tenth centuries—the easternmost themes closest to Armenia proper were Charsianon, Lykandos, Sebasteia, Koloneia, Mesopotamia, and Chaldia. Most of these themes were subdivisions of the original great theme of Armeniakon, with some additions of territory taken from themes to the west. By contrast, Lykandos and Mesopotamia consisted mostly of recent acquisitions (i.e., late ninth–early tenth century). Let us discuss the former group first.

These core territories of the theme of Armeniakon had been in Roman possession since antiquity and were ruled in the same way as other Roman territories elsewhere, although they were probably more heavily militarized. We do not have much evidence about everyday life and the nonelite population in these provinces, but their civilian and military administration, the networks of local elites, and the Church organization were all mainstream Roman (i.e., Greek-speaking and Orthodox). We have only one source that attests an Armenian population presence in these provinces. Konstantinos VII says that the theme of Koloneia in particular was mostly inhabited by Armenians.[62] As this occurs in a survey of the theme of Armeniakon and is followed by separate chapters on the smaller themes that were split off from it, we can tentatively conclude from his statement that Armenians were less present in the other themes.

This is exactly what we would expect based on the historical geography of Armenia and runs contrary to all the loose modern talk about "the Byzantine east" being populated by Armenians.[63] The theme of Koloneia represented the westernmost tip of ancient Lesser Armenia, which was the portion of Armenia allotted to Rome in late antiquity (the larger part had been claimed by Persia). This westernmost tip was all that Rome kept of ancient Lesser Armenia after the Arab conquests. The themes of Chaldia and Sebasteia also contained Armenian populations,[64] but we must also remember that by 930 these areas had been governed by Rome for almost one thousand years. Even so, "Armenian" soldiers are attested in the theme of Sebasteia in the tenth century. An expedition in 911 against the Arabs and Crete involving some 35,000 soldiers and marines of the regular army and fleet also included 1,000 Armenian cavalry from Sebasteia as well as two units of 500 Armenians from other places that cannot be precisely identified. The relative size of the numbers is telling, as is the fact that the Armenians seem to be treated as a distinctively ethnic auxiliary unit.[65]

In the early eighth century, Armenians in the empire may have been so few that the emperor Philippikos Bardanes (711–713) could think of expelling all of them from the empire, and he seems to have carried it out, at least against the non-Chalcedonian Armenians.[66]

By contrast, Armenians made up a larger part of the population of the new but smaller militarized themes that the empire created during its expansion in the east during the tenth century. The theme of Lykandos was founded by the Armenian military entrepreneur Melias (Mleh). He found the place deserted, in the no-man's-land between the Romans and Arabs. Under imperial patronage, he rebuilt the fort and brought in his men.[67] This foundation was among the earliest of the so-called small Armenian themes that began to proliferate in this region during the tenth century. As this phenomenon really picked up during the main phase of expansion, in the second half of the tenth century, we will discuss it in a later section. The nearby theme of Mesopotamia was founded in a similar way.[68]

We do not hear of Armenian communities in central and western Asia Minor. Now, we know from many sources that larger groups had at times left Armenia for Romanía in order to escape the Arabs, or were carried off by the emperors themselves during expeditions and resettled on imperial territory, including in Thrace. A few thousand here, a few thousand there: these groups would not impact imperial demography in a major way. Moreover, they are not heard from again, suggesting that they were assimilated.[69] One group deserves special mention: 12,000 Armenian refugees, including women and children, fled from the Arabs and, with the permission of Konstantinos VI (780–791), entered the empire by way of the Pontos and were resettled. Some historians believe that they were resettled in the Pontos, at a place called Hemshin, and subsequently became the nucleus of the surviving ethnic group that bears that name and spoke a variant of the Armenian language. In that case, we would have a group that maintained its ethnic distinctiveness, assisted by its geographical isolation in the mountains of the Pontos. But the link between Hemshin and that specific group of refugees is tenuous.[70]

Although "the general consensus continues to be that [Armenians] were the largest non-Greek unit of that society,"[71] the existence of large populations of nonassimilated Armenians is hard to document. That consensus was built, and continues to rest, on the presence of mostly assimilated elites. This has to be emphasized: in all the enthusiasm over Armenians in Byzantium, there has been no discussion of Armenian communities or populations living in the core territories the empire, so that we do not really know where or whether they existed. In modern surveys of Armenian history, medieval Armenian historians, and Roman sources, I have not found any references to Armenian populations living in the empire between the mid-seventh and the mid-tenth centuries, with the sole exception of Koloneia, mentioned by Konstantinos VII. All attention has focused on the alleged Armenian origins of the Roman aristocracy, but those origins are placed outside the empire, thus contributing to the silence about "domestic" Armenians before the period of the Roman conquests.

A group related to the Armenians were the Paulicians, proponents of a religious heresy that began in Armenia, spread to Romanía, and seems (unlike most previous heresies) to have formed its own separate ethnoreligious community that broke with Romanía altogether. In the 750s, the Paulicians were regarded as still loyal enough to the empire for Konstantinos V to transfer some to Thrace to reinforce local defenses against the Bulgars.[72] Subsequently, in the mid-ninth century, those in Asia Minor were severely persecuted—allegedly, tens of thousands were put to death—but the operation was botched, driving many, including renegade Roman officers, to seek refuge with the Arabs in Melitene.[73] The Paulicians eventually established their own separate state at Tephrike and the surrounding forts, from where they launched raids into Asia Minor, sometimes collaborating with Arab raiders. Their numbers grew and the empire had to wage open war against them until they were finally defeated under Basileios I in the 870s. After the mid-ninth century, there were not many Paulicians left inside the empire. A Roman visitor to Tephrike before its capture, Petros of Sicily, reports that there were many Orthodox people living in the Paulician state as well, and that the Paulicians did not consider themselves to be Romans: they used the term "Roman" to refer to what we call Orthodoxy, and called themselves Christians. This makes them a distinct self-conscious ethnicity, which is what we would expect.[74] Therefore, in addition to calling them heretics (usually "Manichaeans"), the Byzantine sources call them "barbarians" in contrast to "Romans."[75]

What became of the Paulicians after the conquest of Tephrike? The empire would not have allowed a large number of them to remain in this strategically sensitive region, so the emperor likely dispersed or exiled them, as would occur a full century later with the Muslims of Cilicia. As Petros attested, there was already an Orthodox population in Tephrike, which probably stayed in place, whereas the Paulician leadership fled to Muslim lands or Armenia.[76] Many rank-and-file Paulicians likely converted to Orthodoxy. A military unit of Paulicians is soon recorded as active under Roman command in southern Italy.[77] Some scattered groups remained in the east, for we will see below that they were moved by Ioannes I Tzimiskes to Philippopolis in Thrace, but that was after a phase of further conquest in the east.

The Paulicians are an interesting, even exceptional, group in that many of them began as Romans who espoused a heresy that caused them to be viewed as non-Roman barbarians when they founded a separatist state. In 930, their numbers in the empire were small.

In 1929, surveying the state of the empire around 930, Steven Runciman observed that "the Asiatic population [i.e., Asia Minor] had long since been welded into a harmonious whole; but in Europe there were still undigested masses, tribes consciously distinct from, and hostile to, their neighbors and resentful of the imperial government." In particular, he meant "the Slavs of the Peloponnese."[78] In addition to the Peloponnese, the empire's main European provinces included Greece, part of Epeiros, Thessaly, coastal Macedonia, and Thrace (beyond this line in the interior lay the Bulgarian empire). All of these territories had been invaded and settled by Slavs in the seventh century, and the empire had gradually been reestablishing control over them and absorbing them, as we saw above.[79] The Slavic presence was thicker in some areas than in others, though it is possible that they nowhere entirely displaced the preexisting Roman population. This was, therefore, a strange kind of "imperialism" on the part of Romanía: it was not so much expanding aggressively into a neighboring land as reclaiming its own lands and peoples who had been invaded by the Slavs. We cannot gauge the ethnic composition at this time of southern Greece, Thessaly, Macedonia, and Thrace. As we saw, Leon VI tells us that his father Basileios I converted the Slavs, taught them Greek, and made them into Romans, and their last known ethnic *archons* date from a century before Leon. In 904, the Sklabenoi in the hinterland of Thessalonike were part of the imperial system. These are all signs that the empire was successfully assimilating them. But purely for the sake of argument, to give maximum leeway to ethnic diversity, let us hypothesize that these European territories remained 40 percent minority Slavic, possibly more Roman in southern Greece and more Slavic around Thessalonike.

This estimate makes greater allowance for the survival of Slavic groups as separate groups than some historians do. Judith Herrin, for example, has written that by the end of the process of assimilation Hellas was again a normal Roman province: Orthodox, Greek-speaking, and with a familiar Roman culture. The Slavs

> could not dislodge the Greek tongue or the Christian faith. Instead, the Slavs gradually embraced both, adopting in addition the medieval Byzantine style of city life (as cities slowly revived), of coinage, trading organization, ecclesiastical structure, and Hellenic culture.... The newcomers were converted to Christianity and inducted into Hellenic culture to become the not-always obedient subjects of the Byzantine emperors.[80]

Herrin may well be right. But as I will be making a case for national homogeneity rather than "empire" in this section, I want my own subjective estimates to err in the opposite direction.

We have slightly better indicators regarding the Peloponnese, which was a center of elite Roman culture and appears frequently in the narrative sources for this period. After 930, the only foreign "tribes" that are mentioned there are the Ezerites and Milengoi living around Mt. Taygetos, and these are who Runciman had in mind. As we saw, the Milengoi continued to have an "ethnic *doux*" in the later tenth century. They were probably in a tributary relationship with the empire (rather than absorbed into its regular tax-surveying administration), and they still appear as a distinct group in the early thirteenth century. Otherwise we know little about them. They were almost certainly Orthodox and possibly spoke Greek, but somehow their group identity survived, the only such group in the Peloponnese who "successfully resisted assimilation."[81] Still, we should make maximum allowance for ethnic diversity. For example, we do not know who lived in the remote mountains of Arcadia. I would not use the tired metaphor of an ethnic "mosaic" for the Peloponnese, certainly not for the tenth century,[82] but I would estimate ethnic minority groups at no more than 20 percent in the mid-tenth century. It is perhaps significant that in the lives of the saints of Greece from the ninth and early tenth centuries there is only a single solitary mention of internal barbarians, though the texts do otherwise refer to Arab raiders and other kinds of disruptive local elements.[83]

In the seventh and eighth centuries, the emperors resettled Slavs from the Balkans to Asia Minor or allowed them to move there. Excluding military units, which are a separate category, one group was later carried off by Arab raiders;[84] another defected to the Arabs, and the emperor who settled them in Asia Minor (Justinian II) massacred or sold the rest into slavery;[85] a third group, by contrast, which fled from a war in Bulgaria to Konstantinos V and was settled at Artanas in Bithynia, on the coast, is said to have numbered 208,000, an impossible figure, especially for a group that is said to have crossed the Black Sea.[86] There probably were other resettled groups that are not recorded in the sources, but none were sufficiently impactful on the demography of Asia Minor as to ever be mentioned again.[87] It is therefore not clear that they merit a place in the ethnic profile of the tenth century, any more than do the Arab and Khurramite defectors who were also accepted and assimilated. As Rustam Shukurov recently wrote, "Byzantine authorities, as a rule, divided the immigrants into small groups and sent them to different provinces of the empire to speed up their assimilation with the local population. Usually, the immigrants, scattered in the vast expanses of the empire, lost their ethnic and religious identity by the second generation."[88]

A case in point are the Bulgars. A number of them defected along with their families under Michael I (811–813) and were resettled "in various areas" of the empire.[89] Presumably there were other such groups. Some Bulgarians are attested in 959 in a village near Mt. Athos.[90] But that is all we can say safely about Bulgarians in the empire of 930. The eleventh-century vita of Lazaros of Galesion mentions a village near Ephesos called Boulgarin, from which some scholars deduce the presence of Bulgarians, though the text says nothing about that when the protagonist meets its inhabitants. Even if they were Bulgarians, they may have been settled there by Basileios II after his conquest of Bulgaria (he regularly moved conquered subjects around).[91]

Another interesting theory concerns Saint Ioannikios (ca. 760–846 AD) and the Roman family of Boïlas (plural: Boïlades). Ioannikios began as a soldier in the Roman army and was present at the battle of Markellai (792), a Bulgar victory, after which he turned to the religious life. During the battle, the future saint encountered the emperor, who asked him who he was. Ioannikios replied, "I am from the province of Bithynia, from the village of Marykaton and the family of Boïlas; my name is Ioannikios, and I am an *exkoubitor* in rank."[92] The name Boïlas is a Greek rendition of a Bulgar noble rank. It is a stretch to conclude from this alone that Ioannikios himself was biologically descended from resettled Bulgars, but it is not impossible. Vryonis, who proposed the theory, concluded that their "assimilation . . . seems to have been rapid and complete," facilitated by the Church and the army.[93] Ioannikios' parents were Christians, and as a Roman soldier he fought against the Bulgars (who, at the time, were not Christians).

Groups of Syrian Orthodox (Jacobites) were taken in three raids in the eighth century and resettled in Thrace (once with some Armenians too, who included Paulicians in their midst).[94] At this time, the members of the Syrian Church were becoming a separate ethnicity,[95] so initially at least they might have formed an ethnoreligious minority in Thrace. Some would have resisted conversion to Byzantine Orthodoxy, but we do not know for how long. The first of these three groups is said to have survived until the early eighth century, so for fifty or sixty years, but they are not attested after that. (They would become much more important after the imperial expansion of the later tenth century, as we will see in Chapter 7.)

It was in southern Italy that the empire's presence was most imperial in nature; that is where the management of ethnic differences was a central feature of provincial administration. Two provinces were reconstituted in the ninth century, Calabria and Longobardia (i.e., Apulia). Although they were governed almost as regular themes by governors and armies sent from Constantinople, they "represented too different and too distant a world to be directly relevant to the history of the central lands of the empire."[96] Italy highlights by contrast how homogeneous the central lands were. But it would be special pleading to exclude it from this survey. Unfortunately, the Greek sources pay little attention to Italy and so it is difficult to talk about their perception of local ethnicities. The *Taktika* of Leon VI says that when the general Nikephoros Phokas was sent in the 880s to subdue Calabria his operations at least in part targeted "the nation of the Lombards," whom he subdued and made to feel "free from all slavery" by not imposing high taxes on them.[97] In another text, this act is called "restoring them to the former sovereignty of the Roman *arche*."[98] Even so, they are represented as a distinct ethnic group.

The documentary evidence from these provinces indicates that Calabria had a large Greek-speaking population, whereas in Apulia the majority was Lombard or Latin Italian, so overall there was a significant Latin-rite presence. By 930, the Churches of Rome and Constantinople had not yet decided to insist on their differences to the point of schism. The non-Greek population of these provinces was allowed to live according to its own customs and follow Lombard laws, an arrangement with few parallels in the rest of the empire. For example, the legal status of women was different within their respective two communities. Administrative personnel sent from the center formed a thin layer in Apulia that ruled through the cooperation of Lombard notables, some of whom bore the non-Roman title of *gastald*.[99] A visitor from the core lands of Romanía would have found in southern Italy the greatest diversity, regimented by language or ethnic categories. There were also Jewish communities, as elsewhere throughout the empire, which used Hebrew for some purposes (e.g., tombstones).[100] The fiscal documents of the churches and monasteries of these provinces, which are mostly in Latin, sometimes classify individuals by their language or ethnicity. They can refer, for instance, to a Greek, Armenian, Jew, and (later) a Norman.[101] A privilege in Latin given by an imperial official to the monastery of Montecassino gives an ethnic inventory of people in imperial service in the region: "Armenians, Greeks, and Lombards."[102] Many deeds are explicitly executed according to the "laws" or the "customs" of the Lombards.[103] As it was not the purpose of those documents to provide ethnological information, these glimpses provide valuable evidence for wider social perceptions of ethnicity.

We have little evidence about how the "Greek" minority in southern Italy perceived itself. We cannot say for certain that they called themselves Romans, though that is by no means to be ruled out.[104] A tenth-century Jewish scholar in Byzantine Italy, Shabbatai Donnolo, who knew Greek, Latin, and Hebrew, referred to his life in lands "under the Romans' rule," suggesting that the term had local valence.[105] But local terminology may have also been shaped by the linguistic habits of the Latinate majority, making it possible that the Greek-speakers there called themselves *Graikoi* (in Greek). We must also be careful because Latin texts could at times subsume various ethnic groups from the east under the lump linguistic term *Greci*.[106] Moreover, the proximity of the city of Rome and the presence there of a "Roman" community distinct from that of Romanía would have complicated the local use of the typical Byzantine terminology of "Romans" and "others."[107] The southern Italian context was tricky, caught as it was between rival linguistic taxonomies. But the Greek-speakers, who would be "Romans" in the core territories, definitely perceived themselves as ethnically different from the Latin majority. When Neilos, from Rossano in Calabria, traveled to Rome, he lodged in a monastery of "men from the same race as himself," that is, of Greek-speakers.[108]

A final oddity remains to be mentioned. Konstantinos VII notes the existence of a group living on the very tip of the Mani peninsula (of the Peloponnese) who were called Hellenes by the locals, not because they were descended from the ancient Greeks—Konstantinos says specifically that they were descended from "the ancient Romans"—but because they remained pagans until the reign of his grandfather Basileios I (867–886). Yet they continued to be called Hellenes even after their conversion to Christianity. Moreover, they appear not to have been fully integrated into the imperial administration as they received an *archon* from the local general (*strategos*), a policy that was used for nonassimilated groups. Konstantinos' solitary mention of this group has fueled more speculation than it can bear.[109] Unfortunately, we do not know how this group saw itself. Whatever its nature, it was seen by him as standing outside the mainstream. Now, for the Romans of Byzantium a "Hellene" was one of two things: an ancient Greek or a pagan regardless of ethnicity. The group in the Peloponnese may have actually been descended from ancient Greeks, but that is not how Konstantinos and their local neighbors saw them: they saw them as descended from the ancient Romans and called them Hellenes because of their religion.[110] At any rate, by the eleventh century, the Mani presents an Orthodox profile with a dense cluster of newly built churches. We know a stoneworker active in the southwestern Peloponnese who carved his name on his productions ("Niketas"), in one case adding "from the country of Mani."[111]

That, in outline, is the ethnic profile presented by the main territories of the empire around 930 AD. I have generally excluded client states, outposts, small groups that are not reliably attested as still surviving in the tenth century or that were not ethnoreligiously different from the Roman majority, as well as ethnic monasteries, which were religious outposts of foreign groups.[112] A single example can demonstrate that perceptions of ethnicity governed these groups as well. When the Georgian monk Hilarion (ninth century) and his followers traveled to the monastic center of Mt. Olympos in Bithynia, they were treated with suspicion by some of the local monks because of their foreignness; note that the Georgians were, from the Byzantine point of view, perfectly Orthodox. After Hilarion's death, the emperor Basileios I wanted to give a monastery in Thessalonike to his disciples but they refused on the grounds that it would not be appropriate for a monastery to be taken away from the natives "and given to us, who are foreign men."[113] Orthodoxy was united by faith but riven by ethnicity.

Constantinople and the Army

Byzantine Constantinople is routinely called a multiethnic, even a cosmopolitan, city—indeed, a "mosaic"—and the Byzantine armies are also said to have been multiethnic. Both of these impressions are wrong.

First, a note on demography. In 930, Constantinople may have had a population of around 250,000,[114] and the nominal strength of the empire's armies may have been around 150,000 men. If the empire's total population was around 10 million, then the first represented 2.5 percent of the total while the second was 1.5 percent. Yet for all that they were small, these two sites of Romanness were disproportionately powerful in relation to their size. They appear frequently in the sources and were often regarded as stand-ins for the empire as a whole, by both medieval and modern writers.

Our image of Constantinople as home to a number of ethnic or religious communities comes from the later Byzantine period and especially the Ottoman period. During the twelfth and thirteenth centuries, Italian cities such as Venice and Genoa established outposts there that functioned as "branch offices" of their polities back home, confined to specific locations (see below). We also know from the Spanish Jewish traveler Benjamin of Tudela (1170s) that Constantinople's Jews had their own "quarter." Specifically, there were two thousand Rabanite Jews and five hundred Karaite Jews, both required to live in Pera, across the Golden Horn, but they so disliked each other that they had built a wall between them.[115] It is debatable whether such segregation counts as cosmopolitanism, but here we are interested more in numbers and presence. The City's diversity, meaning the number and size of its ethnic enclaves, grew during the later Byzantine period and exploded under the sultans. But what was it in 930?

We can certainly assume a Jewish presence.[116] Beyond that, as noted above, studies of Byzantine Constantinople list under the category of cosmopolitanism prisoners of war, foreign mercenaries, foreign ambassadors, itinerant merchants, and a small Muslim community.[117] However, none of these groups were certainly natives of the City. At some point, the Muslims (mostly Arabs) were allowed to have a mosque, the object of negotiation between the emperors and various Muslim powers who acted as the patrons or sponsors of the City's Muslims. The latter cannot have been more than a few hundred, but their existence is at least documented. However, there is no definitive evidence that this group contained more than prisoners of war (some of them of high rank and so treated well by the Roman authorities), envoys, and merchants, some of whom apparently resided in the City for ten years or more.[118] There is no other evidence for foreign or ethnic communities. For example, no Armenian community has been identified in the sources, though we know that notables came to settle there from Armenia on an individual basis or in small groups. Some of them were important enough to be given manors by the emperors, and they brought their families and retinues with them.[119] But it does not seem that they formed a coherent ex-patriot community, and these types of immigrants assimilated quickly. They were quite unlike the Italian colonies that built up in Constantinople in the twelfth century.

It is likely that there were more foreigners in Constantinople than our sources reveal, though unlikely that demographically significant groups have passed completely unnoticed. For example, it is only by a chance reference in Liudprand of Cremona, a western bishop who traveled on official business to Constantinople, that we know of some Amalfitans, Gaetans, and Romans (from Rome) there in 945 and even of some Latin beggars in 968.[120] Liudprand says that the authorities in Constantinople, who were hostile to him, seized those beggars and did not allow them to approach him. There is another chance reference to a Khazar living in, or passing through, tenth-century Constantinople.[121]

In general, the movement of foreigners seems to have been subject to rigorous restrictions. A treaty of around 907 with the Rus' stipulated where their merchants visiting the City could stay and for how long; they could enter only in small groups whose names were recorded.[122] "The activities of foreign merchants . . . were regulated and controlled."[123] This was not an "open city." Soldiers guarded the major crossroads inside, patrolled the City at night, and arrested people who were out and about.[124] A number of saints who looked odd or had spent time abroad and so looked like foreigners were arrested as spies when they approached Roman cities.[125] For example, in the tenth century Basileios the Younger got into trouble because he was acting weirdly and wearing foreign clothes: he was arrested in Asia Minor and taken in chains to the capital for interrogation.[126] The story may be fictitious but reveals contemporary perceptions and possibly policies.

Let us turn from the City to the army. The emperors of Romanía were, at times, wealthy enough to hire thousands of foreign soldiers and mercenaries. Their armies were often mocked by enemies for consisting of a medley of various ethnicities with no cohesion or patriotic morale.[127] But these caricatures were true only in unusual circumstances, and we should not rely on their image of the Roman armies as a "mosaic" of nations. In the middle Byzantine period before 1081, soldiers were recruited overwhelmingly among Romans in the provinces; there was an elaborate system for doing so.[128] In fact, all but a tiny fraction were Roman recruits. The Byzantine sources regularly distinguish between Roman soldiers and "ethnics *(ethnikoi)*,"[129] though sometimes the Romans are listed by province, which should not confuse us: Macedonians, Cappadocians, and the like were just provincial Roman units. When the system of indigenous recruitment began to break down in the 1060s, we hear about it. A historian says that when the emperor Konstantinos X Doukas (1059–1067) needed to assemble an army in a hurry and under pressure, he did so "not in a manner that was fitting for an emperor of the Romans, but only in the way allowed by circumstances, including Macedonians, Bulgarians, Cappadocians, Ouzes, and the other foreigners who happened to be present, in addition to the Franks and Varangians."[130]

Ethnic units were recruited in small numbers for their specialized skills or in order to enforce treaty obligations.[131] Such units typically included fewer than 1,000 men, though they tended to be used more heavily in actual operations: an expedition would be likely to include a higher proportion of foreign soldiers than did the paper strength of the armed forces as a whole.

Consider two surviving inventories of soldiers, pay, and equipment that relate to the expeditions against the Arabs and Crete in 911 and 949. These texts present complex problems of interpretation, but these affect our understanding of Byzantine accounting more than the numbers of foreign soldiers.[132] For the expedition of 911, the text stipulates 700 Rus' auxiliaries in the fleet and 2,000 Armenian cavalry from Sebasteia and other themes to join a Roman army numbering perhaps 35,000; there would also be 5,087 Mardaïtes of the west (see below for them).[133] For the expedition of 949, whose overall size was between 20,000 and 30,000, the fleet was to include 629 Rus' (in nine of their ships), 368 Dalmatians, and 3,000 Mardaïtes; and the cavalry would include 1,000 recently enlisted Armenians from the east (i.e., the eastern themes) and 220 Sthlabesianoi (Slavs) from the Opsikion theme.[134] The true foreigners here were only the Rus', while the Dalmatians came from nearby client states. The Armenians were likely domestic ethnic minorities. The two other groups require some explanation, but we can already see that this was an "OSU" level of diversity: many ethnic names in a row, but small numbers.

Some ethnonyms occur exclusively in connection with military units. The Sklabesianoi (spelled variously) were units of Slavs stationed in Asia Minor, mostly in the Opsikon theme, from where they could be dispatched to trouble areas throughout the empire or beyond. They may have had a Slavic ethnicity (whatever that looked like), for the emperor Romanos I Lakapenos was eager to settle an uprising of the "Slavs" in the Peloponnese (i.e., the Milengoi and the Ezerites) before they could join forces with some "Slavesians" who were causing trouble there too. Be that as it may, the Sthlabesianoi are attested only for the half century 911–961, and cannot have numbered more than a few hundred.[135]

The Mardaïtes (called Jarajima in Arabic) appear immediately after the Arab conquests as a martial Christian group inhabiting the

Amanos mountains, between Cilicia and Syria. They helped the emperors against the Arabs but were basically autonomous, until Justinian II made a deal with the caliph around 687 and resettled 12,000 of them in the empire.[136] Scholars have debated the ethnic origin of the Mardaïtes but the sources give no clear indication; they appear to have been a mixed group that effectively constituted their own new identity. They were dispersed to the naval themes of Asia Minor and Greece, where they are attested in the ninth and tenth centuries, serving as oarsmen. The expedition of 911 included 5,087 Mardaïtes of the west, whereas that of 949 included 3,000.[137] Their captain in the Kibyrraiotai theme (Attaleia) seems not to have been under the direct orders of the local military governor and was appointed directly by the emperor.[138] It is not clear what kind of group the Mardaïtes constituted after they entered Roman service. They were Christian to begin with, and by the tenth century, if not before, they spoke Greek, so it is not clear that they constituted a separate ethnic group at all. The most that we can say based on the evidence is that they formed a distinct military corps in the empire, but one that was perhaps eventually manned completely by ordinary Romans. Possibly it was kept alive by military tradition, not the presence of a separate ethnic group. At any rate, it is not heard from again after the mid-tenth century.

In sum, foreign ethnic units complemented the Roman armies but only in marginal ways; they did not constitute its core. A force could include Rus', Armenians, Slavs, and others and still be 90 percent Roman. This proportion holds for the use of Frankish mercenaries in the eleventh century: whenever numbers are cited, they are quite small, a few hundred here, a few hundred there.[139] The age of conquest would provide two significant exceptions to this pattern: a greater reliance on Armenians and the recruitment of the Varangian Guard, initially of six thousand men. We will discuss these groups in Chapter 7.

Conclusions

Was Romanía an empire in 930 AD? The short answer is that it was not. The vast majority of its population was Roman, and even beyond them it did not always exercise an "imperial" manner of rule over all its non-Roman subjects. A historian of ancient Rome has recently proposed that we think about Roman state power under three aspects: national power exercised by Romans over other Romans; imperial power by Romans over the non-Romans in their empire; and Roman power over people outside the empire. He finds that Byzantium after the seventh century does not really qualify as an empire.[140] My findings support this conclusion. A great deal of power had slid from the second (imperial) category into the first one (national). Romanía was the state of the Roman people and less of an empire.

To summarize our ethnic inventory of Romanía, the theme of Koloneia had a significant Armenian population, and there were Armenian minorities in Sebasteia and other neighboring themes. However, these populations had been living in the Roman empire for almost a millennium. It is likely that they were highly Romanized and Chalcedonian,[141] and they were not, as far as we know, treated differently by the state compared to provincial Romans. We do not know if auxiliary, ethnic Armenian units in the army were recruited primarily among them or in Armenia "proper." Macedonia and Greece still had significant Slavic minorities, though these too had converted to Christianity and were Romanized to varying degrees. The imperial state had ceased to appoint or recognize local ethnic "chiefs" there and the territories in which Slavs had settled were under regular administration. The Sklabenoi of the theme of Strymon, in the hinterland of Thessalonike, seem by 904 to have been a regular part of the Roman army (if an unreliable one when the Arabs attacked the city in that year). We do not know what marked them as ethnically distinct at this point beyond the name attached to their units.

By contrast, some people were subject to special arrangements. Jews could in theory and even practice be regarded as Roman citizens, but were also subject to discrimination, expulsions, and attempts to baptize them. The Ezerites and Milengoi in the Peloponnese also retained some sense of ethnic difference and a separate leadership, whatever their cultural profile was exactly. They formed a separate, quasi-autonomous enclave within Romanía. Apparently, so did the recently converted Hellenes of the Mani. The frontier in Thrace may, in 930, still have been home to Armenian and Syrian communities transplanted from the east almost two centuries earlier; or else they too may have been assimilated. Finally, the most "imperial" provinces were in Italy, where the local population was probably majority Lombard and Latin-speaking, though Calabria had a significant Greek-speaking population. Here the empire allowed its non-Romans to live according to their own norms and even laws, an important codification of difference. But it does not appear that they had lesser or fewer rights there in the eyes of the state as a result of this concession. No discrimination is attested in the sources on the grounds of ethnicity or religious rite.

What does all this mean in practice? The vast majority of the subjects (or citizens) of Romanía were Romans. Even those subjects of Romanía who were described as ethnically different—primarily Slavs and Armenians at this time—were not subject to special legal regimes, especially if they were Orthodox, as most of them seem to have been. If they were treated differently it would have been in the regular course of social life, based on ethnic biases that seem to have permeated Roman society. But at the level of the state and its law of persons, the same institutions governed them as governed the Romans themselves. Members of these minorities could rise to the top, so long as they learned Greek and were Orthodox, but this brought them to the verge of becoming Romans themselves. Elite Romans who are described as having an ethnic origin occupied that liminal point. It is significant that the upper leadership of Romanía was almost entirely Greek-speaking and Orthodox: this means that ethnic minorities, even while subject in theory and likely in practice to the same laws and fiscal regimes as everyone else, faced ethnic or cultural impediments in their bids for positions of power. In this respect, Byzantium would have been perceived as "an empire of the Romans" to these minorities. On the other hand, it is clear that Jews (at select moments) and Paulicians (before their dispersal) could be targeted by the state for primarily religious reasons.

In short, most subjects of Byzantium in 930 did not have an "imperial" relationship to the state. They were ruled by institutions that could at times be oppressive, as institutions tend to be, but that otherwise operated within the undifferentiated framework of Romanía, a national state. For 930, at least, it is hard to justify the label "empire." Its levels of ethnic diversity are strikingly low when compared to all other empires.

7

The Apogee of Empire in the Eleventh Century

> *"Qui vos estis?"*, *inquit, responsum invicem,*
> *"Romani gentium domini."*

In the century after 930, Romanía conquered and annexed more territory than it ever had since the reign of Justinian (527–565), which greatly expanded the ethnic diversity of its subject population. Romanía became more like a bona fide empire—but how much?

We can generally assume that people incorporated into the empire during these conquests were not Romans, whether in religion, language, or some other component of their ethnicity. To be sure, some of them immediately began the process of assimilation to Romanía, though in many places this process was cut short (in the east) or could not hope to take in such large new populations (in Bulgaria). At least initially, then, the change between 930 and 1064 represents an almost pure gain in the column of empire, dramatically shifting the balance between Romans and non-Romans. This change can be seen in the maps included at the start of this volume, which identify the empire's major ethnic populations at the two points in its history discussed in this and the previous chapter. One area taken off the map by the later eleventh century was southern Italy, where Norman aggression confined the Roman administration to a few coastal cities before expelling it altogether, from Bari, in 1071.

However, ethnic and religious difference between conquerors and the conquered is only one criterion of empire. Another is whether the ruling power relies on mechanisms of governance that enforced that difference economically, socially, or legally. The following survey will track both criteria.

Empire in the Balkans

In conquering the Bulgarian empire, Romanía also inherited its diverse subject populations that lived south of the Danube and east of Duklja and Serbia. Before discussing them, it is worth noting that the Bulgarian empire may well have included a Roman population. Its cis-Danubian territories were, after all, former Roman provinces, conquered in the seventh century, and the rulers of Bulgaria frequently carried off groups of captives from Romanía and resettled them in their own lands. Some were ransomed, others not,[1] and defections went in both directions.[2] In the early tenth century, the Bulgarian ruler Simeon (893–927) began to insist on titular parity with the Roman emperor. On one of his seals he even claimed the title "*basileus* of the Romans," albeit without mentioning there either Bulgaria or Bulgarians.[3] The Romans duly protested. The diplomat Theodoros Daphnopates assumed that through this title Simeon was staking a claim to rulership over a community of Romans, and asked the tsar which one he had in mind. Daphnopates assumed that it could refer only to captives of war or slaves, but it is possible that there were other Roman communities within the Bulgarian state, although probably they were small and statistically insignificant.[4]

The majority of the population of Roman-occupied Bulgaria was likely Bulgarian, Slavic-speaking, and Orthodox (by this point, it is pointless to try to distinguish between original Bulgars and Slavs). Due to the lack of discursive narrative texts from Bulgaria, such as we have in abundance for Romanía, it is difficult to reconstruct the contours, nature, and scope of Bulgarian identity. In inscriptions, the rulers of Bulgaria juxtaposed the Bulgarians to the Romans (or "Greeks," which is what they often called them, following western usage) and to the Magyars.[5] A few quasi-historical Bulgarian texts survive from the period of the Roman occupation—in reality, they are prophetic visions that garble history and eschatology—and they reveal the enduring importance of the Bulgarian state tradition and of Bulgarian peoplehood under Roman rule.[6]

For their part too, the Romans continued to regard the Bulgarians as a separate nation, a culturally inferior one to be sure, but categorically equivalent to "Roman." Notoriously, even the Bulgarians' conversion to Christianity did not always cause the Romans to think more highly of them. Many texts, including in religious genres, continued to depict them as a heathen or barbaric nation. An exception was Theophylaktos, their Roman-appointed archbishop at Ohrid (ca. 1100), who tried hard to find a nicer image for the majority of his flock, though even he did not think that they had become Romans.[7] It seems that "people like the Bulgarians, who were subjects of the empire and converts to Orthodoxy but nevertheless failed the ethnic test as Romans, were [an] anomaly."[8] Religious conversion did not bridge the gap between Romans and non-Romans.

Bulgarians could, however, assimilate to Roman norms. Basileios II, who waged a thirty-five-year war against Bulgaria, began to absorb its top men by giving them Roman offices even before he conclusively conquered their state in 1018. This process accelerated after the conquest, not only among the officer class. Soldiers were presumably recruited by the thousands into the new Roman army of the *doukaton* (the regional military command) of Bulgaria.[9] The Bulgarian imperial family was also carted off to Constantinople and eventually married to prominent Romans; they and their descendants rose to high positions in the army, administration, and court. A striking example is provided by Aikaterine, daughter of the last Bulgarian tsar, Ivan Vladislav. In 1019, she was paraded along with the whole of her family in Basileios' triumphal celebrations. But the husband to whom she was married off in 1025, Isaakios I Komnenos, ascended the throne thirty years later, in 1057. Aikaterine thereby became a Roman Augusta and was honored along with Isaakios in the triumphal celebration of his victories as a "joint victor."[10] She had thus been both the conquered and the conqueror in a Roman triumph. I know of one precedent for this in Roman history: as a child

Ventidius Bassus had been led as a captive in a triumph after the Social War, but later, as a Roman consul, he celebrated his own triumph.[11]

If we ask whether occupied Bulgaria was governed in a way that reflected or maintained ethnic differences, the answer is mixed. Basileios gave court titles to Bulgarian nobles, accepted them into the Roman hierarchy, and sought "to put an end to the mutual hatred that formerly prevailed between the two peoples."[12] A Roman historian, the continuator of Skylitzes, claims that Basileios "did not want to change the Bulgarians' customs but decreed that they should live under their own rulers and manners, just as they had under Samuil."[13] This can be seen in two complementary ways: as a policy of accommodation that tolerated local practices and ethnic differences, and also as a policy to maintain that difference, presumably for the benefit of the Romans. It points to a two-tiered system of administration in which Romans and Bulgarians were ruled differently, thereby replicating ethnic or former political differences.

However, it is unclear what "customs" and "rulers" are meant here. The only specific measure that Skylitzes mentions is the allowance that Bulgarians could continue to pay their taxes in kind rather than in coin, as they had under Samuil (the Bulgarian tsars did not mint coins). But this allowance was revoked in 1040, presumably after the Bulgarian economy had become sufficiently monetized. The change sparked a revolt.[14] At any rate, this fiscal concession was due to pragmatic calculations and not a desire to preserve Bulgarian customs. Occupied Bulgarians saw their economy monetized to quasi-Roman levels, transforming their relationship to the state and to each other in a more "Roman" direction. The Romans wanted more uniformity and enforced it as soon as it was possible, or even before that, judging from the revolt.

Basileios left the ecclesiastical structure of Bulgaria more or less in place, subordinating it to the archbishop of Ohrid, a position that, after a brief grace period, was given to a Roman imperial appointee.[15] But the organization of the Church was already the most Roman aspect of the Bulgarian empire even before the conquest; in this respect, at least, Romans and Bulgarians, who had the same faith, were on an equivalent footing. Moreover, at the level of high politics, we do not in fact find a continuation of prior Bulgarian arrangements. Bulgaria was now divided into broad spheres of Roman command (*doukata* or *katepanata*), each of which encompassed a number of military themes. Basileios took over Bulgarian forts, dismantled some, and placed Roman officers in charge of the rest. The generals of the imperial army in Bulgaria were Romans, but the rank and file included Bulgarian recruits.[16] Those forces are called the (Roman) army of Bulgaria or sometimes "the Bulgarians."[17] Military service provided Bulgarians with opportunities for advancement along with incentives to learn Roman ways. But apart from the former imperial family, which was absorbed into the upper echelons of the Roman court, we do not hear of Bulgarian officers rising high in the Roman military officer class. So Bulgarian territory was reorganized, its military was placed in the hands of Roman officers, while the locals provided mostly recruits and (likely) mid-level officers.

The dismantling of the Bulgarian court would have stripped the former boyar class of much of its support, access to influence, and military power.[18] If Bulgarian leadership had survived the prolonged and bloody war, it was on a much reduced local level. The letters of Theophylaktos of Ohrid, written almost a century after the conquest of Bulgaria, do not give the sense that the archbishop had significant contacts among local Bulgarian notables; that stratum is almost completely absent from his network. Theophylaktos dealt primarily with Roman notables, whether in Constantinople or the provinces, and with the Bulgarian general population, not with Bulgarian elites.[19] While no legal mechanism was put in place to suppress the latter, the choices made by the court in political matters and in appointments to office had the same effect. If former Bulgarian elites rose high in the Roman ranks, they presumably did so under Hellenized names and it is possible that they remain invisible to us.

Before the conquest, there had been little bureaucracy beneath the former Bulgarian elite, but now officers of the imperial fisc were sent out to survey the new territory so that taxes could be levied efficiently.[20] Over time this introduced a great deal of bureaucracy to daily life, changing the Bulgarians' relationship to the state and making it much more Roman-like. Toward the end of the eleventh century, Theophylaktos of Ohrid was complaining in his letters about the rapaciousness of imperial tax collectors and naming all the exotic taxes that they were collecting, a typically Roman preoccupation.[21] His letters reveal that a complex bureaucratic apparatus was in place. One scholar has spoken of "the alignment of Bulgaria to the policies, aspirations, and tastes of Constantinople."[22] We have an indirect gauge for how pervasive this was. It has been estimated that roughly three-fourths of the juridical and administrative vocabulary used in the second Bulgarian empire (formed after the rebellion of 1185) was of Roman origin, in contrast to what we know of its predecessor, conquered in 1018.[23] It would appear, then, that the Romans governed Bulgaria through the same fiscal mechanisms by which they governed themselves.

This new bureaucracy did not hover at an elite level in a way that left the majority of the population unaffected or unconcerned. In conquered Bulgaria too, the Roman state penetrated all the way down. Consider the case of Lazar, a dependent farmer *(paroikos)* of the Bulgarian Church, socially just a step up from being a slave. Apparently, in an effort to secure greater freedom for himself he had conspired with agents of the fisc *(praktores)* and accused the archbishop, Theophylaktos, of serious felony charges before no less an authority than the emperor Alexios Komnenos. Theophylaktos had to enlist his most heavyweight patrons in Constantinople to defend himself against "this Bulgarian nature that nourishes every form of evil."[24] Lazar was a Bulgarian peasant, but not only was he enmeshed in the political intrigues of the provincial administration, it seems that the ancient Roman right of petitioning the emperor was available to him. Let us remember here that the founders of the second Bulgarian empire, the brothers Petar and Asen, decided to rebel when they petitioned the emperor in person for a small grant of land, were denied, and Asen was slapped across the face for speaking insolently.[25] This, then, was not indirect rule from a distance ("pay us x amount of taxes and we will leave you alone to manage your own affairs"). The Roman administration took on the nuts and bolts of governance at the local level.

The evidence of seals and the letters of Theophylaktos suggests that the Roman administration of Bulgaria was primarily military and fiscal, and less civilian, in nature. In sum, the royal family was taken off to Constantinople and broken up, the former elites were politically "decapitated," and Bulgaria was governed by Romans through primarily military and fiscal institutions, without giving its people much opportunity to rise in the Roman system. In this sense, it looks more like an occupation, for all that Bulgarians and Romans shared the same religion and were, after the conquest, probably subject to the same laws.

Therefore, some Bulgarians may have felt that they were under foreign occupation, whereas others had access to opportunities available to Romans. Yet they were not Romans, and so it was easier to say that they formed a part of the *territory* of the Romans than their *polity*.[26] This points to the distinction, found in some sources, between Romanía and the *arche* of the Romans.[27] It is significant that Bulgarians mounted three rebellions against Constantinople, in 1040, 1072, and 1185, the last one of which succeeded. The Roman sources state that they were moved in part by a desire for national independence.[28] Modern scholars were for long trained to instinctively reject such motives for premodern people, but there is no reason to deny that this was at least part of the picture, supported as it is by so many sources. For resentful Bulgarians, Roman rule felt a lot more like "empire." But there were also many times during the occupation when the Bulgarian army under Roman command remained loyal to the empire under difficult circumstances. Occupied Bulgaria therefore presents a mixed picture.

The greater level of documentation produced by the Roman state and by Roman authors immediately shed light on at least two ethnic groups that had been living in the broader Bulgarian realm but had so far remained invisible: the Albanians and the Vlachs. This is not the place to rehearse the contentious debates that surround the origin and early history of both groups, as we are interested only in their relation to the Roman state. Unfortunately, it is almost impossible to see what that was, especially in the case of the Albanians, located in the hinterland of the theme of Dyrrachion. They are mentioned for the first time in the eleventh century, as they formed ethnically distinct military units, for example, "an army of Romans, Bulgarians, and Arvanites."[29] It is not known what kind of administrative presence the empire maintained in their mountainous homeland; possibly it was indirect. When Bohemond invaded the empire in 1107, some of them sided with him and showed him the mountain paths.[30]

The Vlachs, a mostly pastoral people who spoke a Romance language, are attested immediately in the *sigillia* that Basileios II issued in 1020 to confirm the rights and jurisdiction of the former Church of Bulgaria.[31] Unfortunately, he does not say much about them or specify the administrative arrangements by which he intended them to be governed (ecclesiastical *sigillia* were not for that). Our sources for the Vlachs under Roman rule are poor. In the 1070s, Kekaumenos wrote a manual with advice to emperors and governors, and he was personally familiar with central Greece. He claims that one of his ancestors, Nikoulitzas, who formerly held a military post in Greece, was, in 979, given the command *(arche)* of the Vlachs of Greece by Basileios II.[32] Apparently there were Vlachs in Romanía long before the war with Bulgaria was over and they performed military service as an ethnic unit under a Roman-appointed *archon*. This arrangement was similar to that which governed the Slavs of central Greece in the seventh and eighth centuries: a quasi-autonomous ethnic group providing soldiers to the empire but not fully assimilated to its administration or cultural life.[33] We do not, however, know Nikoulitzas' ethnicity, and this area of central Greece, along with Kekaumenos' ancestors themselves, would oscillate between Bulgaria and Romanía during Basileios II's long war.[34]

The next window opens in 1066. Kekaumenos gives a detailed account of a rebellion that took place in Thessaly in 1066 that involved the people of Larissa along with some Vlachs and Bulgarians, who were all protesting a tax hike. The (reluctant) leader of the rebellion was one Nikoulitzas Delphinas, a descendant of the *archon* of the Vlachs in 979, which may have been part of the reason why the Vlachs now turned to him. Nikoulitzas Delphinas was related by marriage to Kekaumenos and was the source for the account that he gives of the events. He presents the Vlachs as pastoralists who moved their flocks between Thessaly and the former territory of the Bulgarian empire, but they also maintained a presence in the towns of Thessaly.[35] Kekaumenos' accounts of their activities and lifestyle makes it seem that they were not entirely under the control of imperial authority, but they were planning an armed rebellion and showed up ready to fight, so they must have had some kind of military organization. It appears that they no longer had a separate *archon* appointed by the emperor.[36] Kekaumenos follows his account of the rebellion with a brief ethnography of the Vlachs. He calls them a faithless and perverse *genos* that is not to be trusted. He advises governors to secure the Vlachs' wives and children in "the cities of Romanía" as hostages to their good behavior.[37]

A mobile group of Vlach pastoralists was known as a *katouna*. In the early twelfth century, one such group, consisting of three hundred families, had settled near Mt. Athos, causing a headache to imperial authorities for reasons that we need not get into here. One of the documents generated by their presence claims that the emperor Alexios I Komnenos was basically treating a *katouna* as a taxable unit equivalent to a Roman *chorion* (or village, a fiscal unit).[38] This is one way in which the Roman authorities tried to place the Vlachs under familiar rubrics. Later in the twelfth century Anna Komnene noted that the Vlachs had their own villages but lived a nomadic life; the Roman army once mistook them for Cumans.[39] All this suggests both ethnic alterity and quasi-autonomy. The Vlachs are mentioned repeatedly as a source of soldiers, probably as ethnic auxiliaries.[40] In 1162, the Jewish traveler Benjamin of Tudela says that the Vlachs come down from the mountains of central Greece to rob and pillage, and no state authority resists them; the emperors have failed to tame them. He hyperbolically added that "they do not even profess the Christian faith."[41] A twelfth-century governor of Greece was praised for waging war against the "outlandish barbarians who live in the most inaccessible mountains of Greece, who are highway robbers and tax-evaders."[42] The Vlachs of Thessaly, then, along probably with the Vlachs in many parts of the former Bulgarian empire, were not fully "pacified," to use an ancient Roman term. They occupied the gray area between the polity and the empire of the Romans, and were not even fully subject to the latter. Even before 1204, mountainous Thessaly was being called Vlachia.[43]

Even though they were orthodox, in some contexts Vlachs from the mountains could be regarded as essentially different from the

Romans. We have scant information about this, but it is suggestive of systemic discrimination on ethnic grounds. In the early thirteenth century, the bishop of Naupaktos, Ioannes Apokaukos, granted a divorce and cited, among other reasons, the fact that the wife was "a barbarian and did not speak Greek correctly"—he says this twice in his ruling—adding that she was from the mountainous regions of Velahatouïa and was accordingly given the baptismal name Rousa, an ethnic association that he assumed his readers would understand. She may have been a Vlach or a Slav—we do not know—but we have here a Roman bishop dissolving an orthodox marriage in part because of the couple's ethnic differences, along with their great age difference. On all these grounds, he deemed it "absurd" that they had been married in the first place.[44]

Immediately after the Vlachs, Basileios' *sigillion* refers to the Turks of the Vardar valley (i.e., the Axios). These were probably Hungarian mercenaries who were hired and settled there, north of Thessalonike, either by Samuil or Basileios himself. By the eleventh century they had their own bishop. The unit, with the same ethnogeographical name, is attested in the later Byzantine period, but by then its ethnic composition had changed; it is likely that only the original name remained, linked to the place or to the unit recruited from it.[45]

Moving our focus to Thrace, the emperor Ioannes I Tzimiskes moved many Paulicians from the eastern frontier to Philippopolis in Thrace, to guard the passes there. These Paulicians were presumably incorporated by the empire in its recent conquests in the east, as the request for their transfer came from the new Byzantine bishop of Antioch. One century later, these Paulicians were still in Philippopolis, forming a large part of the local population and providing soldiers to the empire. Alexios Komnenos converted many of them to Orthodoxy, after which they are rarely mentioned.[46] A smaller community of Paulicians or Bogomils was destroyed by Bohemond at Pelagonia in 1097, when his contingent of the First Crusade marched across the Balkans.[47]

Finally, the lower Danube delta, the corner of imperial territory where the river met the Black Sea, was occupied by Pechenegs. Two groups of them had entered the empire in the late 1040s. Konstantinos IX Monomachos had tried to settle both groups on imperial territory and recruit them into the army, but it went horribly wrong. After years of fighting, the two sides came to an agreement: the Pechenegs would recognize the emperor but remain mostly autonomous. For the Romans, the Pechenegs were nomadic Scythians, as far from being civilized Romans as possible, and even after the agreement they occasionally raided the Roman provinces when the Romans were preoccupied, for example during civil wars.[48] As they were not settled in predominantly Roman lands, despite their nominal conversion to Orthodoxy there was no question of their assimilation. Moreover, they had entered with their own women and children and were not successfully dispersed (though that had been the original plan). So the Pechenegs ended up forming an ethnic enclave; in fact, it is not clear that we should treat them as part of the empire. Kekaumenos, who wrote a book with advice in the 1070s, warned against such experiments: "If the enemy asks you to cede part of your territory to him, do not agree unless he agrees to be subject to you and pay you taxes, and even then do it only in great need. The Romans have suffered many disasters from such things . . . for example, the Pechenegs entered Romanía in this way."[49] The Pechenegs were finally crushed by Alexios Komnenos at the battle of Lebounion in 1091, after which they were incorporated into the imperial army. In this capacity, they served the empire well, albeit in smaller dispersed units.

New Armenian Subjects

Turning to the east, the largest non-Roman ethnicity absorbed by the empire in its expansion were the Armenians. The empire annexed the realm of Taron around 968 (it was voluntarily ceded by its ruler); then a portion of the mixed Georgian-Armenian realm of Upper Tao in 1000 (its ruler had backed the wrong side in a Roman civil war in the 980s and had to bequeath part of his state to Rome in his will); Vaspurakan around 1020 (voluntarily ceded); Ani in 1045 (its ruler had also backed the wrong side in the war of 1022 and had to bequeath his realm, but its annexation was resisted when he died); and Vanand (Kars) in 1064/5 (voluntarily ceded while the Seljuks were conquering the Caucasus). The majority of Armenians thereby became imperial subjects, albeit briefly: the most important of the former principalities were held by the empire for fifty years (Vaspurakan), twenty (Ani), and a handful (Vanand). This constricts our ability to see how the empire governed them. The window narrows even more if we assume, as we must, that local practices were generally left in place and changes made only gradually, as in Bulgaria.[50]

It was not only in the annexed principalities that Armenians could be found in the empire. Roman expansion into the Caucasus had been preceded in the tenth century by a push against the Muslim emirates of Cilicia, Syria, Melitene, and Mesopotamia. As it annexed territories there, in the southeast, the empire established many smaller frontier themes that were manned largely by Armenian soldier-settlers. Melias had pioneered these when he founded the fort theme of Lykandos. These relatively short-lived formations came to be known as the smaller "Armenian themes" that were juxtaposed to the older "large Roman themes."[51] In the second half of the tenth century, therefore, Armenians began to play a more prominent role in the imperial army,[52] which was expanding and in need of manpower, although prejudices against their reliability persisted on the Roman side.[53] "Roman" and "Armenian" soldiers are juxtaposed in narrative accounts of operations composed by both Roman and Arab writers.[54] Beyond the empire's reliance on Armenian frontiersmen, its settlement of Armenians in an arc from the Caucasus to the Mediterranean initiated a population drift from Armenia, which later enabled the formation of Armenian states in Cilicia, among other places.

How did the empire govern Armenians? In sum, Roman policy toward them was not much different from its policy toward the Bulgarians, despite the different ways in which Armenian territories were acquired and the confessional split between the Byzantine and Armenian Churches. The new territories—both the smaller Armenian themes and the annexed principalities—were grouped into broader military commands under a *doux* or *katepano*, who was usually a Roman career officer.[55] The armies beneath him, by contrast, led by the regional generals, were probably recruited to a considerable degree among the local population. Unfortunately, we know little about the administrative structures that were put in place in

Armenia. Narrative notices are few. The Armenian historian Aristakes says that when Basileios II annexed part of Tao he appointed "officials, judges and overseers" in the forts and the cities there.[56] Later in his narrative, Aristakes twice records "judges" being sent out from Constantinople to Iberia and Taron, where they adjudicated local disputes; we sorely want to know by what laws they governed.[57] From lead seals we know that men were posted to all the top positions in the Roman administration, both military and civilian-judicial, that we can expect to have left a record. This was true in both the small Armenian themes and the big regional commands formed out of the former principalities, suggesting that the empire intended to install the full apparatus of governance that it used in the Roman themes, just as it did in Bulgaria. These officials were a mix of Romans and locals.[58]

Like the former Bulgarian empire, the former Armenian principalities had not minted coins. To the degree that their economies were monetized, they had relied on Roman and Muslim coinage. The Roman presence would have increased monetization, if only because of the influx of pay given to the soldiers and officers stationed in the new commands, but we do not know how this intersected with tax policy. I have found no studies of the monetization of the local economies during this period, though thousands of Byzantine coins have been discovered.[59] Aristakes refers in one place to a tax official sent from Constantinople and elsewhere records the court's desire to tax the Armenian Church, a plan that was abandoned.[60] But he does not say what form these taxes took (or would have taken). Two imperial governors of Ani posted inscriptions that reveal that the city, if not its surrounding territory, had been regimented by a full apparatus of requisitions, taxes, corves on labor, and exemptions; these typically Roman administrative and fiscal arrangements had no counterpart in the former Armenian royal tradition. To display this new order prominently in the minds of locals, the governors had the inscriptions carved outside the public door of the cathedral of Ani.[61] Unfortunately, we do not know how deeply the Roman bureaucracy penetrated into the newly acquired territories around the city in the two decades that it controlled them. In general, it would be safest to assume that local norms continued in force outside the context of the army and the higher levels of political power, with the additional caveat that the nature of elite society and the ideology projected by politicized spaces was significantly transformed.

As in Bulgaria, the bureaucratization of the armed forces undermined the power of Armenian aristocrats, the "feudal" lords of the former principalities, some of whom had been required to give up their lands and forts. This by itself had massive effects on local society. The former nobility could preserve their high status by seeking positions in the Roman army and administration, but that would have embedded them further in the Roman order. Any doubts that a new and different power was now in charge would have been lain to rest when Basileios II established an army of Bulgarians in Vaspurakan;[62] Varangians and Franks were soon to follow. Most forts, at least initially, were placed in the hands of Roman officers. In the early 1050s, Konstantinos IX Monomachos sent a fiscal official to reorganize the armies of Iberia and possibly Mesopotamia, altering previous arrangements regarding funding, land, and service. This reform was regarded as disastrous at the time and has a notorious reputation in scholarship, even though its nature remains opaque. Whatever it was, it seems to have rested on typical Roman technologies of administration, including registers of lands, soldiers, and payments to and by the state. These probably introduced to the east practices that were being used in the core territories of the empire.[63]

The empire also established many Chalcedonian ecclesiastical sees in the new territories to match those of the (anti-Chalcedonian) Armenian Church; a minority of Armenians were already Chalcedonian and a number switched at this time.[64] But the Armenian Church also began, in the 960s or 970s, to establish its own sees inside imperial territory, especially in Syria but also at Sebasteia.[65] For the first time in over three hundred years, a significant presence of non-Chalcedonian Christians was felt within the empire. The eleventh century did witness a rise in Orthodox polemics against Armenian Christianity, attacks that were, through complicated channels that we need not explore here, caught up in the emerging schism between Rome and Constantinople.[66] But the emperors did not persecute the Armenian Church, as they did, at times, the Syrian Church (see below).[67] Instead, the authorities took a more pragmatic approach.

An attack against Armenian priests instigated by the bishop of Sebasteia is reported for 986–987, but the emperor put a quick stop to it—if we can believe the report.[68] After the annexation of Ani (in ca. 1045), the Armenian *katholikos* (chief prelate) Petros was removed to Constantinople before being relocated to Asia Minor. But these movements may not have been forced, and he seems to have received rock star treatment in the capital.[69] More importantly, we know of a number of non-Chalcedonian Armenians who were appointed to high offices and given court titles.[70]

Thus, while there is abundant evidence for ethnic difference and even for virulent expressions of prejudice between Romans and Armenians, there is no evidence for an overt or systematic politics of difference in the empire's rule over Armenians. The latter could rise in the hierarchy, and many did so. Toward the end of the eleventh century, when the Roman east collapsed, its fragments fell into the hands of officers such as Philaretos Brachamios, Gabriel of Melitene, and Theodoros of Edessa, all of whom the sources call both Armenian and Roman in alternating ways or in various combinations. These figures, who are cherished today for being so complex and ambiguous in their identity,[71] were the product of an unfinished assimilation of local Armenian officers. In better times, they would have advanced their careers by going to the capital, intermarrying with the Roman elite, and being posted to non-Armenian provinces. That path, as we have seen, had been followed by many Armenian nobles in previous centuries and, in the later tenth century, by the rulers of Taron, who went on to become the Taronites, a Roman family that joined the Komnenian aristocracy.[72] But those options were blocked by the fall of Asia Minor to the Turks, which cut these lands off from Constantinople and opened up other, more local opportunities for personal self-aggrandizement in the post-Roman east.

This brings us to the major demographic shift experienced by the Roman east during the eleventh century: a migration of Armenians who moved from their annexed principalities into Cappadocia, Cilicia, and Syria. This move was facilitated by the empire's expansion but likely caused by the Turkish raids into the Caucasus and the increasing instability of the area. Armenian military themes had already been established in an arc down the Caucasus to Cilicia, but there was one more vector of migration: the transfer of the former royal families to Roman Cappadocia. One chronicle, simplifying considerably, directly links the migration of Armenians to the transplantation of their royal families.[73] But that transplantation has been described in misleading terms by some scholars. As it concerns the mechanisms by which Romanía managed its ethnic minorities, a word must be said about it. According to a "maximalist" interpretation of the transfer of the royalty of Vaspurakan, Ani, and Kars, the royals were granted largely autonomous ethnic Armenian "principalities" within Cappadocia, principalities that were both massive in size and hereditary and that they ruled with the feudal armies that they brought from Armenia. They even conducted their own "foreign policy," sometimes against the empire itself.[74]

The maximalist position is untenable and is not supported by the sources, whether Roman or Armenian. Such a grant would be a radical departure from prior imperial policy, an unprecedented and unnecessary surrender of sovereignty made, puzzlingly, from a position of strength, for the first of these grants was made by Basileios II around 1020. He was not one to devolve power, especially after having fought so many wars to consolidate it into his hands. The sources for the period, many of them written by contemporaries, are unaware of the existence of such huge Armenian statelets in the heart of Roman Asia Minor. The actual arrangement was far more prosaic. The facts support a minimalist interpretation according to which the royals were given land, titles, and minor commands of a more limited geographical scope, not new personal principalities in exchange for their old ones.[75] Let us look at the evidence.

The sources say that in exchange for Vaspurakan, its ruler was given the title of *patrikios* and placed in command of the cities of Sebasteia, Larissa, and Abara. He was also given much landed property, to which he moved with a large following. His family and retinue are thereafter associated with Sebasteia.[76] There is uncertainty about whether this grant was received by Senekʻerim or his son Davitʻ, who was also known as Senekʻerim.[77] If it was the former, then an allowance was made for the "hereditary" transmission of the grant from father to son in 1027, when the father died—the only instance of such transmission that the entire settlement of all the royals entailed. This would not have been difficult for Basileios to arrange, as he had experimented with heredity in his imperial arrangements before.[78] If Davitʿ was the original recipient, as seems more likely, then we face no such issue: he was simply accommodated within the existing imperial administration. Now, the twelfth-century Armenian historian Matthew of Edessa claims that two years later Basileios gave Kaisareia, Tzamandos, and Gabadonia to Davitʿ as a reward for his murder of the rebel Nikephoros Phokas, in 1022. This information about the additional grant appears only in Matthew and must be treated with caution, in fact with skepticism. Matthew is unreliable, often purveying fiction as history (see below). It is possible that Basileios gave Davitʿ *lands around* Kaisareia or *in* Tzamandos, but it is virtually impossible that he gave that city and that district to him. Kaisareia (in Charsianon theme) was a central node in the empire's military organization and is never associated in Byzantine sources with Davitʿ.[79]

Gagik II of Ani had surrendered Ani to the empire reluctantly, after it had been pledged by his uncle. In around 1045 Konstantinos IX Monomachos gave him the title of *magistros* and lands in Cappadocia, Charsianon, and Lykandos—not command of the themes, just lands *in* them. Matthew of Edessa names the lands as Kalon-Peghat and Pizu.[80] Two contemporary Roman sources say that Gagik "thereafter lived a peaceful and untroubled life" (Skylitzes), and "spent the rest of his charmed life in luxury and enjoyment on account of the properties and superlative titles that he was given" (Attaleiates).[81] It is important to quote these passages because they refute the hagiographic-heroic account of Gagik's later career in Matthew of Edessa. Matthew has the deposed king deliver long sermons on Armenian Christianity to the imperial court; order his Armenian soldiers to rape Roman women by Kaisareia as he was passing through; then murder the bishop of Kaisareia who was prejudiced against Armenians; and plot to have his throne restored by the Seljuks—all in the time before both Attaleiates and Skylitzes were writing. For Matthew, Gagik symbolized Armenian strength and uncompromising faith.[82]

Matthew also believed that Davitʿ (formerly of Vaspurakan) died in the mid-1030s and passed the command of Sebasteia to his brother

Atom, which would make this the second hereditary transfer in the settlement of the royals of Vaspurakan.[83] But he was mistaken. Aristakes, a more reliable historian who was writing closer to the events, says that, "by order of the emperor Konstantinos IX, Gagik married Davitʿs daughter and ruled that sector [i.e., Sebasteia], since when Davitʿ died he had left no other heir."[84] There was, then, no hereditary transfer, only an imperial reassignment.[85] Sebasteia passed to Gagik, which explains why he is often present there in Matthew's subsequent narrative, although he did not know about the reassignment.[86] In the 1070s, after the battle of Mantzikert, Gagik was given the position of *megas doux* of Charsianon, though it is unknown what (if any) responsibilities it entailed at that point.[87] By contrast, Davitʿs brothers Atom and Abusahl are not attested with titles or offices, despite their prominence in Matthew's narrative. Finally, the last Armenian king to cede his realm to the empire was Gagik of Kars, around 1064. Matthew claims that the emperor (Konstantinos X Doukas) gave him Tzamandos (in Lykandos) in which to settle with his noblemen (that theme had been settled by Armenians from its tenth-century beginnings).[88]

In sum, there is no proof for quasi-autonomous Armenian principalities established within Roman territory. The royals were given lands on which to settle and one command, that of Sebasteia, which was reallocated to Gagik of Ani when Davitʿ died; Gagik may later have been given a command in Charsianon. The question then arises not only about how Romans ruled Armenians, but how former Armenian kings ruled Romans in the theme of Sebasteia. Unfortunately, we have no evidence about that.

Be that as it may, these resettlements did not result in surrogate Armenian statehood, nor were they intended to do so. Still, they played a crucial historical role, one that was enabled by the emperors. The deposed royal families supported the Armenian Church in the empire, hosting the *katholikoi* on their new lands, building churches and monasteries, and forming a nucleus that drew more Armenians from the homeland, as it became increasingly unsafe.[89] The royals did not have private or royal armies, but they did have retinues and wealth, with which they attracted more clients. In these ways, they facilitated the Armenian drift westward and southward. What is important for our purposes is that the emperors let them do this. The idea that the royals turned violent against Romanía is due entirely to the nationalist and theological polemics of Matthew of Edessa, who treats the deposed royals as heroic champions against the wicked Byzantines. But the stories that he tells about this are unbelievable, for instance that Romanos IV Diogenes sacked the city of Sebasteia on his way to Mantzikert out of sheer hatred of the Armenian faith.[90] Despite Matthew's polemics and his hints of persecutions that were intended but did not actually happen, Romanía tolerantly accommodated its anti-Chalcedonian Armenians. The latter, especially the former royals, resisted the allure of Constantinople by refusing to convert, and their families accordingly did not advance high in imperial service. Nina Garsoïan concludes that "the overwhelming mass of the Armenian inhabitants of the empire, isolated by language more than by ethnic background, by religion . . . and at last by the mythology surrounding their lost king [Gagik], remained alien and alienated—incorporated but not assimilated."[91]

The attitudes toward the empire of its new Armenian subjects reflected this sense of incorporation without assimilation. Basileios II had sent a fragment of the True Cross to a monastery in Vaspurakan (outside his dominions), which earned him a panegyric by the Armenian poet Grigor of Narek in the 990s. Here doctrinal differences were set aside. But the works produced by Armenians in the eleventh century keep their distance and do not identify with the empire. The historian Step'anos was born around the time that his homeland Taron was voluntarily annexed—an event that he mentions—and he used at least one Greek source in writing about recent events (he finished writing in 1003 or 1004). But he seems to have worked in Ani, outside the empire. He does not depict the empire as an evil foreign oppressor, but he did regard it as a threat to Armenian identity and its Church; he does not engage in polemics against the Romans, only their theology.[92] Aristakes of Lastivert, a historian of the eleventh century, was from a town near the Roman command center of Theodosioupolis (annexed in 1000). He also used a Greek source and is not overtly hostile to the Romans as such, though he bewails and castigates their failure to defend the east from the Turks. Thus, like the Jews of southern Italy and the Bulgarians, Armenians under Roman rule continued to produce narratives that affirmed their ethnic or national distinction from the imperial core.

Georgians, Syrians, Melkites, Muslims, Jews

Georgians (also known as Kartvelians, called Iberians by the Byzantines) had the same religion as the Romans, but we lack unambiguous evidence for assimilation on their part. The largest concentration of Georgians in the empire were in the part of Tao that was annexed in 1000, and Basileios II had prepared the ground before 1000 by bestowing imperial titles on local notables. But the impression left by the Georgians is that they maintained their ethnic separation even when they were actively involved in the affairs of the empire. They founded a separate monastery on Mt. Athos, called Iviron ("of the Iberians"), which had around three hundred monks in the eleventh century.[93] The imperial general Gregorios Pakourianos was of mixed Georgian-Armenian ancestry and culture but claimed to belong to "the most glorious race of the Georgians." He had a distinguished career in Roman service in the eleventh century and died in battle against the Pechenegs. In the charter for the monastery that he founded in Bulgaria (Bačkovo), he notes that many of his relations had shed their blood fighting for the Roman empire and that he too was proud of serving it, but at the same time he stipulated that the monastery was for Georgians only, and he specifically excluded Romans from it because they were too violent and greedy, a remarkable assertion of ethnic stereotypes and boundaries.[94]

In a compilation of decisions made by the early eleventh-century judge Eustathios Romaios, we find a case of an "ethnic" man of Georgian origin who held a high court title but had not followed "the laws of the Romans" in drawing up his will. Instead, he had followed his national custom, and the judge emended the will in accordance with Roman law in order to process the dispute.[95] In both cases (of founding monasteries and drawing up wills) it was the Georgians who maintained their own separation, not the imperial authorities who enforced it.

As the empire expanded in the southeast, it incorporated members of the Syrian Orthodox faith (also known as Jacobites), who also did not recognize the Council of Chalcedon and were therefore regarded by the Byzantine Church effectively as heretical; by this point, the Syrian Orthodox were functionally an ethnicity too, distinguished by language, ecclesiastical organization, and a shared history.[96] Initially, the empire not only incorporated them, it actively encouraged them to leave Muslim-controlled lands and resettle on imperial territory. Nikephoros II Phokas (963–969) invited their patriarch Yuhannan VII Sarigta to relocate to Melitene, under assurance of toleration. The offer was accepted, but that same emperor later hauled the patriarch and his bishops to Constantinople, where they were forced to debate doctrinal issues. Toleration was restored by the more pragmatic Ioannes I Tzimiskes (969–976), and soon the Jacobites expanded their presence and built monasteries in the Roman-ruled east, especially around Melitene and Antioch, with financial assistance provided by court officials. The immigration of Jacobites and Armenians presumably filled the demographic and economic gap left by the Muslims who were expelled in the course of the Roman conquest (see below). The period of toleration of the Jacobites lasted sixty years, whereupon persecution of their ecclesiastical leadership was initiated again by Romanos III Argyros in 1029 and, after another hiatus, Konstantinos X Doukas in the 1060s, with more arrests, forced "debates," and exiles. Konstantinos X allegedly intended to expel all non-Chalcedonians from Melitene.[97]

Clearly, a politics of difference marked the empire's treatment of Jacobites, especially their priesthood, more so, it seems, than its treatment of the equally non-Chalcedonian Armenians. As we saw, some of the latter were appointed to high Roman offices in the east, but I know of no Jacobites similarly promoted between the bouts of ecclesiastical persecution.[98] A synod convened in 1030 in Constantinople to condemn the Jacobites reminded the emperors that the laws of the Christian Roman empire forbade such heretics from holding court titles as well as civic and military positions.[99] And yet Armenian non-Chalcedonians were being appointed to high offices. Moreover, it appears that the ancient laws against heretics were not always enforced on the Jacobites either. The Byzantine Orthodox bishop of Melitene Ioannes complained to the patriarch and Synod of Constantinople about this, and they drafted a resolution protesting the nonenforcement of the relevant laws. Apparently, Orthodox families were marrying their daughters to the Jacobites; the latter were being allowed to draft legal wills naming other heretics as their heirs; and judges were admitting testimony given by Jacobites against the Orthodox, all of which was prohibited by law.[100] It seems that a politics of difference was not being vigorously enforced in Melitene, and the two religious communities were being treated as legally interchangeable.

We need more research on the selective enforcement of these laws by region, community, and date. Among the nonreligious factors relevant to the exclusion of the Syrians from high office was their lack of prior experience in running states and armies, whether their own or those of a host empire, whereas many Armenians had such experience.

The multiethnic demography of the major cities in the Roman east is illustrated by a history of the Coptic patriarchs of Alexandria (an Arabic text), which records that in 1072 Edessa had 20,000 Syrians, 8,000 Armenians, 6,000 Romans, and 1,000 Latins (including probably Frankish mercenaries).[101] Even if these figures are accurate, they do not necessarily reflect the city's demography in the more settled decades before the Turkish invasions that were taking place at that time.

Imperial expansion also brought in a large population of Arabic-speaking Orthodox (also known as Melkites). They may have formed a majority of the population in Cilicia, especially after the expulsion of the Muslims, as well as in Antioch and its hinterland. Antioch became a forward base or second capital of the empire on the frontier. It was only to be expected that the empire would favor Melkites in the new territories. It relied on them to govern Antioch at the local level, preferring them over the Armenians and Jacobites. The Melkite Church consolidated its power there and sometimes harassed the Churches of its rivals, even when the latter were being tolerated by the imperial authorities elsewhere. The Melkite population of Antioch and Laodikeia was also boosted by refugees fleeing the chaotic regime of the Fatimid caliph al-Hakim in Egypt in the mid-1010s; among them was the later historian Yahya of Antioch, a Melkite who wrote in Arabic.[102] His chronicle, one of the best works of history of its time, does not focus on his Church or its dispersed membership, though it does recount the events of the tenth and eleventh centuries from its perspective. But the fascinating and complex history of Antioch during the century of Roman rule has not yet been written in full, nor have studies yet been devoted to the treatment of Arabic-speaking Christians in Byzantium.[103]

I have not found characterizations of Melkite Christians in Roman texts of this period from which we might gauge their perception of ethnic or cultural difference. The twelfth-century Armenian historian Matthew of Edessa says that the Melkites of Antioch (or some subgroup) "consider themselves Romans in faith but in essence should be regarded as Muslims because of the language they use and because of their deeds." But he is a hostile witness, going on to call them "blasphemers of the Orthodox faith [he means his own anti-Chalcedonian faith] . . . resembling sick and feeble women who sit in the streets and babble with their tongues."[104] The Romans would obviously have had a different view. The empire had in the past accepted Christians from the caliphate and resettled them, though before the ninth century most would have been Greek-speakers.[105] Some Arabic-speakers among them were promoted to high offices in the administration.[106] In our period, the empire did give court titles to Melkites. It is likely that an Arabic-speaking Christian, Kulayb, who was promoted to the highest position available locally, governor of Antioch, was a Melkite. However, such appointments were made under tense circumstances of conquest and civil war; thereafter that post was held by career Roman officers.[107]

The leadership of the Melkite community, both lay and clerical, possibly retained a knowledge of Greek, which had remained an important language in the Christian East long after the Arab conquests. This means that they would have been able to interface seamlessly with the Roman administration and even pass in Roman society. The epitaph of one Basileios, who died in Antioch in 999, was written in both Greek and Arabic.[108] More light on this question will likely be brought by the publication of bilingual Arabic-Greek seals from the collection at Dumbarton Oaks, especially those that record offices and titles.[109]

Another Melkite, Petros Libellisios, was appointed governor of Antioch around 1068. He is described as follows by the historian Michael Attaleiates: "He was Assyrian by race, born in Antioch, and he had been superbly educated in both Roman and Saracen wisdom and letters."[110] In other words, he was bilingual, perhaps bicultural, and educated in a way that an elite Roman could respect. It would be curious to know how Melkites who spoke no Greek were perceived by Romans, say, for example, by Constantinopolitans, for Melkites were not Arabic-speaking Romans: they had their own, separate identity.[111] Still, imperial policy seems not to have enforced or even formally recognized ethnic, linguistic, or cultural differences between these two Orthodox groups, however Greek- and Arabic-speakers perceived each other.

Muslims bore the brunt of the empire's military expansion in the east, which targeted a number of frontier emirates from Cilicia, up through Melitene, to those nestled more deeply in the southern Caucasus.[112] The Roman expansion was perceived by Muslims abroad as an unmitigated disaster, eliciting calls for jihad and, when those failed, lamentations and fiery sermons. It was inevitable that the empire would now have Muslim subjects, but they were perhaps not as many as one might conclude from looking at a map. The Roman campaigns of conquest against the emirates were brutal, targeting the civilian population, destroying agriculture, and enslaving those who were caught in the countryside. Many of those captives were brought back to the core territories and dispersed as slaves. Nikephoros II Phokas in particular tended to expel Muslims from the cities that he captured during the fifteen years when he was in command of the army (955–969), or to demand that they convert. This caused depopulation. The sources, both Roman and Arab, contain many references to columns of refugees departing for more distant Muslim lands, sometimes under military escort. In order to keep or reclaim their homes, some Muslims converted, presumably to the Melkite Church, sometimes after they had been initially deported. With regard to Muslims, then, Romanía practiced an imperial "politics of difference" at its most extreme, at least initially.[113]

After reducing the Muslim presence in the conquered territories, the state brought in Roman, Armenian, and Jacobite settlers (the last especially to the region of Melitene). It is possible also that the Christian population had been in the majority in Cilicia before the conquest, even if the emirates were governed by Muslims.[114] But after the conquests, Muslims were allowed to remain in some of the territories controlled by the *doukaton* of Antioch. Unfortunately, we have no systematic study of how the empire governed them. It is likely that they largely governed themselves and interfaced with imperial authorities only at the highest local level. In some places, they were governed internally by their own judges, laws, and customs, while paying tribute to the empire.[115] A Nestorian Christian physician from Baghdad, Ibn Butlan, wrote in the mid-eleventh century that the main mosque of Laodikeia (on the Syrian coast) had been turned into a church but local Muslims prayed at another mosque and had their own judge *(qadi)*; at a village between Antioch and Aleppo there were four Byzantine Orthodox (or Melkite) churches and one mosque.[116]

The empire did not want or seek out Muslim subjects, but it acquired and tolerated some because it needed their lands and cities for strategic reasons, for example in coastal Syria. As far as I know, Roman sources do not refer to them at all after the period of the conquests, or make ethnic distinctions among them (e.g., Arabs, Turks, Daylami, etc.). The Romans so hated their religion that this overrode finer internal distinctions. Progress in understanding the standing of these Muslim minorities in the Christian empire will likely come from further research in eastern sources.

Imperial expansion in the east also brought more Jewish communities into the empire. Also, the intolerant climate of Fatimid Egypt led many Jews (as well as Melkites) to migrate to Romanía, which was flourishing economically. The empire was now crisscrossed by denser Jewish networks that extended throughout the eastern Mediterranean and into Muslim-ruled lands. Overall, these Jewish communities appear to have flourished too. The Nestorian bishop Elias of Nisibis (d. 1046) wrote that the Romans "tolerate a large population of Jews in their realm. . . . They afford them protection, allow them openly to adhere to their religion, and to build their synagogues. . . . The Jew in their lands may say 'I am a Jew.' No one brings it up to him, restrains him, or puts any difficulties in his way." Yet in another part of the same treatise Elias says the Jews "endure humiliation and hatred."[117]

The letters of the Cairo Genizah illustrate both aspects, but primarily the brighter one. In around 1090, a blind scholar, formerly from Egypt but now resident in Thessalonike, talks about the economic motives and concern for his safety that led him to migrate to the empire. Now, he says, "my situation is very good."[118] In 1137, a Jew in Seleukeia (Isauria) claimed that he was prospering and that his contact would not regret joining him "here in the Land of the Romans.... This is a place which has everything in the world, just like the Fayyum." The letter writer had married a local girl and referred to the Roman armies as "our commanders." He was doing well and identified with Romanía.[119] By contrast, a letter from around 1096, obsessed with Messianic signs, says that in Thessalonike the Christians have always hated the Jews most intensely, but it also appears from this letter that the authorities were not being aggressive toward the Jewish community.[120]

Constantinople and the Armies

A baseline profile for Constantinople and the armies in 930 AD was established in Chapter 6, so here we need only briefly note major developments that occurred since that time.

There is no evidence that Constantinople had become significantly more multiethnic by 1064, though it probably grew in population and was home to numerous royal hostages and deposed royal families. By the mid-eleventh century there was a permanent Latin community, which we know largely because some Latin-rite churches became bones of contention in the lead-up to the schism of 1054.[121] At first, the community was probably Amalfitan. In 992, the Venetians were made a favored trading partner with the empire: the treaty imagines that many of their ships would come to Constantinople, but it does not yet envisage a permanent presence.[122] The Latin community altogether probably numbered no more than a few hundred. In 1043, as a Rus' naval attack became immanent, the authorities arrested all the Rus' merchants in the City and dispersed them to the provinces, which suggests, first, that they were not too many; second, that there were no full-time Rus' residents in the City; and third, that the authorities kept track of their whereabouts, which is what we would expect on the basis of the empire's past treaties.[123]

Moreover, the capital was now home to an array of dethroned kings and royal families, hostages from many surrounding polities and nations, embassies, and honored foreigners, but these did not significantly change its demography. A later Syriac source claims that Konstantinos IX expelled all the Armenians, Arabs, and Jews who had come to the capital in the past thirty years, allegedly because they had incited the riot against him in 1044 (which is nonsense). No reliable conclusions can be drawn from this testimony, as the author ridiculously says that the expulsion affected a hundred thousand people.[124] But it was under Konstantinos IX that we first hear of Roma (i.e., Gypsies) in Romanía. The emperor hired them to clear out some wild animals infesting the suburban Philopation park.[125]

A Latin description of Constantinople, by the "Anonymous Tarragonensis" and written toward the end of the eleventh century, says that the City contained many different *gentes:* Greeks, Armenians, Syrians, Lombards, English, Dacians (probably Vlachs), Amalfitans, Franks, Jews, and Turks (or "Turkopouloi"), but that the Greeks occupied the largest and best part of the City.[126] The text strongly implies that each of these groups was assigned to a specific region, which we know was the case with the Jews and the growing Latin communities of that time. The City had become more multiethnic, though no ratios can be extracted from this list. The English mentioned here were Anglo-Saxon refugees who fled to Romanía after the Norman conquest of their homeland; many of them joined the Varangian Guard, which is likely who the author means here.[127] The Franks were likely also the mercenaries whom Alexios I Komnenos hired. The Syrians and Armenians had moved to Constantinople in the aftermath of the empire's great expansion eastward or were pushed there by the Turkish expansion into Asia Minor, along with many Romans from Asia Minor.

But before this period of dislocation, it is hard to accept the image of Constantinople as a cosmopolitan city; that is, beyond the boutique diversity of hostages, mercenaries, and merchants. The dominant attitude among the local authorities was likely the one expressed by Isaakios II Angelos when he said in a chrysobull of 1189 that, whereas it was not desirable to let the "nations" spread themselves in

Constantinople, he was willing to except the Venetians, who loved Romanía so much that they were virtually like native Romans.[128]

The Roman army definitely became more multiethnic in the later tenth and eleventh centuries, but not, as many historians believe, because it (allegedly) began to rely increasingly on foreign mercenaries. Actually, the numbers of such mercenaries were still low, consisting of groups of a few hundred here and there. Rather, the chief source of ethnolinguistic diversity in the army was the fact that the regular armies of the *doukata* of Bulgaria, Paradounabon, Vaspurakan, Iberia, and Edessa were surely recruited to some degree among the local populations, including Bulgarians, Georgians, and Armenians. In addition, a greater diversity of ethnic units is attested, raised among tributary or theoretically dependent people along the periphery, such as the Arvanites (Albanians), the Pechenegs in the lower Danube, and even Bedouin tribes from the Jazira. My sense is that they were hired or called up on an ad hoc basis and were not part of the standing forces. There was, however, one ethnic unit formed in this period that became a permanent institution, namely the self-consciously foreign Varangian Guard. Its very purpose was to be a corps that would have no Roman political interests and would therefore be exclusively loyal to its employer, the emperor. It was, after all, originally hired to fight against Roman armies in a civil war. Its "otherness" was therefore highlighted in many ways, and it is possible that its members were subject to separate legal status defined by the corps, comparable to other ethnic enclaves within the empire.[129] The Varangian Guard was an experiment in maintained but controlled ethnic difference.

Law, Ethnicity, and Policy at the Apogee

Some empires used formal instruments of law to enforce the unequal status of the conquerors and the conquered, to limit the latter's access to the highest levels of power in the ruling hierarchy, and even to mark them off socially. Romanía was not such an empire. Within the lands governed by its formal institutions, its own legal system recognized the existence of only one law—Roman law—that applied to all its subjects. In a narrowly legal sense, the state "saw" only Roman citizens: "Those who live within the circumference of the Roman world, namely those who live under the authority of the Romans, even if they do not live in Rome itself, are still Roman citizens, on the basis of the decree issued by the emperor Antoninus" (i.e., the *Constitutio Antoniniana* of 212).[130] After 212, Roman law eventually replaced the local laws of provincial cities, which, if they survived at all, become local customs operating at a sublegal level. The transition from an *imperium* full of *gentes* to a single-law Romanía can be traced in the sources.

What is more difficult to discern is the legal treatment of foreign groups that entered the empire after 212, especially those that did so in large enough numbers to sustain a sense of their separate ethnicity, such as the Goths.[131] A legal scholion of the sixth century implies that the allied Gothic unit of the *phoideratoi* was perceived as ethnically foreign and those who wished to join it had somehow to prove their ethnic eligibility.[132] And ethnic distinctions persisted within the empire's core population, with the Bessians (Thracians) and Isaurians, for example, regarded sometimes as distinct groups. It is possible that Justinian appointed officers to "catch" Syrians and Egyptians and drive them away from the capital, an identification that would have been made on the basis of speech and other ethnic markers.[133] Roman legal homogeneity had not yet overridden all ethnic differences, though it was moving in that direction.

We are in the dark when it comes to the legal status of foreign peoples conquered or annexed by the empire, such as the Tzanoi and Armenians placed under direct imperial rule by Justinian; also of lands in the core territories that were lost to foreign settlers and then reabsorbed along with their new ethnic populations, such as Bulgaria and the Sklabinias in Greece; and of foreign lands that had never been part of the core of the empire but were annexed in the later tenth and eleventh centuries, such as the various Caucasian principalities. Was Roman law introduced to these territories? Did the state treat their inhabitants as (notional or actual) Roman citizens, even if they did not assimilate culturally and ethnically, as so many clearly did not in the period that interests us here? They may have been viewed by Roman society as ethnically different, but did the state treat them as Roman citizens whenever they interacted with it formally?

The basic principle of the law, quoted above, required that these people be seen as Roman citizens. In practice, however, we do not know how this played out. Small groups admitted to the empire and resettled, would, as we have seen, have been absorbed and fallen under the same legal regime as other Romans; indeed, with few exceptions, over time they became ethnic Romans as well. But the treatment of larger groups such as the Bulgarians and Armenians remains opaque. We have little evidence. In the sixth century, Justinian tried to align some "barbaric" social practices in the newly annexed Armenian territories (e.g., regarding inheritances) with Roman norms, proclaiming that Armenia should not have different laws from the rest of the Roman state, a statement that implies an intention of universal legal homogenization on his part.[134] According to the ideology of his regime, moreover, barbarians brought within the orbit of the empire had to be civilized, converted, and assimilated to Roman norms.[135] In time, this could have made them into Roman citizens indistinguishable from others across the empire. But we do not know the extent to which such a global program was implemented or enforced, what its impact was on daily life in the new provinces, or whether it was accompanied by reforms in areas beyond inheritance and (inevitably) taxation and recruitment.

Turning to the tenth and eleventh centuries, we have no programmatic statements advocating the legal homogenization of newly annexed territories comparable to that of Justinian in the sixth. Court writers of the middle period certainly assumed that lawful rule by Romans would make the barbarians more civilized in all respects, but they do not show us what was happening on the ground in the provinces. The penetration of Roman law surely accompanied the extension of the imperial administration to the new territories, the evidence for which we surveyed above (probably minimal when it came to the Vlachs, deeper in Bulgaria, as-yet unknown in Armenia). This process would have faced two obstacles, one pragmatic, the other religious. Pragmatically, the empire would have had to tolerate the customs, norms, and even laws of its new subjects, at least initially, since it was not possible to change them overnight, or even in the long term. There was precedent for this. The Latin-Lombard population of the southern Italian provinces lived under its own laws, upon which the imperial administration was superimposed. It is likely that the Vlachs of Mt. Pindos, the Albanians further north, and the Milengoi on Mt. Taygetos also lived under conditions of quasi-autonomy, beyond providing tribute and soldiers to the empire. The Varangians had their own corps-code. Also, Basileios II initially allowed the Bulgarians to continue living under their own "customs," though the exact legal implications of this rather general statement are unclear.[136] We do not know what Bulgarian law looked like, and the Bulgarians would in any case have been subject to Orthodox canon law, which was entangled with imperial law on multiple levels. But there was room within the empire for local "custom" as a sublegal norm.[137]

This brings us to religious limitations on legal homogeneity. Whereas late Roman law had effectively eliminated distinctions among the *gentes* and *civitates* of the empire, starting in the fourth century it re-created a new set of distinctions based on doctrinal affiliation: full rights were enjoyed by those who adhered to the doctrine preferred by the imperial authorities, while all others suffered under various degrees of legal discrimination.[138] Heresy was defined as a quasi-criminal act that potentially carried severe legal consequences. As communities coalesced around deviant doctrines in the fifth and centuries, these laws alienated them from Constantinople. Thus, the former Roman distinction between conquerors and conquered was replaced by that between the Orthodox Romans and others, the latter including pagans, Jews, and Christian heretics. In theory, one could not enjoy the full rights of Roman citizenship without being Orthodox.

Thus, specific categories of imperial subjects would have remained under a differentiated system of law. Jews were in some respects treated as Romans, in other areas their rights were curtailed, and beyond that, as non-Christians, they would have been subject to the authority of their own religious leadership. The Muslim communities that lived in the empire after the age of the great conquests were probably subject to the jurisdiction of their *qadis*, except when they entered into legal disputes with Romans. It would have been difficult, if not impossible, to integrate Muslims into the Roman legal system by this point. Turning to the Syrian Jacobites, imperial law would have classified them as heretics of some kind. As we saw, however, the imperial authorities and other Romans in Syria were apparently willing to treat the Jacobites as full Roman citizens with equal rights (intermarrying with them, accepting them as equals in court, etc.). This elicited protests by the Church, which demanded that the Jacobites be subjected to the restrictions codified in the antiheretical laws of the earlier period. But when the state cracked down on the Jacobites, it targeted only their leadership. Thus, legal distinctions based on religious differences were blurred in this case. The Roman authorities do not seem to have used the law to enforce differences to the full extent that they could. To the contrary, the state (as opposed to the Church) appears to have been willing to overlook religious differences for the purposes of legal and administrative convenience. Even some non-Chalcedonian Armenians were appointed to high office.

It is also possible that, long before the conquests, Roman law had already influenced the legal traditions of the Bulgarians, Armenians, Georgians, Syrians, and Melkites, thereby smoothing the interface between them and the imperial administration in the eleventh century. This avenue for homogenization is an area that deserves more attention.[139] On the other hand, law could go only so far in structuring how the Romans governed their non-Roman subjects. Perceptions of ethnic difference did not necessarily follow legal definitions. Orthodox Slavs, Bulgarians, Armenians, and Georgians who lived in the empire and were subject to some kind of Roman law were still viewed as ethnically different from the Romans on the basis of traits that were invisible to the law. Even without a strict legal basis, these differences could result in state policies and social attitudes with real consequences. There is evidence that the Roman state treated its non-Roman subjects differently, albeit not on the basis of explicit legal distinctions. This is another area where ethnicity and empire intersected.

Romans of the eleventh century were certainly aware that they were living in a diverse, expansive state. Yet the only place where they expressed satisfaction about this new state of affairs was in imperial orations, where they praised the emperor for ruling over so many nations. Otherwise, when they came face to face with this diversity they did not like it, which was another reason why the literary elite preferred to stay in Constantinople if they could. Eustathios Boïlas complained when he had to leave his native land, Orthodox Cappadocia, and go settle, still within the empire, "among alien nations with a strange religion and tongue," that is, Armenians.[140] The monastic founder Nikon of the Black Mountain who settled near Antioch demonstrated his Orthodox faith by stating that he had received it "from his ancestors; these were *not* people who had been raised and lived in any of the places and lands where the heresies are all mixed up together, but were a Roman root, via the grace of Christ."[141] Being Roman functioned for him as a marker of Orthodoxy.

When the historian Michael Attaleiates sought to explain the empire's many defeats in the later eleventh century, he began by refuting the religious explanations given by the pious. To explain why so many of those who lived under Roman authority were being cut down by the Turks, they supposed at first that the Armenians and Jacobites were paying the price for their impiety. But then the troubles reached the Orthodox too, and the Romans did not know what to make of it.[142] This reveals that the Romans placed their non-Orthodox subjects into a different moral category from themselves, even when it came to foreign attacks against their own empire. It revealed also that distinctions had become muddled. As Psellos put it in a letter: "Romanity and barbarity are no longer clearly distinguished, but are all mixed up together."[143] Needless to say, he was not celebrating its greater diversity. He was referring to foreign barbarians who were invading the empire, not to its ethnic subjects.

The empire seems to have exerted minimal or almost no institutional or infrastructural control over certain groups in mountainous areas, such as the Vlachs and Albanians. Unfortunately, the evidence is scanty and does not extend to the crucial details, but it points to a loose relationship mediated by local ethnic leaders who interfaced with the imperial authorities. Both groups were capable of raiding imperial territories or striking deals with foreign invaders, but in times of peace they did owe the empire soldiers and tribute. This loose arrangement had a precedent in the empire's relationship with the Ezerites and Milengoi in the Peloponnese, who were ruled by their own ethnic *archons*. Religious groups, as we have seen in the case of the Jews, Muslims, and Jacobites, were also treated as "others" in some ways or in some contexts, for example in having their own religious authorities and their own "laws"; in being occasionally persecuted by the imperial Church; and so on.

There is another criterion that demonstrates clearly that the state treated these minorities differently from the way it treated Romans: there is no evidence of Jacobite, Jewish, and Muslim subjects of the empire receiving court titles and offices and placed in command positions (unlike what happened with select Armenians and Bulgarians). This discrimination effectively made these groups into a third-class category of subjects (the Armenians and Bulgarians being second-class).

Turning from people and cultures to geography, the Byzantine state in the eleventh century exhibits the hub-and-spoke image of segmented empires. The Vlach, Albanian, and Bulgarian subjects in the European provinces were linked to each other through proximity and history and to the imperial capital but not to the Georgian, Armenian, and Syrian subjects of the Asian provinces. Here the empire's fundamental geographical feature, the fact that it was divided into two by the sea, played a fundamental role in allowing it to keep its holdings isolated from each other and segmented. It was also advantageous that the capital was so situated as to control the narrowest point of passage from one continent to the other, the Bosporos. Therefore, the Vlachs could collaborate with Bulgarians, and eventually did so, when they jointly broke away from the empire in 1185, and the Armenians could collaborate with the Syrians, but the empire's two halves were largely independent worlds, linked only through Constantinople. The Adriatic functioned in a similar way for the Italian provinces. Even when they were lost to foreign invaders, the Normans, the latter ultimately proved unable to expand to the empire's core Balkan territories.

Let us consider also the distinction posed at the beginning of Chapter 6: looking at Romanía as an empire, should we say that it *was* an empire or that it *had* an empire? To the extent that it may be understood as an empire at all, the answer is clearly that Romanía *had* an empire. It was a core national state, Romanía or "Romanland," that at times acquired territories or ethnic subjects whom it governed in an imperial way. Romanía existed before, during, and after those acquisitions. It lost the east after 1071 and it lost Bulgaria in 1185, but it still retained its own identity. It was always the *politeia* of the Romans plus their *arche* over non-Romans, whether the latter was larger or smaller.

Around 1064 the empire was marked by a higher degree of ethnic and religious diversity than at any point in the previous four centuries. Many of its new ethnic subjects expressed their distinctiveness through narratives in Latin, Hebrew, Slavonic, Armenian, Syriac, and Arabic. These works foregrounded these communities' separate experience of those two centuries. One day they might be studied together as comparable products of the Byzantine imperial periphery, rather than segregated, as they are today, into siloed fields defined by linguistic training, nationality, or religious confession.

The majority of the population of the empire always remained Roman. This was unlike most empires, in which the ruling ethnic group is a minority. Moreover, the default setting of the Roman state in this phase of its expansion was, wherever possible, to homogenize its administration of conquered territories, even to the degree of disregarding religious differences that would otherwise produce radically unequal subject populations. Islam could not, of course, be overlooked in this way, but the anti-Chalcedonian otherness of the Jacobites and Armenians was accommodated, up to a point. Hence it could justly be said by a court orator in the 1040s that "New Rome ruled over many nations *(ethne)*."[144]

It has been said that "in losing its frontiers and opening itself to the world, it is a bit as if Byzantium had lost its definition."[145] We might reformulate this and say that it had become a bit less like a nation-state and a bit more like an empire, however briefly. Whether the balance swung categorically from the former type of state to the latter is an artificial question. Overall, "Byzantium" was not really an empire. In terms of population, geography, and political orientation, it was overwhelmingly the ethnic or national state of the Romans, their "polity," as they called it, which at various times exercised a looser or tighter hegemony over non-Romans: Romanía *had* an empire, or rather it entered into imperial relationships at times with conquered subjects along the margins, but its own essence was not that of an empire.

Conclusion

For over a thousand years, the western European world has falsely denied the Romanness of the eastern empire and its majority population. Prejudice and polemic were piled on top of the original sin of denialism in an orgy of contempt that lasted well into the twentieth century. The eastern Romans were viewed as effeminate "Greeks," then as schismatics and heretics, as degenerate Christians, servile subjects of an oriental theocratic despotism, and the source of Soviet oppression. The "Greek" label was a fundamental distortion of east Roman culture, but it nevertheless preserved the idea that it represented a nation. Even that was lost, however, in the later nineteenth century due to the imperial anxieties of the Great Powers. When Byzantine Studies emerged as a professional academic discipline, the field retreated from the politically charged "Greek" label and fully embraced the empty abstraction of "Byzantium," whose majority population was seen as lacking ethnicity and nationality. The "Byzantines" were henceforth defined by their faith, Orthodoxy, which therefore drew the lion's share of both scholarly and popular attention during the twentieth century. The unambiguous evidence of the sources for the polity of the Romans was disregarded, a feat of intellectual discipline that can be accomplished only after years of graduate training. The national basis of Romanía was marginalized in favor of theological abstractions lifted from the writings of a few bishops, such as Eusebios of Kaisareia.

At the same time, the existence of minority ethnic groups in the empire, urged by modern national states and their historians, was taken at face value. The result was a monstrously inverted riddle, the only "empire" in history about which it was possible to identify ethnic minorities but not the majority. More than that, it became unclear whether this was an empire or some other kind of state. Were there ruling and ruled ethnic groups specific enough to be named, or only a deracinated Orthodox "elite" that ruled over a majority with no name and various minorities that could be named if only they enjoyed the advantage of modern national spokesmen? Were "the Byzantines" the ones ruling this state, and were they the ones who are called "Romans" in the sources? Or were all of the empire's subjects "Byzantines," both those who "called themselves Romans" and the rest? Could minorities exist with no majority?

Such were the confusions that resulted when the empirical commitments of scholarship yielded to the ideological commitments of denialism. As a result, our books are full of baffling statements. Consider, for example, the claim that a Greek identity and the Greek language were not requirements for anyone to be considered a Byzantine.[1] What is this trying to say, if we were to translate it from the invented terminology of modern scholarship into real-world terms? That one did not have to be a Roman to be a subject of the emperor? But isn't that merely to say that the Romans had an empire? This is true but also redundant, because there were never any requirements for being the subject of an empire. The field of Byzantine Studies, tangled up in the terminological weeds that it itself has sown, has operated in this state of cognitive dissonance for over a century. Its scholars read the name "Roman" in the sources, but many of them cannot "see" it. The goal of this book has been to make it harder to unsee.

To remove this blockage and understand Byzantium as an empire, we have to take the evidence of our sources regarding ethnicity seriously. This requires that we remove the edifices of denial that have been built up to block our view.

As the evidence piles up, the dissonance can mount until it becomes too much to bear and the opinion topples over, a phenomenon called the affective tipping point. The tipping point depends on the balance between how badly the opinion holder's reputation would de damaged by relinquishing the opinion and whether the counterevidence is so blatant and public as to be common knowledge: a naked emperor, an elephant in the room.[2]

The evidence is extensive and incontrovertible. What we call Byzantium was a Roman polity populated overwhelmingly by identifiable ethnic Romans and a number of ethnic minorities. "Roman" was not an elite court identity or a literary affect: it was a nationality that extended to most of the population regardless of its location, occupation, gender, and class (i.e., roughly to all who were Greek-speaking and Orthodox). It was common Romans who began to call their land and state *Romanía*, "Romanland," and to call their language *Romaic*. They had a reasonably clear awareness of who in their state were not Romans. The size of these ethnic minorities was usually quite small (e.g., in the early tenth century), although it grew in phases of imperial expansion (in the late tenth and early eleventh centuries). Therefore, for most of its history in this period, the Roman state was not much of an "empire." Even in those phases, the size of unassimilated ethnic minorities was probably not so great in relation to the Roman population that it necessarily tilted the balance toward "empire" as the primary category that we should be using. To be sure, historians have not found a minimum threshold ratio of ethnic diversity for a state to qualify as an empire, nor have they sought one. But generally speaking Byzantium usually lay closer to the national state end of the spectrum (as Romanía), though it made occasional forays in a more imperial direction (as the hegemony of the Romans over others).

All states, including nation-states, are multiethnic. The standard for empire is found in the regimes of difference by which nonruling groups are governed. In Romanía, there is evidence for assimilation and inclusion as well as for intolerance, persecution, second-class citizenship, guest-elite status, grudging toleration, and differential access to power. Now that we have a working model of ethnicity and empire we can begin to write the history of Byzantium along these lines, as historians have long been doing for other empires. But to study the management of difference, we have to first be able to "see" the ethnoreligious distinctions on which it was based. This, in turn, requires that we recognize the Romans as a group distinct from the rest, as in fact they are consistently presented in all the sources, both Byzantine and foreign.

It also requires that we discard notions of immutable ethnicity, or race, which retain a hold on Byzantine Studies due to the claims pressed by nationalist schools of historiography and the field's own unreconstructed view of ethnicity, which predates the mid-twentieth century. In most fields of research since then, ethnicity is understood as mutable, as a cultural artifact produced by societal change, not something that inheres in biologically defined groups. Historians of Byzantium in particular have to accept this approach for two reasons. First, ever since antiquity foreign groups and individuals who entered the empire could assimilate and become Roman, discarding their former identities or retaining only symbolic traces of them. Romanness was a cultural-political identity that could on occasion represent itself through largely symbolic narratives of shared ancestry. By assimilating to its institutions, foreigners could make themselves part of those narratives of belonging. And second, the very existence of Romanía itself was the product of ethnic change among the eastern subjects of the ancient Roman empire. It emerged from specific processes at a particular time in history, and likewise later disappeared. There are now no more eastern Romans. But that does not authorize us to deny that they ever existed.

At the same time, I would caution against the extreme use of "fluidity" for studying ethnicity. In fields that have accepted the paradigm of ethnic change, it has become fashionable in some quarters to treat ethnicity as infinitely malleable, negotiated and renegotiated on a daily or instantaneous basis, and ultimately as an evanescent or unreal social artifact. One can allegedly wake up in a Serbian household, play the Greek in the marketplace in the morning, then switch to an Albanian persona at a wedding in the evening, pray at a Muslim shrine, and correspond with Jewish relatives at night. I suspect that such models reflect the ideals and hopes of late modern liberalism and are inherently political. They are a misleading and even fictional basis for studying historical ethnicities, which are not that easy to perform in a native way. Most people can manage only one in a convincing way, two at most. Truly "fluid" people are extremely rare. Moreover, ethnicities are social and not individual constructs, and, if they survive for a significant period, are deeply grounded in the maintenance among a large group of narratives, institutions, and specific markers such as language. These are hard to change. It can happen, but it takes time, effort, powerful incentives, or a dramatic change of circumstances. If we must use the metaphor, the "fluid" in question is more like honey, tar, or glue, and less like water or blood. If you doubt this, go to any group with a fairly well-defined identity and try to change its narrative about itself.[3]

The Romans of Byzantium did come into being and did go extinct, but both events were processes that lasted for centuries and were precipitated by conquest, incentives, and dramatic historical change on either end. In between, however, they kept their Romanness together for over a thousand years through the maintenances of their narratives, institutions, and specific culture. Now, a group of this size that names its homeland, state, language, common culture, and monarch after itself is what we call a nation. This has significant implications.

One set of implications has to do with Byzantine history as a national narrative. Consider, for example, the reaction of the Romans to the loss of their capital in 1204 and the dismemberment of their polity. That reaction in all ways refutes the attenuated and anemic versions of Roman identity served up by the denialist tradition, while conversely it exactly matches what we would expect of an ethnic group deprived through aggression of its national state. The language of ethnic and even racial difference between Romans and others is pervasive in this period. Moreover, the Romans could recognize each other across the lines of the different and competing states that they set up in the aftermath of 1204: they knew who was Roman, independent of statehood. They were, moreover, insistent on reclaiming and restoring their lost homeland, by which they meant more than just Constantinople. Also, they did not have an "Orthodox" state in mind, as the Bulgarians and Vlachs were among their major opponents. All these elements of ethnicity did not suddenly appear out of nowhere in 1204. They had been there all along and were only amplified now by outrage and loss.[4]

The second set of implications is more theoretical and points to a need for more research on the formation and subsistence of premodern national states. Many historians are slowly but surely rejecting the modernist doctrine, which avers that only modern developments (e.g., telegraphs, newspapers, industry, and universal schooling) can create nation-states. I intend to situate Romanía within the growing rejection of this doctrine in a separate book, which will focus, beyond ethnicity, on institutions and governmentality. Yet it is still common to read that "cultural homogeneity of the kind the modern nation-state produced was beyond the reach of even the most infrastructurally developed of these ancient states." The concern is with "technological constraints," even though the footnote then refers to the "remarkably complex and efficient communicative apparatuses [that] ancient empires developed."[5]

This reasoning places the cart before the horse. Cultural homogeneity is one of the most striking features of Byzantine society. Rather than denying it on dubious a priori grounds, we should instead be searching for the mechanisms—both the institutions and processes—that created and sustained it. Consider the following double standard. The same scholars who might deny that premodern means created cultural homogeneity on a national level, and who also deny that the Byzantines were Romans, will at the same time readily admit—even insist—that Byzantine society was thoroughly Christianized, indeed that Christianity had created radically new subjectivities and through these reshaped the entire population on a deep personal level. But if the "means" existed for the one transformation, they existed for the other. The two were not so different. Both created identities associated with specific labels that entailed distinctive beliefs about one's place in the world and one's relations with others; constitutive practices; and public and private performative scripts. Why do we believe that the ancient world could spread a religious belief that reformatted people "all the way down," both socially and personally, but that the same could not be done with their political and ethnic identities? The same argument can be made for Islamization and Arabization in the eastern provinces after the seventh century. Those were also deep and broad developments that changed ethnicities, beliefs, practices, narratives, and languages for the majority. This too happened, and institutions played a key role in promoting them.

It remains then to show in detail how the institutions and public ideology of the state could create, sustain, reflect, or be enmeshed with the Romanness of the majority of its subjects. Through what mechanisms did Romanía constitute itself as a national state, and by what channels was governmentality disseminated? Were average Romans so oppressed by their own elites, as some believe, that there could be no meaningful community of interest between them, or was Romanía a state whose existence and extraordinary survival required the efforts and attachment of an entire people and not just the short-term ambitions of a narrow elite?

ABBREVIATIONS

NOTES

BIBLIOGRAPHY

INDEX

Abbreviations

AASS	*Acta Sanctorum*
BMGS	*Byzantine and Modern Greek Studies*
BS	*Byzantinoslavica*
BZ	*Byzantinische Zeitschrift*
CJ	*Codex Iustinianus*, ed. P. Krueger, *Corpus Iuris Civilis*, vol. 2 (Berlin, 1895).
DOP	*Dumbarton Oaks Papers*
GRBS	*Greek, Roman, and Byzantine Studies*
JöB	*Jahrbuch der österreichischen Byzantinistik*
MGH Epp.	*Monumenta Germaniae Historica Epistolae*
MGH SS	*Monumenta Germaniae Historica Scriptores*
ODB	A. P. Kazhdan et al., eds., *The Oxford Dictionary of Byzantium*, 3 vols. (Oxford, 1991).
PBE	M. Jeffreys et al., *Prosopography of the Byzantine World* (2011), http://pbw.kcl.ac.uk.
PG	J.-P. Migne, ed., *Patrologiae cursus completus, Series graeca*, 161 vols. (Paris, c. 1857–1866).
PLRE	A. H. M. Jones and J. R. Martindale, eds., *The Prosopography of the Later Roman Empire*, 3 vols. (Cambridge, 1971–1992).
PmbZ	Berlin-Brandenburg Academy of Sciences, *Prosopographie der mittelbyzantinischen Zeit* (Berlin, 2000–).

REA	*Revue des études arméniennes*
REB	*Revue des études byzantines*
SHMESP	Société des Historiens Médiévistes de l'Enseignement Supérieur Public
TIB	Austrian Academy of Sciences, *Tabula imperii byzantini* (Vienna, 1976–).
TM	*Travaux et mémoires*

Notes

CHAPTER 1 ▪ *A History of Denial*

1. Kaldellis, *Byzantine Republic.*
2. Konstantinos VII, *Book of Ceremonies* 1.91 (pp. 419–420).
3. Juxtaposition: Ioannes of Antioch, *History* fr. 239.5 (Mariev) = 308 (Roberto); *ethnos:* Eutropios (Greek trans.), *Breviarium* 6.3; Theodoretos, *Letter* 40 (greed); Prokopios, *Secret History* 6.4; see Lenski, "Assimilation."
4. *CJ* 9.12.10, probably a response to the incident in Ioannes of Antioch, *History* fr. 229 (Mariev) = 298 (Roberto).
5. Marcellinus Comes, *Chronicle* s.a. 473.
6. *Chronicle of Pseudo-Joshua the Stylite* 12.
7. Kandidos, *History* fr. 1.
8. *Pace,* e.g., Greatrex, "Roman Identity." This view will be discussed extensively below.
9. Kaldellis, "Christodoros."
10. *Miracles of Saint Demetrios* 2.284–287, alluding to Exod. 12:31–49. I use naive terms such as "tribe" deliberately in translations to evoke the loose language of the sources. A similar tale is told by Prokopios (sixth century) regarding Roman soldiers in northern Gaul who were cut off when the barbarians conquered that province: for a century they passed down their sense of identity along with their "ancestral customs" and "ancestral laws," including their distinctive clothes and shoes (*Wars* 5.12.17–19).
11. Konstantinos VII, *De administrando imperio* 13.114–116 (trans. Jenkins, mod.).
12. Konstantinos VII, *De administrando imperio* 13.175–181 (trans. Jenkins, mod.). For being raised in the customs of the Roman court, cf. Theophanes, *Chronographia,* 455.

13. Konstantinos VII, *De administrando imperio* 13.197–199.
14. See Chapter 2, section on "Ethnicity in the Black Hole."
15. Averil Cameron, *Byzantine Matters*, 55.
16. Canon 72 of the Council in Trullo (691–692 AD).
17. Kaldellis, "Ethnicity and Clothing."
18. Choniates, *History* 336–338.
19. Barzos, Γενεαλογία, vol. 2, 515. His sons were Alexios and David, founders of the empire of Trebizond.
20. G. Akropolites, *History*, 44; commentary in Macrides, *George Akropolites*, 233.
21. G. Akropolites, *History*, 54.
22. Stouraitis, "Roman Identity."
23. For western recognition of eastern Rome, see, among many studies, Hänssler, *Byzanz*, 147; Ekonomou, *Byzantine Rome*.
24. Gantner, "The Label 'Greeks'"; Forrai, "The Sacred Nectar."
25. Pope Nicolaus I, *Letter 88 to Michael III* (865 AD); Emperor Louis II, *Letter to Basileios I* (871 AD); see below for Louis' letter.
26. Isaac, *Invention*, 381–406; Hunger, *Graeculus perfidus*.
27. Liudprand, *Embassy to Constantinople*, 47.
28. J. M. H. Smith, *Europe after Rome*; for an early phase, Reimitz, *History*, 1, 117.
29. Messis, "Lectures sexuées"; in general, see Carrier, *L'Autre à l'époque des croisades*.
30. Shawcross, "Re-Inventing the Homeland."
31. Fowden, "Gibbon on Islam," 265n10.
32. For a preliminary study, see Kaldellis, "Political Freedom"; see also Wood, *Modern Origins*, 64, 66.
33. J. Bell Burnell quoted in Richardson, *The Language of Empire*, 6–7.
34. Eagleman, *Incognito*, 88.
35. See now Raffensperger, *Reimagining Europe*.
36. Gutas, *Greek Thought*, 84–95; Connelly, *Contesting the Greek Past*; in general, see El Cheikh, *Byzantium*.
37. Sixteenth-century: Beck, *Der Vater*; Reinsch, "Hieronymus Wolf"; Ben-Tov, *Lutheran Humanists*, 106–109.
38. Kaldellis, "From 'Empire of the Greeks' to "Byzantium."
39. Frary, *Russia*; Figes, *Crimea*, 12–13, 113, 150–153, 163, 187.
40. Koubourlis, Οι ιστοριογραφικές οφειλές, documents such views in eighteenth- and nineteenth-century western historiography.
41. Eger, *Islamic-Byzantine Frontier*, 243, translating Arabic *Rumi*; Lefort, "Population et démographie," e.g., 209–211.
42. Skopetea, Φαλλμεράϋερ.
43. Kaldellis, *New Herodotos*, 229–236.
44. Ostrogorsky, *History*, 27; still a productive model for some: Chitwood, *Byzantine Legal Culture*, 187, 190.
45. Respectively: Laiou and Maguire, *Byzantium: A World Civilization*, 49 (Shahîd), and 20 (Vryonis); cf. 95 (Vikan): "The Byzantines continued to call

themselves *Romanoi.*" This reveals a lack of familiarity with the sources, for this is not how "Romans" is spelled in Greek (it is *Romaioi*).

46. Averil Cameron, *The Byzantines*, 14, ix. Cameron studiously avoids calling the Byzantines Romans after the seventh century or puts the word in quotation marks, and always firmly distinguishes between the Roman and Byzantine empires, for all that the she recognizes that the distinction is "moot" (ix). She thus gives mixed signals about her position.

47. Averil Cameron, *The Byzantines*, 27.

48. Louis II, *Letter to Basileios I*, p. 390; see Fanning, "Imperial Diplomacy"; Muldoon, *Empire and Order*, 48–50.

49. Louis II, *Letter to Basileios I*, p. 389.

50. Kaldellis, *Byzantine Republic.*

51. *Annales Laureshamenses* s.a. 801, p. 33: *cessabat a parte Graecorum nomen imperatoris, et femineum imperium apud se abebant.* For the context, see Reimitz, *History*, 351–353, 360–368.

52. Anastasius: Forrai, "The Sacred Nectar."

53. Liudprand, *Embassy to Constantinople* 51.

54. Gibbon, *History*, vol. 3, 416.

55. Jeffreys, "Rhetoric in Byzantium," 166.

56. Respectively: Lounghis, Η κοινωνική εξέλιξη, 56; Lambakis et al., *Byzantine Diplomacy*, 123 (Vlysidou) and 57 (Lounghis).

57. Herodian, *History after Marcus Aurelius* 1.6.5.

58. See Chapter 3, section on "The Vernacular Ontology of Romanía."

59. Jerome, *Letter* 146.6–7 *(si auctoritas quaeritur, orbis maior est urbe).*

60. Agathias, *Histories* 5.14.1, has been misread to support this criterion. What he says is that by conquering Italy, Libya, and other lands, Justinian made himself *autokrator* of the Romans in deed and not merely in name, referring to the military aspect of *imperator.* It is wrong to read this as saying that only with the conquest of Italy was Justinian made a proper *Roman* emperor.

61. Angold, *Byzantium*, 2, 20.

62. Angold, *Byzantium*, 22, 57.

63. Angold, *Byzantium*, 57.

64. Angold, "Venetian Chronicles," 59: Venice had a "splendid history, which may just possible outshine both Byzantium and the crusades."

65. Jeffreys, "Byzantine Studies," 3: "[They] thought of themselves as Roman."

66. J. Harris, *Lost World*, 5; cf. Cameron, *Circus Factions*, 309: "From Romulus to the Crusades . . . [there is] a deceptive line of continuity" (because "change").

67. Flower, *Roman Republics*, 37.

68. W. V. Harris, *Roman Power*, 5. See the commonsensical view of Bury, *History*, vol. 1, vi, already in 1899. For another breath of fresh air, see Whittow, *Making*, 96: "It had changed, but no more than one would expect in the history of a state over several centuries. It was still the Roman empire, and known as such to its citizens and enemies."

69. Dench, *Romulus' Asylum*, 368.

70. Heather, *Empires and Barbarians*, 381 (its "self-proclaimed imperial Romanness... is a chimera"), 385; cf. Angold, *Byzantium*, 114; Hoyland, *Theophilus*, 3–4. Cf. Heather, *Fall of the Roman Empire*, 431, for an arbitrary distinction between a continuation of the Roman empire and a successor state, which is what he says Byzantium was.

71. S. Morris, "When Brothers Dwell in Unity," 5. Yet modern studies of Roman culture do not emphasize the *res pubica*.

72. Hammer, "Russia and Roman Law," 1.

73. Gerkan, *Griechische Städteanlagen*, 168.

74. Sheldon, *Intelligence Activities*, xii ("oriental monarchy," in the foreword by Bernard Knox), 287 (same words by the author); "distant ruler": Cline and Graham, *Ancient Empires*, 293, who even use the term "Dominate." Autocratic fundamentalist state: Takács, *Construction of Authority*, xx, xxii, 120, 125, 134–135, 146, 154 (the shadows of Hitler, Stalin, and 9/11 lie over this book). Many more books with similar claims could be cited.

75. Bryce, *Life and Society*, 15.

76. Papadopoulou, Συλλογική ταυτότητα, 13, 59.

77. Louth, *Greek East and Latin West*, 20.

78. Kaegi, *Heraclius*, 316.

79. Geanakoplos, *Greek Scholars*, 205n17.

80. O'Donnell, "Late Antiquity," 210.

81. O'Donnell, *Ruin*, 354; at 217 he implies that *Byzantium* was a contemporary term, rather than a modern invention.

82. E.g., Mango, "Byzantinism"; Alexander, "Strength of Empire"; Obolensky, *Byzantium and the Slavs*, 13; Metcalf, *Byzantine Cyprus*, 301.

83. J. Harris, *Lost World*, 211.

84. Kazhdan and Constable, *People and Power*, 120.

85. Dölger, *Byzanz*, 70–115; Papadopoulou, Συλλογική ταυτότητα, 13, 59 (presented correctly as a consensus, though unfortunately agreeing with it).

86. Stouraitis, "Roman Identity," apparently endorsed by Haldon, *Empire*, 320n130, and ostensibly relying on T. Eagleton, M. Mann, L. Althusser, and P. Bourdieu; but see Kaldellis, "The Social Scope."

87. Magdalino, "Hellenism and Nationalism," 5–7.

88. Kaldellis, *Hellenism*, ch. 6; and "Hellenism and Identity."

89. Curta, *Edinburgh*, x, 1 (and throughout the introduction and last chapter).

90. Variants of this position can be found in many publications in Greeks. For versions in English, see Kaldellis, *Hellenism*, 112n215.

91. Freeman, *Historical Essays*, 231–278.

92. Bury, *History*, vol. 1, v–viii.

93. Cf. Ando, "Decline," 32n7.

94. Bury, "Introduction."

95. Sykoutris, Εμείς και οι αρχαίοι, 73.

96. Kaldellis, *Byzantine Republic*.

97. Chrysos, "Roman Political Identity," 8.

98. Franklin, "Empire of the Rhomaioi," 518–519: "The 'Roman' aspect of the Byzantine self-image involves not only the political heritage of empire,

but also a broader cultural identity. The Byzantines were 'Romans' not only by political succession, but also (as they saw it) in their culture. In its literary and rhetorical forms, in its codes of civil law, in its institutions, in its geographical, ethnographic, bureaucratic and political terminology, Byzantium expressed and described itself in terms of the 'Roman' past. It matters little whether or not we regard the Byzantine view of 'Romanness' as historically accurate or consistent; the Byzantines were, or thought themselves to be, mimetic of antiquity because they admitted no distinction or discontinuity of substance."

99. Curta, *Edinburgh*, ch. 10.

100. Kennedy, *Great Arab Conquests*, 6–7: "No one at that or any other time ever described themselves in normal life as 'Byzantines'. They themselves knew that they were Romans and they called themselves as such. . . . Despite the violence it does to the language of the sources, I have, with some reluctance, accepted the general scholarly usage and refer to Byzantines and the Byzantine Empire throughout."

101. Wickham, *Inheritance of Rome*, 4–5.

102. Kaegi, *Byzantine Military Unrest*, 6; Curta, *Southeastern Europe*, xi; Canepa, *Two Eyes*, 3, 228–229n5; Ando, "From Republic to Empire," 39–40.

103. Fox, "What, If Anything, Is a Byzantine?"

104. The website is called Philosophy of History (http://www.friesian.com/philhist.htm).

105. Holt, *Meadowland*, 193. For another novel of Varangians in Byzantium, published in the same year and set in the same period, which follows scholars rather than the sources and so gets the Roman identity of the Byzantines entirely wrong, see Severin, *Viking*, vol. 3: *King's Man*, 41–47, 101.

CHAPTER 2 ▪ *Roman Ethnicity*

Epigraph: Cicero, *Against Verres* 2.5.172. ("We must esteem the blood of all Roman citizens as kindred blood.")

1. Agathias, *Histories* 1.2.3–4 (trans. Frendo, mod.).
2. Zonaras, *Chronicle* 15.4 (vol. 3, 261); cf. Prokopios, *Wars* 3.3.1, 5.11.29, 5.12.8.
3. Skylitzes, *Synopsis of Histories*, p. 151; see Martin, *Byzance et l'Italie*, 42.
4. Antonaccio, "(Re)Defining Ethnicity," 47.
5. Martin, *Byzance et l'Italie*, 45, 125.
6. *Life of Saint Neilos of Rossano* 41.
7. Curta, *Edinburgh*, 295.
8. Skylitzes, *Synopsis of Histories*, p. 329.
9. E.g., *Life of Saint Epiphanios*, in *PG* 41: 37; *Life of Basileios I*, 68; see Kaldellis, "Ethnicity and Clothing."
10. A number of episodes are attested: Koutrakou, "Spies of Towns," 264.
11. Gregoras, *Roman History* 11.11 (vol. 1, 567–568).
12. Gregoras, *Roman History* 37.46 (vol. 3, 555).
13. Mango, *Byzantium*, 26.

14. Averil Cameron, *The Byzantines*, 1, 6—a double evasion: attribution *and* quotation marks.

15. E.g., Laiou, "The Foreigner and the Stranger," 76.

16. Averil Cameron, *The Byzantines*, 8; a curiously indirect nod to the subjectivity of ethnicity appears at the bottom of 14.

17. Seneca, *To Helvia on Consolation* (= *Dialogues* 12[11]) 7.5, 7.10.

18. Moatti, *Critical Thinking*, 271–290.

19. Strabo, *Geography* 14.2.28.

20. For a recent volume by social scientists on the dynamics of ethnic change, see Chandra, *Constructivist Theories*, esp. ch. 4 (though the volume defines ethnicity more tightly around descent—a deliberately "minmalist definition"—than I and others would: see below).

21. For definitions of ethnicity, see the programmatic statements by the contributors to McInerney, *A Companion to Ethnicity*, esp. 2, 35, 67, 104, 112, 115, 122, 143, 158, 178, 216, 217, 221, 298, 341, 350, 371, 517; and the social-scientific definitions listed by Chandra, *Constructivist Theories*, 69–93. For an excellent study of how concepts of ethnicity can be applied to the early (western) Middle Ages, see Pohl, "Introduction." Many scholars now push back against descent as the prime criterion of ethnicity.

22. Buell, *Why This New Race*, 9, 40–41, 193n72; see the citations in the previous note for the variable role of ancestry.

23. Spira, "Ethnicity and Nationality"; De Vos, "Ethnic Pluralism," 24–25; Brubaker, Loveman, and Stamatov, "Ethnicity as Cognition," 48; Chandra, *Constructivist Theories*, 63; Pohl, "Introduction," 20.

24. Kaldellis, *Hellenism in Byzantium*, 87–95, "From Rome to New Rome." But cf. Curta, "Burial," 420.

25. Much recent scholarship has pushed back against the modernist fallacy, according to which nations can emerge and be sustained only by the specific mechanisms that brought *some* modern nations into being (e.g., museums, industrialization, newspapers, schools). This notion is embarrassingly outdated, but certain names (e.g., Gellner, Anderson, Hobsbaum) exert talismanic force.

26. See Chapters 4 and 5.

27. Weber, *Economy and Society*, 389; see Webb, *Imagining the Arabs*, 195–196.

28. Ciggaar, "Une description," 119–120 (the Anonymous Tarragonensis).

29. See my review in the *Medieval Review* 09.04.10, which insists on too sharp a distinction between ethnicities and civic nations (as explained above).

30. In part, this was because Page did not spell out the implications of her findings for the prevailing views. She just presented and analyzed what she found in the sources.

31. E.g., Laiou, "The Foreigner and the Stranger," 77–79; Harris, *Lost World*, 211; Stouraitis, "Roman Identity," 201–202.

32. Hall, *Ethnic Identity*; Luraghi, "Study of Greek Ethnic Identities," 217: "Not even invoking Bourdieu's magical name can eliminate this hurdle. Archaeologists need to resign themselves and look at the written sources." But cf. Antonaccio, "(Re)Defining Ethnicity"; Curta, "Burial" and "Medieval Archaeology."

33. Reimitz, *History*, 3–4, resulting, at 121, in "Frankishnesses."
34. Surveys in Walbank, "Nationality"; Fraser, *Greek Ethnic Terminology;* Papadopoulou, Συλλογικὴ ταυτότητα, 221–315; Laniado, *Ethnos et droit*, 161.
35. Bouraselis, ΘΕΙΑ ΔΩΡΕΑ; Ando, *Citizenship and Empire*. Certain legal distinctions that were left over (at least in theory) were abolished by Justinian in *Novel* 78, which established an undifferentiated Roman citizenship for all.
36. Ulpian in *Digest* 1.5.17 *(in orbe Romano qui sunt . . . cives Romani effecti sunt)*; *Basilika* 46.1.14: Οἱ ἐν τῇ Ῥωμαϊκῇ γῇ ὄντες πολῖται Ῥωμαίων εἰσίν, with the scholion: Οἱ ἐν τῷ κύκλῳ ὄντες τῷ Ῥωμαϊκῷ, τουτέστιν οἱ τελοῦντες ὑπὸ Ῥωμαίους, κἂν μὴ αὐτὴν οἰκοῦσι τὴν Ῥώμην, ὅμως πολῖται Ῥωμαίων ἐκ τῆς Ἀντωνίνου τοῦ βασιλέως διατάξεώς εἰσιν.
37. Mathisen, *"Peregrini"*; Laniado, *Ethnos et droit*.
38. Julian, *Panegyric in Honor of Constantius (Oration* 1) 5c.
39. Weisweiler, "Populist Despotism," 152; cf. Lavan, *Slaves to Rome*.
40. John Chrysostom, *Homily 47 on Acts of the Apostles* 22.25 in *PG* 60: 333–334; see Inglebert, "Christian Reflections," 106–108. For the mistaken attribution to Hadrian, see Chrysos, "Roman Political Identity," 9n12.
41. Konstantinos VII, *Book of Ceremonies* 1.69 (pp. 316–317).
42. Prokopios, *Wars* 7.33.8.
43. Prokopios, *Wars* 7.14.11–16.
44. Prokopios, *Secret History* 18.21.
45. Theophylaktos Simokattes, *History* 7.2.1.
46. Nikephoros, *Short History* 12; more examples in Theophanes, *Chronographia*, pp. 341 (not necessarily soldiers), 346.
47. G. Akropolites, *History*, 13.
48. Prokopios, *Wars* 2.29.19. It is sometimes claimed that they were Laz, e.g., by Bryer, "Some Notes on the Laz," 177–178, but Prokopios knew the Laz and makes no such connection.
49. Prokopios, *Secret History* 6.23, 11.38.
50. Agathias, *Histories* 2.17.5.
51. Attaleiates, *History* 48; cf. Gregoras, *Roman History* 37.46 (vol. 3, 554): not just the *Byzantioi* (people of Constantinople) but the Romans everywhere.
52. Genesios, *On the Reigns* 3.3; Theophanes Continuatus 3.21, 3.29; see Chapter 4.
53. Theophanes Continuatus 4.15; Skylitzes, *Synopsis of Histories*, p. 91.
54. Gregoras, *Roman History* 2.6.4.
55. Nikephoros II Phokas, *On Skirmishing* 23 (p. 230).
56. Vári, "Zum historischen Exzerptenwerke."
57. Zosimos, *New History* 4.9.4.
58. Kaldellis, "Social Scope," 189, citing the relevant works by John Haldon.
59. Attaleiates, *History* 284.
60. D. Angelov, "Three Kinds of Liberty."
61. Kinnamos, *History* 6.8: ἐλευθέρων γὰρ ἄρχειν Ῥωμαίων, οὐμενοῦν ἀνδραπόδων αὐτὸς ἤθελεν.
62. In the east: Vryonis, "Will of a Provincial Magnate," 270; southern Italy: Dain, "Une formule"; Thessalonike (probably): Eustathios of Thessalonike, *Letter* 27 (p. 80).

63. E.g., Page, *Being Byzantine*, 49–50, citing previous scholarship to the same effect.

64. E.g., Greatrex, "Roman Identity," an often-cited article; this definition is treated as a viable alternative by Page, *Being Byzantine*, e.g., 43–44, 47, though her sources support only the ethnic definition.

65. Laiou, "The Foreigner and the Stranger," 81.

66. Obolensky, *Byzantium and the Slavs*, 13.

67. Vryonis, "Byzantine Images," 66.

68. See Laniado, "Aspar," for sample pushback.

69. Justinian, *Novel* 117.4.

70. Philotheos, *Kletorologion*, pp. 177–179.

71. Eustathios Romaios, *Peira* 14.16, 54.6; cf. Laiou, "L'étranger" and "Institutional Mechanisms," 164.

72. *Life of Saint Basileios the Younger* 1.26, with the commentary on p. 117.

73. Psellos, *Chronographia* 6.134; Choniates, *History* 204–205 (Manuel preferred barbarians at his court over "native" Romans). For the same complaint by Kekaumenos, see the end of Chapter 4; for prejudices against Armenians, see Chapter 5.

74. Manuel I Komnenos, *Novel* 71, in I. Zepos and P. Zepos, *Jus Graecoromanum*, vol. 1, 416 (money-changers).

75. Kaldellis, "Classicism"; Theotokis, "Rus, Varangian and Frankish Mercenaries."

76. Alexios I, *Sigillion on the Monastery of St. John on Patmos*, in Miklosich and Müller, *Acta*, vol. 6, 47.

77. E.g., Theophanes, *Chronographia*, pp. 366, 393 (for the eighth century); Leon VI, *Taktika* 20.89; Leon the Deacon, *History* 2.8; Kekaumenos, *Strategikon* 80, 88; Attaleiates, *History* 116, 297; Zonaras, *Chronicle* 18.20; Choniates, *History* 29–30.

78. Choniates, *History* 166; cf. Anna Komnene, *Alexiad* 2.10.4.

79. Skylitzes, *Synopsis of Histories*, p. 491.

80. Justinian, *Novel* 130.8.

81. E.g., Ibn al-Athir in Vasiliev, *Byzance et les Arabes*, vol. 2, pt. 2, 151.

82. Leon VI, *Taktika* 12.90; cf. *On Strategy* 42: spies must never be of the same race as the enemy.

83. Leon VI, *Taktika* 17.89.

84. Vári, "Zum historischen Exzerptenwerke," esp. sections 6–8 of the speech.

85. Agathias, *Histories* 4.8.5.

86. Vryonis, "Will of a Provincial Magnate," 264.

87. Laniado, *Ethnos et droit*, 120–123.

88. Psellos, *Orationes forenses* 1.2659–2661.

89. Skylitzes, *Synopsis of Histories*, p. 17; cf. Ditten, *Ethnische Verschiebungen*, 90–92. A conceptually similar group identified by Page, *Being Byzantine*, 7, included ethnic Romans who fought against their own state.

90. Lavan, *Slaves to Rome*, esp. 34, 91–92, 234.

91. E.g., Num. 23:9.

92. Magdalino and Nelson, "Introduction," 12–19, 25–27; for the terminology, see Ahrweiler, "Byzantine Concepts," 1–15, here 2–4. For the early Christian adoption of the Jewish sense of *ethnos*, see Jones, *Between Pagan and Christian*, 3.

93. For the latter, see *Life of Saint Maria the Younger* 23 (referring to Christian Bulgarians), with the note by the translator, Laiou, at 276n119.

94. Konstantinos VII, *Book of Ceremonies*, pref.; Skylitzes, *Synopsis of Histories*, p. 104.

95. Curta, *Edinburgh*, 295.

96. Doane, "Dominant Group Ethnic Identity"; cf. Jenkins, *Rethinking Ethnicity*, 11 (no minority without a majority) and 14–15 (ethnicity not just for *them*); Pohl, "Introduction," 13, in premodern contexts.

97. Bauer, *A Greek-English Lexicon*, 155.

98. Antiquity: Goodblatt, *Elements of Ancient Jewish Nationalism*; subsequently: A. D. Smith, *Chosen Peoples*.

99. For "holy *ethnos*," see Papadopoulou, Συλλογικὴ ταυτότητα, 231–232, 314. Biblical precedents for it and for holy *laos* include Exod. 19:6 and 1 Pet. 2:9–10.

100. *Digenis Akritis* (G) 4.50–51: ἐθνικὸς μὲν ἀπὸ πατρός, ἐκ δὲ μητρὸς Ῥωμαῖος. Cf. Pomponius Porphyrion (second century AD) on Horace, *Satire* 1.7.2, on Persius "the Hybrid," who was by birth Greek on one side and Roman on the other.

101. Skoutariotes, *Chronicle*, p. 171 (the attribution of this text is debated).

102. Malamut, "De l'empire des Romains," 166; at 167 she predictably equates Romans and Christians. The same is implied in many publications, e.g., Pohl, "Telling the Difference," 68.

103. Konstantinos VII, *De administrando imperio* 13.175–181. Cf. Theophylaktos, *History* 1.5.6, 6.2.14 (the *ethnos* of the Romans); pseudo-Stephanos, *Horoscope of Islam*, p. 274 (the *ethnos* of the Romans will be driven out of Syria by the Arabs); Leon VI, *Taktika* 11.9 (the constitution and survival of the *ethnos* depend on farming and soldiering, linked to our *basileia*); *Disputation of Gregentios with the Jew* 2.476 (the prophesy in Mic. 4:6–7 about a mighty *ethnos* pertains to the *basileia* of the Romans, which is a mighty *ethnos*); Attaleiates, *History* 195 (Romans these days do not care about the well-being of their *ethnos*); Zonaras, *Chronicle*, pref. (vol. 1, 12), promises to tell the history of the *ethnos* of the Romans down to his own time; cf. also 6.29 (vol. 1, 562) (how the *ethnos* of the Romans was formed); Anna Komnene, *Alexiad* 1.13 (the Romans of Alexios are called an *ethnos* in a letter sent by the pope to Robert Guiscard, which is probably an invention or free version by Anna herself); Doukas, *History* 14.5 (the misfortunes of the *ethnos* of the Romans).

104. Four of his passages to this effect are cited by Ivanov, "*Pearls before Swine*," 36.

105. Kosmas Indikopleustes, *Christian Topography* 3.65–66; see Ivanov, "*Pearls before Swine*," 69–70; for Kosmas' views of Romanía, see Chapter 3, section "Patriots for Romanía."

106. E.g., Ioseph Bryennios, *Dialogue with a Muslim* 43.

107. *Digenis Akritis* (G) 4.50–51, 5.69. Cf. *Miracles of Saint Demetrios* 2.293 (some who were of the Roman *phylon*, as opposed to foreign ethnic types);

Kinnamos, *History* 6.2 (Demetrios from a Roman by *genos*, from the town of Lampe).

108. E.g., Theodoros Anagnostes, *Ecclesiastical History* 3.185; Kinnamos, *History* 2.8 (a Gavras); Manuel II Palaiologos, *Funeral Oration for His Brother Theodoros*, pp. 128–131, 160; cf. Theophylaktos, *History* 5.13.7 (the wife of the Persian shah).

109. E.g., Agathias, *History* 2.20.7; Kinnamos, *History* 2.14, 5.13; Choniates, *History* 639; see Chapter 4.

110. Planoudes, *Basilikos* 18 (p. 61.472–475); see D. Angelov, *Imperial Ideology*, 174.

111. Photios, *Homily* 18.2 (p. 174).

112. Lauxtermann, *Byzantine Poetry*, 236–238.

113. E.g., patriarch Nikolaos, *Letter* 170 (pp. 496–499); Theophanes Continuatus 1.9, 2.15, 2.17, 3.38; *Life of Basileios I* 62; Leon the Deacon, *History* 7.3, 8.9; Mauropous, *Speech of Thanksgiving for the Defeat of the Rebellion = op.* 186.2 (p. 178), 186.39 (p. 187); Psellos, *Letters KD* 156 (p. 181) and 190 (p. 214); Attaleiates, *History* 55, 195–196; Skylitzes, *Synopsis of Histories*, pp. 37, 39, 292, 315; Kinnamos, *History* 2.7; Choniates, *History* 387, 625. Photios' famous *Letter to Boris* (*Letter* 1) presents this as a general principle that every ruler should follow: serve and protect the people of your own race.

114. Syrianos, *Rhetorica militaris* 37.6–8 ('Ρωμαίους τε ὄντας καὶ τὴν τῶν πατέρων ἀρετὴν ἀπομιμουμένους); cf. Julian in Ammianus, *Res Gestae* 23.5.19: "The blood of our relatives on the swords of the enemy."

115. Syrianos, *Rhetorica militaris* 33.1, 40.1, 49.3.

116. Leon VI, *Taktika* 2.31; cf. Marcus Aurelius in Cassius Dio, *Roman History* 72.3.3 (Xiphilinos epitome): extra payments to the soldiers would have to be wrung from their parents and relatives.

117. Leon VI, *Taktika* 12.57, cf. also 14.31, 18.127. For the problem of Christian Bulgaria, see Kaldellis, *Ethnography*, 84–85.

118. Attaleiates, *History* 193–198.

119. Euodios, *Forty-Two Martyrs of Amorion* 9 and 26.

120. *Life of Saint Elias the Younger* 49; for contemporary Romans, see 25.

121. Justinian, *Novel* 31.1.3.

122. Kazhdan, "Constantine imaginaire"; Dagron, *Constantinople imaginaire*.

123. Ammianus, *Res Gestae* 23.5.19–20; cf. the historian's own view of the distant Roman past as "ours": 25.9.9–11.

124. Euagrios, *Ecclesiastical History* 6.11.

125. Détorakis and Mossay, "Un office inédit," at vv. 43–44, 101 ('Ρώμης γεννήματα).

126. Kinnamos, *History* 2.16.

127. Markopoulos, "Roman Antiquarianism," 287–290; Angelov, *Imperial Ideology*, 108–109; Kaldellis, *Hellenism in Byzantium*, 89. For genealogies in late antiquity, see Kaldellis, "The Politics of Classical Genealogies."

128. Theophanes Continuatus 3.17.

129. Kinnamos, *History* 2.14; see Chapter 4.

130. Dench, *Romulus' Asylum*, 22, and ch. 4, e.g., 258; cf. Isaac, *Invention*, 134–137, 165.

131. Orlin, *Foreign Cults*, 21–22. The dynamic is excellently described in Woolf, "Inventing Empire," 316–317.

132. Buell, *Why This New Race*, 75; cf. Isaac, *Invention*, 110 ("Common ancestry justified contemporary structures, enmities, friendships, and diplomatic ties"); cf. Redgate, *The Armenians*, 23; Reynolds, "Nations."

133. Mango, *Byzantine Literature*.

134. Stouraitis, "Roman Identity." For a response, see Kaldellis, "Social Scope." For evidence that overturns this thesis from a different direction, see Kaplanis, "Antique Names." "The leading men" etc.: Attaleiates, *History* 270.

135. Kyrillos (Cyril) of Skythopolis, *Life of Saint Ioannes the Hesychast*, p. 211.

136. *Life of Saint Epiphanios*, in *PG* 41: 41, 45; see Rapp, "Epiphanius of Salamis," 178–184.

137. *Life of Saint Nikolaos the Younger* 3 (pp. 446–447); Sabas, *Life of Saint Petros of Atroa* 48.

138. *Chronicle of Pseudo-Joshua the Stylite* 68.

139. Some Arab writers also called the inhabitants of western half of the former Roman empire Rum as well. But in dealing with the Byzantines they were consistent. In general, see Samir, "Quelques notes"; Durak, "Who Are the Romans?" For the "Greeks" of Asia Minor (the scholar's term) called *Rumi* by the Seljuks of Rum in the eleventh and twelfth centuries, see Korobeinikov, "How 'Byzantine' Were the Early Ottomans?," 219. In general, see Miquel, *La géographie humaine*, vol. 2, 368–481; El Cheikh, *Byzantium*.

140. P. Webb, *Imagining the Arabs*, 186 (here Muqatil's *Tafsir*).

141. Quoted and discussed by Morony, "Religious Communities," 155.

142. El Cheikh, *Byzantium*, 115–137.

143. Al-Baladhuri, *Origins*, vol. 1, pp. 86, 248 (translated as "Greeks"). For more Rumi slaves, see, e.g., al-Tabari, *History*, vol. 33: *Storm and Stress*, 116 (1253).

144. Al-Jahiz, trans. in Connelly, *Contesting the Greek Past*, 116.

145. E.g., Serhan, "Οι όροι «Βυζάντιο»," 446.

146. Quoted and translated by El-Huni, *The Poetry of Ibn al-Rùmî*, 4–5.

147. E.g., Abû Firâs, *Les Byzantines*, poem 19 (p. 48): "I sometimes fear the Roman relatives of my mother"; poem 18 (p. 46): "my low blood" (stressing her low social class); see El Tayib, "Abū Firās," 315.

148. Merendino, "Quattro Lettere," 322. Friedrich may have been repeating back claims made originally to him by Batatzes in a previous letter.

149. Shawcross, *Chronicle*.

150. Uberti, *Dittamondo* 3.23 (v. 36; vol. 1, 249); see the commentary at vol. 2, 298–301. I owe this reference, with gratitude, to Andreas Kyropoulos.

151. Chandler, *Travels*, 136.

152. Koubourlis, Οι ιστοριογραφικές οφειλές, 53n12, 161–162.

153. E.g., that of the Georgian Gregorios Pakourianos, in his *Typikon*.

154. E.g., *Life of Saint Maria the Egyptian* 36, in *PG* 87: 3724; *Martyrdom of Gondilouch* 7 (p. 356); *Life of Saint Thomais* 26; K. Akropolites, *On Saint Barbaros*, pp. 419–420; for disparagement in provincial Byzantine saints' *Lives* of the Christian Bulgarians for attacking the empire, see Kaldellis, *Ethnography*, 129.

155. See Chapter 3, section on "Religion and Ethnicity."

156. Krueger, "Practice of Christianity," 9–10.

CHAPTER 3 ▪ *Romanland*

Epigraph: Cicero, *Against Verres* 2.5.167. ("And not only among Roman citizens, who are united [to each other] by a community of language, rights, and many other things.")

1. Louis II, *Letter to Basileios I*, p. 390; see Chapter 1, section on "The Quandaries of Denialism."
2. Leon VI, *Taktika* 18.95; see Chapter 4.
3. Nikolaos, *Letter* 1 (p. 3).
4. Liudprand, *Embassy to Constantinople* 51.
5. Vryonis, "Will of a Provincial Magnate," 264–265.
6. See below, in the section "Patriots for Romanía."
7. Shawcross, *Chronicle*, 192–193.
8. K. Akropolites, *On Saint Barbaros*, 405–406.
9. Gregoras, *Florentios*, 71.
10. This is well put by Conant in *Staying Roman*, 7.
11. This will be argued in a future study on the governmental aspect of Roman nationality.
12. Treadgold, *History*; Jeffreys et al., *Oxford Handbook*. They mention only the name of the modern country.
13. E.g., Wolff, "Romania"; Jacoby, "After the Fourth Crusade."
14. E.g., Van Tricht, *Latin Renovatio*; many of the papers in Balard et al., *Byzance et le monde extérieure*, esp. part 1, on westerners living in Byzantine lands.
15. E.g., Genesios, *On the Reigns* 2.10, 3.3; Kinnamos, *History* 2.8; Theodoros Prodromos, *Historical Poems* 4.21 and 4.231; Theodoros II Laskaris, *Letter* 214.
16. E.g., Alexander, "Strength of Empire," 340–341; Kazhdan, "Romania," 1805; and the glossary in Shepard, *Cambridge History*, 900.
17. Athanasios, *History of the Arians* 35. Date (357 AD): Barnes, *Athanasius and Constantius*, 126. For a similar notion of Rome as the head of the world, see Jerome, cited and discussed in Ando, *Imperial Ideology*, 2.
18. *Digest* 50.1.33; cf. *Basilika* 7.5.5, 38.1.6. The emperor Herakleios said that many people were coming to Constantinople as "the common fatherland of all": *Novel* 24 in Zepos, *Jus Graecoromanum*, vol. 1, 33.
19. Themistios, *Oration* 7.94c–d.
20. *Panegyrici Latini* 9.21.3. Possibly he meant only that the emperors had brought the world under Roman control.
21. For theories and models of empire, see Chapter 6.
22. Ando, "Sovereignty," 24; cf. Burbank and Cooper, *Empires*, 58.
23. Ando, "Empire, State, and Communicative Action," 226–227; for the impact of this transformation on imperial self-presentation, see Weisweiler, "Populist Despotism," 160–161.
24. Ando, "Empire as State," 179–180.
25. *Martyrdom of Saba* 4 (p. 218), 8 (p. 221); trans. in Heather and Matthews, *Goths*, 114, 117; context: Lee, *Information*, 75.
26. Orosius, *Seven Books of History against the Pagans* 7.43.5–6. For the Latin sources, see Zeiller, "L'apparition."

27. Weisweiler, "From Empire to World-State," 194, drawing conclusions from the data in Noreña, *Imperial Ideals*.
28. Epiphanios of Salamis, *Panarion* 66.1.10, 66.1.12, 66.5.9, 66.5.11, 69.2.1.
29. Epiphanios of Salamis, *Panarion* 69.9.3.
30. Aristeides, *Oration* 26.63.
31. Magdalino, "Byzantium = Constantinople," 43.
32. Kaldellis, "How Was a 'New Rome' Even Thinkable?"
33. E.g., Aristeides, *Oration* 26.36, 61, 63, 75.
34. Rutilius Namatianus, *De reditu suo* 1.63–66.
35. Edwards and Woolf, *Rome the Cosmopolis*.
36. Malalas, *Chronicle* 16.19 (ἄλλον βασιλέα τῇ Ῥωμανίᾳ; Ἀρεόβινδον βασιλέα τῇ Ῥωμανίᾳ); *Paschal Chronicle*, p. 622 (Πρόβον βασιλέα τῇ Ῥωμανίᾳ).
37. Theophylaktos, *History* 5.13.4 (who says that the letter was written in Greek).
38. Kaldellis, *Byzantine Republic*.
39. Smyth, *Greek Grammar*, 338.
40. Burbank and Cooper, *Empires*, 58.
41. J. Brunshmid in *Eranos Vindobonensis* (1893), 331–333: Χρ(ιστέ) Κ(ύριε) βοήτι της πόλεως κ' έρυξον τὸν Ἄβαριν κὲ πύλαξον τὴν Ῥωμανίαν κὲ τὸν γράψαντα ἀμήν (Archaeological Museum of Zagreb).
42. Malalas, *Chronicle* 16.19; cf. 16.21: "in every city of Romanía."
43. Konstantinos VII, *Book of Ceremonies* 1.65 (vol. 1, 295).
44. Keroularios, *Letter I to Petros of Antioch*, 175.
45. Geography: Kosmas Indikopleustes, *Christian Topography* 2.29, 2.45, 11.23; Epiphanios of Jerusalem, *Proskynetarion*, p. 81 (eighth–ninth century). State territory: *Digenis Akritis* (G) 5.81. Something to be attacked by barbarians: Kosmas Indikopleustes, *Christian Topography*, 2.75; Petros the Sicilian, *History of the Paulicians* 178; Symeon Logothetes, *Chronicle* 119.2, 121.18, 130.20, 130.27, etc. These are indicative citations for each category.
46. Petros the Sicilian, *History of the Paulicians* 185 (ninth century).
47. Petros the Sicilian, *History of the Paulicians* 184.
48. Nikephoros II Phokas, *On Skirmishing* 4 (p. 156), 7 (p. 162).
49. Theophanes Continuatus (ed. Bekker, p. 427), on the wars of Ioannes Kourkouas, summarizing a lost eight-book account by one Manuel. Judging by the sudden frequency of the term *Romanía* and its cognates here, that lost work featured them heavily, and it also made comparisons to Roman heroes of the past, such as Trajan and Belisarios. For the lost work, see Whittow, *Making*, 344–345; Treadgold, *Middle Byzantine Historians*, 197–203.
50. Vasiliev, *Byzance et les Arabes*, vol. 2, pt. 2, 400; he also spells Romanos I as "Armanus" on 96.
51. I thank Kevin van Bladel for helping me with the Arabic and Persian grammar. The Persian expression can be found, e.g., in Naser-e Khusraw's *Safarnama* (eleventh century).
52. E.g., Holo, *Byzantine Jewry*, 69.
53. Psellos, *Letter S* 3 (p. 225).
54. Miklosich and Müller, *Acta*, vol. 4, 235–236: τοὺς κόπους ὑπὲρ τῆς Ῥωμανίας (1250s); see Angold, "Byzantine 'Nationalism,'" 66.

55. *Actes de Lavra*, vol. 1, 286 (no. 55).
56. In Papadopoulos-Kerameus, Ἀνάλεκτα, vol. 4, 109–113, here 112: σπουδάζω δὲ ἐπὶ πᾶσι παντοίως εἰς τὰ συμφέροντα τῇ τιμῇ τοῦ περιποθήτου σου υἱοῦ καὶ τῆς ῾Ρωμανίας; discussions in Svoronos, "Le serment"; Medvedev, "Ἡ συνοδικὴ ἀπόφαση."
57. Miklosich and Müller, *Acta*, vol. 3, 25–37.
58. E.g., Christophilopoulou, *Το πολίτευμα και οι θεσμοί*, 7n1, 351.
59. Psellos, *Orationes forenses et acta*, p. 181; for the background, see McQueen, "Relations."
60. Nikephoros II Phokas, *On Skirmishing* 4 (p. 156), 7 (p. 162).
61. Romanía: Konstantinos VII, *De administrando imperio* 9.113, 22.22, 44.126–127, 46.15, 46.135–139, 47.24, 53.530; style: 1.8–15.
62. See Chapter 2, section on "A Prima Facie Ethnicity." I am preparing a separate study of Byzantine patriotism, which will explore the concept of *patris*, its extension to the whole of Romanía, and the institutions that promoted it.
63. For Eusebios and Rome, see Johnson, *Ethnicity and Argument*, ch. 6.
64. Kosmas Indikopleustes, *Christian Topography* 2.75; for Kosmas in general, see L. Brubaker, "The *Christian Topography*."
65. Kekeumenos, *Strategikon* 18; *paideia*: 76.
66. Kekeumenos, *Strategikon* 11 and 18.
67. Kekeumenos, *Strategikon* 30; for his ancestry, see the very end of Chapter 4.
68. Kekeumenos, *Strategikon* 81.
69. Ševčenko, "Constantinople," 733; in general, see de Boel, "L'identité 'romaine.'" The poem has come down in various patchy versions. The version from which they derive may be placed around 1100. For this poem and Kekaumenos, see the excellent discussion of Magdalino, "Honour among the Romaioi," who notices the importance of Romanía.
70. *Digenis Akritis* (G) 1.49 and 2.191.
71. *Digenis Akritis* (G) 3.9–15; cf. 2.52–85.
72. Family: *Digenis Akritis* (G) 3.52–54: ἐν τοῖς μέρεσιν ἔλθωμεν τῆς καλῆς ῾Ρωμανίας; also 2.3, 2.191, 3.15; religion: 1.306, 3.201–202.
73. *Digenis Akritis* (G) 3.138–139, 3.201.
74. E.g., Goodblatt, *Elements of Ancient Jewish Nationalism*, 134.
75. Herodotos, *Histories* 8.144; see Isaac, *The Invention of Racism*, 112, 263n25.
76. E.g., Attaleiates, *History* 43, here the Pechenegs; Eustathios, *Funeral Oration for Manuel I Komnenos* 18 ("a language, I mean an *ethnos*"). This usage probably has biblical roots: Bauer, *A Greek-English Lexicon*, 161, s.v. *glossa* 2.3. See also Choniates, *History* 204–205, 209, 322. For the limits of linguistic pluralism in Byzantium, see Dagron, "Formes et fonctions"; Oikonomides, "L''unilinguisme.'"
77. Obolensky, *Six Byzantine Potraits*, 125; see also 67, 69.
78. *Life of Saint Neilos of Rossano* 14.
79. Psellos, *Letter KD* 190 (p. 214).
80. E.g., Choniates, *History* 191, 300 (though the meaning is unclear); in general, see Schreiner, "Bilinguismus."

81. Daphnopates, *Oration on the Peace* 16 (p. 278).
82. Theophylaktos, *History* 5.10.4.
83. Choniates, *History* 125.
84. Judg. 12:5–6.
85. Kramer, "Ῥωμαῖοι und Λατῖνοι."
86. Cupane, "Ἡ τῶν Ῥωμαίων γλῶσσα." Cupane argues that references to the Roman language in Byzantine texts, which had previously been taken to refer to Greek (including by the present author), actually refer to Latin, and I am persuaded that in most cases she is right (I am not sure about the case in the seventh-century *Acta of St. Anastasios the Persian*, which probably refers to Greek, or Anna Komnene, *Alexiad* 7.8.3); also Papadopoulou, Συλλογικὴ ταυτότητα, 146–156. See below for later references that refer to Greek.
87. Burgmann, "Byzantinische Rechtslexika," 109–111. For "Roman" and "Italian" matters as law, see Kazhdan, "Some Observations," 209 (Psellos); Magdalino, "Prosopography," 49–50. For the military context, see Maurikios, *Strategikon*, pref. and 1.8; Leon VI, *Taktika*, pref. and 4.6.
88. E.g., Konstantinos VII, *On the Themes*, p. 82.
89. For studies, see Kaldellis, *Hellenism*, 69–70.
90. Nicolaus I, *Letter* 88 (p. 459).
91. Themistios, *Oration* 6.71c; see the survey by Basilikopoulou, "Ἡ πάτριος φωνή."
92. Ioannes Lydos, *On the Magistracies* 1.50, 2.3, 2.12, 3.42, 3.68; see Kaldellis, *Hellenism*, 73–74.
93. Theophylaktos, *History* 3.4 (not realizing that it was a Germanic word), 4.9, 6.7, 7.2, 7.14.
94. Justinian, *Novels* 66.1.2, 7.1, 22.2; see Dagron, "Aux origines."
95. Konstantinos VII, *On the Themes*, p. 60.
96. Goodblatt, *Elements of Ancient Jewish Nationalism*, 69–70.
97. *Chronicle of the Morea* 4130.
98. Korobeinikov, "How 'Byzantine' Were the Early Ottomans?," 222.
99. *Life of Basileios I* 68; possibly also Anna Komnene, *Alexiad* 7.8.3.
100. E.g., Leon the Deacon, *History* 2.7 (the battering "ram").
101. *Digenis Akritis* (G) 1.115.
102. See the citations and discussion in Cupane, "Ἡ τῶν Ῥωμαίων γλῶσσα," 154. At 154 she cites a passage from Neophytos the Recluse (late twelfth century), which says that "in the Roman language, Mamma means *manna*" (and this is in fact the "modern" Greek word for mother): *Panegyrike Biblos* A: 2.5 (p. 131).
103. E.g., de Boel, "L'identité 'romaine,'" 178, citing previous bibliography also in support of that position. Mackridge, *Language* 48n57, takes it only as far back as the *Chronicle of the Morea*.
104. Beaton, *The Medieval Greek Romance*, 140, 253n35; for more, see Cupane, "Ἡ τῶν Ῥωμαίων γλῶσσα," 152–156.
105. E. Fisher, "Alexios of Byzantium"; for the second translator's preface, see *Catalogus Codicum Astrologorum Graecorum*, vol. 12 (1936), 153.
106. Priest at Serres: Synadinos, *Conseils* 4.13; bizarre: a letter written by Ioannes Oikonomou, quoted in Siniosoglou, Ἀλλόκοτος Ἑλληνισμός, 238n4;

Russian newspaper: Frary, *Russia*, 30. Many texts can be cited from between the seventeenth and nineteenth centuries that make this distinction.

107. Manuel Malaxos, *Historia Patriarchica*, p. 114. I thank Andreas Kyropoulos for this and the following reference.

108. Çelebi, *Book of Travels*, pp. 283–284, for the Peloponnese; for his view of the Melkites of Syria, who, he was surprised to discover, did not speak *Rumca*, see Masters, *The Arabs*, p. 15.

109. Chandler, *Travels*, 136.

110. De Lange, "Hebrews, Greeks or Romans?," 117.

111. Connelly, *Contesting the Greek Past*, 19 (n. 36 for al-Ya'qubi), 183. For a fascinating exchange on ethnicity and language, using these terms, see the text translated by Canard, "Les aventures," 54; the reference now is Al-Tanūḥī, *Kitāb al-faraj ba'da l-šidda*, vol. 2 193.17–194.7 (I thank Coleman Connelly for his help with the original Arabic).

112. G. Fisher, *Between Empires*, 132–131, citing relevant scholarship. Not until late in their history did some Byzantines themselves believe that their language made them "Greeks": Kaldellis, *A New Herodotos*.

113. Adams, *"Romanitas"*; also Dench, *Romulus' Asylum*, 314–315; Clackson, *Language and Society*, 31, 40–41, 66–67; Ando, *Imperial Rome*, 57; Wallace-Hadrill, *Rome's Cultural Revolution*, 57.

114. Konstantinos IX Monomachos, *Novel on the Nomophylax* 16.

115. Mehl, *Roman Historiography*, 12–14: should the book focus on Roman or Latin texts? He wisely opts for the former.

116. Kaldellis, *Hellenism*, 64–71.

117. Euodios, *Forty-Two Martyrs of Amorion* 4.

118. E.g., the Isaurian emperors in the *Ekloge*: Chitwood, *Byzantine Legal Culture*, 24, 185.

119. Inglebert, "Christian Reflections," 101.

120. Sozomenos, *Ecclesiastical History* 2.15.5.

121. E.g., Nikephoros, *Short History* 1, 65; *Life of Saint Basileios the Younger* 3.23, 3.27. This happens in Leon VI's *Taktika* too. See Whittow, *Making*, 162–163.

122. A random sample: Obolensky, *Byzantium and the Slavs*, 13; Mango, *Byzantium*, 29–31; Whittow, *Making*, 126; Ahrweiler, "Byzantine Concepts," 9–10; Angold, *Byzantium*, 22, 28, 44; Metcalf, *Byzantine Cyprus*, 301; Ruggieri, "Carians," 207; Dark and Özgümüş, *Constantinople*, xv, 105. By contrast, Page, *Being Byzantine*, 57–58, 125, 161, 170–172, 174, 252, 276, got it right.

123. Petros of Sicily, *History of the Paulicians* 37 (p. 21).

124. Kaldellis, *Ethnography*, 126–139.

125. The *Life of Saint Neilos of Rossano* 96; Mesarites, *Funeral Oration for His Brother Ioannes* 49 (I, p. 62); see Kaldellis, *Hellenism*, 357–358.

126. Kanaboutzes, *Commentary on Dionysios of Halikarnassos* 35. This passage conclusively proves that the author was Orthodox; the reference to "our emperor Justinian" (at 12) indicates that too (but westerners could claim Justinian too). A similar list in Bryennios, *Dialogue with a Muslim* 43, quoted above.

127. Pakourianos, *Typikon*, p. 44.

128. Kaldellis, *Byzantine Republic*, 189–190.

129. Choniates, *History* 606; see Kaldellis, *Hellenism*, 365.
130. Manuel II Palaiologos, *Funeral Oration for Theodoros*, 161.
131. Choniates, *History* 238–239.
132. Leon VI, *Taktika* 20.39: Ῥωμαίοις καὶ μάλιστα Χριστιανοῖς.
133. Nikon, *Taktikon*, p. 15.
134. See now Kaldellis, "Did the Byzantine Empire Have 'Ecumenical' or 'Universal' Aspirations?"
135. A. D. Smith, *Chosen Peoples*.
136. Pitsakis, "Pour une définition," esp. 172, exemplifies this school of thought.
137. A notable recent exception that gets it right is Ivanov, *"Pearls before Swine."*
138. Whitby, "Emperors and Armies," 178–179; Magdalino, "Enlightenment and Repression," 371; L. Brubaker and Haldon, *Byzantium*, 16.
139. McCormick, *Eternal Victory*, 244–252 ("God and Country"); Trombley, "War, Society and Popular Religion"; Haldon, *Warfare*, ch. 1; Kolia-Dermitzaki, Ὁ βυζαντινός ἱερός πόλεμος, passim, esp. 232–260.
140. See Chapter 2, section on "A Fiction of the Sources?"
141. McCormick, *Eternal Victory*, 237–238.
142. Photios, *Homily* 2.15 (p. 28).
143. Photiadis, "A Semi-Greek"; Kaegi, *Heraclius*, 296; for other cases and the prayer books, see McCormick, *Eternal Victory*, 243.
144. Text in Brightman, *Liturgies*, 407–408; trans. Jasper and Cuming, *Prayers*, 102–103; the main liturgy: Krueger, *Liturgical Subjects*, 115.
145. Pertusi, "Acoluthia," 157; for the fossils of this tradition, see Pitsakis, "Pour une définition," 170.
146. The subtitle of Krueger's *Liturgical Subjects*, a groundbreaking book from this standpoint.
147. Konstantinos VII, *Book of Ceremonies* 1.69 (pp. 316–318).
148. Sen, *Identity and Violence*, 83.
149. P. Webb, *Imagining the Arabs*, 12.
150. Cf. Koder, "Byzanz, die Griechen und die Romaiosyne."
151. An important study, albeit looking at the west, is Woolf, *Becoming Roman*; for elites in the east, Madsen, *Eager to Be Roman*; the best framework for understanding the process is Ando, *Imperial Ideology*; a preliminary sketch of my own in Kaldellis, *Hellenism*, ch. 2. For a summary of modern debates over late antique ethnogenesis, but not touching on the Romans of the east, see Wood, *Modern Origins*, 310–329.
152. Isaac, *The Invention of Racism*, 8.
153. W. V. Harris, *Roman Power*, poses the question explicitly in his later chapters, ultimately deciding against it, though tentatively. I am curious what he would make of Byzantium after the seventh century. In many publications, Ando also sees Rome on a trajectory away from "empire" and toward a unified state: see the section "The Vernacular Ontology of Romanía."
154. Hippolytos, *Commentary on Daniel* 4.8.
155. Themistios, *Oration* 16.211c–d; trans. (mod.) and analysis by Heather and Moncour, *Politics, Philosophy and Empire*, 281.

156. For a modern study of the process in Galatia, see Mitchell, "Galatians," 280 (and in other publications by the same scholar on Galatia, cited there); Isaac, *The Invention of Racism*, 89–90.

157. Augustine, *Expositions on the Psalms* 58.1.21 (vol. 39, 744): *qui iam cognoscit gentes in imperio Romano quae quid erant, quando omnes Romani facti sunt, et omnes Romani dicuntur?* Augustine intuitively saw his fellow provincials as Romans entitled to due legal rights: see his *Letter* 10* on the operation of slavers, discussed by Inglebert, "Christian Reflections," 109.

158. Conant, *Staying Roman*, 1, 192.

159. See Chapter 2, section on "Who Was Included?"

160. Translation by Connelly, *Contesting the Greek Past*, 18.

161. Konstantinos VII, *On the Themes*, p. 62.

162. Photios, *Letter* 103 (vol. 1, 139–143).

163. Stegemann, "War der Apostel Paulus ein römischer Bürger?"; Harrill, *Paul the Apostle*, 98–99.

164. τῇ Ῥωμαϊκῇ κλήσει καὶ τῇ πολιτείᾳ.

165. Gen. 46:21.

166. Cicero, *De legibus* 2.2.5; *Pro Balbo* 28–29; *Pro Caecina* 100; see Sherwin-White, *The Roman Citizenship*, 57–58, 73, 153–154, 304–306.

167. τὸ Ῥωμαίων γένος ὑπέδυ ὥσπερ οὖν οὗτοι πάντες, ἔθνους καὶ πατρίδος ὄντες ἀλλοφύλου, εἰς τὴν Ῥωμαϊκὴν ἐτέλεσαν πολιτογραφίαν.

CHAPTER 4 ▪ *Ethnic Assimilation*

Epigraph: Cicero, *Guide to Elections* 14. ("This is Rome, a state formed by a gathering of nations.") For the idea, see Moatti, *Birth of Critical Thinking*, 47–48; it was understood across the ages: Vergil, *Aeneid* 12.823–28; Claudian, *On the Consulship of Stilicho* 3.150–154; Paul the Deacon, *Historia Romana* 1.2.

1. Moatti, *Birth of Critical Thinking*, 271–290; see also Farney, *Ethnic Identity*; Dench, *Romulus' Asylum*, 5–6, 22. Even so, recent scholarship has emphasized ancient notions of Roman ethnicity. For the absorption of refugees, immigrants, and barbarian soldiers in earlier Roman imperial history, see Barbero, *Barbari*.

2. Laiou, "Institutional Mechanisms," focuses on fiscal and judicial systems, and considers minorities who "clearly retained their identity" (162); that is, experienced integration rather than assimilation. Ahrweiler, "Citoyens," 346, refers correctly to the integration of these groups into the "national community" of Byzantium, but offers no definitions or documentation.

3. Lenski, *Failure of Empire*, 351.

4. *Panegyrici Latini* 8.9.1–4, 8.21.1 (Constantius I), and 2.36.3 (Theodosius I).

5. Eustathios, *Funeral Oration for Manuel I Komnenos* 18–19, 65; see Bourbouhakis' commentary (p. 130) on the viticultural metaphor of grafting.

6. Agathias, *Histories* 1.20.3 (βαρβαρικὰ διαιτήματα).

7. Agathias, *Histories* 2.20.7: ἦν δέ τις τῶν ἐπισημοτάτων ἐν τοῖς ταξιάρχοις Θεόδωρος ὄνομα, τὸ μὲν γένος ἕλκων ἐκ τοῦ ἔθνους τῶν Τζάνων, παρὰ Ῥωμαίοις

δὲ τεθραμμένος καὶ ἤδη τὸ βαρβαρικὸν τοῦ τρόπου, εἰ καὶ πάτριον ἦν, ἀποσκευασάμενος καὶ ἐς τὸ ἀστειότατον μετακοσμήσας; for a similar case, see Prokopios, *Wars* 8.26.13 (a Herul).

8. Anna Komnene, *Alexiad* 8.7.4.
9. Kinnamos, *History* 2.14, 5.13.
10. Agathias, *Histories* 1.20.4.
11. Crone, *Nativist Prophets*, esp. 46–76, for their rebellion.
12. Theophanes Continuatus 3.29.
13. Zuckerman, "Emperor Theophilos," 146–147.
14. Genesios, *On the Reigns* 3.7.
15. Pseudo-Symeon: see Zuckerman, "Emperor Theophilos," 107.
16. Theophanes Continuatus 3.21; Genesios, *On the Reigns* 3.3.
17. Michael the Syrian, *Chronicle*, vol. 3, 88.
18. E.g., al-Tabari, *History*, vol. 33: *Storm and Stress*, 3 (1165).
19. Ibn Hawqal (writing not long after the events in question and hailing from the region of their origin) in Vasiliev, *Byzance et les Arabes*, vol. 2.2, 419–421; commentary at vol. 2.1, 270–273.
20. Cf. Signes Codoñer, *Theophilos*, 140–141.
21. *Life of Saint Athanasia of Aigina* 4 (p. 181; trans. Sherry, p. 143); the same story (albeit in different wording) in the *Synaxarion of Constantinople*, p. 611 (app.), from the version of 1301.
22. *Forty-Two Martyrs of Amorion*, version 3, p. 27; cf. Signes Codoñer, *Theophilos*, 128–129.
23. *Forty-Two Martyrs of Amorion*, version 3, p. 27; *Life of Saint Methodios* 7, in *PG* 100: 1249d.
24. Sherry, "Life of St. Athanasia," 143n22.
25. Haldon, *Warfare*, 259.
26. Zosimos, *New History* 4.30.4–5.
27. Signes Codoñer, *Theophilos*, 153–172, quotation from 167; eloquence: Genesios, *On the Reigns* 3.4; Theophanes Continuatus 3.19.
28. Symeon Logothetes, *Chronicle* 131.50–52. Though the source explicitly states that the language was Persian, the Armenian nationalist historian N. Adontz tried to twist it into "Persarmenian" in order to claim that it was really "Armenian": *Études*, 77; but see Cheynet, "Théophile," 48. For the Armenian bias in Byzantine scholarship, see Chapter 5.
29. Konstantinos VII, *Book of Ceremonies* 2.49 (vol. 1, 694–695).
30. Eger, *Islamic-Byzantine Frontier*, 292.
31. Ibn Hawqal in Vasiliev, *Byzance et les Arabes*, vol. 2, pt. 2, 420.
32. Cheynet, *La société byzantine*, 627–646.
33. Psellos, *Letters S* 38–39, 172, and esp. 189 (at p. 483).
34. Christides, *Image of the Pre-Islamic Arab*, 177.
35. For more on Digenis Akritis, see Chapter 3, the section on "Patriots for Romania."
36. *Digenis Akritis G* 1.32 (fair); 1.115 (language), 1.305 (defect), 1.332 (miracle), 2.23–25 (values), 3.257 (dress), 2.53–55 (his mother).
37. Holmes, *Basil II*, 207–208.
38. K. Akropolites, *On Saint Barbaros*, pp. 405–406.

39. K. Akropolites, *On Saint Barbaros*, pp. 412–413.

40. K. Akropolites, *On Saint Barbaros*, p. 420.

41. Konstantinos VII, *De administrando imperio* 50.202–203; probably a Christian: Kaldellis, *Christian Parthenon*, 92–94.

42. Theophanes, *Chronographia*, p. 385 (eighth century); *Life of Saints David, Symeon, and Georgios* 34 (ninth century) (p. 256).

43. Other groups too settled in Greece (e.g., Avars), but they left a far smaller trace on the processes analyzed below.

44. Konstantinos VII, *On the Themes*, p. 91: "The entire country was Slavicized" under Konstantinos V, during a plague (but this account is obviously political, given what follows; see section on "The Politics of Slavic Ethnicity" below). Cf. the ninth- or tenth-century *Chrestomathia of Strabo*, which says in reference to the ancient Greeks that "many *ethne* have been lost and now there is not even a name for the Macedonians and the Thracians. . . . The whole of Epeiros, practically all of Hellas, the Peloponnese, and Macedonia are held by Scythian Slavs" (7.37, 7.47). The *Chronicle of Monembasia*, by contrast, presents a more mixed picture of what happened in the Peloponnese. Curta, *Edinburgh*, 125–126, believes that it was not Slavs in the Peloponnese but Avars. For these sources, see Anagnostakis and Kaldellis, "Textual Sources."

45. I hesitate to attribute this picture to specific works of scholarship because of the national politics involved and the quibbling that would inevitably be required. Curta, *Edinburgh*, is an excellent survey, though I would quibble over his caginess regarding Slavs.

46. Stamatoyannopoulos et al., "Genetics." I am troubled by the notion of a "Slavic homeland" situated between the Oder and Dnieper Rivers and used as the benchmark for Slavic DNA. How can we know that people perceived by the Byzantines as Slavs in eighth-century Greece were genetically related to the current inhabitants of that alleged "homeland"?

47. Ševčenko, "Three Paradoxes," 229 (what follows there about Byzantine policies in conquered Bulgaria is, we now know, completely wrong).

48. For two models, see Herrin, "Aspects of the Process of Hellenization"; Dunn, "Evangelization or Repentance?" *Hellenization* is the term preferred by (a) Greek national historians (for obvious reasons) and (b) western scholars who do not want to say "Romanization" for fear of conceeding that there was something Roman about Byzantium. For an approach to the question through personal names, see Kravari, "L'hellénisation des Slaves."

49. Leon VI, *Taktika* 18.95; cf. *Life of Basileios I* 54 on the alleged baptism and submission to Rome of the Slavs of the western Balkans, a narrative that does not imply cultural assimilation.

50. Wilson, *Holy Roman Empire*, 78.

51. *Miracles of Saint Demetrios* 2.1.179–180 (invasions), 2.4.254 and 268 (peace and trade).

52. Theophanes, *Chronographia*, pp. 474–475, with the notes by Mango and Scott; Curta, *Edinburgh*, 126.

53. Curta, *Edinburgh*, 127.

54. Oikonomides, "L'archonte Slave," esp. 117; additional seals in Seibt, "Seigel" (34 for Ioannes); Curta, *Edinburgh*, 116–117. We do not know if these

archons with Slavic names were appointed by the court from within the groups that they governed or were brought in from other Slavic groups that had previously accepted imperial suzerainty.

55. *Miracles of Saint Demetrios* 2.4.231–235.
56. *Miracles of Saint Demetrios* 2.4.255–257, 289–290.
57. Curta, *Edinburgh*, 285 (bishop and theme); cf. 286: "That after c. 800 no mention is made of the Bel(ege)zites may indicate that their polity had by then been absorbed within the theme of Hellas," and 287: "the Berzetes and the Rynchines of the *Miracles of Saint Demetrios* are not known from any subsequent sources." Cf. Kaminiates, *Capture of Thessalonike* 6 (villages and taxes). For the evolution of the Drogoubites, see also Malingoudis, Σλάβοι, 151–153.
58. Konstantinos VII, *On the Themes*, p. 89; see Ditten, *Ethnische Verschiebungen*, 163–176; Curta, *Edinburgh*, 109 and 131n34.
59. Konstantinos VII, *Book of Ceremonies* 2.37 (pp. 634–635).
60. Kaminiates, *Capture of Thessalonike* 20, 41.
61. *Life of Saint Athanasios of Athos (B)* 77.
62. Liudprand, *Antapodosis* 3.24.
63. *Actes d'Iviron*, vol. 2, 85 (*Actum Leonis judicis*, a. 1059–1074), citing documents from the tenth century; and the Georgian *Life of Saint George the Athonite* 13 (pp. 120–121, trans. Grdzelidze); cf. Curta, *Edinburgh*, 173–174.
64. Curta, "Linear Frontiers," 27–28; Malingoudis, Σλάβοι, 155.
65. Our main sources are the *Chronicle of Monembasia*, on which see Anagnostakis and Kaldellis, "Textual Sources"; and Konstantinos VII, *De administrando imperio* 49–50.
66. *Life of Saint Nikon "Metanoeite!"* 59, 62; cremation: Oikonomides, "Ὄψιμη ἱεραποστολή," 32–33.
67. *Chronicle of the Morea* 1715–1738 (Milengoi); 3040 and 4605 (Slavs).
68. Avramea, "Ὁ τζάσις τῶν Μεληγγῶν"; for the early fifteenth century, see Isidoros of Kiev in Regel, *Analecta*, 65.
69. Laskaris Kananos, *Travel Account*, p. 16. He calls them "Zygiotai," from the Zygos of Mani, associated with the Milengoi in many prior Byzantine texts.
70. *Miracles of Saint Demetrios* 2.5.289.
71. Theophanes, *Chronographia*, p. 486. For Nikephoros' similar policies in the Peloponnese, see the *Chronicle of Monembasia*; Ditten, *Ethnische Verschiebungen*, 331–360.
72. Parpola, "The Construction of Dur-Sarrukin"; for Assyrian identity, construed even on "national" terms, see Bedford, "The Neo-Assyrian Empire."
73. Brubaker and Haldon, *Byzantium*, 583, who use the correct ethnonym.
74. Theophanes, *Chronographia*, p. 440; for the other reports, see *PmbZ* I: 5404.
75. For Thomas, see now Signes Codoñer, *Theophilos*, 25–59, who argues that a Thomas the Armenian and a Thomas the Slav were mistakenly conflated. A native of the empire: Symeon Logothetes, *Chronicle* 129.4; Michael the Syrian, *Chronicle*, vol. 3, 75.

76. *Life of Basileios I* 16; *Patria of Constantinople* 3.161. For a ninth-century general (Andreas) who was possibly of Slavic origin, see Genesios, *On the Reigns* 4.30.

77. The following analysis is a restructured and heavily modified form of Anagnostakis and Kaldellis, "Textual Sources," 128–135, with permission from the journal and my coauthor. Readers should consult that article for a fuller bibliography of nonessential items and scholarly dead-ends.

78. Niketas, *Letter* 2.

79. Niketas, *Letter* 5.

80. Niketas, *Letter* 4.

81. Niketas, *Letter* 20.

82. Jazdzewska, "Hagiographic Invention."

83. Niketas, *Life of Saint Theoktiste* 4.

84. Niketas, *Letters* 11, 23, 30, 31.

85. I am confused by Curta's unexplained rejection of Niketas' Roman identity (*Edinburgh*, 296n13: "He cannot be regarded as a Roman . . . never claimed to be a Roman"). This overlooks his *Life of Saint Theoktiste;* directly contradicts Curta's understanding of Roman identity in Byzantium (294–295); does not consider Niketas' career ; fails to explain what his ethnicity was if not Roman; and is a weak argument anyway: in our extant evidence, it is also likely that Scipio, Lucretius, or Vergil also did not "claim to be Romans." As Curta himself says on the previous page, specifically with regard to Roman identity in the Byzantine provinces, "There was no need to stress the obvious" (295).

86. Konstantinos VII, *On the Themes*, p. 91. The word may come from Slavic *gorazd*, "shrewd": Curta, *Edinburgh*, 280.

87. Kaldellis, *Hellenism in Byzantium*, 93–95.

88. Theophanes Continuatus p. 394 (ed. Bekker).

89. Konstantinos VII, *De administrando imperio* 13.146–194.

90. Theophanes Continuatus p. 413 (ed. Bekker). According to the chronicles, Niketas was later (927–928) implicated in a plot to dethrone Romanos in favor of Christophoros, Romanos' son, and was exiled to northwest Asia Minor: Westerink, *Nicétas*, 30–31.

91. Shepard, "A Marriage Too Far?," 132–133 (who does not discuss Niketas).

92. Shepard, "A Marriage Too Far?," 122n4.

93. *Life of Basileios I* 12; Konstantinos VII, *On the Themes*, p. 85.

94. Anagnostakis, "Μονεμβασία-Λακεδαίμων," 111–113; Anagnostakis, "Ελλαδικά παραμύθια," 125–128; Curta, *Edinburgh*, 236, 280, 288, 295.

95. Theophanes Continuatus p. 399 (ed. Bekker). On the Rentakioi, see Ditten, "Prominente Slawen," 104–108.

96. Westerink, *Nicétas*, 24.

97. Curta, *Edinburgh*, 284.

98. Westerink, *Nicétas*, 24–25; in more detail, Anagnostakis, "Ελλαδικά παραμύθια," 121–122, 126, with a prosopography of the Eladikoi-Helladikoi at 129–132; Anagnostakis, "Byzantium and Hellas," 15–29.

99. Runciman, *Emperor Romanus*, 47–48, 52; see Anagnostakis, "Ελλαδικά παραμύθια," 129–130.

100. Theophanes Continuatus p. 388 (ed. Bekker).
101. Niketas, *Letter* 8.
102. Garsoïan, "Armenian Integration," 101–102.
103. Pseudo-Symeon, *Chronicle*, p. 673.
104. Skylitzes, *Synopsis of Histories*, p. 285.
105. Lauxtermann, "John Geometres," 378.
106. Katrares, *Anakreontic Verses against the Philosopher Neophytos* 50–54.
107. Page, *Being Byzantine*, 48–49. For ethnic stereotypes in humor, see Haldon, "Humour," 58–59.
108. For the swift linguistic shift within certain families from Coptic to Arabic in postconquest Egypt, see Mikhail, *From Byzantine to Islamic Egypt*, 94.
109. For this distinction cast in the ideal types of France and Germany, see W. Brubaker, "Immigration" (things have changed since 1990, when this was published).
110. "Cultural genocide" as an aspect of genocide was proposed by the Polish Jewish lawyer Rafael Lemkin in 1944. He had more direct assaults in mind, but epigones have applied it to incentivized assimilation as well.
111. Theophanes Continuatus 1.5.
112. I have collected many statements to this effect by Byzantine authors. It was a conventional notion.
113. Isaac, *The Invention of Racism*, 20, 18, 24, 37.
114. Laiou, "The Foreigner and the Stranger," 96.
115. Psellos, *Orationes panegyricae* 4.299 (p. 68).
116. Attaleiates, *History* 31; see Kaldellis, *Ethnography*, 117–126.
117. He recounts his background at Anna Komnene, *Alexiad* 7.8.7. It does not matter whether the story was true.
118. Choniates, *History* 9–10; Brand, "Turkish Element."
119. For his Roman patriotism, see Chapter 3, section on "Patriots for Romanía."
120. Kekaumenos, *Strategikon* 81 (foreigners), 30 (Dvin), 31 (Demetrios Polemarchios), 73 (Kekaumenos); see Roueché, "Defining the Foreign," 209. The best analysis of his family background is by C. Roueché on the *Sharing Ancient Wisdoms* project website: http://www.ancientwisdoms.ac.uk (my only correction would be that Kamenos is not an Armenian name but the vernacular Greek form of Kekaumenos).

CHAPTER 5 ▪ *The Armenian Fallacy*

Epigraph: Jordanes, *Romana* 90. ("Thus out of diverse elements, as it were, he [Romulus] assembled a single body and created the Roman people.")
1. Prokopios, *Wars* 7.26.25–27, 7.31–32 (respectively).
2. Garsoïan, "Armenian Integration," 56–58, 62–63.
3. Ditten, *Ethnische Verschiebungen*, 72–82.
4. Charanis, *Armenians in the Byzantine Empire*, 13–18 (though uncritically repeating dubious information from some sources).

5. See, for example, the introduction by S. Der Nersessian to Charanis, *Armenians in the Byzantine Empire*, 7–9.
6. Charanis, *Armenians in the Byzantine Empire*, 39.
7. Adontz, *Études* (collected articles); Charanis, *Armenians in the Byzantine Empire*; and Kazhdan, *Armiane*; for the last item, see the summary in Vryonis, "Armenians and Greeks," as well as Kazhdan, "The Armenians in the Byzantine Ruling Class." Settipani, *Continuité*, is a valuable resource but it often pushes murky evidence or outright guesswork too far, producing specific genealogical connections and thereby reconstructing family trees based on too many conjectures. It also subscribes heavily to the Armenian fallacy.
8. Ayvazyan, *Armenian Military*, 98n155.
9. Garsoïan, "Armenian Integration," 60, also 93–103.
10. Cheynet, *Pouvoir*, 283 (but see below).
11. Seibt, "Stärken," 331–332.
12. Preiser-Kapeller, "Complex Processes," 296–297.
13. E.g., Genesios, *On the Reigns* 1.10.
14. Kaldellis, *Genesios*, xv–xxi; and Markopoulos, "Genesios," 138–140, based on more information than is discussed here.
15. Genesios, *On the Reigns* 4.3; cf. 4.10; he is *PmbZ* I: 3962.
16. For the institution of fosterage in medieval Armenia, see Redgate, *The Armenians*, 105.
17. Genesios, *On the Reigns* 4.18 (and see the passage quoted above); *Life of Basileios I* 12.
18. *Life of Basileios I* 12; he is *PmbZ* I: 8476 and II: 28290.
19. Skylitzes, *Synopsis of Histories*, p. 3 (pref.).
20. Genesios, *On the Reigns* 1.24; Cf. Strabo, *Geography* 11.14.12–13; Justin, *Epitome of Trogus* 42.2.10–12; Stephanos of Byzantion, *Ethnika* s.v. *Armenia*.
21. Markopoulos, "Genesios," 139; Kountoura-Galake, "Origins"; Cheynet, "Les Génésioi."
22. *PmbZ* I: 193; Settipani, *Continuité*, 150–158.
23. Respectively: Symeon Logothetes, *Chronicle* 130.11; Theophanes Continuatus 3.18; he is *PmbZ* I: 195. The manor is apparently known only in this connection: Janin, *Constantinople*, 375.
24. Signes Codoñer, *Theophilos*, 115–117, 257.
25. *PmbZ* II: 20241 and 26844.
26. Garsoïan, "Armenian Integration," 98. For the Taronites in general, see Adontz, "Les Taronites"; Settipani, *Continuité*, 343 ff.; for the Byzantine Taronites in the tenth century, see Cheynet, "Les Arméniens." Attempts to retain native forms of Christians names (e.g., Armenian Krikorikios for Gregorios) did not catch on: Cheynet, *La société byzantine*, vol. 1, 143.
27. Nikephoros Bryennios, *Materials* 1.11.
28. Theophylaktos of Ohrid, *Letters* 81, 66.
29. Anna Komnene, *Alexiad* 13.1.3.
30. Peters-Custot, *Les grecs*, 6.
31. Manganeios Prodromos (?) in *Recueil des historiens des croisades: Historien grecs*, vol. 2, pp. 288–292, esp. vv. 179, 181, 193–194, 198–199. The groom was Ioannes Komnenos, son of Andronikos, son of Ioannes II.

32. Kazhdan, *Armian*, 140–141, summarized by Ayvazyan, *Armenian Military*, 107. For possible such communities in the Balkans, see Garsoïan, "Armenian Integration," 58; Cyprus: Metcalf, *Byzantine Cyprus*, 433, 489, 538, 590–593 (discussing the use of DNA to identify them).

33. Eustathios of Thessalonike, *Capture of Thessalonike* 113–114 (pp. 124–126) implies that at least some Armenians, like the Jews, lived in a separate quarter outside the city (though we know that they had a church inside the walls too).

34. Confessional bias: Mahé, "Confession religieuse"; for Armenian identity in historiography, see Mahé, "Entre Moïse et Mahomet"; T. L. Andrews, "Identity, Philosophy, and the Problem of Armenian History," 30–32. For Chalcedonian Armenians, see Yarnley, "Armenian Philhellenes"; Arutjunova-Fidanjan, "Ethno-Confessional Self-Awareness."

35. Redgate, "Armenian Identity," 292.

36. Charanis, *Armenians in the Byzantine Empire*, 38–40 (not quite there yet, but almost); Garsoïan, "Armenian Integration," 98n170; Seibt, "Stärken," 340; salutary skepticism in Redgate, *The Armenians*, 237, including about nomenclature; also correctly in Papadopoulou, Συλλογική ταυτότητα, 76n1.

37. Garsoïan, "Armenian Historiography," 56.

38. Cheynet, *The Byzantine Aristocracy*, I:12, sees these names as distinctively Mamikonian.

39. Chitwood, *Byzantine Legal Culture*, 16; Chitwood muddies the waters at 42 (his "likely ethnic origins"). For Symbatios' view of Roman history, see his preface to the *Epitome of the Laws* in Schmink, *Studien*, 112–119.

40. Signes Codoñer, *Theophilos*, Section II: The Armenian Court, is over seventy pages long (63–136). Another study thick in Armenian fictions about this period is Kountoura-Galaki, "Armeniac Theme."

41. Theophanes Continuatus 4.6.

42. Signes Codoñer, *Theophilos*, 79–81.

43. *PLRE* III: p. 963.

44. *PmbZ* I: 5680 (astrologer) and 5682 (his father, the *skiastes*); antiquity: Potter, *Roman Empire*, 33–34.

45. Bartikian, Αρμενοβυζαντινά, 234; cf. Signes Codoñer, *Theophilos*, 113–114 ("whatever his ethnic origins may have been").

46. Signes Codoñer, *Theophilos*, 73–74.

47. Signes Codoñer, *Theophilos*, 63; he is *PmbZ* I: 766; Thekla is *PmbZ* I: 7259. *PBE* admits that his first name is the only evidence of his Armenian ethnicity.

48. Signes Codoñer, *Theophilos*, 105n13.

49. Theophanes, *Chronographia*, p. 463; for this problem, see below in this same section.

50. *Life of Saint Philaretos* 379, 447.

51. Bardas: *Life of Saint Philaretos* 475–486; Romans: 379, 447. Maria is *PmbZ* I; 4727. A different, wholly conjectural argument for Euphrosyne's Armenian ethnicity is offered by Treadgold, *Byzantine Revival*, 432n375. Cf. Rydén, *Life of St Philaretos*, 25: "There is no proof that Philaretos' family was Armenian, although an Armenian origin remains a possibility." Yet no one explains what "Armenian" might have meant in that context.

52. Genesios, *On the Reigns* 3.2; Theophanes Continuatus 4.1.
53. Signes Codoñer, *Theophilos*, 74–75, here 83; Marinos: *PmbZ* I: 4812; Theodora: *PmbZ* I: 7286; Manuel: *PmbZ* I: 4707.
54. Vardan, *History* 41 (p. 182).
55. Signes Codoñer, *Theophilos*, 246.
56. Signes Codoñer, *Theophilos*, 130, 160, 176, 443.
57. Signes Codoñer, *Theophilos*, 87.
58. Signes Codoñer, *Theophilos*, 35 (a special relationship between Leon V and Thomas the Armenian) and 111 (marriage, though no source calls either man an Armenian).
59. For the later, "imperial" period, see Cheynet, *Pouvoir*, 397, 399.
60. Quotation: Garsoïan, "Armenian Integration," 65.
61. Cheynet, *La société byzantine*, 339, 413, 473–476; Krsmanović, *Byzantine Province*, 101n121; Polemis, *Doukai*, 5–6.
62. Abastaktos: *PmbZ* II: 28180; Runciman, *Emperor Romanus*, 63.
63. Liudprand, *Antapodosis* 3.36 (*ex Armenorum gente*).
64. Theophanes Continuatus p. 423 (ed. Bekker); cf. *PmbZ* II: 26833 (p. 588).
65. E.g., Theophanes Continuatus pp. 412, 423, 426 (ed. Bekker); Runciman, *Emperor Romanus*, 78, correctly calls her not an Armenian but an Armeniac.
66. Zonaras, *Chronicle* 16.13 (Leon VI's third wife). The pseudo-ethnicization of provincial origins was a lexical convention of the ancient Roman empire that continued in Byzantium: Bertrand, "Langue grecque et administration romaine"; Sherwin-White, *Roman Citizenship*, 437–444; Kaldellis, *Hellenism*, 88; Laniado, *Ethnos et droit*, 10–11. I am preparing a separate study of this phenomenon.
67. E.g., Attaleiates, *History* 180; Skylitzes, *Synopsis of Histories*, p. 155.
68. Grégoire, "Le lieu de naissance." It is only in the later eleventh century that Romanos is associated with Lakape or called Lakapenos.
69. Konstantinos VII, *On the Themes*, p. 75; in general, see *TIB* 2: 85, 224–226; Melias: *PmbZ* II: 25041. The standard study is Dédéyan, "Mleh le Grand"; also Cooper and Decker, *Cappadocia*, 237.
70. Symeon Logothetes, *Chronicle* 132.7; land: *ODB*, vol. 2, p. 1203. *PmbZ* II: 28180 interprets it as a "place" of honor in the emperor's retinue, but the text explicitly says that Abastaktos foreswore "honors," which includes precisely such positions; moreover, a plot of land in the east is more compatible with the humble origins attributed later to Romanos I than a place of honor next to the emperor.
71. Lambakis, in Lambakis et al., *Η Μικρά Ασία των θεμάτων*, 299.
72. E.g., Runciman, *Emperor Romanus*, 150.
73. Haldon, *Byzantium in the Seventh Century*, 215–220.
74. E.g., Adontz, *Armenia*, 158–159; Haldon, *Warfare*, 84: the theme was called *Armeniakon* "because Armenians made up a substantial portion of the populations who were indigenous to the regions in question or who had migrated." The migrations were in fact much later than the name. Garsoïan, "Armenian Integration," 54, is also wrong to say that "the creation of the theme of Armeniakon . . . continued to attest the presence of an important Armenian component in northeastern Asia Minor." No, the name simply followed the army. Ayvazyan, *Armenian Military*, 46, assumes that the army *per Armeniam*

contained many Armenians, in fact the forces of the previous Armenian realms in the region. He offers no proof for this.

75. Sarris, *Empires of Faith*, 143; sources: *CJ* 1.29.5; Prokopios, *Buildings* 3.1.27–29; Malalas, *Chronicle* 18.10. Theophanes, *Chronographia*, p. 175, mangles the minor provision in the law that the general could hire local *scriniarii* because they knew the terrain better into a general statement that the army recruited its soldiers locally. Justinian later added Bulgar soldiers to the army *per Armeniam:* Theophanes, *Chronographia*, p. 219.

76. Konstantinos VII, *On the Themes*, pp. 63–65.

77. Theophanes, *Chronographia*, p. 469; Charanis, *Armenians in the Byzantine Empire*, 20.

78. E.g., Theophanes, *Chronographia*, pp. 418, 469.

79. Symeon Logothetes, *Chronicle* 119.7.

80. Kountoura-Galaki, "Armeniac Theme," 32n35, misquoting Genesios, *On the Reigns* 4.15.

81. Garsoïan, "Armenian Integration," 93n153, also 60n29, 65.

82. Seibt, *Skleroi*, 19–20; *PmbZ* I: 4409 (possibly named Leon). It is unclear whether Seibt's Skleros no. 4 (*Skleroi*, 21–23), a coruler of Muslim Melitene in the mid-ninth century, has anything to do with the later Byzantine family, and no source says that he was an Armenian, despite the fact that scholars sometimes call him that (*PmbZ* I: 6822; Cooper and Decker, *Life and Society*, 233).

83. Garsoïan, "Armenian Integration," 91.

84. Vryonis, "Byzantine Images," 67.

85. Cheynet, *The Byzantine Aristocracy*, II:26; see II:27n68, for another formulation that implies assimilation; for a nuanced reconstruction, where "Hellenization" comes into play along with ethnic solidarity, see Cheynet, *Pouvoir*, 323–324.

86. E.g., Seibt, "Stärken," 341 (pitting his *armenischen Familientradition* against his integration).

87. Grousset, *L'Arménie*, 504.

88. Phokas: Bartikian, Αρμενοβυζαντινά, 13; Whittow, *Making*, 337.

89. Kaldellis, *Streams of Gold*, 83–87, 96–97.

90. Shepard, "Scylitzes on Armenia," 307.

91. Garsoïan, "Armenian Integration," 94, also 66.

92. Birley, *Septimius Severus*.

93. *Chronicle of Pseudo-Joshua the Stylite* 12; Konstantinos VII, *Book of Ceremonies* 1.92 (p. 419).

94. Theophanes Continuatus 2.3–5.

95. Anna Komnene, *Alexiad* 1.8.1.

96. Reprinted in Adontz, *Études*, 125–133; Charanis, *Studies*, VI. Cf. Kaegi, *Early Islamic Conquests*, 64: Maurikios was of "probable Armenian origin." But Redgate, *The Armenians*, 237, finds that the "counter-arguments seem overwhelming."

97. Euagrios, *Ecclesiastical History* 5.19; Paul the Deacon, *History of the Lombards* 3.15; see *PLRE* IIIB: 855.

98. Cumont, *Chroniques byzantines*, 22–29. For the convention of ethnicizing provincial origins, see pp. 175 and 181.

99. Cf. Garsoïan, "Armenian Integration," 57, 68–69.
100. Bartikian, Αρμενοβυζαντινά, 13.
101. *PLRE* III: 586; Kaegi, *Heraclius*, 21, also 30, 32, 97. Settipani, *Continuité*, 115–117, correctly rejects any Armenian connection.
102. Toumanoff, "Caucasia and Byzantium," 135, 157–158.
103. Toumanoff, "Heraclids."
104. Kaegi, *Heraclius*, 22.
105. Runciman, *Byzantine Theocracy*, 55; Kouymijian, "Ethnic Origins."
106. Kaegi, *Heraclius*, 21. Kaegi asserts that "Greek panegyrists would not have wished to call attention to any Armenian origins of Heraclius." This, however, is refuted by the example of Basileios I (see below). Moreover, the entire school of thought that Herakleios was an Armenian rests on our ability to infer this very fact transparently from a passage in a historian who was a panegyrist of Herakleios. The argument wants to have it both ways; that is, that the Greek authors hid his Armenian origin and that they revealed it clearly.
107. Konstantinos VII, *On the Themes*, p. 60; Manasses, *Historical Synopsis* 3608. John of Nikiu, *Chronicle* 106.2 (seventh century) implies that Herakleios' mother and sister were living in Cappadocia under Phokas (602–610).
108. Theophylaktos, *History* 3.1.1 (ἐνεσήμαινε καταλιπόντα τὸ στράτευμα ἐς τὴν ἑαυτοῦ πόλιν ἐπανελθεῖν ἐς τὴν Ἀρμενίαν γενόμενον, Ναρσῇ τε τῷ Κωνσταντίνης πόλεως ἡγεμόνι, μεθιέναι τὸ στράτευμα). Philippikos is *PLRE* III: 1023–1024.
109. Whitby and Whitby, *The History of Theophylact*, 72n1.
110. Theophylaktos, *History* 3.6.2.
111. Redgate, *The Armenians*, 237.
112. Justinian, *Edict* 3; *Novels* 21, 31. The standard study is Adontz, *Armenia*. Roman migration to the area: Preiser-Kapeller, "Complex Processes," 298.
113. Too much has sometimes been made of an unclear and likely corrupt passage later in the work, which some scholars take to imply a family connection between Herakleios' grandson Konstas II (641–668) and Smbat V Bargatuni: pseudo-Sebeos, *History*, p. 145. For some of its problems, see Toumanoff, "Caucasia and Byzantium," 135n98.
114. Leon the Deacon, *History* 6.5 (theme), 5.9 (name).
115. Matthew of Edessa, *Chronicle* 1.18; see the discussion in *PmbZ* II: 22778 (esp. pp. 41, 50); Vest, *Geschichte*, vol. 2, 997–998. For the problems with Matthew as as source here, see Kaldellis, "Did Ioannes I Tzimiskes?"
116. Nikephoros, *Short History* 45 (l. 12); Riedinger, *Acta conciliorum oecumenicorum*, II.2.2, p. 899; see *PmbZ* I: 6150.
117. Louth, *Greek East and Latin West*, 47: "Perhaps because of his Armenian background, he was inclined to return once again to the Christological nostrums of the preceding century"; also Ostrogorsky, *History*, 152–153; Haldon, *Byzantium in the Seventh Century*, 322.
118. Herrin, *Margins and Metropolis*, 193.
119. Garsoïan, "Armenian Integration," 97; and "Armenian Historiography," 54. The Pergamene connection is a manuscript error for Persarmenian: see *PmbZ* I: 5258 and 6150.
120. Herrin, *Margins and Metropolis*, 194, 196–197, 202.

121. Theophanes, *Chronographia*, p. 382; Michael the Syrian, *Chronicle*, vol. 2, 482. For more sources, and the decree in question, see Nichanian, "Byzantine Emperor Philippikos-Vardanes," 46–48, correctly breaking the link between the emperor's ethnic background and his religious policies. For various readings of this episode, see Ditten, *Ethnische Verschiebungen*, 75–76, 176–177.

122. Ostrogorsky, *History*, 144, 152–153 ("an Armenian").

123. *History of the Caucasian Albanians* 3.12 (p. 203).

124. *PmbZ* I: 632.

125. Adontz, *Études*, 37–46; Turner, "Origins"; Signes Codoñer, *Theophilos*, 83–87.

126. *PmbZ* I: 784, e.g., Genesios, *On the Reigns* 2.4.

127. *Acta Conciliorum Oecumenicorum* II.5, p. 71, 31–32.

128. Krumbacher, "Kasia," 363. There is a tradition of scholarship, e.g., Kountoura-Galaki, "Armeniac Theme," 32n35, and Vryonis, "Byzantine Images," 69–73, which attempts to biographize the poem by linking it to an apocryphal story regarding Kasia's participation in a bride show for Theophilos. But (1) we cannot be certain that the poem was written by Kasia, who (2), we now know, did not participate in the bride competition, and (3) her competitor Theodora was not regarded as Armenian (see above). No part of this rationalization holds up.

129. *Life of Saint Euthymios the Younger* 18: ἦν γὰρ οὐ κρυπτός τις καὶ ὕφαλος, κἂν ἀπ' Ἀρμενίων τὸ γένος κατήγετο, ἀλλ' ἀπόνηρος ἅμα καὶ ἁπλοῦς τὸν τρόπον καὶ ἄδολος.

130. Vryonis, "Will of a Provincial Magnate," 264–265. There are many later texts with hostile images of the Armenians, even of those living in the empire, e.g., Eustathios of Thessalonike, *Capture of Thessalonike* 113–114 (pp. 124–126); Choniates, *History* 403; cf. Mesarites, *Ekphrasis of the Church of the Holy Apostles* 21.1–4.

131. Nikephoros II Phokas, *On Skirmishing* 2 (trans. Dennis, mod.); more texts in Garsoïan, "Armenian Integration," 63, 76, 79; McGeer, "Legal Decree."

132. Garsoïan, "Armenian Integration," 66–67.

133. Zonaras, *Commentary on the Canons of the Council in Troullo*: Canon 51 (vol. 2, 425); see R. Webb, *Demons*, 123–124.

134. Choniates, *History* 253.

135. Gans, "Symbolic Ethnicity"; Waters, *Ethnic Options*.

136. Anagnostou, "Critique of Symbolic Ethnicity": symbolic ethnicity's theoretical emphasis on "choice" in forging identities is ideological, given the multiple constraints that groups and individuals actually face in the United States.

137. *PLRE* IIIA: 720 (Isaacius 8); for the inscription, and a discussion, see Lauxtermann, *Byzantine Poetry*, 221–223. Cf. Arsakes the Arsacid at Justinian's court: Prokopios, *Wars* 7.32.1; Aspietes (Oshin?) serving under Alexios I Komnenos: Anna Komnene, *Alexiad* 12.2.1–2.

138. Markopoulos, "Anonymous Laudatory Poem."

139. Leon VI, *Homily* 14, pp. 199–200; for the genre, see Agapitos, "Ἡ εἰκόνα," 297–306; for the evolution of Basileios' mythology, see Markopoulos, "Οι μεταμορφώσεις."

140. Niketas David of Paphlagonia, *Life of Patriarch Ignatios* 89; pseudo-Symeon, *Chronicle*, p. 689.
141. *Life of Basileios I* 2–4.
142. *Pro:* Adontz, "L'age et l'origine"; *contra:* Schminck, "Beginnings and Origins," who says (67) that Basileios was of "pure Greek birth" (which I take to mean "Roman," whatever "pure" means in this context); a survey of previous scholarship and the sources in all languages are in Tobias, *Basil I*, 1–50.
143. Blaum, "Diplomacy," 43.
144. Anagnostakis, "Η Σολομώντεια αμφιθυμία."
145. *Life of Basileios I* 19 (with the commentary ad loc. by Ševčenko, 78 app. crit.); Vardan, *History* 45 (p. 186); see Garitte, "La vision."
146. For the Paulicians, see Chapter 6.
147. Vardan, *History* 45 (p. 186).
148. Konstantinos VII, *Book of Ceremonies* 2.48 (pp. 686–687); Yovhannēs Drasxanakertc'i, *History of Armenia* 29.13.
149. Redgate, *The Armenians*, 238.
150. Redgate, "Armenian Identity," 291–293; cf. Bartikian, Αρμενοβυζαντινά, 45, comes close to reading Basileios' ostensible Armenian ethnicity as a political fiction useful in this arena.
151. *Life of Basileios I* 12 (the fight with the Bulgarian).
152. Genesios, *On the Reigns* 4.26.
153. Curty, *Les parentés légendaires*.
154. *Life of the Patriarch Euthymios* 1.
155. Cf. Kazhdan, *History*, vol. 2, 104 (also Samonas, the Arab chamberlain). The *Life* does not independently support the claims about Basileios' ancestry; its author was merely repeating what we know the court was already saying. But it has given rise to another case of the Armenian fallacy: Psellos' wife (a century and a half later) is said to have been "of Armenian origin" because she may have been descended from Stylianos Zaoutzes. See Lauritzen, "Courtier," 258.
156. Garsoïan, "Armenian Integration," 53.
157. Cf. Van Lint, "Formation of Armenian Identity." I am aware of, and remain unpersuaded by, efforts to "deconstruct" medieval Armenian identity by showing that none of its constituent elements was true of *all* Armenians. One day these exercises will no longer be considered sophisticated.
158. The great historian of medieval Armenia Nina Garsoïan paints a grim picture in "Armenian Historiography."
159. Cf. Redgate, *The Armenians*, 22, 276.

CHAPTER 6 ▪ *Was Byzantium an Empire in the Tenth Century?*

Epigraph: Panegyrici Latini 9.21.3. ("Now it is delightful to see a painting of the world, because we see nothing foreign in it.")

1. Haldon, "Byzantine Empire," 208, also 205. Cameron, *Byzantine Matters*, 30, realizes that the field must define "empire," but avoids doing so. She quickly switches to "state," then drops the issue.

2. General bibliography: Doyle, *Empires*, 19; Darwin, *After Tamerlane*, 23; Barfield, "Imperial State Formation," 29–30; Maier, *Among Empires*, 7; Pitts, "Political Theory of Empire," 213; Burbank and Cooper, *Empires*, 6–13 (and note the book's subtitle: *Power and the Politics of Difference*); Rome and its heirs: Nicolet, *Space*, 15; Goldstone and Haldon, "Ancient States," 17; Muldoon, *Empire and Order*, 63, 139; Mattingly, *Imperialism*, 6, 10; Woolf, *Rome*, 24–27; and Barkey, *Empire of Difference*, 9–12 (and in the title). A similar definition is used programmatically in two recent encyclopedic projects: MacKenzie, *The Encyclopedia of Empire*; and Bang et al., *The Oxford World History of Empire*. Chrysos, "Das byzantinische Reich," uses different categories for his analysis, primarily the practice of imperialism and the significance of imperial titles.

3. Goldstone and Haldon, "Ancient States," 17; see also Haldon, "Comparative State Formation," 1112–1113.

4. Maier, *Among Empires*, 23, 31.

5. Nexon and Wright, "What's at Stake"; Barkey, *Empire of Difference*, esp. 9–10.

6. The distinction seems to have first been made by G. Hosking in the *Times Literary Supplement*, March 10, 1995, p. 27, and has since been echoed widely, e.g., Maier, *Among Empires*, 5–6; de Waal, *Caucasus*, 37; Ando, "From Republic to Empire," 39–40.

7. Cf. Nicolet, *Space*, 1, 15.

8. Richardson, *Language of Empire*, traces the evolution of the term; see 60 (*imperium* of Rome over other people); 35 (triumphs); also Muldoon, *Empire and Order*, 17–19.

9. Mason, *Greek Terms*, 189.

10. Cf. W. V. Harris, *Roman Power*, 159; see also 150, 154; "slaves": Lavan, *Slaves*.

11. Ando, *Roman Social Imaginaries*, 87–88; also Ando, *Law*, 19.

12. Ando, *Imperial Rome*, 1, 77.

13. Ando, "Empire, State, and Communicative Action," 226–227.

14. See, e.g., Suleiman the Magnificent's famous letter to King Francis I of France (February 1526).

15. Rösch, *Onoma*, 53–62, 159–171. Manuel I Komnenos styled himself "Isauricus, Cilicius, Armenicus, Dalmaticus, Ugricus, Bosniacus, Chrobaticus, Lazicus, Ibericus, Bulgaricus, Serbicus, Zikhicus, Azaricus, Gothicus" in an edict that he posted in Hagia Sophia: *Novel* 70 in Zepos and Zepos, *Jus Graecoromanum*, vol. 1, 410, with analysis in Vasiliev, *Goths*, 140–145.

16. For interesting reflections on which states called themselves or were subsequently called empires, see Woolf, *Rome*, 19–23.

17. Cf. Necipoğlu, *Byzantium*, 18. But *empire* is not a Byzantine term.

18. E.g., Arnold, *Medieval Germany*, 75–97, for this and other definitions of the imperial title in the west; also Folz, *Concept of Empire*, 6–7, 13–14, 17, 27, 41–44, 48–49, 54, 63, 65; Muldoon, *Empire and Order*, 34.

19. Ioannes Lydos, *On the Magistracies* 1.6 and 1.4; for the client kings, see Braund, *Rome and the Friendly King*; Chrysos, "Der Kaiser und die Könige."

20. I. Morris, "The Greater Athenian State," 129 and 132.

21. Berger and Miller, "Building Nations," 13.

22. Kazhdan and Constable, *People and Power*, 152–154 (see below); Nicol, *Byzantium*, I:317 ("the heterogeneous mixture of races that made up the Byzantine empire"); Haldon, *Byzantium in the Seventh Century*, 351 ("multiethnic and polyglot"); Harris, *Lost World*, 87 ("a truly multiracial society"); Stouraitis, "Roman Identity," 196. More citations would be otiose.

23. Burbank and Cooper, *Empires*, 64.

24. Rathbone, *Last English King*, 21: eleventh-century Asia Minor was inhabited "by ancient tribes who acknowledged the Eastern Emperor as their lord, paying him tribute, but no loyalty."

25. Kazhdan and Constable, *People and Power*, 152–154.

26. See the section "Constantinople and the Army" below.

27. The Ohio State University, Statistical Summary (Autumn 2017), https://www.osu.edu/osutoday/stuinfo.php.

28. Rutgers University, "We Are Diverse," http://newbrunswick.rutgers.edu/about/we-are-diverse.

29. Cf. Manjoo, *True Enough*.

30. Haldon, *Byzantium in the Seventh Century*, 351; the same in P. Angelov, "Byzantines as Imagined," 47; Obolensky, *Byzantine Commonwealth*, 355 (who then immediately contradicts himself).

31. Vryonis, "Byzantine Images," 66.

32. E.g., Mango, *Byzantium*, 26, looking at the empire of 560 AD. But Cheynet, *Pouvoir*, 379–404, analyzes the contours of imperial rule in the eleventh century largely through the ethnicity of the population in the frontier provinces.

33. E.g., in Stouraitis, "Roman Identity."

34. See Chapter 2, section on "Ethnicity in the Black Hole."

35. Goldstone and Haldon, "Ancient States," 17–18; also Barkey, *Empire of Difference*, 18.

36. Goldstone and Haldon, "Ancient States," 17; also Haldon, "Byzantine Empire," 205.

37. Kekaumenos, *Strategikon* 88.

38. E.g., Leon VI, *Taktika* 9.24 ("ours" versus "some other subject land").

39. Konstantinos VII, *De administrando imperio* 44.125–128.

40. Konstantinos VII, *De administrando imperio* 46.134–135.

41. Attaleiates, *History* 120 (Romanos IV enters the land of the Romans when he crosses the Tauros mountains, even though empire extended well to the southeast of them); 158 (a general moved from Roman-controled Mesopotamia "into the land of the Romans"); 172–173 (from the standpoint of Cilicia, Roman land is defined as the interior of Asia Minor). For more, see Arutjunova-Fidanjan, "New Socio-Administrative Structure," esp. 83–86.

42. Berger and Miller, "Building Nations," 2–5, 10.

43. Konstantinos VII, *De administrando imperio* pref. 23–24, 48.22–27. Pace Magdalino, "Constantine VII," 39, there is no reason to assume that for Konstantinos the *"politeia* did not stretch beyond the Sea of Marmara." The most obvious reading of the text is that the polity of the Romans stretched as far as there were Romans.

44. Cf. Lounghis, "Some Questions."
45. Psellos, *Chronographia* 6.189.
46. See Kaldellis, "Did the Byzantine Empire Have 'Ecumenical' or 'Universal' Aspirations?"
47. *Codex Theodosianus* 2.1.10 = *Codex Iustinianus* 1.9.8 = *Basilika* 1.1.36 (more condensed each time). See the papers in Bonfil et al., *Jews in Byzantium*, esp. Linder, "Legal Status," and Laiou, "Institutional Mechanisms," 168–170. For language and attitudes, see de Lange, "Hebrews, Greeks." For Jewish integration, see Holo, "Both Byzantine and Jewish?"
48. General: Holo, *Byzantine Jewry*, 79, 104; divorce and assets: 107–110.
49. Schwartz, *Were the Jews a Mediterranean Society?*, 118.
50. *Life of Saint Nikon "Metanoeite!"* 35.
51. Forced conversions: Holo, *Byzantine Jewry*, 32–49; immigration in the eleventh century: 53–57, 60–64, 69–70, 198.
52. Bowman, "Survival in Decline," 105n6.
53. Holo, *Byzantine Jewry*, 28–30, 50. For Byzantine demography in general, see Stathakopoulos, "Population, Demography, and Disease."
54. Jacoby, "Jews in the Byzantine Economy," 255.
55. Holo, *Byzantine Jewry*, 3.
56. Holo, *Byzantine Jewry*, 128.
57. Holo, *Byzantine Jewry*, 7.
58. For the intellectual life of Jewish Apulia under Byzantine rule, see Mancuso, "Historical Introduction" to the translation of Shabbatai Donnolo, *Sefer Hakhmoni*, 5–11; Bonfil, *History and Folklore*. I do not know what to make of the lost Hebrew history, written in Constantinople, of the wars between the emperors and the Khazars: Starr, *Jews*, 166 (no. 112).
59. Kazhdan, *Armiane*; see Vryonis, "Byzantine Images," 71; "Armenians and Greeks," 96–100.
60. E.g., Tatzates (*PmbZ* I: 7241); see also possibly a number of *strategoi* of the Armeniakon theme in the seventh and early eighth centuries: E. Kountoura-Galake in Lambakis et al., Η Μικρά Ασία των Θεμάτων, 113–121.
61. Charanis, *Armenians*, 20–21 (Theophanes, *Chronographia*, p. 469); followed by Toumanoff, "Caucasia and Byzantium," 131.
62. Konstantinos VII, *On the Themes*, p. 64; cf. Attaleiates, *History* 96–97, localizes the heretical foreign nation of the Armenians in Iberia, Mesopotamia, Lykandos, Melitene, and their immediate regions.
63. For the historical geography of Armenia, the maps in Hewsen, *Armenia*, are invaluable.
64. Charanis, *Armenians*, 20. Leon VI had invited some Armenian leaders to govern part of the theme of Sebasteia, but it did not work out: Konstantinos VII, *De administrando imperio* 50.133–152. The account does not mention large forces coming with them.
65. Konstantinos VII, *Book of Ceremonies* 2.44 (pp. 651–660); for the other two locations, which remain obscure, see Haldon, "Theory and Practice," 251nn49–50.
66. See Chapter 5, section on "'Armenian' Emperors."
67. See Chapter 5, section on "The Fallacy in Action."

68. Konstantinos VII, *On the Themes*, p. 73; *De administrando imperio* 50.111–132.

69. Ditten, *Ethnische Verschiebungen*, 74–82 (the "Pergamon" colony has since been shown to be a textual error for the "Persarmenian" ancestry of the emperor Philippikos Bardanes).

70. For various views, see the papers in Simonian, *Hemshin*. The main source for the 12,000 is the eighth-century Armenian historian Ghewond, *History* 42 (p. 149), who does not say that they were settled in the Pontos, only that they entered the empire there.

71. Garsoïan, "Armenian Integration," 53.

72. Theophanes, *Chronographia*, p. 429.

73. Theophanes, *Chronographia*, p. 495; Theophanes Continuatus 4.16; Zonaras, *Chronicle* 14.2 (vol. 3, 390). In general, see Huxley, "Historical Geography."

74. Petros of Sicily, *History of the Paulicians* 5 (p. 9); 37 (p. 21).

75. E.g., *Life of Basileios I* 41–42.

76. Theophanes Continuatus pp. 283–284 (ed. Bekker); see Garsoïan, *Paulician Heresy*, 147, 150; Ditten, *Ethnische Verschiebungen*, 203–207.

77. Genesios, *On the Reigns* 4.37; Theophanes Continuatus p. 313 (ed. Bekker).

78. Runciman, *Emperor Romanus*, 72.

79. See Chapter 4, section on "Slavs to Romans."

80. Herrin, *Margins and Metropolis*, 5–6, see also 12, 16, 18, 34, 37, and, for the end result, 48.

81. Curta, *Edinburgh*, 225.

82. Curta, *Edinburgh*, 225, uses the term *mosaic* on the basis of the notoriously unreliable *Chronicle of Monembasia*, which is discussing the early ninth century.

83. I. Polemis and I are preparing a translation of these *Lives*. The solitary reference is in the *Life of Saint Petros of Argos* 9, which says only that some barbarians came to the saint. The text does not say where these barbarians came from; the event is dated to the early tenth century based on the bishop's career. Curta, *Edinburgh*, 151–152, 172–173, argues that these were not Slavs but either Bulgarians or Arabs, so presumably from outside the province.

84. Theophanes, *Chronographia*, p. 349; see Ditten, *Ethnische Verschiebungen*, 211–212.

85. Theophanes, *Chronographia*, p. 364; Nikephoros, *Short History* 38; Michael the Syrian, *Chronicle*, vol. 2, 470; see Oikonomides, "Silk Trade," 51–53; Hendy, *Studies*, 631–634; Ditten, *Ethnische Verschiebungen*, 86–88, 216–234 (esp. 224–225 on exaggerated numbers).

86. Nikephoros, *Short History* 75 (the figure is only here); Theophanes, *Chronographia*, p. 432; see Ditten, *Ethnische Verschiebungen*, 83–86.

87. A search for Slavs in Asia Minor does not turn up much, or anything: Ditten, *Ethnische Verschiebungen*, 255–257. See below for the Boïlades.

88. Shukurov, *Byzantine Turks*, 86.

89. Theophanes Continuatus 1.5; Skylitzes, *Synopsis of Histories*, p. 12; see Ditten, *Ethnische Verschiebungen*, 90–92. Their khan Krum demanded their

return, but the Romans refused, eventually going to war with him. For another group under Romanos I Lakapenos, see Skylitzes, *Synopsis on Histories*, p. 226.

90. See Chapter 4, section on "Slavs to Romans."

91. *Life of Saint Lazaros of Galesion* 91 (p. 537); see the bibliography cited by the translator, Greenfield, at 182n410.

92. Sabbas, *Life of Saint Ioannikios*, pp. 337–338.

93. Vryonis, "St. Ioannicius the Great"; Ditten, *Ethnische Verschiebungen*, 255, 259; Brubaker and Haldon, *Byzantium*, 583; Malingoudis, Σλάβοι, 161–164; for possible descendants of this group attested in later documents, see Malingoudis, Σλάβοι, 167–170.

94. Group 1: Theophanes, *Chronographia*, p. 422 ("to this day"); Nikephoros, *Short History* 67 (only the expedition, not the captives). Group 2: Theophanes, *Chronographia*, pp. 427, 429; Nikephoros, *Short History* 70, 73; Michael the Syrian, *Chronicle*, vol. 2, 518, 521–522 (and in the cognate chronicles), and 523 (their resistance to conversion). Group 3: Theophanes, *Chronographia*, pp. 451–452; Michael the Syrian, *Chronicle*, vol. 3, 2; Ghewond, *History* 37 (whose claims, reported from hearsay, that they numbered 150,000 cannot be accepted). See Ditten, *Ethnische Verschiebungen*, 178–193.

95. Romeney, "Ethnicity."

96. Haldon, *Byzantium in the Seventh Century*, 4; cf. Whittow, *Making*, 3: "Southern Italy . . . is hardly representative of the heartlands of the empire in Asia Minor."

97. Leon VI, *Taktika* 15.32.

98. *Life of Basileios I* 71: the operations are presented as targeting Arab raiders from Sicily.

99. Scholarship cited in Kaldellis, *Streams of Gold*, 29–30, esp. Martin, *La Pouille*, 491–492, 531–532, 709–714; *Byzance et l'Italie*, esp. part 1; Peters-Custot, *Les grecs*, 32–154. Women: Peters-Custot, "Convivencia," 213–214 (this paper also provides useful ethnic maps). Conciliatory relations between Latin and Greek religious autorities before the eleventh century: Martin, *Byzance et l'Italie*, 73–74.

100. Falkenhausen, "Jews"; Holo, "Both Byzantine and Jewish?," 194; *Byzantine Jewry*, 81.

101. *Codice diplomatico Barense* vol. 1, no. 9 (p. 16, 1017 AD) mentions a Kaloioannes "the Armenian"; no. 18 (p. 31, 1032 AD) mentions "monachi greci"; vol. 3, no. 4 (p. 9, 1041 AD) *Umfreida ex genere Normannorum*; no. 5 (p. 10, 1041 AD) *sum uxor Michali grecus viro meo*; no. 10 (p. 19, 1066 AD) *Michaili, qui est de genere grecorum . . . Greco* (he appears in other documents too). Jew: Falkenhausen, "Jews," 290. Lombard: *Life of Saint Neilos of Rossano* 83.

102. Trinchera, *Syllabus Graecarum membranarum*, no. III (p. 3, 892 AD); for the Armenians settled by the emperors in Italy, see Martin, *Byzance et l'Italie*, 43n24.

103. E.g., Carabellese, *L'Apulia*, no. 2 (pp. 453–454, 1034 AD); no. 5 (p. 459, 1040 AD); no. 7 (p. 463, 1047 AD); no. 13 (p. 475, 1065 AD); no. 13c (p. 478, 1067 AD): the *lex* or *consuetudo gentis Langobardorum*; see Lombard law in Byzantine Italy, see Martin, *Byzance et l'Italie*, 131–132, 393–413.

104. Peters-Custot, *Les grecs*, 140 with n. 278; see also Snapshot 7.

105. Shabbatai Donnolo, *Sefer Hakhmoni*, p. 227 (trans.).
106. Peters-Custot, "Grecs et Byzantines," 186.
107. Peters-Custot, "Le barbare," 161n81.
108. *Life of Saint Neilos of Rossano* 96.
109. Konstantinos VII, *De administrando imperio* 50.71–82; see the studies cited by Anagnostakis and Kaldellis, "Textual Sources," 125.
110. For Byzantine notions of Hellenism, and their overlap, see Kaldellis, *Hellenism*.
111. Curta, *Edinburgh*, 188–195.
112. The Laz formed a client state in the fifth and sixth centuries, but it is not clear whether they lived in areas governed from Constantinople in the tenth (in the theme of Chaldia). Bryer, "Some Notes on the Laz," hedges by saying that they were under Byzantine rule but de facto autonomous, yet there is no proof either way. It is perhaps significant that they are mentioned in sources relating to the empire of Trebizond, but not earlier. For the Laz today, see P. A. Andrews, *Ethnic Groups*, 176–178; and Benninghaus, "Laz." The Athinganoi were a heretical group in central Asia Minor, attested between the sixth and the ninth centuries, but not viewed as a separate ethnicity: Panagiotopoulos, Περὶ Ἀθιγγάνων, 35 (citing previous bibliography). The emperor Michael II was believed to be associated with them somehow. Nothing indicates that the Tzakones (southeastern Peloponnese) were anything other than provincial Romans: Ilias Anagnostakis (pers. comm. and unpublished lectures). For the later meanings of the term, see Arhweiler, "Les termes Τσάκωνες"; Caratzas, *Les Tzacones*. For ethnic monasteries, see Janin, "Les monastères nationaux," and Kaldellis, *Ethnography*, 220n227; for monasteries in the sixth century named after provincial populations, possibly with ethnic or linguistic connotations, see Holl, "Das Fortleben," 245 (e.g., "of the Lykaonians," "Egyptians," "Cretans," but also "Antiochenes"). Arabs lived on Cyprus in the "condominium" phase, but they were presumably (and by definition) not under Roman jurisdiction.
113. The Georgian life is translated by Tchoidze, Ἕνας Γεωργιανός προσκυνητής, see esp. 224, 228; see her commentary at 42–43, 115–119 (variant texts), 126–127.
114. Jacoby, "La population de Constantinople."
115. Benjamin of Tudela, *Itinerary*, pp. 13–14.
116. Jacoby, "Jews of Constantinople."
117. Simeonova, "Constantinopolitan Attitudes"; Rapp, "Medieval Cosmopolis"; Page, *Being Byzantine*, 67–68.
118. Reinert, "Muslim Presence," 130–140; Anderson, "Islamic Spaces." Ten years: *Book of the Eparch* 5.2.
119. Garsoïan, "Armenian Integration," 59–61.
120. Liudprand, *Antapodosis* 5.21; *Embassy to Constantinople* 46.
121. Holo, *Byzantine Jewry*, 159.
122. *Russian Primary Chronicle* s.a. 903–907 (trans. pp. 64–65); see Shepard, "Constantinople," 253.
123. Laiou, "Exchange and Trade," 724.
124. Liudprand, *Antapodosis* 1.11; *Life of Saint Andreas the Fool* 5 (probably a tenth-century composition).

125. Koutrakou, "Spies of Towns," 264.
126. *Life of Saint Basileios the Younger* 1.4: τὸ ξένον τοῦ ἤθους καὶ τοῦ σχήματος αὐτοῦ.
127. Already in Tacitus, *Agricola* 32; Prokopios, *Wars* 8.28.2, 8.30.17–18 (the Goths); Larkin, *Al-Mutanabbi*, 54–55 (for Sayf al-Dawla).
128. Haldon, *Recruitment*; and "Military Service," among many of his studies.
129. See Chapter 2, section on "Who Was Excluded?"
130. Skylitzes Continuatus p. 125.
131. Theotokis, "Rus, Varangian and Frankish Mercenaries."
132. For differing interpretations, see Treadgold, "Army"; Haldon, "Theory and Practice."
133. Konstantinos VII, *Book of Ceremonies* 2.44 (pp. 651–652).
134. Konstantinos VII, *Book of Ceremonies* 2.45 (pp. 662–669, 673).
135. Konstantinos VII, *De administrando imperio* 50.58–70; see Ditten, *Ethnische Verschiebungen*, 263–289; Curta, *Edinburgh*, 172; Anagnostakis, "From Tempe to Sparta," 138–139. For references in Arabic sources to a fort by the Cilician Gates named after Slavs, see Cooper and Decker, *Cappadocia*, 246.
136. Theophanes, *Chronographia*, pp. 363–364; see Ditten, *Ethnische Verschiebungen*, 138–158; Treadgold, *Byzantium and Its Army*, 72; Curta, *Edinburgh*, 289; Letsios, "Byzantine Foreign, Defence and Demographic Policy"; and, for the Arabic evidence, see Eger, *The Islamic-Byzantine Frontier*, 295–299.
137. Konstantinos VII, *Book of Ceremonies* 2.44 (p. 654) and 2.45 (p. 668). Attested for the ninth century too: Theophanes Continuatus pp. 304, 311 (ed. Bekker).
138. Konstantinos VII, *De administrando imperio* 50.169–221.
139. Shepard, "Uses of the Franks"; Kaldellis, *Streams of Gold*, 275–276 (and the narrative information itself).
140. W. V. Harris, *Roman Power*, 2, 5, 219.
141. Non-Chalcedonian Armenians are attested at Sebasteia in 986–987: Step'anos of Taron, *Universal History* 3.20 (unless this is an error for Melitene; cf. Matthew of Edessa, *Chronicle* 1.34).

CHAPTER 7 ▪ *The Apogee of Empire in the Eleventh Century*

Epigraph: Florus, *Epitome of Titus Livius* 2.26. When the Romans were conquering Moesia, a local leader asked them who they were, to which they answered: "We are the Romans, the lords of nations."

1. See, e.g., the almost certainly fictional story about Basileios I as a child: *Life of Basileios I*, 4.
2. An inscription of Khan Krum from 813 mentions five military commanders with Byzantine names: Petkov, *Voices*, 7 (no. 14); and see the deserter Konstantinos, son of Patzikos: *PmbZ* I: 3920. I thank Ian Mladjov for help with the Bulgarian material.
3. Jordanov, "Pečati na Simeon"; Petkov, *Voices*, 34 (no. 35).
4. Daphnopates, *Letter* 5.

5. Romans: Petkov, *Voices*, 6–7 (no. 13), 37 (no. 47); Greeks: 5 (no. 11), 6 (no. 12), 11 (no. 22), 12 (no. 25), 39 (no. 53); Magyars: 44 (no. 70, a miracle story adapted early on into Bulgarian).

6. Petkov, *Voices*, 194–212.

7. Surveys of these Byzantine prejudices in Ivanov, "*Pearls before Swine*," esp. 83–155; Kaldellis, *Ethnography*, 126–139. Additional evidence for enduring perceptions of difference can be found cited throughout Nikolaou and Tsiknakis, Βυζάντιο και Βούλγαροι.

8. Page, *Being Byzantine*, 53.

9. Kolia-Dermitzaki, "Η εικόνα των Βουλγάρων," 88–89; for the twelfth century, see Gjuzelev, "L'empereur byzantine Manuel," 144.

10. Basileios' victory celebrations: Skylitzes, *Synopsis of Histories*, pp. 364–365; marriage to Isaakios: Nikephoros Bryennios, *Materials* 1.2; joint victor: Psellos, *Letter S* 161 (p. 419). For a narrative of the war and Basileios' policies, see Kaldellis, *Streams of Gold*, esp. 125–126, for the settlement. For Bulgarians given ranks and titles, see Kolia-Dermitzaki, "Η εικόνα των Βουλγάρων," 65, citing prior bibliography; and Hondridou, "Η ενσωμάτωση," 111–120.

11. Farney, *Ethnic Identity*, 191.

12. Yahya of Antioch, *Chronicle*, vol. 3, 407.

13. Skylitzes Continuatus p. 162.

14. Skylitzes, *Synopsis of Histories*, p. 412. Taxation in kind under the tsars is confirmed by the so-called *Bulgarian Apocryphal Annals*, an eleventh-century text: Petkov, *Voices*, 196.

15. The ecclesiastical organization of Byzantine Bulgaria is outlined in Basileios' *sigillia*, which confirm the status quo of Samuil and Petar: Gelzer, "Ungedruckte und wenig bekannte Bistumsverzeichnisse," 42–46.

16. Cheynet, *Byzantine Aristocracy*, XI:183–184; Kaldellis, *Streams of Gold*, 124–126.

17. E.g., Attaleiates, *History* 29, 297.

18. For Bulgarian society and politics before the conquest, see Fine, *Early Medieval Balkans*, 164–171.

19. I owe this point to Dimiter Angelov. Theophylaktos' correspondents are listed in Mullett, *Theophylact*, 349–381.

20. Cf. Yahya of Antioch, *Chronicle*, vol. 3, 407.

21. Mullett, *Theophylact*, 99, 125–127, 130–132, and Curta, *Southeastern Europe*, 287, provide the references.

22. Curta, *Southeastern Europe*, 285.

23. Biliarsky, "Some Observations"; Nystazopoulou-Pelekidou, "Βυζαντινή ορολογία."

24. Theophylaktos of Ohrid, *Letters* 96, 98 (quotation from p. 485).

25. Choniates, *History* 369.

26. Psellos, *Chronographia* 4.39.

27. See Chapter 6, section on "Empire and Difference in Byzantium."

28. Psellos, *Chronographia* 4.40; *Orationes panegyricae* 2.340–344 (p. 32); Attaleiates, *History* 9, 11, 34, and esp. 54; Skylitzes, *Synopsis of Histories*, p. 409; Skylitzes Continuatus p. 163. Not all historians dismiss such claims, e.g.,

Cheynet, *Pouvoir*, 388–389; Kolia-Dermitzaki, "Η εικόνα των Βουλγάρων," 66–67; Hondridou, "Η ενσωμάτωση," 114, 120–121.

29. Attaleiates, *History* 297; Anna Komnene, *Alexiad* 4.8.4, 6.7.7. For the first attestations, see Vranousi, "Οἱ ὅροι «'Αλβανοὶ»"; for the Albanians and Byzantium in later centuries, see Ducellier, *L'Albanie;* Gasparis, *Οι Αλβανοί.*

30. Anna Komnene, *Alexiad* 13.5.2.

31. Gelzer, "Ungedruckte und wenig bekannte Bistumsverzeichnisse," 46. In general, see Năsturel, "Les Valaques balkaniques"; Dvoichenko-Markov, "Vlachs"; Curta, "Constantinople and the Echo Chamber."

32. Kekaumenos, *Strategikon* 81. A later addition to the text of Skylitzes, *Synopsis of Histories,* p. 329, places some vagabond Vlachs between Kastoria and Prespa; they killed Samuil's brother David.

33. See Chapter 4, section on "Slavs to Romans."

34. For the careers and political allegiances of this Nikoulitzas and his relatives, see the analysis by C. Roueché at http://www.ancientwisdoms.ac.uk/library/kekaumenos-consilia-et-narrationes/intro-kekaumenos/.

35. Kekaumenos, *Strategikon* 74, is his account of the rebellion; see Curta, *Southeastern Europe,* 280–281.

36. The *prokritos archon* of the Vlachs named Sthlabotas Karmalakes, who was arrested as a ringleader, was only a leader among the Vlachs rather than an imperial appointee. The text then mentions other *prokritoi* of the Vlachs and people of Larissa.

37. Kekaumenos, *Strategikon* 75.

38. Text in Meyer, *Die Haupturkunden,* 164; see Dasoulas, "Οι μεσαιωνικές κοινωνίες," 17–18.

39. Anna Komnene, *Alexiad* 5.5.3, 8.3.4, 8.4.5.

40. Dasoulas, "Οι μεσαιωνικές κοινωνίες," 29.

41. Benjamin of Tudela, *Itinerary,* p. 11.

42. Euthymios Malakes in Papadopoulos-Kerameus, *Noctes Petropolitanae,* 145.

43. Avramea, *Ἡ βυζαντινὴ Θεσσαλία,* 38–39.

44. Apokaukos, doc. 19 (p. 80).

45. Gelzer, "Ungedruckte und wenig bekannte Bistumsverzeichnisse," 46; see Ditten, *Ethnische Verschiebungen,* 107–110; Shukurov, *Byzantine Turks,* 171–173. Basileios II used Turks against the Bulgarians in his campaigns in Macedonia: *Life of Saint Athanasios of Athos (B)* 58; see Curta, *Edinburgh,* 251, 289.

46. Skylitzes, *Synopsis of Histories,* p. 286; Anna Komnene, *Alexiad* 14.8.5–9 (she says they came from the Chalybes and from Armenia). For various classical references to the Chalybes, placing them between the Pontos and Armenia, see W. Smith, *Dictionary of Greek and Roman Geography* (s.v.), but Chalybon was also a district near Aleppo, which is more likely what is meant here. For the Paulicians as a minority within the empire, see Cheynet, *Pouvoir,* 392; Lilie, "Zur Stellung," 312–315, citing previous bibliography.

47. *Gesta Francorum et aliorum Hierosolimitanorum* 1.4; Robert the Monk, *History of the First Crusade* 2.11–15.

48. Perceptions: Kaldellis, *Ethnography,* 117–126; wars and agreement: Kaldellis, *Streams of Gold,* 192–194, 198–201.

49. Kekaumenos, *Strategikon* 19.

50. Studies of the annexed realms look only at the big picture, not at what was happening on the ground: Yuzbashian, "L'administration byzantine"; Arutjunova-Fidanjan, "Some Aspects"; Leveniotis, Κατάρρευση, 53–195.

51. Oikonomides, *Listes*, 344–363; Dagron, *Le traite*, 239–245; Seibt, "Armenika themata." They should not be confused with the themes that emerged from the breakup of the old Armeniakon theme. For Lykandos, see Dédéyan, "Les Arméniens en Cappadoce," 80–81.

52. Cheynet, "Les Arméniens dans l'armée," focusing on the officer class.

53. See Chapter 5, section on "The Politics of Armenian Ethnicity."

54. Arab sources: Dédéyan, "Les Arméniens en Cappadoce," 80. In Byzantine sources the distinction is pervasive.

55. Cheynet, *Byzantine Aristocracy*, XI:185–186; Arutjunova-Fidanjan, "Some Aspects," 318. Calling many of these individuals "Armenians" runs into the problems discussed in Chapter 5, such as that the claim often lacks any proof.

56. Aristakes, *History* 1.4.

57. Aristakes, *History* 18.122, 23.156–159.

58. Leveniotis, Κατάρρευση, 534–584, magisterially presents the relevant prosopography in tables.

59. Greenwood, "Armenian Neighbors," 362, cites the excavation reports.

60. Aristakes, *History* 2.10, 14.90.

61. Mahé, "Ani sous Constantin X."

62. Skylitzes, *Synopsis of Histories*, p. 352; Aristakes, *History* 1.5–6.

63. Kaldellis, *Streams of Gold*, 210–212.

64. Arutjunova-Fidanjan, "Some Aspects"; Garsoïan, "Armenian Integration," 71, 103–109; Redgate, *Armenians*, 223, 250–254. Cheynet, *Pouvoir*, 384: there were conversions to Byzantine Orthodoxy, but not enough to change the balance.

65. Step'anos of Taron, *Universal History* 3.31; see Garsoïan, "Armenian Integration," 71; Leveniotis, Κατάρρευση, 35, 467. Sebasteia: Hild and Restle, *Kappadokien*, 274–275.

66. Kolbaba, *Byzantine Lists*, 37–38, 68–69.

67. The Armenian historians record the persecution of the Syrian Orthodox Church by Romanos III and Konstantinos X (e.g., Aristakes, *History* 6.32–33), but, when it comes to the Armenian Church, they recount threats that didn't lead anywhere (e.g., Matthew of Edessa, *Chronicle* 2.14, 2.25, 2.30) or impossible fables (Matthew of Edessa, *Chronicle* 2.57).

68. Step'anos of Taron, *Universal History* 3.20; see Garsoïan, "Armenian Integration," 83, for skepticism regarding some aspects; Dédéyan, "Les Arméniens en Cappadoce," 83–84, for the buildup of Armenian sees.

69. Garsoïan, "Armenian Integration," 71, 76, 80–81.

70. Arutjunova-Fidanjan, "Some Aspects"; Garsoïan, "Armenian Integration," 100; Cheynet, "Duchy of Antioch," 12, along with, I suspect, most mid- and lower-level Armenian functionaries in the new eastern themes and *doukata*.

71. Among many treatments, see Yarnley, "Philaretos." Cf. Kaldellis, *Streams of Gold*, 298.

72. See Chapter 5, section on "Some Family Chronicles."

73. Michael the Syrian, *Chronicle*, vol. 3, 133, misdating it to 988 (the event he links it to occurred around 1020); in general, see Dédéyan, "Les Arméniens en Cappadoce."

74. The architect of this idea seems to be Dédéyan in "L'immigration arménienne" and "Les Arméniens en Cappadoce," 90–94. Dédéyan is heavily dependent on fictional episodes in Matthew of Edessa (see below); whence Thierry, "Données archéologiques," esp. 119–124; and Hewsen, *Armenia*, 126.

75. Seibt, "Stärken," 337, citing previous publications. Leveniotis, Κατάρρευση, 493–506, tries valiantly to adjudicate between the maximalist and minimalist views, and makes some good points, but generally treats everything recorded in a source, even in later Armenian traditions, as a fact, not realizing how problematic Matthew of Edessa is.

76. Skylitzes, *Synopsis of Histories*, pp. 354–355; Aristakes, *History* 3.19; Matthew of Edessa, *Chronicle* 1.49; the title only: Kekaumenos, *Strategikon* 81. Skylitzes confuses matters by making him the *strategos* of Cappadocia; that theme did not include Sebasteia, but he may be thinking of the broader region of Cappadocia rather than the theme; see Leveniotis, Κατάρρευση, 465. If he was *strategos* of Cappadocia, it would have been for only a brief time, as the roster of the theme's known officials is rather full compared to that of Sebasteia: Leveniotis, Κατάρρευση, 643–650, 652–653.

77. See the debate in Leveniotis, Κατάρρευση, 464.

78. E.g., with Davitʿ of Tao, the principality of Ani, and Eustathios Maleïnos.

79. Matthew of Edessa, *Chronicle* 1.51; for the known officers of the theme, see Leveniotis, Κατάρρευση, 637–642.

80. Skylitzes, *Synopsis of Histories*, p. 437; Aristakes, *History* 10.60 ("villages and cities in the Mesopotamian borders"); Matthew of Edessa, *Chronicle* 1.84.

81. Skylitzes, *Synopsis of Histories*, p. 437; Attaleiates, *History* 80.

82. Matthew of Edessa, *Chronicle* 2.30 (the sermon follows), 2.42–43; see 1.77 for a hagiography of Gagik. For skepticism, see Cheynet, *Pouvoir*, 401–402; "Arméniens," 68–69. Matthew had no understanding of the Roman centralized state and intuitively viewed history through the lens of Armenian "feudal" relations, so he gives the impression that the royals were ruling their own domains. He sometimes makes it seem as if they brought their royal sovereignty to their Byzantine possessions (1.54, 1.62), although he knows they followed the emperor's orders (1.80). The problem extends to a propensity for tall tales that cannot be taken at face value, as scholars have recognized. When his account can be checked against sober or contemporary sources, he often fails. For some examples regarding the tenth century, see Kaldellis, "Did Ioannes I Tzimiskes Campaign in the East in 974?"

83. Matthew of Edessa, *Chronicle* 1.62.

84. Aristakes, *History* 10.61.

85. Davitʿ actually had potential heirs, his brothers Atom and Abusahl (see below), but this was irrelevant to the emperor, for all that hereditary succession was ingrained in Aristakes' thinking.

86. Matthew of Edessa, *Chronicle* 2.54, 2.57; at 2.30 he was sought out by the Artsrunis at Kalon-Peghat, one of his original grants. It is often assumed that the wording in Skylitzes, *Synopsis of Histories*, p. 491 (τοὺς Σεβαστηνοὺς καὶ τοὺς Μελιτηνοὺς καὶ τοὺς ἐκ τῆς Τεφρικῆς καὶ τῶν λοιπῶν Ἀρμενίων), regarding the civil war of 1057, reveals that Sebasteia and Melitene were among "the Armenians," but the grammar links "the other Armenians" only to Tephrike (via the parallel genitive construction). Nevertheless, it could well be that there were significant Armenian forces at Sebasteia and Melitene as well.

87. Seibt, "War Gagik II von Grossarmenien?"

88. Matthew of Edessa, *Chronicle* 2.23.

89. Petros and churches: Aristakes, *History* 14.89; Matthew of Edessa, *Chronicle* 1.93, 2.7.

90. Matthew of Edessa, *Chronicle* 2.57.

91. Garsoïan, "Armenian Integration," 124; 111–124 on the "Royals"; cf. Cheynet, *Pouvoir*, 397.

92. Basileios II: Kaldellis, *Streams*, 111; Step'anos: introduction to the translation by Greenwood.

93. R. Morris, "The Athonites and Their Neighbors," 158.

94. Gregorios Pakourianos, *Typikon* prol. ("race"), 1 (relations), 24 (no Romans allowed), on pp. 21, 35, 105, respectively; in general, see Lemerle, *Cinq études*, 115–191. For Armenian stereotypes of Romans as greedy in this period, see also Step'anos of Taron, *Universal History* 3.3.

95. Eustathios Romaios, *Peira* 14.16, 54.6; cf. Laiou, "L'étranger" and "Institutional Mechanisms," 164.

96. Romeney, "Ethnicity."

97. Context and sources in Kaldellis, *Streams of Gold*, 48, 62, 67, 160, 233; see now also Todt and Vest, *Syria*, vol. 1, 356–360. For the Jacobite immigration, see Dagron, "Minorités ethniques," esp. 189 and 192, for assistance by the *protospatharios* Ioseph and the *patrikios* Eutychios (Kulayb). For Melitene and its surrounding territories in particular, see Vest, *Geschichte*, esp. vol. 2, 1077–1107, 1151–1153, 1171–1252, and vol. 3, 1332–1334.

98. The *krites* "Chrysobourgios" (probably Chrysoberges) seems to have been well disposed toward the Jacobite patriarch rather than a member of his Church: Michael the Syrian, *Chronicle*, vol. 3, 140; cf. Vest, *Geschichte*, vol. 2, 1201–1203; Leveniotis, Κατάρρευση, 583 (no. 198).

99. Patriarch Alexios Stoudites in Ficker, *Erlasse*, 17; see Chitwood, *Byzantine Legal Culture*, 133–149.

100. Synodal Memorandum of September 1039 in Ficker, *Erlasse*, 28–42.

101. Atiya and Abd al-Masih, *History of the Patriarchs of the Egyptian Church*, vol. 2, pt. 3, 305.

102. Kaldellis, *Streams of Gold*, 130. For Melkite literary production at this time, see Nasrallah, *Histoire*.

103. A series of useful articles are only prolegomena: Kennedy, "Antioch"; Todt, "Antioch"; Cheynet, "Duchy of Antioch"; and the introduction and entries in Todt and Vest, *Syria*.

104. Matthew of Edessa, *Chronicle* 2.48.

105. Ditten, *Ethnische Verschiebungen*, 61–68; Auzépy, *L'histoire des iconoclastes*, 221–257.

106. E.g., *Life of Saint Antonios the Younger*, p. 199 (ninth-century).

107. Kulayb: *PmbZ* II: 24209. Context: Kaldellis, *Streams of Gold*, 147; full, revised list of governors of Antioch: Cheynet, *Sceaux de la collection Zacos*, 22–23; other Melkite title holders: Todt, "Antioch," 184–185. ʿUbayd Allah (*PmbZ* II: 28392) converted from Islam to Christianity, but we should not thereby regard him as a Melkite.

108. Dagron and Feissel, "Inscriptions," 457–459.

109. Jonathan Shea, personal communication.

110. Attaleiates, *History* 110.

111. Cf. Monferrer-Sala, "Between Hellenism and Arabicization"; Griffith, *The Church in the Shadow*, 139.

112. Ter-Ghewondyan, *Arab Emirates*, esp. 109–119.

113. Narrative, with sources, in Kaldellis, *Streams of Gold*, 24–64; in brief: Dagron, "Minorités ethniques," 179–186; perceptions from the Muslim side: El Cheik, *Byzantium*, 162–178.

114. Von Sivers, "Taxes and Trade," 75–76; Bosworth, *The Arabs, Byzantium and Iran*, XII–XIII.

115. Todt, "Antioch," 188; Holmes, *Basil II*, 321 (the unusual case of the Marwanid emir Muhhamid al-Dawla), 375, 487.

116. Holmes, "East," 44; see Le Strange, *Palestine*, 457; Schlacht and Meyerhof, *Medico-Philosophical Controversy*, 54–57.

117. Translations from Starr, *Jews*, 190, and Holo, *Byzantine Jewry*, 57 (who change Elias' "Romans" to "Byzantines"); Horst, *Des Metropoliten Elias*, 42, gets it right. See Holo, *Byzantine Jewry*, 51–64, 69–70, for Jewish immigration in this period.

118. Holo, *Byzantine Jewry*, 52–53, 56.

119. Goitein, "A Letter," 300–301.

120. Starr, *Jews*, 205.

121. See the debate between Kolbaba, "On the Closing of the Churches"; Ryder, "Changing Perspectives"; and Kolbaba, "1054 Revisited."

122. Balard, "Amalfi et Byzance"; Nicol, *Byzantium and Venice*, 39–42, 61.

123. Arrest: Skylitzes, *Synopsis of Histories*, p. 430 (who is explicit that their presence was governed by a treaty); past treaties: see p. 226 above.

124. Bar Hebraeus, *Chronography*, p. 227 (trans. Budge). The uprising of 1044 was a Roman political matter.

125. Grdzelidze, *Georgian Monks*, 119 *(Atsinkians)*. The word for them in Georgian is a derivative of Byzantine *Atsinganoi*, used for the Roma: Soulis, "Gypsies in the Byzantine Empire," 145–146. Later the Byzantines took to calling them Egyptians, whence the name "Gypsies."

126. Ciggaar, "Une description," 119–120.

127. Ciggarr, *Western Travellers*, 140–141, citing previous studies; Blöndal, *Varangians*, 141–152, for the English Varangians.

128. Quoted with discussion by Magdalino, "Isaac II, Saladin, and Venice," 102.

129. Blöndal, *Varangians*, 24, 95, 182 (cf. Skylitzes, *Synopsis of Histories*, p. 394).

130. Ulpian in *Digest* 1.5.17 *(in orbe Romano qui sunt . . . cives Romani effecti sunt)*; *Basilika* 46.1.14: Οἱ ἐν τῇ Ῥωμαϊκῇ γῇ ὄντες πολῖται Ῥωμαίων εἰσίν, with the scholion: Οἱ ἐν τῷ κύκλῳ ὄντες τῷ Ῥωμαϊκῷ, τουτέστιν οἱ τελοῦντες ὑπὸ Ῥωμαίους, κἂν μὴ αὐτὴν οἰκοῦσι τὴν Ῥώμην, ὅμως πολῖται Ῥωμαίων ἐκ τῆς Ἀντωνίνου τοῦ βασιλέως διατάξεώς εἰσιν.

131. Cf. Mathisen, *"Peregrini"*; Kerneis, "Rome et les barbares."

132. Laniado, *Ethnos et droit*, discusses the scholion and its background. It is *Basilika* 22.1.1, sch. 2 (vol. 4, 1327).

133. Laniado, *Ethnos et droit*, esp. 245–249, 252. A. Gkoutzioukostas, review of Laniado in *Byzantiaka* 32 (2015) 359–371, here 368–370, argues that this refers not to ethnicity but to provincial origins (specifically to runaway dependents).

134. Justinian, *Novel* 21 pref.; cf. *Edict* 3.

135. Maas, "Delivered," 160–171, mostly on the Tzanoi.

136. Skylitzes Continuatus, p. 162 (*ethima*, not *nomoi*).

137. Kaldellis, *Byzantine Republic*, 206nn42–44; Kerneis, "Loi et coutumes."

138. A striking early formulation is the so-called edict of Thessalonike issued by Theodosius I: *Codex Theodosianus* 16.1.2 = *Codex Iustinianus* 1.1.1 = *Basilika* 1.1.1–3.

139. Outlined by Chitwood, *Byzantine Legal Culture*, 124–127.

140. Vryonis, "The Will of a Provincial Magnate," 264–265.

141. Nikon, *Taktikon*, p. 15.

142. Attaleiates, *History* 96–97; see Kaldellis, "Argument."

143. Psellos, *Letter KD* 207 (p. 239).

144. Psellos, *Orationes panegyricae* 2.133–134 (p. 24).

145. Dagron, "Minorités ethniques," 216.

CONCLUSION

1. Rosenqvist, *Die byzantinische Literatur*, 5.

2. Pinker, *Enlightenment Now*, 377.

3. The high threshold required by ethnic change is stressed by Gil-White, "How Thick Is Blood?," 812, 814.

4. Kaldellis, *Hellenism in Byzantium*, ch. 6; Page, *Being Byzantine*, ch. 4; Chrissis, "Ideological and Political Contestations."

5. Lavan, Payne, and Weisweiler, "Cosmopolitan Politics," 2, 5, and 5n11.

Bibliography

Primary Sources

Modern translations of the following sources are referenced below for the reader's convenience, not necessarily because I have quoted from them. If I have, I say so in the relevant endnote.

Abû Firâs al-Hamdânî, *Les Byzantines: La voix d'un prisonnier*, trans. A. Miquel (Paris, 2010).
Acta Conciliorum Oecumenicorum, II.5: *Concilium Universale Chalcedonense (Collectio Sangermanensis)*, ed. E. Schwartz (Berlin, 1936).
Actes de Lavra, vol. 1: *Des origines à 1204*, ed. P. Lemerle et al. (Paris, 1970).
Actes d'Iviron, vol. 2: *Du milieu di XIe siècle à 1204*, ed. J. Lefort et al. (Paris, 1990).
Agathias, *Histories*, ed. R. Keydell, *Agathiae Myrinaei Historiarum Libri Quinque* (Berlin, 1967); trans. J. D. Frendo, *Agathias: The Histories* (Berlin, 1976).
Akropolites, Georgios, *History*, ed. A. Heisenberg, *Georgii Acropolitae opera*, rev. P. Wirth, vol. 1 (Stuttgart, 1978); trans. R. Macrides, *George Akropolites: The History* (Oxford, 2007).
Akropolites, Konstantinos, *On Saint Barbaros*, ed. A. Papadopoulos-Kerameus, Ἀνάλεκτα ἱεροσολυμιτικῆς σταχυολογίας, vol. 1 (St. Petersburg, 1891), 405–420.
Al-Baladhuri, *The Origins of the Islamic State*, trans. P. K. Hitti (New York, 1961).
Al-Tabari, *The History of al-Tabari*, vol. 33: *Storm and Stress along the Northern Frontiers of the 'Abbasid Caliphate*, trans. C. E. Bosworth (New York, 1991).
Al-Tanūḫī, *Kitāb al-faraj ba'da l-šidda*, ed. 'Abbūd al-Šālijī, 2 vols. (Beirut, 1971–1973).

Anna Komnene, *Alexiad*, ed. D. R. Reinsch and A. Kambylis, *Annae Comnenae Alexias* (Berlin, 2001); trans. E. R. A. Sewter, rev. P. Frankopan, *Anna Komnene: Alexiad* (London, 2009).
Annals of Lorsch, ed. G. H. Pertz, *Annales Laureshamenses*, in *MGH SS*, vol. 1 (Hannover, 1826), 22–39.
Apokaukos, Ioannes, [Dossier of documents], ed. E. Bei-Seferli, "Aus dem Nachlass von N.A. Bees," *Byzantinisch-neugriechische Jahrbücher* 21 (1971–1974).
Aristakes of Lastivert, *History of the Calamities Caused by the Foreign Nations*, trans. M. Canard and H. Berbérian, *Aristakes de Lastivert: Récit des malheurs de la nation arménienne* (Brussels, 1973); trans. R. Bedrosian, *Aristakes Lastivertc'i's History* (New York, 1985).
Aristeides, Ailios, *Oration 26 ("To Rome")*, ed. and trans. J. H. Oliver, *The Ruling Power: A Study of the Roman Empire in the Second Century after Christ through the Roman Oration of Aelius Aristides* (Philadelphia, 1953).
Athanasios, *History of the Arians*, ed. H. G. Opitz, *Athanasius Werke*, vol. 2.1 (Berlin, 1940), 183–230.
Attaleiates, Michael, *History*, ed. and trans. I. Pérez Martín, *Miguel Ataliates: Historia* (Madrid, 2002); ed. and trans. A. Kaldellis and D. Krallis, *Michael Attaleiates: History* (Washington, DC, 2012).
Augustine, *Expositions on the Psalms*, ed. E. Dekkers and J. Fraipont, *Augustinus: Enarrationes in Psalmos* (Turnhout, 1956).
Bar Hebraeus, *Chronography*, trans. E. A. W. Budge, *The Chronography of Gregory Abu'l Faraj, the Son of Aaron, the Hebrew Physician Commonly Known as Bar Hebraeus Being the First Part of His Political History of the World* (London, 1932).
Basilika, ed. H. J. Scheltema et al., *Basilicorum Libri LX*, 8 vols. (Groningen, 1953–).
Benjamin of Tudela, *Itinerary*, ed. and trans. M. N. Adler (London, 1907).
Book of the Eparch, ed. and trans. J. Koder, *Das Eparchenbuch Leons des Weisen* (Vienna, 1991).
Bryennios, Ioseph, *Dialogue with a Muslim*, ed. A. Argyriou, "Ἰωσὴφ τοῦ Βρυεννίου μετά τινος Ἰσμαηλίτου διάλεξις," Ἐπετηρὶς Ἑταιρείας Βυζαντινῶν Σπουδῶν 35 (1966–1967): 158–195.
Bryennios, Nikephoros, *Materials for a History*, ed. and trans. P. Gautier, *Nicephori Bryennii Historiarum libri quattuor (Nicéphore Bryennios: Histoire)* (Brussels, 1975).
Canons of the Council in Trullo, ed. P. Joannou, *Les canons des conciles oecuméniques* (Rome, 1962), 98–241.
Çelebi, Evliya, *Book of Travels*, trans. R. Dankoff and S. Kim, *An Ottoman Traveller: Selections from the Book of Travels of Evliya Çelebi* (London, 2010).
Choniates, Niketas, *History*, ed. J.-L. van Dieten, *Nicetae Choniatae Historia* (Berlin, 1975); trans. H. J. Magoulias, *O City of Byzantium, Annals of Niketas Choniates* (Detroit, 1984).
Chrestomathia of Strabo, ed. S. Radt, *Strabons Geographika*, vol. 9 (Göttingen, 2010), 243–246.

Chronicle of Monembasia, ed. P. Lemerle, "La chronique improprement dite de Monemvasie: Le contexte historique et légendaire," *REB* 21 (1963): 5–49; and I. Dujčev, *Cronaca di Monemvasia* (Palermo, 1976).
Chronicle of Pseudo-Joshua the Stylite, trans. F. R. Trombley and J. W. Watt (Liverpool, 2000).
Chronicle of the Morea, Greek ed. J. Schmitt, *The Chronicle of Morea* (London, 1904); French ed. J. Longnon, *Livre de la conqueste de la Princée de l'Amorée: Chronique de Morée* (Paris, 1911); trans. H. E. Lurier, *Crusaders as Conquerors: The Chronicle of Morea* (New York, 1964).
Codice diplomatico Barense, vol. 1: *Le pergamene del Duomo di Bari (952–1264)*, ed. G. B. N. de Rossi and F. Nitti (Bari, 1897); vol. 3: *Le pergamene della cattedrale di Terlizzi (971–1300)*, ed. F. Carabellese (Bari, 1899).
Daphnopates, Theodoros, *Letters*, ed. J. Darrouzès and L. G. Westerink, *Théodore Daphnopatès: Correspondance* (Paris, 1978).

———, *Oration on the Peace*, ed. and trans. I. Dujčev, "On the Treaty of 927 with the Bulgarians," *DOP* 32 (1978): 219–295.

Digenis Akritis: The Grottaferrata and Escorial Versions, ed. and trans. E. Jeffreys (Cambridge, 1998).
Digest, ed. T. Mommsen, *Corpus Iuris Civilis*, vol. 1, pt. 2 (Berlin, 1899); ed. and trans. A. Watson, *The Digest of Justinian* (Philadelphia, 1985).
Disputation of Gregentios with the Jew, ed. and trans. A. Berger, *Life and Works of Saint Gregentios, Archbishop of Taphar* (Berlin, 2006).
Doukas, *History*, ed. and trans. V. Grecu, *Istoria Turco-Bizantina* (Bucharest, 1958); trans. H. Magoulias, *Decline and Fall of Byzantium to the Ottoman Turks, by Doukas* (Detroit, 1975).
Epiphanios of Jerusalem, *Proskynetarion*, ed. H. Donner, "Palästina-Beschreibung des Epiphanios Hagiopolita," *Zeitschrift des deutschen Palästina-Vereins* 87 (1971): 42–91.
Epiphanios of Salamis, *Panarion*, ed. K. Holl, *Epiphanius*, vols. 1–3: *Ancoratus und Panarion* (Leipzig, 1915–1933); trans. F. Williams, *The Panarion of Epiphanius of Salamis*, 2 vols. (Leiden, 1987–1994).
Euagrios, *Ecclesiastical History*, ed. J. Bidez and L. Parmentier, *The Ecclesiastical History of Evagrius* (London, 1898); trans. M. Whitby, *The Ecclesiastical History of Evagrius Scholasticus* (Liverpool, 2000).
Euodios, *Forty-Two Martyrs of Amorion*, ed. V. Vasil'evskij and P. Nikitin, *Skazanija o 42 amorijskich mucenikach* (St. Petersburg, 1905), 61–78.
Eustathios of Thessalonike, *Capture of Thessalonike*, ed. and trans. J. Melville-Jones, *Eustathios of Thessaloniki: The Capture of Thessaloniki* (Canberra, 1988).

———, *Letters*, ed. F. Kolovou, *Die Briefe des Eustathios von Thessalonike* (Munich, 2006).

———, *Funeral Oration for Manuel I Komnenos*, ed. and trans. E. C. Bourbouhakis, *Not Composed in a Chance Manner: The Epitaphios for Manuel I Komnenos by Eustathios of Thessalonike* (Uppsala, 2017).

Eustathios Romaios, *Peira*, ed. I. Zepos and P. Zepos, *Ius Graecoromanum*, vol. 4 (Athens, 1931).

Eutropios (Greek translation), *Breviarium*, ed. S. P. Lampros, "Παιανίου μετάφρασις εἰς τὴν τοῦ Εὐτροπίου Ῥωμαϊκὴν ἱστορίαν," *Νέος Ἑλληνομνήμων* 9 (1912): 9–113.
Forty-Two Martyrs of Amorion, ed. V. Vasil'evskij and P. Nikitin, *Skazanija o 42 amorijskich mučenikach* (St. Petersburg, 1905).
Genesios, Ioseph, *On the Reigns of the Emperors*, ed. A. Lesmüller-Werner and I. Thurn, *Josephi Genesii regum libri quattuor* (Berlin, 1978); trans. A. Kaldellis, *Genesios: On the Reigns of the Emperors* (Canberra, 1998).
Gesta Francorum et aliorum Hierosolimitanorum, ed. and trans. R. Hill, *The Deeds of the Franks and the Other Pilgrims to Jerusalem* (London, 1962).
Ghewond, *History*, trans. Z. Arzoumanian, *History of Lewond, The Eminent Vardapet of the Armenians* (Philadelphia, 1982).
Gregoras, Nikephoros, *Roman History*, ed. I. Bekker and L. Schopen, *Nicephori Gregorae historiae Byzantinae*, 3 vols. (Bonn, 1829–1855).
———, *Florentios*, ed. and trans. P. L. M. Leone, *Niceforo Gregora: Fiorenzo o Intorno alla sapienza* (Naples, 1975).
Hippolytos, *Commentary on Daniel*, ed. M. Lefèvre, *Hippolyte: Commentaire sur Daniel* (Paris, 1947).
History of the Caucasian Albanians, trans. C. J. F. Dowsett, *The History of the Caucasian Albanians by Movses Dasxuranc'i* (London, 1961).
Ioannes Lydos, *On the Magistracies of the Roman State*, ed. and trans. A. Bandy, *Ioannes Lydus: On Powers or The Magistracies of the Roman State* (Philadelphia, 1983).
Ioannes of Antioch, *History*, ed. and trans. S. Mariev, *Ioannis Antiocheni fragmenta quae supersunt omnia* (Berlin, 2008); ed. and trans. U. Roberto, *Ioannis Antiocheni fragmenta ex historia chronica* (Berlin, 2005).
John Chrysostom, *Homily 47 on Acts of the Apostles* 22.25 in *PG* 60.
John of Nikiu, *Chronicle*, trans. R. H. Charles, *The Chronicle of John, Coptic Bishop of Nikiu* (Amsterdam, 1916).
Julian, *Panegyric in Honor of Constantius (Oration 1)*, ed. J. Bidez, *L'empereur Julien: Oeuvres complètes*, vol. 1.1 (Paris, 1932), 10–68; trans. W. C. Wright, *The Works of the Emperor Julian*, vol. 1 (London, 1913), 4–127.
Justinian, *Novels* and *Edicts*, ed. R. Schoell and G. Kroll, *Corpus Iuris Civilis*, vol. 3 (Berlin, 1899); trans. S. P. Scott, *The Civil Law*, vols. 16–17 (Cincinnati, 1932).
Kaminiates, Ioannes, *Capture of Thessalonike*, ed. G. Böhlig, *Ioannis Caminiatae de expugnatione Thessalonicae* (Berlin, 1973); trans. D. Frendo et al., *John Kaminiates: The Capture of Thessaloniki* (Perth, 2000).
Kanaboutzes, Ioannes, *Commentary on Dionysios of Halikarnassos*, ed. M. Lehnerdt, *Ioannis Canabutzae magistri ad principem Aeni et Samothraces in Dionysium Halicansasensem Commentarius* (Leipzig, 1890); with corrections by S. Reiter, "Zu Joannes Kanabutzes Magister," *Wiener Studien* 13 (1891): 329–332; trans. A Kaldellis, *Byzantine Readings of Ancient Historians* (New York, 2015), 113–170.
Kandidos, *History*, ed. and trans. A. Kaldellis, in I. Worthington, ed., *Brill's New Jacoby*, online resource, http://referenceworks.brillonline.com.

Katrares, Ioannes, *Anakreontic verses against the philosopher Neophytos*, ed. P. Matranga, *Anecdota graeca* (Rome, 1850), 675–682.
Kekaumenos, *Strategikon*, ed. G. G. Litavrin, *Sovety i rasskazy Kekavmena* (Moscow, 1972); ed. and trans. D. Tsoungarakis, Κεκαυμένος: Στρατηγικόν (Athens, 1993).
Keroularios, Michael, *Letter I to Petros of Antioch*, ed. C. Will, *Acta et scripta quae de controversiis ecclesiae graecae et latinae saeculo undecimo composita extant* (Leipzig, 1861), 172–185.
Kinnamos, Ioannes, *History*, ed. A. Meineke, *Ioannis Cinnami epitome rerum ab Ioanne et Alexio Comnenis gestarum* (Bonn, 1836); trans. C. Brand, *John Kinnamos: Deeds of John and Manuel Comnenus* (New York, 1976).
Konstantinos VII Porphyrogennetos, *Book of Ceremonies*, ed. J. J. Reiske, *Constantini Porphyrogeniti imperatoris de cerimoniis aulae byzantinae*, 2 vols. (Bonn, 1829–1830); trans. A. Moffatt and M. Tall, *Constantine Porphyrogennetos: The Book of Ceremonies*, 2 vols. (Canberra, 2012).
———, *On the Themes*, ed. A. Pertusi, *Costantino Porfigorenito: De thematibus* (Vatican City, 1952).
———, *De administrando imperio*, ed. G. Moravcsik and trans. R. J. H. Jenkins, *Constantine Porphyrogenitus: De administrando imperio* (Washington, DC, 1967).
Konstantinos IX Monomachos, *Novel on the Nomophylax*, ed. A. Salač, *Novella Constitutio saec. XI medii* (Prague, 1954).
Kosmas Indikopleustes, *Christian Topography*, ed. and trans. W. Wolska-Conus, *Cosmas Indicopleustès: Topographie chrétienne*, 3 vols. (Paris, 1968–1973); trans. J. W. McCrindle, *The Christian Topography of Cosmas, An Egyptian Monk* (New York, 1967).
Kyrillos of Skythopolis, *Life of Saint Ioannes the Hesychast*, ed. E. Schwartz, *Kyrillos von Skythopolis* (Leipzig, 1939); trans. R. M. Price, *Cyril of Scythopolis: The Lives of the Monks of Palestine* (Kalamazoo, MI, 1991), 220–244.
Laskaris Kananos, [*Travel Account*], ed. V. Lundström, *Smärre Byzantinska skrifter*, vol. 1: *Laskaris Kananos' Reseanteckningar från de nordiska länderna* (Uppsala, 1902).
Leon VI, *Homily* 14, ed. T. Antonopoulou, *Leontis VI Sapientis imperatoris Byzantini Homilae* (Turnhout, 2008), 195–218.
———, *Taktika*, ed. and trans. G. T. Dennis, *The Taktika of Leo VI* (Washington, DC, 2010).
Leon the Deacon, *History*, ed. C. B. Hase, *Leonis diaconi Historae libri X* (Bonn, 1828); trans. A.-M. Talbot and D. F. Sullivan, *The History of Leo the Deacon: Byzantine Military Expansion in the Tenth Century* (Washington, DC, 2005).
Life of Basileios I, ed. and trans. I. Ševčenko, *Chronographiae quae Theophanis Continuati nomine fertur liber quo Vita Basilii imperatoris amplectitur* (Berlin, 2011).
Life of Saint Andreas the Fool, ed. and trans. L. Rydén, *The Life of St. Andrew the Fool*, 2 vols. (Uppsala, 1995).
Life of Saint Antonios the Younger, ed. A. Papadopoulos-Kerameus, Συλλογὴ Παλαιστινῆς καὶ Συριακῆς ἁγιολογίας, vol. 1 (St. Petersburg, 1907), 186–216.

Life of Saint Athanasia of Aigina, ed. F. Halkin, *Six inédits d'hagiologie byzantine* (Brussels, 1987); trans. L. F. Sherry, "Life of St. Athanasia of Aigina," in A.-M. Talbot, ed., *Holy Women of Byzantium: Ten Saints' Lives in English Translation* (Washington, DC, 1996), 137–157.

Life of Saint Athanasios of Athos (B), ed. J. Noret, *Vitae duae antiquae sancti Athanasii Athonitae* (Turnhout, 1982); trans. A.-M. Talbot in R. P. H. Greenfield and A.-M. Talbot, *Holy Men of Mt. Athos* (Cambridge, MA, 2016), 127–367.

Life of Saint Basileios the Younger, ed. and trans. D. F. Sullivan, A.-M. Talbot, and S. McGrath, *The Life of Saint Basil the Younger* (Washington, DC, 2014).

Life of Saint Elias the Younger, ed. G. Rossi Taibbi, *Vita di sant' Elia il Giovane* (Palermo, 1962).

Life of Saint Epiphanios, in *PG* 41: 23–115.

Life of Saint Euthymios the Younger, ed. L. Petit, "Vie et office de saint Euthyme le Jeune," *Revue de l'Orient chrétien* 8 (1903): 168–205.

Life of Saint George the Athonite, trans. T. Grdzelidze, *Georgian Monks on Mount Athos: Two Eleventh-Century Lives of the Hegoumenoi of Iviron* (London, 2009).

Life of Saint Lazaros of Mt. Galesion: An Eleventh-Century Pillar Saint, ed. H. Delehaye in *AASS Nov. III* (Brussels, 1910); trans. R. P. H. Greenfield (Washington, DC, 2000).

Life of Saint Maria the Egyptian, ed. *PG* 87: 3697–3726; trans. M. Kouli, "Life of St. Mary of Egypt," in A.-M. Talbot, ed., *Holy Women of Byzantium: Ten Saints' Lives in English Translation* (Washington, DC, 1996), 65–94.

Life of Saint Maria the Younger, ed. P. Peeters, *AASS Nov. IV* (Brussels, 1925), 692–705; trans. A. Laiou, "Life of St. Mary the Younger," in A.-M. Talbot, ed., *Holy Women of Byzantium: Ten Saints' Lives in English Translation* (Washington, DC, 1996), 239–289.

Life of Saint Methodios, ed. *PG* 100: 1243–1263.

Life of Saint Neilos of Rossano, ed. G. Giovanelli, Βίος καὶ πολιτεία τοῦ ὁσίου πατρὸς ἡμῶν Νείλου τοῦ Νέου (Grottaferrata, Italy 1972).

Life of Saint Nikolaos the Younger, ed. I. Polemis and E. Mineva, Βυζαντινά υμνογραφικά και αγιολογικά κείμενα (Athens, 2016), 444–455.

Life of Saint Nikon "Metanoeite!," ed. and trans. D. F. Sullivan, *The Life of Saint Nikon* (Brookline, MA, 1987).

Life of Saint Petros of Argos, ed. I. Polemis and E. Mineva, Βυζαντινά υμνογραφικά και αγιολογικά κείμενα (Athens, 2016), 466–500.

Life of Saint Philaretos, ed. and trans. L. Rydén, *The Life of St. Philaretos the Merciful Written by His Grandson Niketas* (Uppsala, 2002).

Life of Saints David, Symeon, and Georgios, ed. J. van den Gheyn, "Acta Graeca ss. Davidis, Symeonis et Georgii Mitylenae in insula Lesbo," *Analecta Bollandiana* 18 (1899): 211–259; trans. D. Abrahamse and D. Domingo-Forasté, "Life of Sts. David, Symeon and George of Lesbos," in A.-M. Talbot, ed., *Byzantine Defenders of Images: Eight Saints' Lives in English Translation* (Washington, DC, 1998), 143–241.

Life of Saint Thomais, ed. H. Delehaye in *AASS Nov. IV* (Brussels, 1925), 234–242; trans. P. Halsall, "Life of St. Thomaïs of Lesbos," in A.-M. Talbot,

ed., *Holy Women of Byzantium: Ten Saints' Lives in English Translation* (Washington, DC, 1996), 291–321.
Life of the Patriarch Euthymios, ed. and trans. P. Karlin-Hayter, *Vita Euthymii patriarchae Constantinopolitani* (Brussels, 1970).
Liudprand of Cremona, *Antapodosis* and *Embassy to Constantinople*, ed. P. Chiesa, *Liudprandi Cremonensis opera* (Turnhout, 1998); trans. P. Squatriti, *The Complete Works of Liudprand of Cremona* (Washington, DC, 2007).
Louis II, *Letter to Basileios I*, in *MGH Epp.*, vol. 7 (Berlin, 1928), 385–394.
Malalas, Ioannes, *Chronicle*, ed. I. Thurn, *Ioannis Malalae Chronographia* (Berlin, 2000); trans. E. Jeffreys et al., *The Chronicle of John Malalas* (Melbourne, 1986).
Malaxos, Manuel, *Historica politica et patriarchica Constantinopoleos*, ed. I. Bekker (Bonn, 1849).
Manasses, Konstantinos, *Historical Synopsis*, ed. O. Lampsides, *Constantini Manassis Breviarium Chronicum*, 2 vols. (Athens, 1996).
Marcellinus Comes, *Chronicle*, ed. and trans. B. Croke (Sydney, 1995).
Manuel II Palaiologos, *Funeral Oration for His Brother Theodoros*, ed. and trans. J. Chrysostomides, *Manuel II Palaeologus: Funeral Oration on His Brother Theodore* (Thessalonike, 1985).
Martyrdom of Gondilouch, ed. A. Papadopoulos-Kerameus, Ἀνάλεκτα ἱεροσολυμιτικῆς σταχυολογίας, vol. 4 (St. Petersburg, 1897), v351–356.
Martyrdom of Saba, ed. H. Delehaye, "Passio S. Sabae Gothi," *Analecta Bollandiana* 31 (1912): 216–221; trans. P. Heather and J. Matthews, *The Goths in the Fourth Century* (Liverpool, 1991), 111–117.
Matthew of Edessa, *Chronicle*, trans. A. E. Dostourian, *Armenia and the Crusades, 10th to 12th Centuries: The Chronicle of Matthew of Edessa* (Lanham, MD, 1993).
Maurikios, *Strategikon*, ed. G. T. Dennis and trans. E. Gamillscheg, *Das Strategikon des Maurikios* (Vienna, 1981); trans. G. T. Dennis, *Maurice's Strategikon: Handbook of Byzantine Military Strategy* (Philadelphia, 1984).
Mauropous, Ioannes, *Poems and Orations*, ed. P. de Lagarde, *Iohannis Euchaitorum Metropolitae quae in codice Vaticano Graeco 676 supersunt* (Göttingen, 1882).
Mesarites, Nikolaos, *Funeral Oration for His Brother Ioannes*, ed. A. Heisenberg, *Neue Quellen zur Geschichte des lateinische Kaisertums und der Kirchenunion, I–III*, in *Sitzungsberichte der bayerischen Akademie der Wissenschaften, Philosophisch-philologische und historische Klasse* (Munich), here 1922 Abh. 5.
Michael the Syrian, ed. and trans. J.-B. Chabot, *Chronique de Michel le Syrien, Patriarche Jacobite d'Antioche (1166–1199)*, 4 vols. (Paris, 1899–1910).
Miracles of Saint Demetrios, ed. and trans. P. Lemerle, *Les plus anciens recueils des miracles de saint Démétrius et la pénétration des Slaves dans les Balkans*, 2 vols. (Paris, 1979).
Neophytos the Recluse, *Panegyrike Biblos A*, ed. T. Giagkou and N. Papatriantafyllou-Theodoridi in D. G. Tsames et al., eds., Ἁγίου Νεοφύτου τοῦ Ἐγκλείστου Συγγράμματα, vol. 3 (Paphos, Cyprus, 1999).

Nicolaus I, pope, *Letter 88 to Michael III*, in *MGH Epp.*, vol. 6 (Berlin, 1925), 454–487.

Nikephoros, patriarch of Constantinople, *Short History*, ed. and trans. C. Mango (Washington, DC, 1990).

Nikephoros II Phokas, *On Skirmishing*, ed. and trans. in G. Dennis, *Three Byzantine Military Treatises* (Washington, DC, 1985), 143–239.

Niketas David, *Life of Patriarch Ignatios*, ed. and trans. A. Smithies, with notes by J. M. Duffy (Washington, DC, 2013).

Niketas *magistros*, *Life of Saint Theoktiste*, ed. H. Delehaye, *AASS Nov. IV* (Brussels, 1925), 224–233; trans. A. C. Hero, "Life of St. Theoktiste of Lesbos," in A.-M. Talbot, ed., *Holy Women of Byzantium: Ten Saints' Lives in English Translation* (Washington, DC, 1996), 95–116.

———, *Letters*, ed. and trans. L. G. Westerink, *Nicétas Magistros: Lettres d'un exilé (928–946)* (Paris, 1973).

Nikolaos Mesarites, *Ekphrasis of the Church of the Holy Apostles*, ed. and trans. G. Downey, in *Transactions of the American Philosophical Association*, n.s. 47 (1957): 855–924.

Nikolaos Mystikos, *Letters*, ed. and trans. R. J. H. Jenkins and L. G. Westerink, *Nicholas I Patriarch of Constantinople: Letters* (Washington, DC, 1973).

Nikon, *Taktikon*, ed. V. Beneshevich, *Taktikon Nikona Chernogortsa* (St. Petersburg, 1917).

On Strategy, ed. and trans. in G. Dennis, *Three Byzantine Military Treatises* (Washington, DC, 1985), 9–135.

Orosius, *Seven Books of History against the Pagans*, ed. M.-P. Arnaud-Lindet, *Orose: Histoire (contre le païens)*, 3 vols. (Paris, 1990–1991); trans. A. T. Fear (Liverpool, 2010).

Pakourianos, Gregorios, *Typikon*, ed. and trans. P. Gautier, "Le typikon du sébaste Grégoire Pakourianos," *REB* 42 (1984): 5–145; trans. R. Jordan, "Pakourianos: *Typikon* of Gregory Pakourianos for the Monastery of the Mother of God Petritzonitissa in Bačkovo," in J. Thomas and A. C. Hero, eds., *Byzantine Monastic Foundation Documents: A Complete Translation of the Surviving Founders'* Typika *and Testaments* (Washington, DC, 2000), 507–563.

Paschal Chronicle, ed. L. Dindorf, *Chronicon paschale* (Bonn, 1832); trans. M. Whitby and M. Whitby, *Chronicon Paschale, 284–628 AD* (Liverpool, 1989).

Patria of Constantinople, ed. T. Preger, *Scriptores Originum Constantinopolitanum* (Leipzig, 1901–1907); ed. and trans. A. Berger, *Accounts of Medieval Constantinople: The Patria* (Washington, DC, 2013).

Paul the Deacon, *History of the Lombards*, ed. L. Bethmann and G. Waitz, *Historia Langobardorum*, in *MGH SS*, vol. 2 (Hanover, 1878), 12–187; trans. W. D. Foulke (Philadelphia, 1907).

Petros the Sicilian, *History of the Paulicians*, ed. and trans. C. Astruc et al., "Les sources grecques pour l'histoire des Pauliciens d'Asie Mineure," *TM* 4 (1970): 2–227, here 6–68; partial trans. in J. and B. Hamilton, *Christian Dualist Heresies in the Byzantine World, c. 650–1450* (Manchester, 1998), 65–92.

Philotheos, *Kletorologion*, ed. N. Oikonomides, *Les Listes de préséance byzantines des IXe et Xe siècles* (Paris, 1972), 81–235.
Photios, *Homilies*, ed. B. Laourdas, Φωτίου Ὁμιλίαι (Thessalonike, 1966).
———, *Letters*, ed. B. Laourdas and L. G. Westerink, *Photii Patriarchae Constantinopolitani Epistulae et Amphilochia*, 3 vols. (Leipzig, 1983–1987).
Planoudes, Maximos, *Basilikos*, ed. L. Westerink, "Le basilikos de Maxime Planude," *BS* 27 (1966): 98–103; and 28 (1967): 54–67.
Prodromos, Theodoros, *Historical Poems*, ed. W. Hörandner, *Theodoros Prodromos: Historische Gedichte* (Vienna, 1974).
Prokopios, *Buildings, Secret History,* and *Wars;* ed. J. Haury, rev. G. Wirth, *Procopii Caesariensis opera omnia*, 4 vols. (Leipzig, 1962–1964); trans. H. B. Dewing, *Procopius*, 6 vols. (Cambridge, MA, 1914–1935); trans. A. Kaldellis, *Prokopios: The Secret History with Related Texts* (Indianapolis, 2010).
Psellos, Michael, *Letters S*, ed. K. N. Sathas, Μεσαιωνικὴ Βιβλιοθήκη, vol. 5 (Venice, 1876).
———, *Letters KD*, ed. E. Kurtz and F. Drexl, *Michaelis Pselli scripta minora*, vol. 2: *Epistulae* (Milan, 1941).
———, *Orationes forenses et acta*, ed. G. T. Dennis (Leipzig, 1994).
———, *Orationes panegyricae*, ed. G. T. Dennis, *Michelis Pselli Orationes panegyricae* (Leipzig, 1994).
———, *Chronographia*, ed. D. R. Reinsch, *Michelis Pselli Chronographia*, 2 vols. (Berlin, 2014); trans. E. R. A. Sewter, *Michael Psellus: Fourteen Byzantine Rulers* (London, 1966).
Pseudo-Sebeos, *History*, trans. R. W. Thomson, with notes by J. Howard-Johnston, *The Armenian History Attributed to Sebeos* (Liverpool, 1999).
Pseudo-Stephanos, *Horoscope of Islam*, ed. H. Usener, "De Stephano Alexandrino," in *Kleine Schriften*, vol. 3 (Leipzig, 1913), 247–322.
Pseudo-Symeon, *Chronicle*, ed. I. Bekker, *Theophanes Continuatus, Ioannes Cameniata, Symeon Magister, Georgius Monachus* (Bonn, 1838).
Robert the Monk, *History of the First Crusade*, ed. P. le Bas in *Recueil des historiens des Croisades: historiens occidentaux*, vol. 3 (Paris, 1866), 717–882; trans. C. Sweetenham (Farnham, UK, 2005).
Russian Primary Chronicle (Laurentian Text), trans. S. H. Cross and O. P. Sherbowitz-Wetzor (Cambridge, MA, 1953).
Sabas, *Life of Saint Petros of Atroa*, ed. V. Laurent, "La Vie merveilleuse de saint Pierre d'Atroa," *Subsidia hagiographica* 29 (1956): 65–225.
Sabbas, *Life of Saint Ioannikios*, ed. J. van den Gheyn, in *AASS Nov. II.1* (Brussels, 1894), 332–383.
Shabbatai Donnolo, *Sefer Hakhmoni*, ed. and trans. P. Mancuso (Leiden, 2010).
Skoutariotes, Theodoros, *Historical Synopsis*, ed. K. Sathas, Μεσαιωνικὴ Βιβλιοθήκη, vol. 7 (Venice, 1894).
Skylitzes Continuatus, ed. E. T. Tsolakis, Ἡ Συνέχεια τῆς χρονογραφίας τοῦ Ἰωάννου Σκυλίτζη *(Ioannes Skylitzes Continuatus)* (Thessalonike, 1968).
Skylitzes, Ioannes, *Synopsis of Histories*, ed. J. Thurn, *Ioannis Scylitzae Synopsis Historiarum* (Berlin, 1973); trans. J. Wortley, *John Skylitzes: A Synopsis of Byzantine History, 811–1057* (Cambridge, 2010).

Step'anos of Taron, *Universal History*, trans. H. Gelzer and A. Burckhardt, *Des Stephanos von Taron Armenische Geschichte* (Leipzig, 1907); trans. F. Macler, *Histoire universelle par Étienne Asołik de Tarôn* (Paris, 1917); trans. T. Greenwood, *The Universal History of Step'anos Taronec'i* (Oxford, 2017).
Stephanos of Byzantion, *Ethnika*, ed. M. Billerbeck, *Stephani Byzantii Ethnika*, 5 vols. (Berlin, 2006–).
Symeon Logothetes, *Chronicle*, ed. S. Wahlgren, *Symeonis Magistri et Logothetae Chronicon* (Berlin, 2006).
Synadinos, *Conseils et mémoires de Synadinos prêtre de Serrès en Macédoine (XVIIe siècle)*, ed. and trans. P. Odorico (Paris, 1996).
Synaxarion of Constantinople, ed. H. Delehaye, *Synaxarium ecclesiae Constantinopolitanae (e codice Sirmondiano nunc Berolinensi)* (Brussels, 1902).
Syrianos, *Rhetorica militaris*, ed. I. Eramo, *Siriano: Discorsi di guerra* (Bari, Italy, 2010).
Themistios, *Orations*, ed. G. Downey and A. F. Norman, *Themistii Orationes*, 2 vols. (Leipzig, 1951–1970); trans. P. Heather and D. Moncour, *Politics, Philosophy, and Empire in the Fourth Century: Select Orations of Themistius* (Liverpool, 2001).
Theodoretos of Kyrros, *Letters*, ed. Y. Azéma, *Théodoret de Cyr: Correspondance*, 3 vols. (Paris, 1955–1965).
Theodoros II Laskaris, *Letters*, ed. N. Festa, *Theodori Ducae Lascaris epistulae CCXVII* (Florence, 1898).
Theodoros Anagnostes, *Ecclesiastical History*, ed. C. Hansen, *Theodoros Anagnostes: Kirchengeschichte* (Berlin, 1971).
Theophanes Continuatus, ed. and trans. J. M. Featherstone and J. Signes Codoñer, *Chronographiae quae Theophanis Continuati nomine fertyur libri I–IV* (Berlin, 2015); book VI, ed. I. Bekker, *Theophanes Continuatus, Ioannes Cameniata, Symeon Magister, Georgius Monachus* (Bonn, 1838).
Theophanes the Confessor, *Chronographia*, ed. C. de Boor, *Theophanis Chronographia*, 2 vols. (Leipzig, 1883–1885); trans. C. Mango and R. Scott, *The Chronicle of Theophanes Confessor: Byzantine and Near Eastern History AD 284–813* (Oxford, 1997).
Theophylaktos of Ohrid, *Letters*, ed. and trans. P. Gautier, *Théophylacte d'Achrida: Lettres* (Thessalonike, 1986).
Theophylaktos Simokattes, *History*, ed. C. de Boor, rev. P. Wirth, *Theophylacti Simocattae Historiae* (Stuttgart, 1972); trans. M. Whitby and M. Whitby, *The History of Theophylact Simocatta* (Oxford, 1986).
Uberti, *Dittamondo*, ed. G. Corsi (Bari, Italy, 1952).
Vardan, *History*, trans. R. W. Thomson, "The Historical Compilation of Vardan Arewelc'i," *DOP* 43 (1989): 125–226.
Yahya of Antioch, *Chronicle*: (I) the years 937–969: ed. and trans. I. Kratchovsky and A. Vasiliev, *Histoire de Yahya*, in *Patrologia Orientalis* 18.5 (1924): 699–832; (II) the years 969–1013: ed. and trans. I. Kratchovsky and A. Vasiliev, in *Patrologia Orientalis* 23.3 (1932): 347–520; (III) the years 1013–1034: ed. I. Kratchovsky and trans. F. Michaeu and G. Trouppeau, in *Patrologia Orientalis* 47 (1997): 373–559; trans. B. Pirone, *Yaḥyā al Anṭākī:*

Cronache dell'Egitto Fāṭimide e dell'Impero Bizantino, 937–1033 (Milan, 1998).
Yovhannēs Drasxanakertc'i, *History of Armenia*, trans. K. H. Maksoudian (Atlanta, 1987).
Zonaras, Ioannes, *Chronicle*, ed. *PG* 134–135; ed. M. Pinder and T. Büttner-Wobst, *Ioannis Zonarae Epitomae historiarum*, 3 vols. (Berlin, 1841–1897).
———, *Commentary on the Canons of the Council in Troullo*, ed. G. A. Rallis and M. Potlis, Σύνταγμα τῶν ἱερῶν καὶ θείων κανόνων etc., vol. 2 (Athens, 1852).

Modern Scholarship

Adams, J. N., "'*Romanitas*' and the Latin Language," *Classical Quarterly* 53 (2004): 184–205.
Adontz, N., "L'age et l'origine de l'empereur Basile I (867–886)," *Byzantion* 8 (1933): 474–500; and 9 (1934): 223–260.
———, "Les Taronites en Arménie et à Byzance," *Byzantion* 9 (1934): 715–738; 10 (1935): 531–551; and 11 (1936): 21–42.
———, *Études arméno-byzantines* (Lisbon, 1965).
———, *Armenia in the Period of Justinian: The Political Conditions based on the Naxarar System*, trans. N. G. Garsoïan (Lisbon, 1970).
Agapitos, P., "Ἡ εἰκόνα τοῦ αὐτοκράτορα Βασιλείου Α΄ στὴ φιλομακεδονικὴ γραμματεία, 867–959," *Hellenika* 40 (1989): 285–322.
Ahrweiler, H., "Les termes Τσάκωνες—Τσακονίαι et leur évolution sémantique," *REB* 21 (1963): 243–249.
———, "Citoyens et étrangers dans l'Empire romain d'Orient," in *La nozione di "Romano" tra cittadinanza e universalità, Atti del Seminario, 21–23 aprile 1982* (Naples, 1984 = *Da Roma alla Terza Roma: Studi* 2): 343–350.
———, "Byzantine Concepts of the Foreigner: The Case of the Nomads," in H. Ahrweiler and A. Laiou, eds., *Studies on the Internal Diaspora of the Byzantine Empire* (Washington, DC, 1998), 1–15.
Alexander, P., "The Strength of Empire and Capital as Seen through Byzantine Eyes," *Speculum* 37 (1962): 339–357.
Anagnostakis, I., "Ελλαδικά παραμύθια και ελλαδική παραμυθία στο Βυζάντιο του 10ου αι.," in *Ελιά και Λάδι, Δ΄ Τριήμερο Εργασίας* (Athens, 1996), 121–150.
———, "Η Σολομώντεια αμφιθυμία των πρώτων Μακεδόνων αυτοκρατόρων και οι αποκαλυπτικές καταβολές της," in A. Lampropoulou and K. Tsiknakis, eds., *Η εβραϊκή παρουσία στον ελλαδικό χώρο (4ος–19ος αιώνας)* (Athens, 2008), 39–60.
———, "Μονεμβασία-Λακεδαίμων: Για μια τυπολογία αντιπαλότητας και για την Κυριακή αργία στις πόλεις," in T. Kiousopoulou, ed., *Οι βυζαντινές πόλεις, 8ος–15ος αιώνας: Προοπτικές της έρευνας και νέες ερμηνευτικές προσεγγίσεις* (Rethymno, Greece, 2012), 101–137.
———, "Byzantium and Hellas: Some Lesser Known Aspects of the Helladic Connection (8th–12th c)," in E. Albani et al., eds., *Heaven & Earth*, vol. 2: *Cities and Countryside in Byzantine Greece* (Athens, 2013), 15–29.

———, "'From Tempe to Sparta': Power and Contestation prior to the Latin Conquest of 1204," in A. Simpson, ed., *Byzantium, 1180–1204: "The Sad Quarter of a Century"?* (Athens, 2015), 135–157.

Anagnostakis, I., and A. Kaldellis, "The Textual Sources for the Peloponnese, A.D. 582–959: Their Creative Engagement with Ancient Literature," *GRBS* 54 (2014): 105–135.

Anagnostou, Y., "A Critique of Symbolic Ethnicity: The Ideology of Choice?," *Ethnicities* 9 (2009): 94–140.

Anderson, G. D., "Islamic Spaces and Diplomacy in Constantinople (Tenth to Thirteenth Centuries C.E.)," *Medieval Encounters* 15 (2009): 86–113.

Ando, C., *Imperial Ideology and Provincial Loyalty in the Roman Empire* (Berkeley, CA, 2000).

———, "Decline, Fall, and Transformation," *Journal of Late Antiquity* 1 (2008): 30–60.

———, "From Republic to Empire," in M. Peachin, ed., *Oxford Handbook of Social Relations in the Roman World* (Oxford, 2011), 37–66.

———, *Law, Language and Empire in the Roman Tradition* (Philadelphia, 2011).

———, "Empire, State and Communicative Action," in C. Kuhn, ed., *Politische Kommunikation und öffentliche Meinung in der antiken Welt* (Stuttgart, 2012), 219–229.

———, *Imperial Rome, AD 193 to 284: The Critical Century* (Edinburgh, 2012).

———, *Roman Social Imaginaries: Language and Thought in Contexts of Empire* (Toronto, 2015).

———, ed., *Citizenship and Empire in Europe 200–1900: The Antonine Constitution after 1800 Years* (Stuttgart, 2016).

———, "Introduction. Sovereignty, Territoriality and Universalism in the Aftermath of Caracalla," in C. Ando, ed., *Citizenship and Empire in Europe: The Antonine Constitution after 1800 Years* (Stuttgart, 2016), 7–27.

———, "Empire as State: The Roman Case," in J. Brooke et al., eds., *State Formations: Histories and Cultures of Statehood* (Cambridge, 2018), 175–189.

Andrews, P. A., ed., *Ethnic Groups in the Republic of Turkey* (Wiesbaden, 1989).

Andrews, T. L., "Identity, Philosophy, and the Problem of Armenian History in the Sixth Century," in P. Wood, ed., *History and Identity in the Late Antique Near East* (Oxford, 2013), 29–41.

Angelov, D., *Imperial Ideology and Political Thought in Byzantium, 1204–1330* (Cambridge, 2007).

———, "Three Kinds of Liberty as Political Ideals in Byzantium, Twelfth to Fifteenth Centuries," in *Proceedings of the 22nd International Congress of Byzantine Studies*, vol. 1: *Plenary Sessions* (Sofia, Bulgaria, 2011), 311–331.

Angelov, P., "The Byzantines as Imagined by the Medieval Bulgarians," in V. Gjuzelev and K. Petkov, eds., *State and Church: Studies in Medieval Bulgaria and Byzantium* (Sofia, Bulgaria, 2011), 47–81.

Angold, M., "Byzantine 'Nationalism' and the Nicaean Empire," *BMGS* 1 (1975): 49–70.

———, *Byzantium: The Bridge from Antiquity to the Middle Ages* (London, 2001).

———, "The Venetian Chronicles and Archives as Sources for the History of Byzantium and the Crusades (992–1204)," in M. Whitby, ed., *Byzantines and Crusaders in Non-Greek Sources, 1025–1204* (Oxford, 2007), 59–94.
Antonaccio, C., "(Re)Defining Ethnicity: Culture, Material Culture, and Identity," in S. Hales and T. Hodoes, eds., *Material Culture and Social Identities in the Ancient World* (Cambridge, 2010), 32–53.
Arnold, B., *Medieval Germany, 500–1300: A Political Interpretation* (Toronto, 1997).
Arutjunova-Fidanjan, V. A., "Some Aspects of the Military-Administrative Districts and of Byzantine Administration in Armenia during the 11th Century," *REA* 20 (1986–1987): 309–320.
———, "The Ethno-Confessional Self-Awareness of Armenian Chalcedonians," *REA* 21 (1988–1989): 345–363.
———, "The New Socio-Administrative Structure in the East of Byzantium," *Byzantinische Forschungen* 19 (1993): 79–86.
Atiya, A. S., and Y. Abd al-Masih, ed. and trans., *History of the Patriarchs of the Egyptian Church, Known as the History of the Holy Church of Sawirus ibn al-Mukaffac, Bishop of al-Asmunin*, vol. 2, pt. 3 (Cairo, 1959).
Auzépy, M.-F., *L'histoire des iconoclastes* (Paris, 2007).
Avramea, A., Ἡ βυζαντινὴ Θεσσαλία μέχρι τοῦ 1204 (Athens, 1974).
———, "Ὁ τζάσις τῶν Μεληγγῶν: Νέα ἀνάγνωσις ἐπιγραφῶν ἐξ Οἰτύλου," *Parnassos* 16.2 (1974): 288–300.
Ayvazyan, A., *The Armenian Military in the Byzantine Empire: Conflict and Alliance under Justinian and Maurice* (Alfortville, France, 2012).
Balard, M., "Amalfi et Byzance (Xe–XIIe siècle)," *TM* 6 (1976): 85–95.
Balard, M., et al., eds., *Byzance et le monde extérieure: Contacts, relations, échanges* (Paris, 2005).
Bang, P., C. A. Bayly, and W. Scheidel, eds., *The Oxford World History of Empire* (Oxford, forthcoming).
Barbero, A., *Barbari: immigrati, profughi, deportati nell'Impero romano* (Rome, 2006).
Barfield, T., "Imperial State Formation along the Chinese-Nomad Frontier," in S. Alcock et al., eds., *Empires: Perspectives from Archaeology and History* (Cambridge, 2001), 10–41.
Barkey, Karen, *Empire of Difference: The Ottomans in Comparative Perspective* (Cambridge, 2008).
Barnes, T. D., *Athanasius and Constantius: Theology and Politics in the Constantinian Empire* (Cambridge, MA, 1993).
Bartikian, H., Αρμενοβυζαντινά: Σχέσεις του αρμενικού έθνους με το μεσαιωνικό ελληνισμό (Ιστορικές Συμβολές) (Thessalonike, 2007).
Barzos, K., Ἡ γενεαλογία τῶν Κομνηνῶν, 2 vols. (Thessalonike, 1984).
Basilikopoulou, A., "Ἡ πάτριος φωνή," in N. G. Moschonas, ed., Ἡ ἐπικοινωνία στὸ Βυζάντιο (Athens, 1993), 103–113.
Bauer, W., trans., and W. F. Arndt and F. W. Gingrich, eds., *A Greek-English Lexicon of the New Testament and Other Early Christian Literature* (Chicago, 1957).
Beaton, R., *The Medieval Greek Romance* (London, 1996).

Beck, H.-G., *Res Publica Romana: Vom Staatsdenken der Byzantiner* (Munich, 1970).
———, *Das byzantinische Jahrtausend* (Munich, 1978).
———, trans., *Der Vater der deutschen Byzantinistik: Das Leben des Hieronymus Wolf von ihm selbst Erzäht* (Munich, 1984).
Bedford, P. R., "The Neo-Assyrian Empire," in I. Morris and W. Scheidel, eds., *The Dynamics of Ancient Empires: State Power from Assyria to Byzantium* (Oxford, 2009), 30–64.
Benninghaus, R., "The Laz: An Example of Multiple Identification," in P. A. Andrews, ed., *Ethnic Groups in the Republic of Turkey* (Wiesbaden, 1989), 497–502.
Ben-Tov, A., *Lutheran Humanists and Greek Antiquity: Melanchthonian Scholarship between Universal History and Pedagogy* (Leiden, 2009).
Berger, S., and A. Miller, "Building Nations in and with Empires—A Reassessment," in S. Berger and A. Miller, eds., *Nationalizing Empires* (Budapest, 2014), 1–30.
Bertrand, J.-M., "Langue grecque et administration romaine: de l'ἐπαρχεία τῶν Ῥωμαίων à l'ἐπαρχεία τῶν Θρακῶν," *Ktéma: civilisation de l'Orient, de la Grèce et de Rome antiques* 7 (1982): 167–175.
Biliarsky, I., "Some Observations on the Administrative Terminology of the Second Bulgarian Empire (13th–14th Centuries)," in J. Shepard, ed., *The Expansion of Orthodox Europe: Byzantium, the Balkans and Russia* (Aldershot, UK, 2007), 327–347.
Birley, A., *Septimius Severus: The African Emperor* (New Haven, CT, 1988).
Blaum, P. A., "Diplomacy Gone to Seed: A History of Byzantine Foreign Relations, A.D. 1047–57," *International Journal of Kurdish Studies* 18 (2004): 1–56.
Blöndal, S., *The Varangians of Byzantium*, trans. B. S. Benedikz (Cambridge, 1978).
Bonfil, R., *History and Folklore in a Medieval Jewish Chronicle: The Family Chronicle of Ahima'az ben Paltiel* (Leiden, 2009).
Bonfil, R., et al., eds., *Jews in Byzantium: Dialectics of Minority and Majority Cultures* (Leiden, 2012).
Bosworth, C. E., *The Arabs, Byzantium and Iran: Studies in Early Islamic History and Culture* (London, 1996).
Bouraselis, K., *ΘΕΙΑ ΔΩΡΕΑ: Μελέτες πάνω στὴν πολιτικὴ τῆς δυναστείας τῶν Σεβήρων καὶ τὴν Constitutio Antoniniana* (Athens, 1989).
Bowman, S., "Survival in Decline: Romaniote Jewry post-1204," in R. Bonfil et al., eds., *Jews in Byzantium: Dialectics of Minority and Majority Cultures* (Leiden, 2012), 102–131.
Brand, C., "The Turkish Element in Byzantium, 11th–12th Centuries," *DOP* 43 (1989): 1–25.
Braund, D., *Rome and the Friendly King: The Character of Client Kingship* (New York, 1984).
Brightman, F. E., *Liturgies Eastern and Western* (Oxford, 1896).
Brubaker, L., "The *Christian Topography* (Vat. gr. 699) Revisited: Image, Text, and Conflict in Ninth-Century Byzantium," in E. Jeffreys, ed., *Byzan-*

tine Style, Religion and Civilization: In Honour of Sir Steven Runciman (Cambridge, 2006), 3–24.
Brubaker, L., and J. Haldon, *Byzantium in the Iconoclast Era, c. 680–850: A History* (Cambridge, 2011).
Brubaker, R., M. Loveman, and P. Stamatov, "Ethnicity as Cognition," *Theory and Society* 33 (2004): 31–64.
Brubaker, W., "Immigration, Citizenship, and the Nation-State in France and Germany: A Comparative Historical Analysis," *International Sociology* 5 (1990): 379–407.
Bryce, T., *Life and Society in the Hittite World* (Oxford, 2002).
Bryer, A., "Some Notes on the Laz and Tzan," *Bedi Karthlisa: Revue de karthvélologie* 21–22 (1966): 174–195; and 23–24 (1967): 161–168.
Buell, D. K., *Why This New Race: Ethnic Reasoning in Early Christianity* (New York, 2005).
Burbank, J., and F. Cooper, *Empires in World History: Power and Politics of Difference* (Princeton, NJ, 2010).
Burgmann, L., "Byzantinische Rechtslexika," *Fontes Minores* 2 (1977): 87–146.
Bury, J. B., *A History of the Later Roman Empire from Arcadius to Irene* (London, 1889).
———, "Introduction," *Cambridge Medieval History*, vol. 4: *The Eastern Roman Empire* (Cambridge, 1923), vii–xiv.
Cameron, Alan, *Circus Factions: Blues and Greens at Rome and Byzantium* (Oxford, 1976).
Cameron, Averil, *The Byzantines* (Oxford, 2006).
———, *Byzantine Matters* (Princeton, NJ, 2014).
Canard, M., "Les aventures d'un prisonnier arabe et d'un patrice byzantine à l'époque des guerres bulgaro-byzantines," *DOP* 9 (1956): 49–72.
Canepa, M. P., *The Two Eyes of the Earth: Art and Ritual of Kingship between Rome and Sasanian Iran* (Berkeley, CA, 2009).
Carabellese, F., *L'Apulia ed il suo comune nell' alto medio evo* (Bari, Italy, 1905).
Caratzas, S. C., *Les Tzacones* (Berlin, 1976).
Carrier, M., "L'Autre à l'époque des croisades: les Byzantins vus par les chroniqueurs du monde latin (1096–1261)" (PhD thesis, Université de Montréal, published online by the Éditions universitaires européennes, 2012).
Chandler, R., *Travels in Greece* (Oxford, 1776).
Chandra, K., ed., *Constructivist Theories of Ethnic Politics* (Oxford, 2012).
Charanis, P., *Armenians in the Byzantine Empire* (Lisbon, 1963).
———, *Studies on the Demography of the Byzantine Empire: Collected Studies* (London, 1972).
Cheynet, J.-C., *Pouvoir et contestations à Byzance (963–1210)* (Paris, 1996).
———, "Théophile, Théophobe et les Perses," in S. Lambakis, ed., *Η Βυζαντινή Μικρά Ασία (6ος–12ος αι.)* (Athens, 1998), 39–50.
———, *Sceaux de la collection Zacos (Bibliothèque nationale de France) se rapportant aux provinces orientales de l'Empire byzantin* (Paris, 2001).
———, *The Byzantine Aristocracy and Its Military Function* (London, 2006).
———, "The Duchy of Antioch during the Second Period of Byzantine Rule," in K. Ciggaar and M. Metcalf, eds., *East and West in the Medieval Eastern*

Mediterranean, vol. 1: *Antioch from the Byzantine Reconquest until the End of the Crusader Principality* (Leuven, 2006), 1–16.

———, *La société byzantine: l'apport des sceaux*, 2 vols. (Paris, 2008).

———, "Les Arméniens dans l'armée byzantine au Xe siècle," *TM* 18 (2014): 175–192.

———, "Les Génésioi," in T. Antonopoulou, S. Kotzabassi, and M. Loukaki, eds., *Myriobiblos: Essays on Byzantine Literature and Culture* (Berlin, 2015), 71–83.

Chitwood, Z., *Byzantine Legal Culture and the Roman Legal Tradition, 867–1056* (Cambridge, 2017).

Chrissis, N. G., "Ideological and Political Contestations in Post-1204 Byzantium: The Orations of Niketas Choniates and the Imperial Court of Nicaea," in S. Tougher, ed., *The Emperor in the Byzantine World* (London, forthcoming).

Christides, V., *The Image of the Pre-Islamic Arab in the Byzantine Sources* (Princeton, NJ, 1970).

Christophilopoulou, Ai., *Τὸ πολίτευμα καὶ οἱ θεσμοὶ τῆς βυζαντινῆς αὐτοκρατορίας, 324–1204* (Athens, 2004).

Chrysos, E., "Der Kaiser und die Könige," in H. Wolfram and F. Daim, eds., *Die Völker an der mittleren und unteren Donau im fünften und sechsten Jahrhundert* (Vienna, 1980).

———, "The Roman Political Identity in Late Antiquity and Early Byzantium," in K. Fledelius, ed., *Byzantium: Identity, Image, Influence (Major Papers)* (Copenhagen, 1996), 7–16.

———, "Das byzantinische Reich: Ein Imperium *par excellence*," in M. Gehler and R. Rollinger, eds., *Imperien und Reiche in der Weltgeschichte: epochenübergreifende und globalhistorische Vergleiche*, vol. 1: *Imperien des Altertums, mittelalterliche und frühneuzeitliche Imperien* (Wiesbaden, 2014), 621–634.

Ciggaar, K. N., "Une description de Constantinople dans le *Tarragonensis 55*," *REB* 53 (1995): 117–140.

———, *Western Travellers to Constantinople. The West and Byzantium, 962–1204: Cultural and Political Relations* (Leiden, 1996).

Clackson, J., *Language and Society in the Greek and Roman Worlds* (Cambridge, 2015).

Cline, E. H., and M. W. Graham, *Ancient Empires from Mesopotamia to the Rise of Islam* (Cambridge, 2011).

Conant, J., *Staying Roman: Conquest and Identity in Africa and the Mediterranean, 439–700* (Cambridge, 2012).

Connelly, C., "Contesting the Greek Past in Ninth-Century Baghdad" (PhD dissertation, Harvard University, 2016).

Cooper, J. E., and M. J. Decker, *Life and Society in Byzantine Cappadocia* (New York, 2012).

Crone, P., *The Nativist Prophets of Early Islamic Iran: Rural Revolt and Local Zoroastrianism* (Cambridge, 2012).

Cumont, F., *Chroniques byzantines du manuscrit 11376* (Ghent, 1894).

Cupane, C., "'Η τῶν 'Ρωμαίων γλῶσσα," in K. Belke et al., eds., *Byzantina Mediterranea: Festschrift für Johannes Koder zum 65. Geburtstag* (Vienna, 2007), 137–156.
Curta, F., *Southeastern Europe in the Middle Ages, 500–1250* (Cambridge, 2006).
——, *The Edinburgh History of the Greeks, c. 500 to 1050: The Early Middle Ages* (Edinburgh, 2011).
——, "Linear Frontiers in the 9th Century: Bulgaria and Wessex," *Quaestiones Medii Aevi Novae* (2011): 15–32.
——, "Medieval Archaeology and Ethnicity: Where Are We?," *History Compass* 9.7 (2011): 537–548.
——, "Burial in Early Medieval Greece: On Ethnicity in Byzantine Archaeology," in B. Borisov, ed., *Prof d-r Boris Borisov uchenici I priiateli* (Veliko Tărnovo, Bulgaria, 2016), 419–448.
——, "Constantinople and the Echo Chamber: The Vlachs in the French Crusade Chronicles," *Medieval Encounters* 22 (2016): 427–462.
Curty, O., *Les parentés légendaires entre cités grecques: catalogue raisonnée des inscriptions contenant le terme ΣΥΓΓΕΝΕΙΑ et analyse critique* (Geneva, 1995).
Dagron, G., "Aux origines de la civilization byzantine: Langue de culture et langue d'État," *Revue historique* 241 (1969): 23–56.
——, "Minorités ethniques et religieuses dans l'Orient byzantin à la fin du Xe et au XIe siècle: l'immigration syrienne," *TM* 6 (1976): 177–216.
——, *Constantinople Imaginaire: études sur le recueil des "Patria"* (Paris, 1984).
——, "Formes et fonctions du pluralisme linguistique à Byzance (IXe–XIIe siècle)," *TM* 12 (1994): 219–240.
Dagron, G., and D. Feissel, "Inscriptions inédités du Musée d'Antioche," *TM* 9 (1985): 421–461.
Dagron, G., and H. Mihăescu, *Le traité sur la guérilla (De velitatione) de l'empereur Nicéphore Phocas (963–969)* (Paris, 1986).
Dain, A., "Une formule d'affranchissement d'esclave," *REB* 22 (1964): 238–240.
Dark, K., and F. Özgümüş, *Constantinople: Archaeology of a Byzantine Megapolis: Final Repors on the Istanbul Rescue Archaeology Project 1998–2004* (Oxford, 2013).
Darwin, J., *After Tamerlane: The Rise and Fall of Global Empires, 1400–2000* (New York, 2008).
Dasoulas, F. G., "Οι μεσαιωνικές κοινωνίες των Βλάχων," *Βαλκανικά Σύμμεικτα* 16 (2014): 7–40.
de Boel, G., "L'identité 'romaine' dans le roman *Digénis Akritis*," in H. Hokwerda, ed., *Constructions of Greek Past: Identity and Historical Consciousness from Antiquity to the Present* (Groningen, The Netherlands, 2003), 157–183.
Dédéyan, G., "L'immigration arménienne en Cappadoce au XIe siècle," *Byzantion* 45 (1975): 41–117.
——, "Les Arméniens en Cappadoce aux Xe et XIe siècles," in C. D. Fonseca, ed., *Le aree omogenee della Civiltà Rupestre nell'ambito dell'Impero Bizantino: La Cappadocia* (Lecce, Italy, 1981), 75–95.
——, "Mleh le Grand, stratège du Lykandos," *REA* 15 (1981): 73–102.

de Lange, N., "Hebrews, Greeks or Romans? Jewish Culture and Identity in Byzantium," in D. C. Smythe, ed., *Strangers to Themselves: The Byzantine Outsider* (Aldershot, UK, 2000), 105–117.

Dench, E., *Romulus' Asylum: Roman Identities from the Age of Alexander to the Age of Hadrian* (Oxford, 2005).

Détorakis, T., and J. Mossay, "Un office inédit pour ceux qui sont morts à la guerre, dans le Cod. Sin. Gr. 734–735," *Le Muséon: Revue des études orientales* 101 (1988): 183–211.

De Vos, G., "Ethnic Pluralism: Conflict and Accommodation," in G. De Vos and L. Romanucci-Ross, eds., *Ethnic Identity: Creation, Conflict and Accommodation*, 3rd ed. (London, 1995), 5–41.

de Waal, T., *The Caucasus* (Oxford, 2010).

Ditten, H., "Prominente Slawen und Bulgaren in byzantinischen Diensten (Ende des 7. bis Anfang des 10. Jahrhunderts)," in H. Köpstein and F. Winkelmann, eds., *Studien zum 8. und 9. Jh. in Byzanz* (Berlin, 1983), 95–119.

———, *Ethnische Verschiebungen zwischen der Balkanhalbinsel und Kleinasien vom Ende des 6. bis zur zweiten Hälfte des 9. Jahrhunderts* (Berlin, 1993).

Doane, A. W., "Dominant Group Ethnic Identity in the United States: The Role of 'Hidden' Ethnicity in Intergroup Relations," *Sociological Quarterly* 38.3 (1997): 375–397.

Dölger, F., *Byzanz und die europäische Staatenwelt* (Ettal, Germany, 1953).

Doyle, M. W., *Empires* (Ithaca, NY, 1986).

Ducellier, A., *L'Albanie entre Byzance et Venise, Xe–XVe siècles* (London, 1987).

Dunn, M., "Evangelization or Repentance? The Re-Christianization of the Peloponnese in the Ninth and Tenth Centuries," *Studies in Church History* 14 (1977): 71–86.

Durak, K., "Who Are the Romans? The Definition of *Bilad al-Rum* (Land of the Romans) in Medieval Islamic Geographies," *Journal of Intercultural Studies* 31 (2010): 285–298.

Dvoichenko-Markov, D., "The Vlachs: The Latin Speaking Population of Eastern Europe," *Byzantion* 54 (1984): 508–526.

Eagleman, D., *Incognito: The Secret Lives of the Brain* (New York, 2011).

Edwards, C., and G. Woolf, eds., *Rome the Cosmopolis* (Cambridge, 2003).

Eger, A. A., *The Islamic-Byzantine Frontier: Interaction and Exchange among Muslims and Christian Communities* (London, 2015).

Ekonomou, A. J., *Byzantine Rome and the Greek Popes: Eastern Influences on Rome and the Papacy from Gregory the Great to Zacharias, AD 590–752* (Lanham, MD, 2007).

El Cheikh, N., *Byzantium Viewed by the Arabs* (Cambridge, MA, 2004).

El-Huni, A. A., "The Poetry of Ibn al-Rùmî" (PhD dissertation, University of Glasgow, 1996).

El Tayib, A., "Abū Firās al-Ḥamdānī," in J. Ashtiany et al., eds., *Abbasid Belles-Lettres* (Cambridge, 1990), 315–327.

Falkenhausen, V. von, "The Jews of Byzantine Southern Italy," in R. Bonfil et al., eds., *Jews in Byzantium: Dialectics of Minority and Majority Cultures* (Leiden, 2012), 272–296.

Fanning, S., "Imperial Diplomacy between Francia and Byzantium: The Letter of Louis II to Basil I in 871," *Cithara* 34 (1994): 3–17.
Farney, G. D., *Ethnic Identity and Aristocratic Competition in Republican Rome* (Cambridge, 2007).
Ficker, G., *Erlasse des Patriarchen von Konstantinopel Alexios Studites* (Kiel, Germany, 1911).
Figes, O., *Crimea: The Last Crusade* (London, 2011).
Fine, J. V. A., Jr., *The Early Medieval Balkans: A Critical Survey from the Sixth to the Late Twelfth Century* (Ann Arbor, MI, 1993).
Fisher, E., "Alexios of Byzantium and the Apocalypse of Daniel: A Tale of Kings, Wars and Translators," in S. Dogan and M. Kadiroglu, eds., *Bizans ve Cevre Kültürler/Byzantium and the Surrounding Cultures (Festschrift in Honor of S. Yildiz Ötüken)* (Istanbul, 2010), 177–185.
Fisher, G., *Between Empires: Arabs, Romans, and Sassanians in Late Antiquity* (Oxford, 2011).
Flower, H. I., *Roman Republics* (Princeton, NJ, 2010).
Folz, R., *The Concept of Empire in Western Europe from the Fifth to the Fourteenth Century*, trans. S. A. Oglivie (London, 1969).
Forrai, R., "The Sacred Nectar of the Deceitful Greeks: Perceptions of Greekness in Ninth Century Rome," in A. Speer and P. Steinkrüger, eds., *Knotenpunkt Byzanz: Wissensformen und kulturelle Wechselbeziehungen* (Berlin, 2012), 71–84.
Fowden, G., "Gibbon on Islam," *English Historical Review* 131 (2016): 261–292.
Fox, C. R., "What, If Anything, Is a Byzantine?," *Celator* 10 (1996), http://www.romanity.org/htm/fox.01.en.what_if_anything_is_a_byzantine.01.htm.
Franklin, S., "The Empire of the Rhomaioi as Viewed from Kievan Russia: Aspects of Byzantino-Russian Cultural Relations," *Byzantion* 53 (1983): 507–537.
Frary, L. J., *Russia and the Making of Modern Greek Identity, 1821–1844* (Oxford, 2015).
Fraser, P. M., *Greek Ethnic Terminology* (Oxford, 2009).
Freeman, E. A., *Historical Essays* (London, 1879).
Gans, H., "Symbolic Ethnicity: The Future of Ethnic Groups and Cultures in America," *Ethnic and Racial Studies* 2 (1979): 1–20.
Gantner, C., "The Label 'Greeks' in the Papal Diplomatic Repertoire in the Eighth Century," in W. Pohl and G. Heydemann, eds., *Post-Roman Transitions: Christian and Barbarian Identities in the Early Medieval West* (Turnhout, 2013), 303–349.
Garitte, G., "La vision de S. Sahak en grec," *Le Muséon* 71 (1958): 255–278.
Garsoïan, N., *The Paulician Heresy: A Study of the Origin and Development of Paulicianism in Armenia and the Eastern Provinces of the Byzantine Empire* (The Hague, 1967).
———, "The Problem of Armenian Integration into the Byzantine Empire," in H. Ahrweiler and A. E. Laiou, eds., *Studies on the Internal Diaspora of the Byzantine Empire* (Washington, DC, 1998), 53–124.

———, "Armenian Historiography in Crisis," in C. Straw and R. Lim, eds., *The Past before Us: The Challenge of Historiographies of Late Antiquity* (Turnhout, 2004), 49–60.
Gasparis, Ch., ed., Οι Αλβανοί στον Μεσαίωνα (Athens, 1998).
Geanakoplos, D. J., *Greek Scholars in Venice: Studies in the Dissemination of Greek Learning from Byzantium to Western Europe* (Cambridge, MA, 1962).
Gelzer, H., "Ungedruckte und wenig bekannte Bistumsverzeichnisse der orientalischen Kirchen," *BZ* 2 (1893): 22–72.
Gibbon, E., *The History of the Decline and Fall of the Roman Empire*, ed. D. Womersley, 3 vols. (London, 1994).
Gil-White, Francisco J., "How Thick Is Blood? The Plot Thickens . . . : If Ethnic Actors Are Promordialists, What Remains of the Circumstantialist/Primordialist Controversy?," *Ethnic and Racial Studies* 22 (1999): 789–820.
Gjuzelev, V., "L'empereur byzantine Manuel Ier Comnène à la lumière de quelques nouvelles sources et opinions," in K. Nikolaou and K. Tsiknakis, eds., Βυζάντιο και Βούλγαροι *(1018–1185)* (Athens, 2008), 141–151.
Goitein, S. D., "A Letter from Seleucia (Cilicia): Dated 21 July 1137," *Speculum* 39 (1964): 298–303.
Goldstone, J. A., and J. F. Haldon, "Ancient States, Empires, and Exploitation: Problems and Perspectives," in I. Morris and W. Scheidel, eds., *The Dynamics of Ancient Empires: State Power from Assyria to Byzantium* (Oxford, 2009), 3–29.
Goodblatt, D., *Elements of Ancient Jewish Nationalism* (Cambridge, 2006).
Grdzelidze, T., *Georgian Monks on Mount Athos: Two Eleventh-Century Lives of the Hegoumenoi of Iviron* (London, 2009).
Greatrex, G., "Roman Identity in the Sixth Century," in S. Mitchell and G. Greatrex, eds., *Ethnicity and Culture in Late Antiquity* (London, 2000), 267–292.
Greenwood, T., "Armenian Neighbors (600–1045)," in J. Shepard, ed., *The Cambridge History of the Byzantine Empire, c. 500–1492* (Cambridge, 2008), 333–364.
Grégoire, H., "Le lieu de naissance de Romain Lécapène et de Digénis Acritas," *Byzantion* 8 (1933): 572–574.
Griffith, S. H., *The Church in the Shadow of the Mosque: Christians and Muslims in the World of Islam* (Princeton, NJ, 2008).
Grousset, R., *Histoire de l'Arménie, des origines à 1071* (Paris, 1947).
Gutas, D., *Greek Thought, Arabic Culture: The Graeco-Arabic Translation Movement in Baghdad and Early 'Abbasid Society (2nd–4th / 8th–10th Centuries)* (London, 1998).
Haldon, J. F., *Recruitment and Conscription in the Byzantine Army, c. 550–950* (Vienna, 1979).
———, *Byzantium in the Seventh Century: The Transformation of a Culture* (Cambridge, 1993).
———, "Military Service, Military Lands, and the Status of Soldiers: Current Problems and Interpretations," *DOP* 47 (1993): 1–67.

———, *Warfare, State and Society in the Byzantine World, 565–1204* (London, 1999).
———, "Theory and Practice in Tenth-Century Military Administration: Chapters II, 44 and 45 of the *Book of Ceremonies*," *TM* 13 (2000): 201–352.
———, "Humour and the Everyday in Byzantium," in G. Halsall, ed., *Humour, History and Politics in Late Antiquity and the Early Middle Ages* (Cambridge, 2004), 48–73.
———, "The Byzantine Empire," in I. Morris and W. Scheidel, eds., *The Dynamics of Ancient Empires: State Power from Assyria to Byzantium* (Oxford, 2009), 205–253.
———, "Comparative State Formation: The Later Roman Empire in the Wider World," in S. F. Johnson, ed., *The Oxford Handbook of Late Antiquity* (Oxford, 2012), 1111–1147.
———, *The Empire That Would Not Die: The Paradox of Eastern Roman Survival, 640–740* (Cambridge, MA, 2016).
Hall, J. M., *Ethnic Identity in Greek Antiquity* (Cambridge, 1997).
Hammer, D., "Russia and Roman Law," *American Slavic and East European Review* 16.1 (1957): 1–16.
Hänssler, F., *Byzanz und Byzantiner: Ihr Bild im Spiegel der Überliefrung der germanischen Reiche im früheren Mittelalter* (Bern, 1960).
Harrill, J. A., *Paul the Apostle: His Life and Legacy in Their Roman Context* (Cambridge, 2012).
Harris, J., *The Lost World of Byzantium* (New Haven, CT, 2015).
Harris, W. V., *Roman Power: A Thousand Years of Empire* (Cambridge, 2016).
Heather, P., *The Fall of the Roman Empire: A New History* (London, 2005).
———, *Empires and Barbarians: Migration, Development and the Birth of Europe* (London, 2009).
Heather, P., and D. Moncour, *Politics, Philosophy and Empire in the Fourth Century: Select Orations of Themistius* (Liverpool, 2001).
Hendy, M. F., *Studies in the Byzantine Monetary Economy, c. 300–1450* (Cambridge, 1985).
Herrin, J., "Aspects of the Process of Hellenization in the Early Middle Ages," *Annual of the British School at Athens* 68 (1973): 113–126.
Herrin, J., *Margins and Metropolis: Authority across the Byzantine Empire* (Princeton, NJ, 2013).
Hewsen, R. H., *Armenia: A Historical Atlas* (Chicago, 2001).
Hild, F., and M. Restle, *Kappadokien* (= *Tabula Imperii Byzantini*, vol. 2) (Vienna, 1981).
Holl, K., "Das Fortleben der Volkssprachen in Kleinasien in Nachchristlicher Zeit," *Hermes* 43 (1908): 240–254.
Holmes, C., "'How the East Was Won' in the Reign of Basil II," in A. Eastmond, ed., *Eastern Approaches to Byzantium* (Aldershot, UK, 2001), 41–56.
———, *Basil II and the Governance of Empire (976–1025)* (Oxford, 2005).
Holo, J., *Byzantine Jewry in the Mediterranean Economy* (Cambridge, 2009).
———, "Both Byzantine and Jewish? The Extent and Limits of Jewish Integration in Middle Byzantine Society," in B. Crostini and S. La Porta, eds.,

Negotiating Co-Existing: Communities, Cultures and Convivencia in Byzantine Society (Trier, Germany, 2013), 189–202.
Holt, T., *Meadowland* (London, 2005).
Hondridou, S., "Η ενσωμάτωση της Βουλγαρικής ηγετικής τάξης στο βυζαντινο κρατικό μηχανισμό και το παρασκήνιο της τακτικής αυτής από το 1018 έως το τέλος περίπου του 11ου αιώνα," in K. Nikolaou and K. Tsiknakis, eds., *Βυζάντιο και Βούλγαροι (1018–1185)* (Athens, 2008), 111–120.
Horst, L., *Des Metropoliten Elias von Nisibis Buch vom Beweis der Wahrheit des Glaubens* (Colmar, Germany, 1886).
Hoyland, R. G., *Theophilus of Edessa's Chronicle and the Circulation of Historical Knowledge in Late Antiquity and Early Islam* (Liverpool, 2011).
Hunger, H., *Graeculus perfidus, Ἰταλὸς ἰταμός: Il senso dell'alterità nei rapporti Greco-Romani ed Italo-Bizantini* (Rome, 1987).
Huxley, G., "The Historical Geography of the Paulician and T'ondrakian Heresies," in T. J. Samuelian and M. E. Stone, eds., *Medieval Armenian Culture* (Chico, CA, 1982), 81–95.
Inglebert, H, "Christian Reflections on Roman Citizenship (200–430)," in C. Ando, ed., *Citizenship and Empire in Europe 200–900: The Antonine Constitution after 1800 Years* (Stuttgart, 2016), 99–112.
Isaac, B., *The Invention of Racicism in Classical Antiquity* (Princeton, NJ, 2004).
Ivanov, S. A., *"Pearls before Swine": Missionary Work in Byzantium* (Paris, 2015).
Jacoby, D., "La population de Constantinople à l'époque byzantine: un problème de démographie urbaine," *Byzantion* 31 (1961): 81–110.
———, "The Jews of Constantinople," in C. Mango and G. Dagron, eds., *Constantinople and Its Hinterland* (Aldershot, UK, 1995), 221–232.
———, "After the Fourth Crusade: The Latin Empire of Constantinople and the Frankish States," in J. Shepard, ed., *The Cambridge History of the Byzantine Empire, c.500–1492* (Cambridge, 2008), 759–778.
———, "The Jews in the Byzantine Economy (Seventh to Mid-Fifteenth Century)," in R. Bonfil et al., eds., *Jews in Byzantium: Dialectics of Minority and Majority Cultures* (Leiden, 2012), 220–255.
Janin, R., "Les monastères nationaux et provinciaux à Byzance (Constantinople et environs)," *Échos d'Orient* 32 (1933): 429–438.
———, *Constantinople Byzantine: Développement urbain et répertoire topographique* (Paris, 1964).
Jasper, R. C. D., and G. J. Cuming, *Prayers of the Eucharist: Early and Reformed* (New York, 1980).
Jazdzewska, K., "Hagiographic Invention and Imitation: Niketas' *Life of Theoktiste* and Its Literary Models," *GRBS* 49 (2009): 257–279.
Jeffreys, E., "Byzantine Studies as an Academic Discipline," in E. Jeffreys et al., eds., *Oxford Handbook of Byzantine Studies* (Oxford, 2008), 3–20.
———, "Rhetoric in Byzantium," in I. Worthington, ed., *A Companion to Greek Rhetoric* (Oxford, 2010), 166–184.
Jeffreys, E., et al., eds., *The Oxford Handbook of Byzantine Studies* (Oxford, 2008).
Jenkins, R., *Rethinking Ethnicity* (London, 2008).
Johnson, A. P., *Ethnicity and Argument in Eusebios' Praeparatio Evangelica* (Oxford, 2006).

Jones, C. P., *Between Pagan and Christian* (Princeton, NJ, 2014).
Jordanov, I., "Pečati na Simeon, vasilevs na romeite (?–927)," *Bulgaria Mediaevalis* 2 (2011): 87–98.
Kaegi, W. E., *Byzantine Military Unrest 471–843: An Interpretation* (Amsterdam, 1981).
———, *Byzantium and the Early Islamic Conquests* (Cambridge, 1995).
———, *Hercalius, Emperor of Byzantium* (Cambridge, 2003).
Kaldellis, A., trans., *Genesios: On the Reigns of the Emperors* (Canberra, 1998).
———, "Classicism, Barbarism, and Warfare: Prokopios and the Conservative Reaction to Later Roman Military Policy," *American Journal of Ancient History* n.s. 3–4 (2004–2005 [2007]): 189–218.
———, "A Byzantine Argument for the Equivalence of All Religions: Michael Attaleiates on Ancient and Modern Romans," *International Journal of the Classical Tradition* 14 (2007): 1–22.
———, "Christodoros on the Statues of the Zeuxippos Baths: A New Reading of the *Ekphrasis*," *GRBS* 47 (2007): 361–383.
———, *Hellenism in Byzantium: The Transformations of Greek Identity and the Reception of the Classical Tradition* (Cambridge, 2007).
———, "From Rome to New Rome, From Empire to Nation State: Reopening the Question of Byzantium's Roman Identity," in L. Grig and G. Kelly, eds., *Two Romes: Rome and Constantinople in Late Antiquity* (Oxford, 2012), 387–404.
———, *Ethnography after Antiquity: Foreign Lands and People in Byzantine Literature* (Philadelphia, 2013).
———, "Did Ioannes I Tzimiskes Campaign in the East in 974?," *Byzantion* 84 (2014): 235–240.
———, *A New Herodotos: Laonikos Chalkokondyles on the Ottoman Empire, the Fall of Byzantium, and the Emergence of the West* (Cambridge, MA, 2014).
———, *The Byzantine Republic: People and Power in New Rome* (Cambridge, MA, 2015).
———, "Did the Byzantine Empire Have 'Ecumenical' or 'Universal' Aspirations?," in C. Ando and S. Richardson, eds., *Ancient States and Infrastructural Power: Europe, Asia, and America* (Philadelphia, 2017), 272–300.
———, "The Social Scope of Roman Identity in Byzantium: An Evidence-Based Approach," *Byzantina Symmeikta* 27 (2017): 173–210.
———, *Streams of Gold, Rivers of Blood: The Rise and Fall of Byzantium, 955 A.D. to the First Crusade* (Oxford, 2017).
———, "Ethnicity and Clothing in Byzantium," in I. Jevtic, K. Durak, and P. Magdalino, eds., volume in preparation.
———, "From "Empire of the Greeks" to "Byzantium": The Politics of a Modern Paradigm-Shift," in N. Ashenbrenner and J. Ransohoff, eds., *The Invention of Byzantium in Early Modern Europe*, volume in preparation.
———, "Hellenism and Identity at the Empire of Nikaia: The Evolution of Modern Narratives vs. the Textual Evidence," in P. Papadopoulou and A. Simpson, eds., *The Empire of Nicaea Revisited*, volume in preparation.

———, "How Was a 'New Rome' Even Thinkable? Premonitions of Constantinople and the Movable Idea of Rome," in Y. Kim and A. E. T. McLaughlin, eds., *Leadership and Community in Late Antiquity: Essays in Honour of Raymond Van Dam*, volume in preparation.

———, "Political Freedom in Byzantium: The Rhetoric of Liberty and the Periodization of Roman History," *History of European Ideas* (forthcoming).

———, "The Politics of Classical Genealogies in the Late Antique Roman East," in I. Tanaseanu-Doebler and S. Anghel, eds., volume in preparation.

Kaplanis, T. A., "Antique Names and Self-Identification: *Hellenes, Graikoi*, and *Romaioi* from Late Byzantium to the Greek Nation-State," in D. Tziovas, ed., *Re-Imagining the Past: Antiquity and Modern Greek Culture* (Oxford, 2014), 81–97.

Kazhdan, A., *Armiane v sostave gospodstvuiushchego klassa Vizantiĭskoĭ Imperii v XI–XII vv.* (Erevan, Armenia, 1975).

———, "The Armenians in the Byzantine Ruling Class, Predominantly in the Ninth through Twelfth Centuries," in T. J. Samuelian and M. E. Stone, eds., *Medieval Armenian Culture* (Chico, CA, 1984), 439–451.

———, "'Constantine imaginaire': Byzantine Legends of the Ninth Century about Constantine the Great," *Byzantion* 57 (1987): 196–250.

———, "Romania," in *ODB*, vol, 3, p. 1805.

———, "Some Observations on the Byzantine Concept of Law: Three Authors of the Ninth through the Twelfth Centuries," in A. Laiou and D. Simon, eds., *Law and Society in Byzantium: Ninth-Twelfth Centuries* (Washington, DC, 1994), 199–215.

———, *A History of Byzantine Literature (850–1000)*, ed. Christine Angelidi (Athens, 2006).

Kazhdan, A., and G. Constable, *People and Power in Byzantium: An Introduction to Modern Byzantine Studies* (Washington, DC, 1982).

Kennedy, H., "Antioch: From Byzantium to Islam and Back Again," in J. Rich, ed., *The City in Late Antiquity* (New York, 1992), 181–198.

———, *The Great Arab Conquests: How the Spread of Islam Changed the World We Live in* (Philadelphia, 2007).

Kerneis, S., "Loi et coutumes dans l'Empire romain. A propos du droit vulgaire," in J.-P. Coriat et al., eds., *Inter cives necnon peregrinos* (Göttingen, 2014), 367–384.

———, "Rome et les barbares: Aux origines de la personnalité des lois," in F. Botta and L. Loschivo, eds., *Civitas, iura, arma: Organizzazioni militari, istituzioni giuridiche e strutture sociali alla origini dell'Europa (s. III–VIII)* (Lecce, Italy, 2015), 103–116.

Koder, J., "Byzanz, die Griechen und die Romaiosyne—eine 'Ethnogenese' der 'Römer'?," in H. Wolfram and W. Pohl, eds., *Typen der Ethnogenese under besonderer Berücksichtigung der Bayern* (Vienna, 1990), 103–111.

Kolbaba, T., *The Byzantine Lists: Errors of the Latins* (Urbana, IL, 2000).

———, "On the Closing of the Churches and the Rebaptism of Latins: Greek Perfidy or Latin Slander," *BMGS* 29 (2005): 39–51.

———, "1054 Revisited: Response to Ryder," *BMGS* 35 (2011): 38–44.

Kolia-Dermitzaki, A., Ὁ βυζαντινός ἱερός πόλεμος: Ἡ ἔννοια καί ἡ προβολή τοῦ θρησκευτικοῦ πολέμου στό Βυζάντιο (Athens, 1991).

———. "Η εικόνα των Βουλγάρων και της χώρας τους στις βυζαντινές πηγές του 11ου και 12ου αιώνα," in K. Nikolaou and K. Tsiknakis, eds., Βυζάντιο και Βούλγαροι (1018–1185) (Athens, 2008), 59–89.

Korobeinikov, D., "How 'Byzantine' Were the Early Ottomans? Bithynia in ca. 1290–1450," in I. V. Zaitsev and S. F. Oreshkova, eds., *Osmanskii mir I osmanistika* (Moscow, 2010), 215–238.

Koubourlis, G., Οι ιστοριογραφικές οφειλές των Σπ. Ζαμπέλιου και Κ. Παπαρρηγόπουλου: Η συμβολή Ελλήνων και ξένων λογίων στη διαμόρφωση του τρίσημου σχήματος του ελληνικού ιστορισμού (1782–1846) (Athens, 2012).

Kountoura-Galaki, E., "The Armeniac Theme and the Fate of Its Leaders," in S. Lambakis, ed., Η Βυζαντινή Μικρά Ασία (6ος–12ος αι.) (Athens, 1998), 27–38.

———, "The Origins of the Genesios Family and Its Connections with the Armeniakon Theme," *BZ* 93 (2000): 464–473.

Koutrakou, N., "'Spies of Towns': Some Remarks on Espionage in the Context of Arab-Byzantine Relations," *Graeco-Arabica* 7–8 (2000): 243–266.

Kouymijian, D., "Ethnic Origins and the 'Armenian' Policy of Emperor Heraclius," *Revue des études armeniennes* 17 (1983): 635–642.

Kramer, J., "Ῥωμαῖοι und Λατῖνοι," in G. W. Most et al., eds., *Philanthropia kai Eusebeia: Festschrift für Albrecht Dihle zum 70. Geburtstag* (Göttingen, 1993), 234–247.

Kravari, V., "L'hellénisation des Slaves de Macédoine orientale, au témoignage des anthroponymes," in M. Balard et al., eds., *Eupsychia: mélanges offerts à Hélène Ahrweiler*, vol. 2 (Paris, 1998), 387–397.

Krsmanović, B., *The Byzantine Province in Change (On the Threshold between the 10th and the 11th Century)* (Belgrade, 2008).

Krueger, D., "The Practice of Christianity in Byzantium," in D. Krueger, ed., *Byzantine Christianity = A People's History of Christianity*, vol. 3 (Philadelphia, 2006), 1–15.

———. *Liturgical Subjects: Christian Ritual, Biblical Narrative, and the Formation of the Self in Byzantium* (Philadelphia, 2014).

Krumbacher, K., "Kasia," *Sitzungsberichte der bayerischen Akademie der Wissenschaften, Philosoph.-phil. und hist. Kl.* 3.1 (1897): 305–369.

Laiou, A. E., "The Foreigner and the Stranger in 12th Century Byzantium: Means of Propitiation and Acculturation," in M. T. Fögen, ed., *Fremde der Gesellschaft: Historische und socialwissenschaftliche Untersuchungen zur Differenzierung von Normalität und Fremdheit* (Frankfurt, 1991), 71–97.

———, "L'étranger de passage et l'étranger privilégié à Byzance, XIe–XIIe siècles," in L. Mayali, ed., *Identité et droit de l'autre* (Berkeley, CA, 1994), 69–88.

———, "Institutional Mechanisms of Integration," in H. Ahrweiler and A. Laiou, eds., *Studies on the Internal Diaspora of the Byzantine Empire* (Washington, DC, 1998), 161–181.

———, "Exchange and Trade, Seventh–Twelfth Centuries," in A. E. Laiou, ed., *The Economic History of Byzantium* (Washington, DC, 2002), 697–770.
Laiou, A. E., and H. Maguire, eds., *Byzantium: A World Civilization* (Washington, DC, 1992).
Lambakis, S., et al., eds., *Η Μικρά Ασία των θεμάτων: Έρευνες πάνω στην γεωγραφική φυσιογνωμία και προσωπογραφία των βυζαντινών θεμάτων της Μικράς Ασίας (7ος–11ος αι.)* (Athens, 1998).
Lambakis, S., et al., eds., *Byzantine Diplomacy: A Seminar* (Athens, 2007).
Laniado, A., "Aspar and His Phoideratoi: John Malalas on a Special Relationship," in U. Roberto and L. Mecella, eds., *Governare e riformare l'impero al momento della sua divisione: Oriente, Occidente, Illirico* (Rome, 2015), 1–18.
———, *Ethnos et droit dans le monde protobyzantin, Ve–VIe siècle: Fédérés, paysans et provinciaux à la lumière d'une scholie juridique de l'époque de Justinien* (Geneva, 2015).
Larkin, M., *Al-Mutanabbi: Voice of the 'Abbasid Poetic Ideal* (Oxford, 2008).
Lauritzen, F., "A Courtier in the Women's Quarters: The Rise and Fall of Psellos," *Byzantion* 77 (2007): 251–266.
Lauxtermann, M., "John Geometres—Poet and Soldier," *Byzantion* 68 (1998): 356–380.
———, *Byzantine Poetry from Pisides to Geometres* (Vienna, 2003).
Lavan, M., *Slaves to Rome: Paradigms of Empire in Roman Culture* (Cambridge, 2013).
Lavan, M., R. E. Payne, and J. Weisweiler, "Cosmopolitan Politics: The Assimilation and Subordination of Elite Cultures," in M. Lavan, R. E. Payne, and J. Weisweiler, eds., *Cosmopolitanism and Empire: Universal Rulers, Local Elites, and Cultural Integration in the Ancient Near East and Mediterranean* (Oxford, 2016), 1–28.
Lee, A. D., *Information and Frontiers: Roman Foreign Relations in Late Antiquity* (Cambridge, 1993).
Lefort, J., "Population et démographie," in J.-C. Cheynet, ed., *Le monde byzantine*, vol. 2 (Paris, 2006), 203–219.
Lemerle, P., *Cinq études sur le XIe siècle Byzantin* (Paris, 1977).
Lenski, N., "Assimilation and Revolt in the Territory of Isauria, from the 1st Century BC to the 6th Century AD," *Journal of the Economic and Social History of the Orient* 42.4 (1999): 413–465.
———, *Failure of Empire: Valens and the Roman State in the Fourth Century A.D.* (Berkeley, CA, 2002).
Le Strange, G., *Palestine under the Moslems: A Description of Syria and the Holy Land from a.d. 650 to 1500* (Boston, 1890).
Letsios, D., "Byzantine Foreign, Defence and Demographic Policy during the Establishment of the Umayyad Caliphate—the Case of the Mardaites," in K. Frangoulis and E. Badawi, eds., *Βυζάντιο και Αραβικός κόσμος: Συνάντηση Πολιτισμών* (Thessalonike, 2013), 297–311.
Leveniotis, G. A., *Η πολιτική κατάρρευση του Βυζαντίου στην ανατολή: Το ανατολικό σύνορο και η κεντρική Μικρά Ασία κατά το Β΄ ήμισυ του 11ου αι.* (Thessalonike, 2007).

Lilie, R.-J., "Zur Stellung von ethnischen und religiösen Minderheiten in Byzanz: Armenier, Muslime und Paulikianer," in W. Pohl et al., eds., *Visions of Community in the Post-Roman World: The West, Byzantium and the Islamic World, 300–1000* (Aldershot, UK, 2012), 301–315.

Linder, A., "The Legal Status of Jews in the Byzantine Empire," in R. Bonfil et al., eds., *Jews in Byzantium: Dialectics of Minority and Majority Cultures* (Leiden, 2012), 149–217.

Lounghis, T., "Some Questions Concerning the Terminology Used in Narrative Sources to Designate the Byzantine State," *Byzantina Symmeikta* 11 (1997): 11–22.

———, *Η κοινωνική εξέλιξη στη διάρκεια των λεγομένων «σκοτεινών αιώνων» (602–867)*, 2nd ed. (Athens, 2013).

Louth, A., *Greek East and Latin West: The Church AD 681–1071* (Crestwood, NY, 2007).

Luraghi, N., "The Study of Greek Ethnic Identities," in J. McInerney, ed., *A Companion to Ethnicity in the Ancient Mediterranean* (Malden, MA, 2014), 213–227.

Maas, M., "'Delivered from Their Ancient Customs': Christianity and the Question of Cultural Change in Early Byzantine Ethnography," in K. Mills and A. Grafton, eds., *Conversion in Late Antiquity and the Early Middle Ages: Seeing and Believing* (Rochester, NY, 2003), 152–188.

MacKenzie, J. M., ed., *The Encyclopedia of Empire* (New York, 2016).

Mackridge, P., *Language and National Identity in Greece, 1766–1976* (Oxford, 2009).

Macrides, R., *Akropolites, George: The History, Translated with Introduction and Commentary* (Oxford, 2007).

Madsen, J. M., *Eager to Be Roman: Greek Responses to Roman Rule in Pontus and Bithynia* (London, 2009).

Magdalino, P., "Honour among the Romaioi: The Framework of Social Values in the World of Digenes Akrites and Kekaumenos," *BMGS* 13 (1989): 183–218.

———. "Enlightenment and Repression in Twelfth-Century Byzantium: The Evidence of the Canonists," in N. Oikonomides, ed., *Το Βυζάντιο κατά τον 12ο αιώνα: Κανονικό δίκαιο, κράτος και κοινωνία* (Athens, 1991), 357–373.

———. "Hellenism and Nationalism in Byzantium," in P. Magdalino, *Tradition and Transformation in Medieval Byzantium* (Aldershot, UK, 1991), chapter XIV.

———, "Prosopography and Byzantine Identity," in A. Cameron, ed., *Fifty Years of Prosopography: The Later Roman Empire, Byzantium and Beyond* (Oxford, 2003), 41–56.

———, "Isaac II, Saladin, and Venice," in J. Shepard, ed., *The Expansion of Orthodox Europe: Byzantium, the Balkans and Russia* (Aldershot, UK, 2007), 93–106.

———, "Byzantium = Constantinople," in L. James, ed., *A Companion to Byzantium* (Chichester, UK, 2010), 43–53.

———, "Constantine VII and the Historical Geography of Empire," in S. Bazzaz et al., eds., *Imperial Geographies in Byzantine and Ottoman Space* (Washington, DC, 2013), 23–42.

Magdalino, P., and R. Nelson, "Introduction," in P. Magdalino and R. Nelson, eds., *The Old Testament in Byzantium* (Washington, DC, 2010), 1–38.

Mahé, J.-P. "Entre Moïse et Mahomet: Refléxions sur l'historiographie arménienne," *REA* 23 (1992): 121–153.

———, "Confession religieuse et identité nationale dans l'église arménienne du VIIe au XIe siècle," in N. Garsoïan and J.-P. Mahé, eds., *Des Parthes au Califat: quatre leçons sur la formation de l'identité arménienne* (Paris, 1997), 59–78.

———, "Ani sous Constantin X, d'après une inscription de 1060," *TM* 14 (2002): 403–414.

Maier, C. S., *Among Empires: American Ascendancy and Its Predecessors* (Cambridge, MA, 2006).

Malamut, E., "De l'empire des Romains à la nation des Hellènes: Évolution identitaire de la fin du XIe au XVe siècle," in SHMESP, *Nation et nations au Moyen Âge* (Paris, 2014), 165–179.

Malingoudis, Ph., Σλάβοι στη μεσαιωνική Ελλάδα, 2nd ed. (Thessalonike, 2013).

Mango, C., "Byzantinism and Romantic Hellenism," *Journal of the Warburg and Courtauld Institutes* 28 (1965): 29–43.

———, *Byzantine Literature as a Distorting Mirror* (Oxford, 1975).

———, *Byzantium: The Empire of New Rome* (New York, 1980).

Manjoo, F., *True Enough: Learning to Live in a Post-Fact Society* (Hoboken, NJ, 2008).

Markopoulos, A., "An Anonymous Laudatory Poem in Honor of Basil I," *DOP* 46 (1992): 225–232.

———, "Roman Antiquarianism: Aspects of the Roman Past in the Middle Byzantine Period (9th–11th Centuries)," in E. Jeffreys, ed., *Proceedings of the 21st International Congress of Byzantine Studies*, vol. 1 (London, 2006), 277–298.

———, "Genesios: A Study," in S. Kotzabassi and G. Mavromatis, eds., *Realia Byzantina* (Berlin, 2009), 137–150.

———, "Οι μεταμορφώσεις της «μυθολογίας» του Βασιλείου Ά," in V. Leontariou et al., eds., *Antecessor: Festschrift für Spiros N. Troianos zum 80. Geburtstag* (Athens, 2013), 945–970.

Martin, J.-M., *La Pouille du VIe au XIIe siècle* (Rome, 1993).

———, *Byzance et l'Italie méridionale* (Paris, 2014).

Mason, H. J., *Greek Terms for Roman Institutions: A Lexicon and Analysis* (Toronto, 1974).

Masters, B., *The Arabs of the Ottoman Empire, 1516–1918: A Social and Cultural History* (Cambridge, 2013).

Mathisen, R., "*Peregrini, Barbari,* and *Cives Romani:* Concepts of Citizenship and the Legal Identity of Barbarians in the Later Roman Empire," *American Historical Review* 111.4 (2006): 1011–1040.

Mattingly, D. J., *Imperialism, Power, and Identity: Experiencing the Roman Empire,* with a new preface (Princeton, NJ, 2011).

McCormick, M., *Eternal Victory: Triumphal Rulership in Late Antiquity, Byzantium and the Early Medieval West* (Cambridge, 1990).
McGeer, E., "The Legal Decree of Nikephoros II Phokas Concerning Armenian *Stratiotai*," in T. S. Miller and J. Nesbitt, eds., *Peace and War in Byzantium: Essays in Honor of George T. Dennis, S.J.* (Washington, DC, 1995), 123–137.
McInerney, J., ed., *A Companion to Ethnicity in the Ancient Mediterranean* (Malden, MA, 2014).
McQueen, W. B., "Relations between the Normans and Byzantium 1071–1112," *Byzantion* 56 (1986): 427–476.
Medvedev, I., "Ἡ συνοδικὴ ἀπόφαση τῆς 24 Μαρτίου 1171 ὡς νόμος γιὰ τὴ διαδοχὴ στὸ θρόνο τοῦ Βυζαντίου," in N. Oikonomides, ed., *Τὸ Βυζάντιο κατὰ τὸν 120 αἰώνα: Κανονικὸ δίκαιο, κράτος καὶ κοινωνία* (Athens, 1991), 229–238.
Mehl, A., *Roman Historiography*, trans. H.-F. Mueller (Malden, MA, 2011).
Merendino, E., "Quattro lettere greche di Federico III," *Atti della Accademia di Scienze, Lettere, e Arti di Palermo* ser. 4, 34 (1974–1975): 293–343.
Messis, Ch., "Lectures sexuées d l'altérité: Les Latins et identité romaine menacée les derniers siècles de Byzance," *JöB* 61 (2011): 151–170.
Metcalf, D. M., *Byzantine Cyprus, 491–1191* (Nicosia, Cyprus, 2009).
Meyer, P., *Die Haupturkunden für die Geschichte der Athosklöster* (Amsterdam, 1965).
Mikhail, M. S. A., *From Byzantine to Islamic Egypt: Religion, Identity and Politics after the Arab Conquest* (London, 2016).
Miklosich, F., and J. Müller, *Acta et diplomata graeca medii aevi sacra et profana*, 6 vols. (Vienna, 1865–1890).
Miquel, A., *La géographie humaine du monde musulman jusqu'au milieu du 11e siècle: les travaux et les jours*, 4 vols. (Paris, 1967–1988).
Mitchell, S., "The Galatians: Representation and Reality," in A. Erskine, ed., *A Companion to the Hellenistic World* (Oxford, 2003), 280–293.
Moatti, C., *The Birth of Critical Thinking in Republican Rome*, trans. J. Lloyd (Cambridge, 2015).
Monferrer-Sala, J. P., "Between Hellenism and Arabicization: On the Formation of an Ethnolinguistic Identity of the Melkite Communities in the Heart of Muslim Rule," *Al-Qantara* 33 (2012): 445–471.
Morony, M. G., "Religious Communities in the Early Islamic World," in W. Pohl, ed., *Visions of Community in the Post-Roman World: The West, Byzantium and the Islamic World, 300–1100* (Aldershot, UK, 2012), 155–163.
Morris, I., "The Greater Athenian State," in I. Morris and W. Scheidel, eds., *The Dynamics of Ancient Empires: State Power from Assyria to Byzantium* (Oxford, 2009), 99–177.
Morris, R., "The Athonites and Their Neighbors in Macedonia in the Tenth and Eleventh Centuries," in J. Burke and R. Scott, eds., *Byzantine Macedonia: Identity, Image, and History* (Melbourne, 2000), 157–167.
Morris, S., *"When Brothers Dwell in Unity": Byzantine Christianity and Homosexuality* (Jefferson, NC, 2016).

Muldoon, J., *Empire and Order: The Concept of Empire, 800–1800* (New York, 1999).
Mullett, M., *Theophylact of Ochrid: Reading the Letters of a Byzantine Archbishop* (Aldershot, UK, 1997).
Nasrallah, J., *Histoire du mouvement littéraire dans l'église melchite du Ve au XXe siècle: Contribution à l'étude de la littérature arabe chrétienne*, vol. 3.1: *969–1250* (Leuven, 1979).
Năsturel, P., "Les Valaques balkaniques aux Xe–XIIIe siècles (mouvements de population et colonisation dans la Romanie grecque et latine)," *Byzantinische Forschungen* 7 (1979): 89–112.
Necipoğlu, N., *Byzantium between the Ottomans and the Latins: Politics and Society in the Late Empire* (Cambridge, 2009).
Nexon, D. H., and T. Wright, "What's at Stake in the American Empire Debate," *American Political Science Review* 101 (2007): 253–271.
Nichanian, M., "Byzantine Emperor Philippikos-Vardanes: Monothelite Policy and Caucasian Diplomacy," in R. Hovannisian and S. Payaslian, eds., *Armenian Constantinople* (Costa Mesa, CA, 2010), 39–51.
Nicol, D. M., *Byzantium: Its Ecclesiastical History and Relations with the Western World* (London, 1972).
———, *Byzantium and Venice: A Study in Diplomatic and Cultural Relations* (Cambridge, 1994).
Nicolet, C., *Space, Geography and Politics in the Early Roman Empire* (Ann Arbor, MI, 1991).
Nikolaou, K., and K. Tsiknakis, eds., Βυζάντιο και Βούλγαροι *(1018–1185)* (Athens, 2008).
Noreña, C. F., *Imperial Ideals in the Roman West: Representation, Circulation, Power* (Cambridge, 2011).
Nystazopoulou-Pelekidou, M., "Βυζαντινή ορολογία στή διοίκηση καὶ τὴν οἰκονομία τῶν μεσαιωνικῶν βαλκανικῶν κρατῶν," in N. G. Moschonas, Ἡ ἐπικοινωνία στὸ Βυζάντιο (Athens, 1993), 607–622.
Obolensky, D., *The Byzantine Commonwealth, Eastern Europe, 500–1453* (New York, 1971).
———, *Six Byzantine Potraits* (Oxford, 1988).
———, *Byzantium and the Slavs* (Crestwood, NY, 1994).
O'Donnell, J., "Late Antiquity," *Transactions of the American Philological Association* 134 (2004): 203–213.
———, *The Ruin of the Roman Empire: A New History* (New York, 2008).
Oikonomides, N., *Les Listes de préséance byzantines des IXe et Xe siècles* (Paris, 1972).
———, "Silk Trade and Production in Byzantium from the Sixth to the Ninth Century: The Seals of Kommerkiarioi," *DOP* 40 (1986): 33–53.
———, "L'archonte Slave de l'Hellade au VIIIe siècle," *Vizantiiskii Vremennik* 55 (1994): 111–118.
———, "L''unilinguisme' officiel de Constantinople byzantine (VIIe–XIIe s.)," *Byzantina Symmeikta* 13 (1999): 9–22.
———, "Ὄψιμη ιεραποστολή στη Λακωνία," in V. Konti, ed., *Ο μοναχισμός στην Πελοπόννησο: 4ος–15ος αι.* (Athens, 2004), 29–35.

Orlin, E. M., *Foreign Cults in Rome: Creating a Roman Empire* (Oxford, 2010).
Ostrogorsky, G., *History of the Byzantine State*, trans. J. Hussey (New Brunswick, NJ, 1969).
Page, G., *Being Byzantine: Greek Identity before the Ottomans* (Cambridge, 2008).
Panagiotopoulos, I., Περὶ Ἀθιγγάνων: Πολιτικὴ καὶ θρησκεία στὴ βυζαντινὴ αὐτοκρατορία (Athens, 2008).
Papadopoulos-Kerameus, A., *Noctes Petropolitanae* (St. Petersburg, 1913).
Papadopoulou, Th., Συλλογικὴ ταυτότητα καὶ αὐτογνωσία στὸ Βυζάντιο: Συμβολὴ στὸν προσδιορισμὸ τῆς αὐτοαντίληψης τῶν Βυζαντινῶν κατὰ τὴν λόγια γραμματεία τους (11^{ος}–ἀρχὲς 13^{ου} αἰ.) (Athens, 2015).
Parpola, S., "The Construction of Dur-Sarrukin in the Assyrian Royal Correspondence," in A. Caubet, ed., *Khorsabad, le palais de Sargon II, roi d'Assyrie* (Paris, 1995), 47–77.
Pertusi, A., "Una Acoluthia militare inedita del X secolo," *Aevum* 22 (1948): 145–168.
Peters-Custot, A., "Le barbare et l'étranger dans l'Italie méridionale pré-normande (IXe–Xe siècles): l'Empire à l'éprouve de l'altérité," in D. Nourrisson and Y. Perrin, eds., *Le barbare, l'étranger: Images de l'autre* (Saint-Étienne, France, 2005), 147–163.
———, *Les grecs de l'Italie méridionale post-Byzantine: Une acculturation en douceur* (Rome, 2009).
———, "*Convivencia* between Christians: The Greek and Latin Communities of Byzantine South Italy (9th–11th Centuries)," in B. Crostini and S. La Porta, eds., *Negotiating Co-Existing: Communities, Cultures and Convivencia in Byzantine Society* (Trier, Germany, 2013), 203–220.
———, "Grecs et Byzantins dans les sources latines de l'Italie (Ixe–XIe siècle)," in SHMESP, *Nation et nations au Moyen Âge* (Paris, 2014), 181–191.
Petkov, K., *The Voices of Medieval Bulgaria, Seventh–Fifteenth Century: The Records of a Bygone Culture* (Leiden, 2008).
Photiadis, P. J., "A Semi-Greek Semi-Coptic Parchment," *Klio* 41 (1963): 234–235.
Pinker, S., *Enlightenment Now: The Case for Reason, Science, Humanism, and Progress* (New York, 2018).
Pitsakis, C. G., "Pour une définition des "étrangers" dans le droit gréco-romain d'après les textes des canonistes orientaux," in. P Castro and P. Catalano, eds., *La condition des "Autres" dans les systèmes juridiques de la Méditerranée* (Paris, 2004), 167–196.
Pitts, J., "Political Theory of Empire and Imperialism," *Annual Review of Political Science* 13 (2010): 211–235.
Pohl, W., "Telling the Difference: Signs of Ethnic Identity," in W. Pohl and H. Reimitz, eds., *Strategies of Distinction: The Construction of Ethnic Communities, 300–800* (Leiden, 1998), 17–69.
———, "Introduction—Strategies of Identification: A Methodological Profile," in W. Pohl and G. Heydemann, eds., *Strategies of Identification: Ethnicity and Religion in Early Medieval Europe* (Turnhout, 2013), 1–78.
Polemis, D. I., *The Doukai: A Contribution to Byzantine Prosopography* (London, 1968).

Potter, D. S., *The Roman Empire at Bay, AD 180–395*, 2nd ed. (London, 2014).
Preiser-Kapeller, J., "Complex Processes of Migration: The South Caucasus in the Early Islamic Empire (7th–10th Century AD)," *Tagungen des Landesmuseums für Vorgeschichte Halle (Saale)* 17 (2017): 295–313.
Raffensperger, Christian, *Reimagining Europe: Kievan Rus' in the Medieval World* (Cambridge, MA, 2012).
Rapp, C., "Epiphanius of Salamis: The Church Father as Saint," in A. Bryer and G. Georgallides, eds., *The Sweet Land of Cyprus: Papers Given at the Twenty-Fifth Jubilee Spring Symposium of Byzantine Studies, Birmingham, March 1991* (Nicosia, Cyprus, 1993), 169–187.
———, "A Medieval Cosmopolis: Constantinople and Its Foreign Inhabitants," in J. M. Asgeirsson and N. van Deusen, eds., *Alexander's Revenge: Hellenistic Culture through the Centuries* (Reykjavíc, 2002), 153–171.
Rathbone, J., *The Last English King* (London, 1997).
Redgate, A. E., *The Armenians* (Oxford, 1998).
———, "Myth and Reality: Armenian Identity in the Early Middle Ages," *National Identities* 9 (2007): 281–306.
Regel, W., *Analecta Byzantino-Russica* (St. Petersburg, 1891).
Reimitz, H., *History, Frankish Identity and the Framing of Western Ethnicity, 550–850* (Cambridge, 2015).
Reinert, W., "The Muslim Presence in Constantinople, 9th–15th Centuries: Some Preliminary Observations," in H. Ahrweiler and A. E. Laiou, eds., *Studies on the Internal Disapora of the Byzantine Empire* (Washington, DC, 1998), 125–150.
Reinsch, D. R., "Hieronymus Wolf as Editor and Translator of Byzantine Texts," in P. Marciniak and D. C. Smythe, eds., *The Reception of Byzantium in European Culture since 1500* (London, 2015), 43–55.
Reynolds, S., "Nations, Tribes, Peoples, and States," *Medieval Worlds* 2 (2015): 79–88.
Richardson, J., *The Language of Empire: Rome and the Idea of Empire from the Third Century BC to the Second Century AD* (Cambridge, 2008).
Riedinger, R., *Acta conciliorum oecumenicorum: Series secunda, volumen secundum: Concilium universale Constantinopolitanum tertium*, parts 1–2 (Berlin, 1990–1992).
Romeney, B.t.H., "Ethnicity, Ethnogenesis and the Identity of the Syriac Orthodox Christians," in W. Pohl et al., eds., *Visions of Community in the Post-Roman World: The West, Byzantium and the Islamic World, 300–1100* (Aldershot, UK, 2012), 183–204.
Rösch, G., *Onoma Basileias: Studien zum offiziellen Gebrauch der Kaisertitel in spätantiker und frühbyzantinischer Zeit* (Vienna, 1978).
Rosenqvist, J. O., *Die byzantinische Literatur vom 6. Jahrhundert bis zum Fall Konstantinopels 1453* (Berlin, 2007).
Roueché, C., "Defining the Foreign in Kekaumenos," in D. C. Smythe, ed., *Strangers to Themselves: The Byzantine Outsider* (Aldershot, UK, 2000), 203–213.
Ruggieri, V., "The Carians in the Byzantine Period," in F. Rumscheid, ed., *Die Karer und die Anderen* (Bonn, 2009), 207–218.

Runciman, S., *The Emperor Romanus Lecapenus and His Reign* (Cambridge, 1929).
———, *The Byzantine Theocracy* (Cambridge, 1977).
Rydén, L., ed., *The Life of St. Philaretos the Merciful Written by His Grandson Niketas* (Uppsala, 2002).
Ryder, J. R., "Changing Perspectives on 1054," *BMGS* 35 (2011): 20-37.
Samir, K., "Quelques notes sur les termes rum et rumi dans la tradition arabe: étude de sémantique historique," in *La Nozione de 'Romano' tra Cittadinanza et Universalita: 21–23 Aprile 1982* (Rome, 1984), 461–478.
Sarris, P., *Empires of Faith: The Fall of Rome to the Rise of Islam, 500–700* (Oxford, 2011).
Schlacht, J., and M. Meyerhof, *The Medico-Philosophical Controversy between Ibn Butlan of Baghdad and Ibn Ridwan of Cairo* (Cairo, 1937).
Schminck, A., *Studien zu mittelbyzantinischen Rechtsbüchern* (Frankfurt, 1986).
———, "The Beginnings and Origins of the 'Macedonian' Dynasty," in J. Burke and R. Scott, eds., *Byzantine Macedonia: Identity, Image, and History* (Melbourne, 2001), 61–68.
Schreiner, P., "Bilinguismus, Biliteralität und Digraphie in Byzanz," in P. Schreiner, *Orbis Byzantinus: Byzanz und seine Nachbaren* (Bucharest, 2013), 399–414.
Schwartz, S., *Were the Jews a Mediterranean Society? Reciprocity and Solidarity in Ancient Judaism* (Cambridge, 2010).
Seibt, W., *Die Skleroi: Eine prosopographisch-sigillographische Studie* (Vienna, 1976).
———, "Armenika themata als terminus technicus der byzantinischen Verwaltungsgeschichte des 11. Jahrhunderts," *BS* 54 (1993): 134–141.
———, "War Gagik II von Grossarmenien ca. 1072–3 *megas doux Charsianou?*," in J. S. Langdon et al., eds., ΤΟ ΕΛΛΗΝΙΚΟΝ: *Studies in Honor of Speros Vryonis, Jr.* (New Rochelle, NY, 1993), vol. 2, 159–168.
———, "Siegel als Quelle für Slawenarchonten in Griechenland," *Studies in Byzantine Sigillography* 6 (1999): 27–36.
———, "Stärken und Schwächen der byzantinischen Intergrationspolitik genüber den neuen armenischen Staatsbürgern im 11. Jahrhundert," in V. Vlyssidou, ed., Η αυτοκρατορία σε κρίση (;) Το Βυζάντιο τον 11ο αιώνα *(1025–1081)* (Athens, 2003), 331–347.
Sen, A., *Identity and Violence: The Illusion of Destiny* (London, 2006).
Serhan, K., "Οι όροι «Βυζάντιο» και «Βυζαντινοί» στις αραβικές πηγές," in K. Frangoulis and E. Badawi, eds., Βυζάντιο και Αραβικός κόσμος: Συνάντηση Πολιτισμών (Thessalonike, 2013), 439–453.
Settipani, C., *Continuité des élites à Byzance durant les siècles obscurs: Les princes Caucasiens et l'empire du Vie au IX siècle* (Paris, 2006).
Ševčenko, I., "Three Paradoxes of the Cyrillo-Methodian Mission," *Slavic Review* 23 (1964): 220–236.
———, "Constantinople Viewed from the Eastern Provinces in the Middle Byzantine Period," *Harvard Ukrainian Studies* 3–4 (1978–1980): 712–747.
Severin, T., *Viking*, vol. 3: *King's Man* (London, 2005).

Shawcross, T., "Re-Inventing the Homeland in the Historiography of Frankish Greece: The Fourth Crusade and the Legend of the Trojan War," *BMGS* 27 (2003): 120–152.
———, *The Chronicle of Morea: Historiography in Crusader Greece* (Oxford, 2009).
Sheldon, R. M., *Intelligence Activities in Ancient Rome: Trust in the Gods, but Verify* (London, 2005).
Shepard, J., "Scylitzes on Armenia in the 1040s and the Role of Catacalon Cecaumenus," *REA* 11 (1975–1976): 269–311.
———, "The Uses of the Franks in Eleventh-Century Byzantium," *Anglo-Norman Studies* 15 (1993): 275–305.
———, "Constantinople—Gateway to the North," in C. Mango and G. Dagron, eds., *Constantinople and Its Hinterland* (Aldershot, UK, 1995), 243–260.
———, "A Marriage Too Far? Maria Lekapena and Peter of Bulgaria," in A. Davids, ed., *The Empress Theophano: Byzantium and the West at the Turn of the First Millennium* (Cambridge, 1995), 121–149.
———, ed., *The Cambridge History of the Byzantine Empire, c.500–1492* (Cambridge, 2008).
Sherry, L. F., "Life of St. Athanasia of Aigina," in A.-M. Talbot, ed., *Holy Women of Byzantium: Ten Saints' Lives in English Translation* (Washington, DC, 1996), 137–157.
Sherwin-White, A. N., *The Roman Citizenship*, 2nd ed. (Oxford, 1973).
Shukurov, R., *The Byzantine Turks, 1204–1461* (Leiden, 2016).
Signes Codoñer, J., *The Emperor Theophilos and the East, 829–841: Court and Frontier in Byzantium during the Last Phase of Iconoclasm* (London, 2014).
Simeonova, L., "Constantinopolitan Attitudes toward Aliens and Minorities, 860s–1020s," *Études balkaniques* 2000: 91–112; and 2001: 83–98.
Simonian, H. H., ed., *The Hemshin: History, Society and Identity in the Highlands of Northeast Turkey* (London, 2007).
Siniosoglou, N., Ἀλλόκοτος Ἑλληνισμός: Δοκίμιο γιὰ τὴν ὁριακὴ ἐμπειρία τῶν ἰδεῶν (Athens, 2016).
Skopetea, E., Φαλλμεράϋερ: Τεχνάσματα του ἀντίπαλου δέους (Athens, 1999).
Smith, A. D., *Chosen Peoples: Sacred Sources of National Identity* (Oxford, 2003).
Smith, J. M. H., *Europe after Rome: A New Cultural History 500–1000* (Oxford, 2005).
Smith, W., *Dictionary of Greek and Roman Geography* (London, 1854–1857).
Smyth, H. W., *Greek Grammar* (Cambridge, MA, 1976).
Soulis, G. C., "The Gypsies in the Byzantine Empire and the Balkans in the Late Middle Ages," *DOP* 15 (1961): 141–165.
Spira, T., "Ethnicity and Nationality: The Twin Matrices of Nationalism," in D. Conversi, ed., *Ethnonationalism in the Contemporary World* (London, 2002), 248–268.
Stamatoyannopoulos, G., et al., "Genetics of the Peloponnesean Populations and the Theory of Extinction of the Medieval Peloponnesean Greeks," *European Journal of Human Genetics* (2017): 1–9.
Starr, J., *The Jews in the Byzantine Empire, 641–1204* (New York, 1939).

Stathakopoulos, D., "Population, Demography, and Disease," in E. Jeffreys et al., eds., *The Oxford Handbook of Byzantine Studies* (Oxford, 2008), 309–316.

Stegemann, W., "War der Apostel Paulus ein römischer Bürger?," *Zeitschrift für die neutestamentliche Wissenschaft* 78 (1987): 200–229.

Stouraitis, I., "Roman Identity in Byzantium: A Critical Approach," *BZ* 107 (2014): 175–220.

Svoronos, N., "Le serment de fidélité à l'empereur byzantine et sa signification constitutionnelle," *REB* 9 (1952): 106–142.

Sykoutris, I., Εμείς και οι αρχαίοι (Athens, 2006).

Takács, S. A., *The Construction of Authority in Ancient Rome and Byzantium: The Rhetoric of Empire* (Cambridge, 2009).

Tchoidze, E., Ένας Γεωργιανός προσκυνητής στον Βυζαντινό κόσμο του 9ου αιώνα: ο Άγιος Ιλαρίων ο Γεωργιανός (Athens, 2011).

Ter-Ghewondyan, A., *The Arab Emirates in Bagratid Armenia*, trans. N. Garsoïan (Lisbon, 1976).

Theotokis, G., "Rus, Varangian and Frankish Mercenaries in the Service of Byzantine Emperors (9th–11th c.)," *Byzantina Symmeikta* 22 (2012): 125–156.

Thierry, M., "Données archéologiques sur les principautés arméniennes de Cappadoce orientale au XIe siècle," *Revue des études armeniennes* 26 (1996–1997): 119–172.

Tobias, N., "Basil I (867–886), The Founder of the Macedonian Dynasty: A Study of the Political and Military History of the Byzantine Empire in the Ninth Century" (PhD dissertation, Rutgers University, 1969).

Todt, K.-P., "Antioch in the Middle Byzantine Period: (969–1084): The Reconstruction of the City as an Administrative, Military, Economic and Ecclesiastical Center," *Topoi* suppl. 5 (2004): 171–190.

Todt, K.-P., and B. A. Vest, *Syria (Syria Prōtē, Syria Deutera, Syria Euphratēsia)* (Vienna, 2014).

Toumanoff, C., "Caucasia and Byzantium," *Traditio* 27 (1971): 111–158.

———, "The Heraclids and the Arsacids," *Revue des études armeniennes* 19 (1985): 431–434.

Treadgold, W., *The Byzantine Revival, 780–842* (Stanford, CA, 1991).

———, "The Army in the Works of Constantine Porphyrogenitus," *Rivista di studi bizantini e neoellenici* 29 (1992): 77–162.

———, *Byzantium and Its Army 284–1081* (Stanford, CA, 1995).

———, *A History of the Byzantine State and Society* (Stanford, CA, 1997).

———, *The Middle Byzantine Historians* (New York, 2013).

Trinchera, F., *Syllabus Graecarum membranarum* (Naples, 1865).

Trombley, F., "War, Society and Popular Religion in Byzantine Anatolia (6th–13th Centuries)," in S. Lambakis, ed., Η Βυζαντινή Μικρά Ασία (6ος–12ος αι.) (Athens, 1998), 97–139.

Turner, D., "The Origins and Accession of Leo V (813–820)," *JöB* 40 (1990): 171–203.

Van Lint, T. M., "The Formation of Armenian Identity in the First Millennium," *Church History and Religious Culture* 89 (2009): 251–278.

Van Tricht, F., *The Latin Renovatio of Byzantium: The Empire of Constantinople (1204–1228)* (Leiden, 2011).
Vári, R., "Zum historischen Exzerptenwerke des Konstantinos Porphyrogennetos," *BZ* 17 (1908): 78–84.
Vasiliev, A. A., *The Goths in the Crimea* (Cambridge, MA, 1936).
Vasiliev, A. A, et al., eds., *Byzance et les Arabes*, 3 vols. (Brussels, 1935–1968).
Vest, B. A., *Geschichte der Stadt Melitene und der umliegenden Gebiete vom Vorabend der arabischen bis zum Anschluss der türkischen Eroberung (um 600–1124)* (Hamburg, 2007).
von Gerkan, A., *Griechische Städteanlagen* (Berlin, 1924).
von Sivers, P., "Taxes and Trade in the 'Abbasid *thughur*, 750–962 / 133–251," *Journal of the Economic and Social History of the Orient* 25 (1982): 71–99.
Vranousi, E., "Οἱ ὅροι «Ἀλβανοὶ» καὶ «Ἀρβανῖται» καὶ ἡ πρώτη μνεία τοῦ ὁμωνύμου λαοῦ τῆς Βαλκανικῆς εἰς τὰς πηγὰς τοῦ ΙΑ'αἰῶνος," *Byzantina Symmeikta* 2 (1970): 207–254.
Vryonis, S., "The Will of a Provincial Magnate, Eustathius Boilas (1059)," *DOP* 11 (1956): 263–277.
———, "St. Ioannicius the Great (754–846) and the 'Slavs' of Bithynia," *Byzantion* 31 (1961): 245–248.
———, "Byzantine Images of the Armenians," in R. Hovannisian, ed., *The Armenian Image in History and Literature* (Malibu, CA, 1981): 65–81.
———, "Armenians and Greeks in Byzantine Taron," in R. G. Hovannisian, ed., *Armenian Baghesh / Bitlis and Taron / Mush* (Costa Mesa, CA, 2001): 91–103.
Walbank, F. W., "Nationality as a Factor in Roman History," *Harvard Studies in Classical Philology* 76 (1972): 145–168.
Wallace-Hadrill, A., *Rome's Cultural Revolution* (Cambridge, 2008).
Waters, M., *Ethnic Options: Choosing Identities in America* (Berkeley, CA, 1990).
Webb, P., *Imagining the Arabs: Arab Identity and the Rise of Islam* (Edinburgh, 2016).
Webb, R., *Demons and Dancers: Performance in Late Antiquity* (Cambridge, MA, 2008).
Weber, M., *Economy and Society*, ed. G. Roth and C. Wittich (Berkeley, CA, 1978).
Weisweiler, J., "From Empire to World-State: Ecumenical Language and Cosmopolitan Consciousness in the Later Roman Aristocracy," in M. Lavan et al., eds., *Cosmopolitanism and Empire: Universal Rulers, Local Elites, and Cultural Integration in the Ancient Near East and Mediterranean* (Oxford, 2016), 187–208.
———, "Populist Despotism and Infrastructural Power in the Later Roman Empire," in C. Ando and S. Richardson, eds., *Ancient States and Infrastuctural Power: Europe, Asia, and America* (Philadelphia, 2017), 149–178.
Westerink, L. G., *Nicétas Magistros: Lettres d'un exilé (928–946)* (Paris, 1973).
Whitby, M., "Emperors and Armies, AD 235–395," in S. Swain and M. Edwards, eds., *Approaching Late Antiquity: The Transformation from Early to Late Empire* (Oxford, 2004), 156–186.

Whitby, M., and, Whitby, M., *The History of Theophylact Simocatta* (Oxford, 1986).
Whittow, M., *The Making of Byzantium 600–1025* (Berkeley, CA, 1996).
Wickham, C., *The Inheritance of Rome: Illuminating the Dark Age, 400–1000* (London, 2009).
Wilson, P. H., *The Holy Roman Empire: A Thousand Years of Europe's History* (London, 2016).
Wolff, R. L., "Romania: The Latin Empire of Constantinople," *Speculum* 23 (1948): 1–34.
Wood, I., *The Modern Origins of the Early Middle Ages* (Oxford, 2013).
Woolf, G., *Becoming Roman: The Origins of Provincial Civilization in Gaul* (Cambridge, 1998).
———, "Inventing Empire in Ancient Rome," in S. Alcock et al., eds., *Empires: Perspectives from Archaeology and History* (Cambridge, 2001), 311–322.
———, *Rome: An Empire's Story* (Oxford, 2012).
Yarnley, C. J., "Philaretos: Armenian Bandit or Byzantine General?," *REA* 9 (1972): 331–353.
———, "The Armenian Philhellenes," *Eastern Church Review* 8 (1976): 45–53.
Yuzbashian, K. N., "L'administration byzantine en Arménie aux Xe–XIe siècle," *REA* 10 (1973–1974): 139–183.
Zeiller, J., "L'apparition du mot *Romanía* chez les écrivains latins," *Revue des études latines* 7 (1929): 194–198.
Zepos, I., and P. Zepos, eds., *Jus Graecoromanum*, 8 vols. (Athens, 1931–1936).
Zuckerman, C., "Emperor Theophilos and Theophobos in Three Tenth-Century Chronicles: Discovering the 'Common Source,'" *REB* 75 (2017): 101–150.

Index

Abara, 248
Abasgians, 60
Abastaktos, Theophylaktos, 174–175
Abbasids, 127–128, 146
Abu Firas, 77
Abusahl (brother of Davitʿ, son of Senekʿerim), 250
Achaea (Frankish principality), 78
Achaemenids, 124, 201
Adontz, Nicholas, 157, 174, 180–182
Adrianople, 151
Adriatic Sea, 5, 266
Aegean Sea, 102
Aelia Capitolina. *See* Jerusalem
Agarenes. *See* Arabs
Agathias, 38–40, 55, 62, 81, 116, 125–126
Ahima'as, 213
Aikaterine (daughter of Ivan Vladislav), 235
Ailios Aristeides, 88–89
Aitolia, 135
Akameros (*archon* of the Slavs of Belzitia), 140
Akamir. *See* Akameros
Akropolites, Konstantinos, 82
Alans, 60
Albanians, 16, 109, 152, 239, 260, 263, 265, 266, 272
Aleppo, 77, 257

Alexander the Great, 187, 192
Alexandria, 95, 254
Alexandrians, 119
Alexandros (emperor), 136
Alexios (brother-in-law of Saint Maria the Younger), 162
Alexios (translator of an *Apocalypse of Daniel*), 103
Alexios I Komnenos, 59–60, 93, 153–154, 166, 181, 238, 241–243, 259
al-Hakim, 254
Aligernos, 125–126
al-Jahiz, 76
Allabroges, 114
al-Masʿudi, 92
al-Ya'qubi, 104
Amalekite, 186
Amalfitans, 49, 226, 258–259
Amanos mountains, 228
Americans, 31, 177, 190
Amorion, 70
Anastasios I (emperor), 4–5, 72, 89
Anastasius the Librarian, 21
Anatolikon (theme), 117
Ando, Cliff, 86, 200
Andronikos I Komnenos (emperor), 9, 68, 189
Andronikos III Palaiologos (emperor), 41
Anglo-Saxons, 259
Ani, 156, 243–245, 247–249, 251

Antioch, 71, 110, 242, 253–255, 257, 265
Antiochenes, 22
Antiochos (*doux* of the Milengoi), 143–144
Antoninus (Caracalla), 52, 84, 261
Apokaukos, Ioannes, 242
Apollos (apostle), 119
Apulia, 177, 222
Arabia, 75
Arabissos, 181–182
Arabs, 35, 96, 112, 129, 132–136, 142, 145, 151, 179, 186, 189, 198, 215–217, 220, 226, 230, 255, 257, 259; conquests of, 215, 228; as ethnic minority in Byzantium, xi, 42, 59; Roman expeditions against, 128, 156, 215, 228; writings of as sources for Romanía, 15, 33, 51, 75–77, 79, 92, 104–105, 116, 127, 244, 256
Aratos, Ioannes, 212
Arcadia, 144, 220
Archon, 139–140, 142–143, 193, 219, 224, 240–241, 266
Areobindos, 89
Arethas (bishop of Kaisareia), 147
Argos, 145
Ariadne (empress), 4–5, 54
Arians, 85–86
Aristakes of Lastivert, 245, 251
Aristotle, 166
Armenia, 71, 92, 154–159, 161, 167–168, 173, 176–178, 182–186, 190–191, 193, 209–210, 215–216, 218, 226, 230, 244–245, 262
Armenia II (province), 181, 187
Armeniakon (theme), 171, 174–177, 184–185, 214–215
Armenians, xi, xiv, 9, 33–34, 40, 42–44, 59–63, 76, 82, 118, 124, 126, 146, 151, 205–206, 221, 226, 230–231, 253–255, 259–262, 264–265; assimilation of, 136, 155–195, 213–217; in Constantinople, 49, 203, 259; and expansion of Romanía, 243–251, 266–267; military service of, 223, 228–229, 254, 260
Armenion, 164
Armenos, 164
Arsaber (brother of Ioannes the Grammarian), 170
Arsacids, 160, 182, 191–193

Arsakes (conspirator against Justinian), 155
Arshakuni, Hovanes, 182
Artabanes (general under Justinian), 155
Artabasdos (commander of the palace guard), 131–132
Artabasdos (usurper), 59, 186
Artanas, 220
Artaxerxes I (king), 191
Arvanites. *See* Albanians
Aryans, 201
Asen (founder of second Bulgarian empire), 238
Asia Minor, xiii, 4, 45, 55, 58, 84, 100, 102, 108, 114–115, 130, 154, 156, 181, 209, 216–218, 227–228, 259; relocation of non-Romans in, 145, 220, 229, 247–248; themes of, 87, 117, 176
Asołik. *See* Step'anos of Taron
Ašot I Bagratuni, 193
Ašot III (king of Armenia), 165
Assyria, 145
Assyrians, 145, 186, 193, 255
Athanasia of Aigina (saint), 129
Athanasios of Alexandria, 85–86, 88–89
Athaulf, 87
Athenians, ix, 90, 97, 147, 151, 202
Athens, 79, 90, 136–137, 140, 145, 197–198
Athinganoi, 181
Atom (brother of Davitʿ, son of Senekʿerim), 250
Attaleia, 55, 229
Attaleiates, Michael, 55, 57, 70, 249, 255, 265
Augustine (saint), 116
Augustus, 68, 95, 115–116
Austrians, 31
Autokrator, 199
Avars, 5, 63, 91, 141, 156
Axios river. *See* Vardar river
Axouch, 154
Ayvazyan, Armen, 159
Azerbaijan, 127, 131

Baanes (son of Saint Maria the Younger), 162
Babylonians, 114
Bačkovo (monastery), 252
Bactrians, 67
Baghdad, 257

INDEX

Baghdadis, 77
Bagratids, 170, 193
Balkans, 5–6, 10, 15, 34, 46, 54–55, 84, 95, 145, 154, 156, 210, 220, 234, 242, 266; Roman provinces in, 87, 176–177, 179
Baltic Sea, 144
Banu Habib, 129, 133, 136
Barbaros (saint), 82, 135
Bardanes (son of Saint Maria the Younger), 162
Bardanes, Philippikos, 180, 185–187, 216
Bardanes the Turk, 171
Bardas (brother of Theodora, wife of Theophilos), 172
Bardas (cousin of Maria of Amnia), 171
Bardas (father of Leon V), 186
Bari, 234
Barlaam the Calabrian, 82
Barnabas (apostle), 119
Basileios I (emperor), 40, 102, 131, 149, 161–162, 175, 217, 225; alleged Armenian ancestry of, 180, 186, 191–194; assimilative policies of, 138–139, 145, 219; and Louis II, 20–21, 28, 65
Basileios II (emperor), 55, 68, 133–134, 179, 240, 242, 245, 248–249, 251–252; and Bulgaria, 142, 154, 221, 235–237, 240, 246, 263
Basileios Lakapenos, 151
Basileios the Younger (saint), 60, 227
Basileus, x, 201–202, 234
Beck, Hans-Georg, 35
Bedouins, 260
Belegezites, 139–141
Belzitia, 140
Benjamin (son of Jacob), 119
Benjamin of Tudela, 212, 225, 241
Bessians. *See* Thracians
Bichetai, 140
Bithynia, 136, 147, 220–221, 224
Black Sea, 40, 92, 220, 242
Bogomils, 242
Bohemond, 240, 242
Boïlas family, 221
Bosporos, 266
Boukellarion (theme), 175
Boulgarin, 221
Bourtzes family, 174
Brachamios, Philaretos, 247
Branas family, 179

Bratzes, Bardas, 161–162
Britain, 15, 198
British, 33, 201
Britons, 98
Bulgaria, 30, 69, 98, 103, 107, 142–143, 220–221, 233–240, 244–246, 252, 260–262, 266–267
Bulgarians, 40–41, 44, 55–56, 60, 62–63, 76, 106, 108–109, 126, 136, 143, 154, 162, 166, 174, 213, 218, 221, 227, 244, 246, 251, 260, 266, 273; assimilation of, 235–236, 266; as ethnically separate from Romans, 7–10, 234–235, 264, 266–267; and ethnicity-as-politics in Romanía, 149, 151; and Roman administration, 236–240, 262–263
Bulgars, 5, 63, 67, 142, 153, 217, 221
Buridan, 179
Bury, John Bagnall, 32
Buyids, 179

Caesar, Julius, 169
Cairo, 257
Calabria, 40, 222–223, 231
Calabrians, 82
Cameron, Averil, 18, 43
Cappadocia, 62, 87, 175, 181, 184, 247–249, 265
Cappadocians, 181, 183, 227
Capua, 210
Caracalla. *See* Antoninus
Carenitis. *See* Karin
Carians, 45
Carthage, 24, 71
Caucasians, 46, 162
Caucasus, 243–244, 247, 256, 261
Çelebi, Evliya, 104
Chalcedonians, 110, 158, 167, 230, 246
Chaldia (theme), 215
Chalkidike, 143
Chandler, Richard, 79, 104
Charanis, Peter, 157, 174, 177, 181–182, 214
Charlemagne (king of the Franks and Roman emperor), 20–21, 33
Charsianon (theme), 175, 215, 249–250
Chasanes (provincial governor), 133
Cheynet, Jean-Claude, 178
Choirosphaktes, Leon, 147
Choniates, Michael, 109
Choniates, Niketas, 109

Christ, 69, 95, 106, 109–110, 113, 119, 201, 265
Christians, 6–7, 39–40, 51, 59, 65–67, 69, 86–87, 94–95, 97, 104, 106–113, 116, 118, 120, 129, 133–136, 140, 143–145, 147, 213, 218, 221, 228–229, 246, 255, 257–258, 263, 269
Christophoros Lakapenos, 148
Chrysos, Evangelos, 35
Cicero, 24, 119, 169
Cilicia, 117, 156, 218, 229, 244, 247, 254, 256
Chomsky, Noam, 35
Commageneans, 114
Conrad (German king), 71
Constantine the Great (emperor), 7, 24, 71, 89, 107, 187, 192
Constantinopolitans, 10, 76, 164, 256
Constantius II (emperor), 52
Copts, 76
Corinth, 137, 145
Cremona, 174
Crete, 134, 145, 148, 156, 215, 228
Croatia, 210
Cumans, 136, 241
Cupane, Carolina, 99
Curta, Florin, 30, 35, 41, 140
Cypriots, 119
Cyprus, 88
Cyrus the Great, 68, 192

Dacia, 54
Dacians, 49, 259
Dalassenos family, 174
Dalmatians, 228
Damianos (*parakoimomenos*), 146–147, 150
Danube, 87–88, 234, 242, 260
Daphnopates, Theodoros, 234
David, 191–192
Davitʿ (grandson of Senekʿerim), 248–250
Daylami, 257
Dench, Emma, 25
Digenis Akritis, 66, 68, 72, 96, 134
Donnolo, Shabbatai, 213, 223
Doukas family, 174
Doux, 143, 220, 244
Drogoubites, 139–141
Drougoubiteia (theme), 141
Droungarios, 162–163

Duklja, 234
Dur-Sharrukin, 145
Dvin, 154
Dyrrachion, 5
Dyrrachion (theme), 239

Edessa, 76, 254, 260
Egypt, 6, 88, 100, 112, 130, 254, 257–258
Egyptians, 67, 71, 86, 130, 261
Eirene (empress), 21, 140
Eladas, Ioannes, 151
Eladikos, Niketas (*protospatharios*), 151
Elias of Nisibis, 257
Elias the Younger (saint), 70
England, 60
English, 31, 49, 60, 259
Epeiros, 218
Ephesos, 221
Epidamnos. *See* Dyrrachion
Epidauros, 145
Epiphanios of Salamis, 75, 85, 88
Erzurum. *See* Karin
Eskimo. *See* Inuit
Ethiopians, 134, 153
Etruscans, 45
Euagrios (historian), 181
Euboia, 145
Eulogios the Persian, 131
Euodios (ninth-century monk), 70
Euphemios (grammarian), 148
Euphrosyne (wife of Michael II), 170–171
Euschemon (bishop of Kaisareia), 117, 119
Eusebios of Kaisareia, 95, 270
Eustathios Boïlas, 62, 82, 188, 265
Eustathios of Thessalonike, 125
Eustathios Romaios, 60, 252
Evidites, 140
Exkoubitor, 221
Ezerites, 143, 220, 228, 230, 266

Fabius Pictor, 105
Fallmerayer, Jakob Philipp, 16
Fatimids, 254, 257
Fayyum, 258
Fazio degli Uberti, 78
Fisher, Elizabeth, 103
Fisher, Greg, 105
Florentines, 78
Flower, Harriet, 24
Fox, Clifton, 36

INDEX

France, 15, 90, 198
Franklin, Simon, 35
Franks, xi, 7, 12–13, 21–22, 51, 67, 76–79, 102, 106, 136, 139, 144, 149, 166, 229, 254; in Agathias, 38–40; in Constantinople, 49, 259; in Roman service, 59–60, 227, 246
Freeman, E. A., 32
French, 78–79
Friedrich II (emperor), 77

Gabadonia, 249
Gabriel of Melitene, 247
Gaetans, 226
Gagik II of Ani, 249–251
Gagik of Kars, 250
Galatia, 116
Galatians, 115–116
Gallipoli (southern Italy). *See* Kallipolis
Garsoïan, Nina, 160, 251
Gastald, 223
Gaul, 52
Genesios (uncle of Ioseph Genesios), 163
Genesios, Ioseph, 127–128, 136, 163–164, 172, 190, 193–194
Genesios family, 164
Genoa, 225
Genoese, 93
Geometres, Ioannes, 151
Georgia, 177
Georgians, 10, 59–60, 103, 106, 109, 162, 178, 225, 243, 252, 260, 264, 266
Georgios Akropolites, 10, 55
Gepids, 54
Germans, 12, 16–17, 19–21, 23, 31, 35, 39, 60, 71–72, 77, 99, 137, 177, 197, 201–202
Germany, 90
Ghewond, 214
Gibbon, Edward, 13, 22
Gilakios (Armenian officer), 155
Gischala, 119
Golden Horn, 225
Goldstone, Jack, 208
Gothia, 87, 92
Goths, 59, 62, 67, 85, 87, 115, 125, 130, 136, 155, 261
Goubazes, 62
Greece, xiii, 16–17, 30, 32, 123, 135, 218, 220, 229, 240–241, 261; settlement of

Slavs in, 137–138, 140, 143–145, 148–150, 219, 230, 240
Greeks, 19, 45, 71, 116, 137, 203, 223–224, 273; as western label for eastern Romans, xii, 11–22, 25–26, 28–34, 37, 49, 77–79, 81–82, 100, 105, 107, 181, 234, 259, 269, 272
Gregoras, Nikephoros, 41, 82
Gregorios (bishop of Antioch), 71
Grigor of Narek, 251
Gulf of Corinth, 150

Hadrian, 24, 53, 120
Hagia Sophia, 7, 150
Haldon, John, 130, 196, 208
Halys, 115
Hamdanids, 77
Harris, William, 24–25
Hasan. *See* Chasanes
Hasé (provincial governor in Athens), 136, 146–147
Hegel, Georg Wilhelm Friedrich, 14
Helene (sister-in-law of Saint Maria the Younger), 162
Helladikoi, 140
Helladikos, Rentakios, 150
Hellas (theme), 140, 148, 219
Hemshin, 216–217
Herakleia (city on Black Sea coast), 40
Herakleios (emperor), 27, 101, 180, 182–185
Herakleios (father of emperor Herakleios), 183–184
Herakles, 182
Herodotos, 97
Herrin, Judith, 219
Hierissos, 143
Hilarion (Georgian monk), 224–225
Hippolytos (commentator on the book of Daniel), 114–116
Hittites, 26
Holo, Joshua, 212
Holt, Tom, 37
Hozat, 185
Hungarians, 242
Huns, 60, 67, 136

Iakobitzes the Persian, 131
Iberia, 177, 245–246, 260
Iberians. *See* Georgians
Ibn al-Rumi, 77

Ibn Butlan, 257
Ibn Hawqal, 133
Iconoclasts, 129, 146, 169, 186
Iconophiles, 146, 169–170, 186
Idumaeans, 114
Illyrians, 63, 181
Imperator, x, 199, 202
Indians, 31, 67
Inuit, 24
Ioannes (*archon* of the Bichetai of Greece), 140
Ioannes (bishop of Melitene), 253–254
Ioannes I Tzimiskes (emperor), 178–179, 180, 184–185, 218, 242, 253
Ioannes II Komnenos (emperor), 154
Ioannes III Doukas Batatzes (emperor), 56, 77
Ioannes the Grammarian (patriarch), 169–170
Ioannikios (saint), 221
Ioseph (monk on Mt. Athos), 188
Iranians, 56, 127, 191
Ireland, 101
Isaak (Arsacid), 193
Isaakios (governor of Ravenna), 191
Isaakios I Komnenos (emperor), 235
Isaakios II Angelos (emperor), 93, 259
Isauria, 258
Isaurians, 4–5, 53, 61–62, 117, 181, 261
Ises, Ioannes, 126
Ishmaelites, 70
Israel, 6
Italians, 37, 68, 70, 85, 98, 108, 222, 225–226
Italos, Ioannes, 152
Italy, 40, 58, 99, 119, 125, 155–156, 174, 191, 218, 233, 251; and claims to the legacy of ancient Rome, 22, 37, 120; ethnic groups of before Roman conquest, 45; Jewish literature from, 213; Roman administration and ethnic differences in, 222–223, 231, 263, 266
Ivan Vladislav, 235
Iviron, 252

Jacobites (Syrian Orthodox), 221, 252–254, 264–266, 267
Jarajima. *See* Mardaïtes
Jason, 164
Jazira, 260
Jenkins, Romilly, 159

Jerome (saint), 23
Jerusalem, 75, 119–120
Jews, xi, 6, 42, 44, 66, 101, 104, 117–120, 126, 145, 169, 205–206, 241, 266, 272; in Constantinople, 203, 225–226, 259; general condition of in Romanía, 211–213, 230–231, 257–258, 263; in Italy, 213, 223, 251
John Chrysostom, 53, 67
Josephos, 120, 213
Judaea, 119
Julian (emperor), 52, 71
Justin I (emperor), 181
Justinian (emperor), 52, 54–55, 71, 86, 90, 155, 184, 233, 262; ethnic policies of, 59, 61, 261; military affairs under, 155, 176–177, 184; and use of the Greek language, 100–101
Justinian II (emperor), 142, 186, 220, 229

Kaegi, Walter, 183
Kaisar, 164
Kaisareia (Cappadocia), 117, 147, 175, 249
Kaisareia (Palestine), 39, 95
Kallipolis, 40
Kalon-Peghat, 249
Kaloyan (Bulgarian tsar), 55
Kanaboutzes, Ioannes, 109
Karaite Jews, 225
Karatzas, Argyros, 126
Karin, 165, 182, 184, 251
Kars. *See* Vanand
Kartli, 177
Kartvelians. *See* Georgians
Kasia (hymnographer), 188
Katepano, 244
Katholikos, 247, 250
Kazhdan, Alexander, 157, 167, 178, 214
Kekaumenos, 95–96, 154, 209, 240–241, 243
Kekaumenos, Katakalon, 179–180
Kennedy, Hugh, 35
Kennedy, John F., 169
Keroularios (patriarch), 92
Khazars, 59, 151, 226
Khurramites, 56, 124, 127–132, 136, 145, 153, 161, 163, 220
Khusrow, 90
Kibyrraiotai (theme), 136, 229
Kinnamos, Ioannes, 57, 126
Kolchis. *See* Lazike

INDEX

Koloneia, 177, 217
Koloneia (theme), 215, 230
Komnene, Anna, 152, 166, 241
Komnenos, Manuel (son of Andronikos I Komnenos), 9, 56, 68
Komnenos dynasty, 166
Konstas II (emperor), 185
Konstantine (city in Osrhoene), 183
Konstantinos (grandfather of Ioseph Genesios), 163–164, 167, 172, 190, 193–194
Konstantinos *(primikerios)*, 60
Konstantinos IV (emperor), 141
Konstantinos V (emperor), 140, 165, 217, 220
Konstantinos VI (emperor), 171, 216
Konstantinos VII Porphyrogennetos (emperor), 39, 41, 56, 94, 143, 163, 177, 191, 194, 215, 217, 224; and ideas about ethnicity, 7–9, 61, 67, 81, 117, 136, 146–151, 209–210; and use of the Greek language, 101
Konstantinos IX Monomachos (emperor), 55, 210, 242, 246, 249–250, 259
Konstantinos X Doukas (emperor), 227, 250, 253
Kosmas Indikopleustes, 67, 95
Koubikoularios, 140
Koulpingoi, 60
Kourkouas family, 174, 178
Krenitai, 165
Krueger, Derek, 80
Kulayb (governor of Antioch), 255
Kurds, 179
Kyrillos of Skythopolis, 75
Kyzikos, 151

Lacedaemonians, 90
Laiou, Angeliki, 153
Lakapa, 174–175
Lakapenos family, 149, 174, 178
Lakonians, 147
Laodikeia, 254, 257
Larissa (Cappadocia), 248
Larissa (Thessaly), 240
Latins, 9, 11–13, 15, 22, 29, 41, 75, 77, 98, 203–204, 226, 254, 258–259, 263
Lazar *(paroikos)*, 238
Lazaros of Galesion, 221
Lazi. *See* Tzanoi
Lazike, 55

Lebounion, 243
Leo I (emperor), 4, 181, 192
Leo II (emperor), 4
Leon III (emperor), 59
Leon IV (emperor), 171
Leon V (emperor), 164, 170, 180, 186–187
Leon VI (emperor), 59, 61, 69, 81, 110, 138–139, 142, 145, 148, 191, 194, 219, 222
Leon the Philosopher, 170
Libellisios, Petros, 255
Libyans, 183
Liudprand of Cremona, 21, 81, 174, 178, 226
Lombards, xi, 49, 81, 222–223, 231, 259, 263
Longobardia (theme), 177, 222
Louis II (German emperor), 20–21, 28, 65, 81
Lucullus, 115
Lydia, 130
Lydos, Ioannes, 100, 202
Lykandos (theme), 175, 215–216, 244, 249–250
Lykaonians, 117

Macedonia, 78, 120, 137–138, 191–192, 218–219, 230
Macedonian dynasty, 20, 179, 186, 191
Macedonians, 90, 192, 194, 227
Magdalino, Paul, 29
Magister militum, 176, 183
Magistros, 147, 150–151, 165, 249
Magyars, 235
Malalas, 90–91
Mamikonians, 172
Mango, Cyril, 43, 74
Manichaeans, 218
Mani peninsula, 223–224, 231
Manlius Torquatus, 71
Mantzikert, 250–251
Manuel (uncle of Theodora, wife of Theophilos), 172–173
Manuel I Komnenos (emperor), 57, 71, 93, 125, 201
Manuel II Palaiologos (emperor), 110
Mardaïtes, 228–229
Maria (granddaughter of Romanos I), 149
Maria of Amnia, 171

Maria the Younger (saint), 161–162, 167, 169, 172, 190
Marinos (father-in-law of Theophilos), 172
Markellai, 221
Mars, 66
Marykaton, 221
Massachusetts, 169
Mas'udi, 116
Matthew of Edessa, 184–185, 249–251, 255
Maurikios, 180–181, 185
Mediterranean, 244, 257
Megas doux, 250
Melias, 175, 216, 244
Melitene, 175, 217, 244, 253, 256
Melkites, 252, 254–257, 264
Melnik, 10
Mesopotamia, 76, 244, 246
Mesopotamia (theme), 177, 215–216
Mexicans, 177
Mexico, 177
Michael I (emperor), 63, 142, 221
Michael II (emperor), 135, 142, 146, 170–171, 181
Michael III (emperor), 68, 99, 131, 142, 147, 151
Michael VII Doukas (emperor), 59, 93
Michael the Syrian, 128
Milengoi, 143–144, 220, 228, 230, 263, 266
Mleh. *See* Melias
Modestinus, 86
Montecassino, 223
Montesquieu, 13–14
Moors, 67
Morocharzanioi (family), 170
Morris, Ian, 202
Mosele, Alexios (admiral), 165
Mosele, Alexios (general), 164
Mosele, Alexios (*kaisar*), 164–165, 172, 190
Mosele, Romanos (*magistros*), 165
Mosele (Mušel) family, 164, 167, 169
Moses, 6
Mt. Athos, 93, 97, 142, 188, 221, 241, 252
Mt. Olympos (Bithynia), 147, 224
Mt. Olympos (Thessaly), 147
Mt. Pindos, 263
Mt. Taygetos, 143, 220, 263

Muslims, xiv, 13, 41, 70, 82, 96, 102, 104, 129, 132–135, 152, 204, 218, 226, 244–245, 252–257, 263–264, 266, 272

Nabataeans, 114
Narses (commander at Konstantine), 183
Narses (general under Justinian), 59
Nasr (Khurramite general), 131
Naupaktos, 242
Nauplion, 145
Neilos the Younger (saint), 40–41, 108, 152, 223
Nestorians, 95, 257
New Mexico, 177
New York, 169
Nicolaus I (pope), 99
Nikaia, 10, 153
Nikephoros (father of Philippikos Bardanes), 185
Nikephoros (historian and patriarch), 55
Nikephoros (husband of Saint Maria the Younger), 162
Nikephoros I (emperor), 145, 180
Nikephoros II Phokas (emperor), 21, 94, 182, 253, 256
Nikephoros III Botaneiates (emperor), 57
Niketas (patriarch), 146, 150
Niketas (provincial governor), 136
Niketas *magistros*, 147–151, 186
Nikolaos Mystikos (patriarch), 81
Nikon "Metanoeite!," 143–145, 212
Nikon of the Black Mountain, 110, 265
Nikoulitzas (ancestor of Kekaumenos), 240
Nikoulitzas Delphinas, 240
Normans, 59–60, 93, 223, 233, 259, 266

Obama, Barack, 136
Ohio, 169, 204
Ohio State University, 204, 228
Ohrid, 235–236
Oikonomides, Nikos, 140
Opsikion (theme), 175, 228
Orestes (son of Saint Maria the Younger), 162
Orosius, 87
Osrhoene, 183
Ostrogorsky, George, 18
Ottoman empire, 15, 79, 103–104, 124, 198, 203, 225

INDEX

Ottomans, 49, 104, 201
Ouzes, 227

Page, Gill, 49
Pakourianos, Gregorios, 59, 103, 109, 252
Palaiologans, 72
Palestine, 75
Pamphylians, 117
Pankratios (eighth-century astrologer), 170
Pankratios (father of Ioannes the Grammarian), 170
Pannonia, 5
Paphlagonia, 172
Paphlagonians, 171
Paradounabon, 260
Parakoimomenos, 147
Paroikos, 238
Parthenon, 136
Patrikios, 147, 150, 163, 186, 193, 248
Paul (saint), 53, 67, 117–120
Paulicians, 108, 189, 193, 217–218, 221, 231, 242
Paul the Deacon, 181
Pechenegs, 60, 109, 124, 136, 153, 242–243, 252, 260
Pelagonia, 242
Pelasgians, 55
Peloponnese, 78, 102, 137–138, 142–145, 147–150, 156, 201, 218–220, 224, 228, 230, 266
Pennsylvania, 169
Pera, 225
Perboundos (*rex* of the Rynchinoi), 141
Perperean, Z. N., 157
Persarmenians, 59, 185
Persia, 98, 215
Persians, 41, 55, 63, 67, 75–77, 90, 92, 102, 107, 114, 124, 126, 128–129, 131–132, 169, 179, 185, 191, 198, 201, 209
Petar (founder of second Bulgarian empire), 238
Petar I (Bulgarian tsar), 41, 149
Petros (Armenian *katholikos*), 247
Petros of Sicily, 108, 218
Philaretos (father of Maria of Amnia), 171
Philippi, 118, 120
Philippians, 118
Philippikos (*magister militum per Orientem*), 183
Philippopolis, 10, 218, 242

Philippus, Lucius Marcius, 169
Philopation, 259
Phoenicia, 75
Phokas (emperor), 183
Phokas, Nikephoros (general), 222
Phokas, Nikephoros (rebel against Basileios II), 249
Phokas family, 174, 178–179
Photios (patriarch), 68, 112, 117–120, 151, 191–192
Phrygians, 71, 117
Pisidians, 117
Pizu, 249
Planoudes, Maximos, 68
Pompey the Great, 5, 72, 115
Pontians, 55
Pontos, 55, 115, 216–217
Preiser-Kapeller, Johannes, 160
Primikerios, 60
Priskos (replacement for Philippikos, general), 183
Probos (Nika Riots), 90
Prokopios of Kaisareia, 39, 54–55, 90
Protospatharios, 151
Psellos, Michael, 62, 98, 133, 265
Psenas (enemy of Ioannes Geometres), 151
Pseudo-Joshua the Stylite, 76
Pseudo-Sebeos, 182, 184

Rabanite Jews, 225
Raffenel, 79
Raphael I (patriarch), 104
Ravenna, 191
Rentakioi, 150
Rex, 141, 201
Robert Guiscard, 93
Roma, 259
Romaniote Jews, 211
Romanos I Lakapenos (emperor), 7, 9, 33, 143, 148–150, 174–175, 177, 180, 228
Romanos II (emperor), 7, 94
Romanos III Argyros (emperor), 253
Romanos IV Diogenes (emperor), 251
Rome (city on the Tiber), 52, 71, 86, 88, 99, 108, 117–118, 123, 181, 200, 223, 226, 261; Church of, 13, 222, 246; and claims to the legacy of ancient Rome, 14, 20–23, 37
Romulus, 73
Ros (ancestor of the Romans), 119

Ross, Kelley, 36
Rossano, 40, 223
Rouselios (general under Michael VII), 59
Rousseau, Jean-Jacques, 14
Rum (millet), 104
Rumi, Jalal al-Din, 102
Runciman, Steven, 33, 43, 218, 220
Rus', 35, 60, 108–109, 227, 228–229, 258
Russia, 15
Russians, 15, 18, 103, 109
Rutgers University, 204
Rutilius Namatianus, 89
Rynchinoi, 141

Saba (Gothic saint), 85, 87
Sagoudates, 141
Salamis (on Cyprus), 88
Samonas (general under Leon VI), 59
Samuil (Bulgarian tsar), 154, 236, 242
San Vitale (basilica), 191
Saracens, 59–60, 75, 81–82, 103, 136, 146, 255
Sasanians, 198, 201
Sayf al-Dawla, 77
Scipio, 24, 71
Scythia (province), 177
Scythians, 67, 126, 142, 151, 177, 243
Sebasteia, 246–251
Sebasteia (theme), 215, 228, 230
Seibt, Werner, 160
Seleukeia (Isauria), 258
Seljuks, 102, 126, 243, 249
Selymbria, 162
Seneca, 45
Senekʿerim (Davitʿ, son of Senekʿerim). See Davitʿ
Senekʿerim (king of Vaspurakan), 248
Septimius Severus, 181
Serbia, 18, 104, 234
Serbians, 41, 104, 272
Serbs, 106, 108
Serres, 103
Ševčenko, Ihor, 138
Sgouros, Leon, 109
Shukurov, Rustam, 220
Signes Codoñer, Juan, 131, 165, 169–173
Simeon (Bulgarian tsar), 98, 150, 234
Sirmium, 54, 91
Sklabenoi, 140–141, 143, 219, 230
Sklabesianoi, 228
Sklabinias, 145, 261

Skleros, Bardas, 178–179
Skleros family, 174, 178
Skylitzes, Ioannes, 40, 82, 236, 249
Slavs, xi, xiv, 14, 16, 33, 43–44, 54–55, 62–63, 76, 81, 118, 126, 136–151, 156, 192, 205–206, 213, 218–220, 228–231, 240, 242, 264
Solomon, 192
Sophia (daughter of Niketas *magistros*), 148
Sophia (niece of husband of Saint Maria the Younger), 162
Soubdelitia, 142
Spain, 71, 212
Spaniards, 21, 201, 225
Sparta, 90, 145
Spartans, 147, 150–151
Step'anos of Taron, 157, 251
Stephanos (son of Saint Maria the Younger), 162
Stouraitis, Ioannis, 74
Strabo, 45
Strategos, 224
Strymon (river), 141–142
Strymon (theme), 142, 230
St. Saba, 75
Sultan Veled (Walad), 102
Swiss, 31
Sykoutris, Ioannes, 34
Symbatios (legal historian), 169
Syria, 134, 229, 244, 246–247, 257, 264
Syrianos, 69
Syrians, 41, 49, 230, 252, 254, 259, 261, 264, 266. *See also* Jacobites (Syrian Orthodox)

Tao, 245, 252
Tarasis Kodissa. *See* Zeno (emperor)
Taron, 156, 165, 243, 245, 247, 251
Taronites, Gregorios, 166
Taronites, Ioannes, 166
Taronites family, 165–167, 247
Tarsos, 117–119
Tephrike, 108, 193, 217–218
Ter Sahakean, G., 157
Thebes, 145
Thekla (mother of Theophilos), 170–171
Themistios, 86, 100, 115
Theodora (empress, daughter of Konstantinos VIII), 192
Theodora (wife of Theophilos), 170, 172

INDEX

Theodoros of Edessa, 247
Theodosios Boradiotes, 189
Theodosioupolis. *See* Karin
Theoktiste Florina (mother of Theodora, consort of Theophios), 172
Theophanes Continuatus, 170
Theophanes the Confessor, 171, 177, 214
Theophano (empress), 151
Theophilos (emperor), 56, 72, 127–132, 153, 161, 163–165, 169–170, 172
Theophobos (Khurramite leader), 127, 130–131, 163
Theophylaktos of Ohrid, 166, 235, 237–238
Theophylaktos Simokattes, 55, 90, 100, 183–184
Thessalonike, 5, 58, 137–139, 141–143, 219, 224, 230, 242, 258
Thessaly, 139–140, 142, 147, 164, 218–219, 240–241
Thomas (father of Ioseph Genesios), 163–164
Thomas the Slav, 146, 150
Thrace, 54–55, 137–138, 162, 192, 216–219, 221–222, 231, 242
Thracians, 67, 181, 261
Tiber, 123
Tiberios II (emperor), 181
Tiridates the Great (king of Armenia), 191
Tralleis, 116
Treadgold, Warren, 84
Trebizond, 164
Troy, 13
Turks, 42, 45–46, 68, 70, 72, 76, 98, 136, 153, 166, 171, 203, 242, 247, 251, 254, 257, 259, 265
Tzachas, 153
Tzamandos, 249–250
Tzanoi, 62, 68, 126, 261
Tzimiskai (family), 178

United Kingdom, 18
United States, 33–36, 43, 177, 189, 196
Upper Tao, 243

Vahagn, 182
Vanand, 243–244, 248
Vandals, 136
Varangians, 37, 60, 227, 229, 246, 259–260, 263
Vardan, 172
Vardan II Mamikonian, 185
Vardar river, 242
Vaspurakan, 156, 243–244, 246, 248–251, 260
Velahatouïa, 242
Venetians, 258, 260
Venice, 24, 225
Ventidius Bassus, 236
Veroia, 142
Vespasian, 120
Vizye, 162
Vlachia, 241
Vlachs, 109, 152, 239–242, 259, 262–263, 265, 266, 273
Voltaire, 14, 79
Vryonis, Speros, 58–59, 205, 221

Weber, Max, 48
Whitby, Michael, 183
Wickham, Chris, 35

Yahya of Antioch, 254
Yuhannan VII Sarigta, 253

Zaoutzes, Stylianos, 194
Zeno (emperor), 4, 181
Zeugma, 76
Zoe (mother of Konstantinos VII), 151
Zonaras, Ioannes, 39
Zoroastrians, 127, 139
Zosimos, 130